Communities of Grain

The Wilder House Series in Politics, History and Culture

The Wilder House Series is published in association with the Wilder House Board of Editors and the University of Chicago.

David Laitin, *Editor*
Leora Auslander, *Assistant Editor*
George Steinmetz, *Assistant Editor*

Communities of Grain: Rural Rebellion in Comparative Perspective by Victor V. Magagna

ALSO IN THE SERIES

State and Society in Medieval Europe: Gwynedd and Languedoc under Outside Rule by James Given

Language and Power: Exploring Political Cultures in Indonesia by Benedict R. O'G. Anderson

Reclaiming the Sacred: Lay Religion and Popular Politics in Revolutionary France by Suzanne Desan

Communities of Grain

RURAL REBELLION IN COMPARATIVE PERSPECTIVE

Victor V. Magagna

Cornell University Press

ITHACA AND LONDON

First published 1991 by Cornell University Press.

International Standard Book Number 0-8014-2361-9
Library of Congress Catalog Card Number 90-55720
Printed in the United States of America
*Librarians: Library of Congress cataloging information
appears on the last page of the book.*

⊗ The paper in this book meets the minimum requirements
of the American National Standard for Information Sciences—
Permanence of Paper for Printed Library Materials, ANSI Z39.48-1984.

TO TERMINUS,
SPIRIT OF BOUNDARIES
AND TERRITORIAL JUSTICE

Contents

Preface

This book results from my rethinking of the basis of political action in traditional rural societies. For decades, historians and social scientists have been engaged in a subtle and far-reaching reinterpretation of the nature of rural society. Their work has shown us that established notions of rural passivity, social incapacity, and historical insignificance cannot be accepted. More important, the detailed investigation of agricultural societies at the "micro" level has begun to undermine any belief in the existence of a universal peasant class that lives as the mute object of history. Instead, we have learned that rural people can act to shape society, and we have begun to understand the ties of kinship and community that render action possible, even in contexts of poverty and subordination. Surprisingly, however, no grand synthesis of the history of rural society has yet been undertaken. James C. Scott, Samuel Popkin, Joel Migdal, Eric Wolf, and others were primarily concerned with the specific question of revolutionary transformation in traditional societies, and their focus on change rather than continuity provides a partial interpretation of rural social formations. In the present work, therefore, I have attempted to reinterpret agricultural politics and society. I argue that community institutions rather than class are the key to collective action in rural societies, and the issue of who holds the power to define the rights and responsibilities of community membership is what determines the lines of conflict and cooperation in rural contexts.

In contrast to many previous writers, I argue that politics is as important as subsistence in agricultural societies, even in conditions of extraordinary scarcity. My argument moves away from the emphasis on macrostructures and elite power that is typical of historical sociology. It focuses instead on action and events as seen from below, from the standpoint of the dominated. Much will be said about ordinary life, and relatively little about state power and the strategies of the powerful. Interestingly, once we have thus refocused on theoretical vision, it becomes much more difficult to talk coherently about a peasant class. Indeed, one of my central themes is the need to move away from debates about the peasantry and toward a radical reconstruction of our understanding of how community and hierarchy constitute the limits of the possible in agrarian societies.

It is my aim here to provide a foundation for a political sociology of the dominated. By this I mean a theoretically informed understanding of the political institutions created by ordinary men and women, in contrast to the institutions of domination constructed by elites. One of the major gaps in classical social and political thought was the absence of a theory of ordinary social and political life. Consequently, we know far too little about the ways in which subordinate populations are organized and why those organizational patterns achieve determinate forms. Fortunately, the explosion of social history and social science written from below has made it possible to think in broad comparative terms about these issues. Unlike Emile Durkheim or Max Weber, we are in a position to know the logic of popular action in a way that will permit us to combine rich contextual knowledge with broad and bold generalizations. What we need in such an enterprise is synthesis, and it is in that spirit that the present book is offered.

Readers will want to know why the analysis relies on certain cases rather than others. Why, for example, have I chosen to investigate England rather than Brazil or Iran? Comparative work often seems to draw on arbitrary cases that have no apparent significance for theory. Even worse, case selection is sometimes driven by the implicit need to find data that are most likely to support a particular argument, and the results are therefore subtly biased in favor of a particular explanation.

In this book I have used two criteria for the inclusion of cases. First, I have selected national case materials for which there is a rich secondary literature. Thus, the apparently lopsided emphasis on Europe has been partly motivated by the extraordinary richness of secondary works. We know so much about agrarian Europe that no synthetic or theoretical treatment of rural society that excludes it can claim genuinely comparative status.

Second, all the cases have been chosen because of their theoretical importance. France, Spain, and Russia have been included because they are central to the established discourse of historical sociology. Within this discourse the terms of debate are framed according to a logic that makes these three national histories crucial to the definition of peasants and peasant revolutions. Consequently, a revisionist reading of these cases must challenge the root concepts and metaphors that currently guide our interpretation of rural politics. In contrast, England and Japan have been included for reason of logic and methodology. England is rightly treated as a model of agricultural progress, and English rural institutions are often described as peculiarly individualistic in their form and functioning. England, in fact, ought to be the least likely of my cases in which a community-based analysis could serve as a plausible framework. The combination of English commercial precocity and rough individualism should defeat the idea that territorial community structures rural action. If it is not defeated we can be much more certain that community is likely to be significant in all the cases that do not share the peculiarities of the English experience. Finally, Japan has been selected because it serves conceptually to guard the book's larger theoretical claims against any gross cultural bias caused by the necessary emphasis on the West. Japan is usually regarded as a distinctive and self-contained culture, and many comparativists continue to view Japanese history requiring non-Western categories of interpretation. The analysis of rural politics in terms of community can only be strengthened if strong traces of community show through the Japanese past, especially if those traces share common characteristics with the West. The Japanese case is also useful as a proxy for the whole sweep of non-Western history prior to the impact of European colonialism. Japan's success with indigenous industrialization makes it easy to ignore the aspects of historical development that Japan shared with the other great non-European civilizations. Yet, like India, China, and the Middle East, Japan produced a complex agricultural society characterized by sophisticated political institutions and strong traditions of cultural identity. Experts in third-world studies are invited to view Japanese rural history in terms of their own areas in order to gauge the degree to which it was comparable to the rural experience of other non-European regions.

Although some of the best writing on the subject has been framed, explicitly or implicitly, in terms of an encounter with the sad history of European empires in the Old and New worlds, the cases chosen for study here do not explicitly consider the impact of European colonialism on non-European rural societies. If rural rebellion in the twentieth century has been so intimately linked to modern colonialism, one might object, how can a writer of a comparative study of rural politics make general claims unless he or she thinks through the colonial experience? Yet it is not at all clear that European colonialism created forms of domination that were unique. The forms of rural hierarchy created in Europe's colonial peripheries may well bear more than a family resemblance to the patterns of rural domination associated with European feudalism and absolutism.

Even stopping short at the colonial frontier, this book should still help to establish an important point about the use and abuse of history in social science. Much of the current debate about rural politics treats history as a flat and linear store of data about the "eternal" uniformities of human behavior. My own approach is to search for broad descriptive and explanatory generalizations, and my discussion of community institutions is in the tradition of those who have sought to create a universal history. But I am uneasy with any facile belief that history can be ignored by those who seek a neat set of covering laws applicable to all human situations. It was that uneasiness that led to a profound dissatisfaction with typical treatments of peasant life. Accordingly, I hope to put to the best possible use the creative tension between history and comparative analysis.

Naturally, any synthetic treatment of complex realities must run the risk of an all-too-facile rendering of social fact, and the more abstract our generalizations the more vulnerable they are to empirical refutation. This is especially true of social theory, because it works largely through a creative rereading of monographs and articles that claim empirical status. Should the reading of the literature prove faulty, or should the texts themselves prove false, no theoretical scaffolding can survive. Yet the potential rewards of theorizing are enormous. By reading texts in a new and convincing way, we can arrive at a more adequate understanding of the social world that lies behind them. It is not the responsibility of the theorist to reinvent the data on which a conceptual framework must rest; but the theorist must pursue real intellectual anomalies generated by specialized research. Theoretical work is intertextual, since its claims must be evaluated in terms of the literature and discourse that give it meaning. Readers of this book should therefore not expect to find previously unknown information. What they ought to look for is a more plausible way of understanding what is known about rural societies.

I thank James Ingram, Frank Sposito, and Jennifer Wooddell, who helped make this book possible. I also thank colleagues whose reading of the text was useful: Arend Lijphart, Peter Gourevitch, Ellen Comisso, Steve Erie, Gary Jacobson, Ann Craig, Tracy B. Strong, and Paul Drake. I am grateful to Samuel Popkin, whose thinking about property rights influenced my own, and to David Laitin, whose keen comments helped orient my thinking. Finally, I thank David Leonard and Kenneth Jowitt, who inspired this book.

VICTOR V. MAGAGNA

San Diego, California

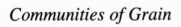

Communities of Grain

CHAPTER I

Vanishing Peasants: Class, Community, and the Anomaly of Rural Collective Action

It is ironic that the late twentieth century has seen a renaissance of rural history. The march of industrial society continues to change the institutional fabric of every region on the globe; yet, intellectual interest in rural life has perhaps never been more pronounced. But the underlying motivation for the efflorescence of rural studies is more complex than a simple desire to expand the stock of knowledge. At one level, it can be explained as a natural attempt to understand the course of rural development in a world still largely tied to the fate of agriculture. At another level, the upsurge in rural science should be seen as the consequence of the United States' difficult involvement in the third world, an involvement that led to Vietnam.

A more fundamental explanation for the scholarly interest in the countryside has to do with the central role that agrarian social relations have assumed in theories of development, especially in theories that link development with revolution. In the work of Barrington Moore, Theda Skocpol, James C. Scott, and Samuel Popkin, the countryside has become the key locus of theoretical interest in the political sociology of revolutionary change.[1] Their work, in turn, has had a profound influence on historians and social scientists interested in rural issues. But here a paradox comes into play that has to do with the very concept of a "peasant" revolution: peasantry, the collective protagonists of the revolutionary

1. Barrington Moore, *Social Origins of Dictatorship and Democracy: Lord and Peasant in the Making of the Modern World* (Boston: Beacon Press, 1966); Theda Skocpol, *States and Social Revolutions: A Comprehensive Analysis of France, Russia, and China* (Cambridge: Cambridge University Press, 1979); James C. Scott, *The Moral Economy of the Peasant* (New Haven: Yale University Press, 1976); and Samuel L. Popkin, *The Rational Peasant* (Berkeley: University of California Press, 1979). Also see Eric Hobsbawm, "Peasant Land Occupations," *Past and Present* 62 (1974), 120; Robert P. Weller and Scott E. Guggenheim, eds., *Power and Protest in the Countryside: Studies of Rural Unrest in Asia, Europe, and Latin America* (Durham: Duke University Press, 1982); and Henry A. Landsberger, ed., *Rural Protests: Peasant Movements and Social Change* (London: Macmillan, 1974).

drama, lack all the characteristics that were once associated with a revolutionary class.[2] Peasants, we are told, lack class consciousness and cohesion, and their "petty" proprietary values and fragmented existence lead them to passivity and reaction.[3] Moreover, rural conditions are not seen as conducive to sustained political action, even when vital interests are at stake. Peasants are the objects rather than subjects of history, and revolutionary moments are too brief and too rare to empower peasants to seize the dynamics of historical change in order to recast the world in their image.[4]

The concept of peasant revolution is ironic and contradictory, and it leaves an uneasy sense that the whole enterprise of studying it is too marginal or too poorly thought through to be of value. Still, the problem of the peasantry is a crucial issue for comparative and theoretical research. On its understanding depends the way in which we will come to explain development and underdevelopment, the meaning of politics in poor societies, and the possibility of peaceful change in the third world. Our interpretation of rural society will also profoundly affect the way basic concepts like class are redrawn to accommodate the tremendous discoveries made by historians and social scientists in the past several decades. Theory, for once, has a very important task to perform, a task that is preparatory to any grand empirical synthesis.

The Elusive Peasant

What is a peasant? The question sounds rhetorical only because the concept has become deeply rooted in our collective imagination. We think we know the referent in the same way that we know the referent of any other proper noun. Peasants are like solid boundary stones. Their identity is too obvious to require comment. Yet if the concept should prove less certain and less empirically

2. This paradox emerges clearly in the literature. See, for example, Harvey J. Kaye, "Another Way of Seeing Peasants: The Work of John Berger," *Peasant Studies* 9 (Winter 1982), 85–105; Joshua B. Forrest, "Defining African Peasants," *Peasant Studies* 9 (Winter 1982), 242–49; Mi Chu Wiens, "Lord and Peasant: The Sixteenth to the Eighteenth Century," *Modern China* 6 (Jan. 1980), 3–39; Alain de Janvry, *The Agrarian Question and Reformism in Latin America* (Baltimore: Johns Hopkins University Press, 1981), 95–106; and Teodor Shanin, ed., *Peasants and Peasant Societies* (London: Basil Blackwell, 1987), esp. 1–14, 57–60, 62–68, and 121–29.

3. The classic statement is from Karl Marx, "The Class Struggles in France: 1848–1850," and "The Eighteenth Brumaire of Louis Bonaparte," in Karl Marx and Frederick Engels, *Selected Works*, vol. 1 (Moscow: Foreign Languages Publishing House, 1951). Also see H. Alavi, "Peasant Classes and Primordial Loyalties," *Peasant Studies* 1 (1973); V. I. Lenin, *The Development of Capitalism in Russia* (Moscow: Progress Publishers, 1967); and Teodor Shanin, "Defining Peasants: Conceptualizations and De-conceptualizations: Old and New in Marxist Debate," *Peasant Studies* 8 (Fall 1978), 38–60.

4. The best recent statement of this position is James C. Scott, *Weapons of the Weak* (New Haven: Yale University Press, 1985).

powerful than is often supposed, we must seriously consider revising much of our thinking about rural society.

According to a fairly well established usage, peasants are low-status cultivators who live close to the margin of subsistence in traditional social formations. Attached to this structural core is also the notion that peasants are characterized by certain cultural peculiarities, especially a commitment to premodern values and institutions. As Teodor Shanin argues in a compendium of rural studies, "As a first approximation we can distinguish peasants as small agricultural producers, who, with the help of simple equipment and the labour of their families, produce mostly for their own consumption, direct or indirect, and for the fulfillment of obligations to holders of political and economic power."[5] Shanin goes on to list several other characteristics of peasants, including a specific cultural identity and an underdog role with respect to established power holders. Shanin's definition is typical, and given its high level of abstraction it seems to apply fairly obviously to a wide range of phenomena. Many societies are marked by problems of subsistence, and the widespread existence of household production requires little comment.[6] More important, anyone who studies agrarian life will recognize the underdog role played by small cultivators in many situations, at least according to the self-evaluations of the actors.

But the extraordinary generality of the concept is exactly what causes it to go awry. To begin with, subsistence-level production is not unique to peasants; it is equally characteristic of traditional artisans and petty manufacturers.[7] So subsistence questions cannot constitute the logical core of the peasant category, because this feature is shared with an indefinite range of other social groups.

Nor does production for use rather than exchange pick out a criterion unique to peasant classes. This is also an element of many urban societies, and it seems odd to reduce an entire class to its orientation toward the market. In any case, the groups we label peasants are tied to markets in many complex ways, ranging from minimal involvement to active participation. It is simply no longer possible to identify peasants with precommercial producers, and the work of authors as diverse as Robert Bates, Popkin, Jan de Vries and Florencia E. Mallon has gone some way toward dispelling any illusions on this score.[8]

5. Shanin, ed., *Peasants and Peasant Societies,* 3–5.

6. See, for example, Marshall Sahlins, *Stone Age Economics* (Chicago: Aldine-Atherton, 1972), 41–148, and A. V. Chayanov, *The Theory of Peasant Economy,* ed. Daniel Thorner et al. (Madison: University of Wisconsin Press, 1986). Also see E. Paul Durrenberger, "Chayanov and Marx," *Peasant Studies* 9 (Winter 1982), 119–29.

7. Frank Ellis, *Peasant Economics: Farm Households and Agrarian Development* (Cambridge: Cambridge University Press, 1988), esp. 102–19.

8. See Robert Bates, *Markets and States in Tropical Africa* (Berkeley: University of California Press, 1981); Robert Bates, ed., *Toward a Political Economy of Development: A Rational Choice Perspective* (Berkeley: University of California Press, 1988); Robert Bates, *Essays on the Political Economy of Rural Africa* (Berkeley: University of California Press, 1987); Samuel Popkin, "Political Entrepreneurs and Peasant Movements in Vietnam," in Michael Taylor, ed., *Rationality and Revolu-*

The notion that peasants are uniquely determined by specific cultural and political traits is also suspect.[9] Peasants are not the only cultural traditionalists in the world, as the behavior of the Iranian bazaar amply demonstrated during the fall of the shah.[10] Traditionalism is a very elastic term, and as social historians have shown, cultural traditionalism can provide the template for both radical and conservative politics. In addition, there seems to be little support for the idea that peasants can be identified with a specific mode of politics. Peasants have been variously described as the most reactionary *and* the most revolutionary of social classes; but the evidence seems to support both views, depending on the time and place at issue.[11]

After subtracting all these items from Shanin's definition, we are left with the uncomfortable feeling that peasants are nothing more than poor farmers, people whose rootedness in the agricultural cycle marks them as the carriers of a unique class tradition. Our intuition tells us that this is correct; yet it is a weak and vague foundation on which to lay a complex theory of rural society. It forces us to lump together people and situations of the most remarkable diversity according to criteria that carry a sense of arbitrariness. What, after all, would motivate us to use the label "peasant" to describe Kansas dirt farmers, Russian smallholders, and Japanese sericulturalists? Surely the shared problem of relative poverty and the

---

tion (Cambridge: Cambridge University Press, 1988), 9–62; Popkin, *The Rational Peasant;* Jan de Vries, *Dutch Rural Economy in the Golden Age, 1500–1700* (New Haven: Yale University Press, 1974); Jan de Vries, "Poverty and Capitalism: Review Essay," *Theory and Society* 12 (2) (1983), 245–55; Florencia E. Mallon, *The Defense of Community in Peru's Central Highlands: Peasant Struggle and Capitalist Transition, 1860–1940* (Princeton: Princeton University Press, 1983), esp. 15–124. A good overview of rural commerce in Europe is in William N. Parker and Eric L. Jones, eds., *European Peasants and Their Markets: Essays in Agrarian Economic History* (Princeton: Princeton University Press, 1975).

9. The classic "culturalist" interpretation is Robert Redfield, *The Little Community: Viewpoints for the Study of a Human Whole* (Chicago: University of Chicago Press, 1955). For recent discussions, see especially Terence Ranger, *Peasant Consciousness and Guerrilla War in Zimbabwe: A Comparative Study* (Berkeley: University of California Press, 1985). Good critiques of "culturalist" interpretations include Sydel Silverman, "Agricultural Organization, Social Structure, and Values in Italy: Amoral Familism Reconsidered," *American Anthropologist* 70 (1968), 1–20; J. D. Berger, "Towards Understanding Peasant Experience," *Race and Class* 11 (1970), 345–59; and Sutti Ortiz, "Peasant Culture, Peasant Economy," in Shanin, ed., *Peasants and Peasant Societies,* 300–303.

10. The best account of Iranian rural society to date is Grace Goodell, *The Elementary Structures of Political Life: Rural Development in Pahlavi Iran* (New York: Oxford University Press, 1986), esp. 302–42. For the role of the bazaar, see Ervand Abrahamian, *Iran between Two Revolutions* (Princeton: Princeton University Press, 1982), 446–538.

11. The best statement of the "peasant" as revolutionary is Eric Wolf, *Peasant Wars of the Twentieth Century* (New York: Harper and Row, 1969), while the classic "reactionary" image is Karl Wittfogel's *Oriental Despotism: A Comparative Study of Total Power* (New Haven: Yale University Press, 1957). How complex and difficult it is to determine whether peasants are one or the other emerges clearly in the study of rural fascism in Italy. See, for example, Anthony L. Cardoza, *Agrarian Elites and Italian Fascism: The Province of Bologna, 1901–1926* (Princeton: Princeton University Press, 1982), 315–39, and Paul Corner, "Fascist Agrarian Policy and the Italian Economy in the Inter-War Years," in John A. Davis, ed., *Gramsci and Italy's Passive Revolution* (New York: Barnes and Noble, 1979), 239–74.

occupation of farming are too contextual and ambiguous to offer much explanatory and comparative power. If it makes sense to talk about peasant classes, it should be possible to identify them precisely and mark out a difference of kind rather than degree between them and other classes.[12]

My starting point is Marx's understanding of the conditions that must be satisfied if we are to be able to categorize a specific group as a class. The purpose here is neither to defend nor attack Marx and Marxism. Rather, it is to show that even a rigorous Marxist interpretation of peasantry cannot save the concept from a series of anomalies and contradictions that force us to move beyond class logic.

A Marxist Critique of Agrarian Class Analysis

It is now well established that Marx did not leave us with a fully developed class theory.[13] He did, however, write an enormous amount about class; and we can piece together enough from his work to construct a Marxist concept of class that picks out its necessary features or "extensional criteria." These features are general structural dimensions of social action, and they recur with sufficient frequency in Marx's work to be relatively uncontroversial dimensions of his thought.

First, class entails a determinate relationship to the means of production, a relationship best described in terms of the kinds of property that each class controls.[14] Thus, the proletariat is defined by its total lack of property, while capital is situated by its ownership and control of the forces of production. Second, class involves similar conditions of life and labor for all members. For example, the working class shares a common existence defined by its insertion in factory-based industry and by the tendency for all kinds of factory labor to become homogenized over time. Finally, classes should be politically homogeneous at the

12. Readers interested in American rural history should see Steven Hahn and Jonathan Prude, eds., *The Countryside in the Age of Capitalist Transformation: Essays in the Social History of Rural America* (Chapel Hill: North Carolina University Press, 1985); Steven Hahn, *The Roots of Southern Populism: Yeoman Farmers and the Transformation of the Georgia Upcountry, 1850–1890* (Oxford: Oxford University Press, 1983), esp. 15–85; Lawrence Goodwyn, *Democratic Promise: The Populist Moment in America* (New York: Oxford University Press, 1976), esp. 33–50; David P. Szatmary, *Shays's Rebellion: The Making of an Agrarian Insurrection* (Amherst: University of Massachusetts Press, 1980), 1–36; and Bruce Palmer, *Man over Money: The Southern Populist Critique of American Capitalism* (Chapel Hill: University of North Carolina Press, 1980), 4–16, 37, 117–20, 173, 197, 211–15.

13. I have drawn heavily in the following discussion on Anthony Giddens, *Capitalism and Modern Social Theory: An Analysis of the Writings of Marx, Durkheim, and Max Weber* (Cambridge: Cambridge University Press, 1971), 35–45; Anthony Giddens, *The Class Structure of the Advanced Societies* (New York: Harper and Row, 1975), 23–51; and Anthony Giddens and Gavin MacKenzie, eds., *Social Class and the Division of Labor: Essays in Honor of Ilya Neustadt* (Cambridge: Cambridge University Press, 1982).

14. Karl Marx and Frederick Engels, *The German Ideology* (London: Lawrence and Wishart, 1970); Marx, *The Poverty of Philosophy* (New York: International Publishers, 1963); and Marx, *Capital*, vols. 1–3 (London: Dent, 1962).

level of political belief and behavior, but only when and if class consciousness has transformed a class-in-itself into a class-for-itself.

Experts in Marx studies might wish to expand this list, but it does seem to capture the core logic of Marx's mature thinking. The more interesting question is whether we can apply this set of criteria to rural societies in an unambiguous fashion. The first problem to address is the relationship between peasants and property. Is there a form of property uniquely determinative of peasant social structure? The question demands a strong affirmative if class analysis is to offer a rigorous and parsimonious grasp of rural societies.

At a very elementary level, the social formations referred to as peasant societies clearly display a remarkable diversity of forms and modes of property holding.[15] This proves true whether we focus on legal forms or underlying patterns of de facto control. For example in eighteenth-century France, a time and place thought of as typically peasant, we can locate a whole range of legal forms of property associated with rural social groups. French cultivators held land in free and servile tenures, and those tenures spanned a continuum from precarious tenancy and sharecropping contracts to allodial land grants.[16] Yet all these modes of tenure have been plausibly connected with the French peasantry, although it is not always clear if a specific mode has been singled out as definitive of the situation of being a peasant.

The comparative task becomes even more difficult when we consider non-Western societies and historical periods that predate the modern era. In many of these cases, the legal definition of property was vested in a highly fragmented and localized customary order, and property rights were held by multiple individuals and groups in hierarchies of tenure that defy neat categorization into landed and landless classes. A good illustration is provided by the pre-British history of southern India. As David Ludden has shown in his innovative study of Tamilnadu, property rights in land were held by caste groups whose individual members could claim specific shares of the village grain heap.[17] Even though these groups were

15. This diversity is emphasized in a more systematic way by Jeffrey M. Paige's *Agrarian Revolution* (New York: Free Press, 1975). Also see Shanin, "Defining Peasants"; Emmanuel Le Roy Ladurie, "Peasants," *The Cambridge Modern History* (Cambridge: Cambridge University Press, 1980), vol. 13, app. 7; Jacques M. Chevalier, "There Is Nothing Simple about Simple Commodity Production," *Journal of Peasant Studies* 10 (1983), 153–86; and J. S. Saul and R. Woods, "African Peasantries," in Shanin, ed., *Peasants and Peasant Societies*, 80–88.

16. The best synthesis in English is P. M. Jones, *The Peasantry in the French Revolution* (Cambridge: Cambridge University Press, 1988), 1–59. Also see Paul Bois, *Paysans de l'Ouest: Des structures économiques et souales aux options politiques depuis l'époque révolutionnaire dans la sarthe* (Paris: Mouton, 1960), and Georges Lefebvre, *Les paysans du Nord pendant la Revolution française* (Bari: Editori Laterza, 1959).

17. David Ludden, *Peasant History in South India* (Princeton: Princeton University Press, 1985), 3–67, 130–63. Also see Burton Stein, *Peasant, State, and Society in Medieval South India* (Delhi: Oxford University Press, 1980), 90–172, and Marshall M. Bouton, *Agrarian Radicalism in South India* (Princeton: Princeton University Press, 1985). For jajman and other prestation relations, see Gloria Goodwin Raheja, *The Poison in the Gift: Ritual, Prestation, and the Dominant Caste in a North*

ritually dominant, they would be classified as peasants under most descriptions, and their ritual hegemony did not allow them to exclude subordinate castes from making legitimate property claims of their own. In other parts of India, especially the north, similar forms of mixed and complex property rights to land and labor were expressed through the etiquette of prestations that informed the jajman system of religious patronage. At least in India it seems impossible to single out a consistent and unambiguous form of peasant property.

Nor do we have to travel to the esoteric shores of medieval Indian historiography in order to see the point. Anyone who has tried to work through the logic of the repartitional Russian commune, or the subtleties of English copyhold, or even the dynamics of the American corp lien will recognize how difficult it is to isolate a form of property determinative of peasant class structure.[18] World agrarian history displays a rich profusion of types of rural property that range from collective tenure and individual freeholds to exotic intermixtures of both. Which is the real, core expression of peasant property? The inability to answer that question decisively casts serious doubt on the existence of a unitary peasant class that cuts across cultural and historical contexts.

A sophisticated Marxist response would be that the whole discussion of legal and customary property relations is beside the point. The relevant issue has to do with control, and once we have identified what groups control scarce resources we have found the key to understanding class power. Since peasants are neither capitalists nor proletarians but occupants of some intermediate position, it should be possible to describe peasant property as the effective control of a specific quantity of scarce resources. That quantity should be large enough to prevent proletarianization, but not so large as to constitute a capitalist enterprise. The idea is that peasants are petty proprietors, occupants of a middle position between elite power and the powerlessness of wage labor.[19]

This is not an unattractive argument, because it seems to cut through the particularities of history without eliminating the peasant as a unit of analysis. Something like this approach underpins Eric Wolf's concept of the "middle peasant," and it also seems to inform the work of Joel Migdal and Teodor

Indian Village (Chicago: University of Chicago Press, 1988), 1–36, and David F. Pocock, "Note on Jajmani Relationships," *Contributions to Indian Sociology* 6 (1962), 78–95.

18. The best discussion of English copyhold is still R. H. Tawney's *The Agrarian Problem in the Sixteenth Century* (New York: Harper and Row, 1967), 19–146, but also see Richard Lachmann, *From Manor to Market: Structural Change in England, 1536–1640* (Madison: University of Wisconsin Press, 1987). For the crop lien, see Michael Schwartz, *Radical Protest and Social Structure: The Southern Farmers' Alliance and Cotton Tenancy, 1880–1890* (New York: Academic Press, 1976), and Roger L. Ransom and Richard Sutch, *One Kind of Freedom: The Economic Consequences of Emancipation* (Cambridge: Cambridge University Press, 1977).

19. This is most clearly stated in Lenin, *The Development of Capitalism in Russia.* Also see R. Firth and B. S. Yamey, eds., *Capital, Saving, and Credit in Peasant Societies* (London: Allen and Unwin, 1964).

Shanin.[20] The notion is ultimately derived from A. V. Chayanov's fertile studies of peasant self-exploitation and household economics, and in the hands of the skillful the approach has been important.[21]

Unfortunately, the equation of peasant property with petty proprietorship does not help us to build a rigorous class analysis of rural society. It is too abstract to delineate the specific logic of peasant property, although it does help us to see what peasants may share with other classes. More important, the equation begs a series of questions. What are the institutional preconditions of autonomy (the collective capacity to make and define rules) and control, and what kinds of resources are crucial to the existence of a peasant mode of production? What is needed is a precise set of boundaries that divide one class from all others, rules of identity distinct to the peasantry as a type, and those rules can be located only in the institutional configurations of property and power that emerge in the historical record. Yet if we return to that record we are faced once more with the problem of trying to specify which legal or customary forms are characteristic of peasant property. Perhaps we could confine our use of the term "peasant" to Wolf's middle proprietors; but to do so arbitrarily disqualifies whole social categories from the scope of peasant studies. What, for example, are we to do with Andalusian field laborers or semilandless villagers in pre–1910 Mexico, groups that are often thought to express the logic of peasant behavior best?[22]

It is instructive that Marx did not fall into these sorts of difficulties in his analysis of the industrial proletariat. Marx was completely clear that the proletariat was defined by its absolute lack of ownership and control of the strategic means of industrial production. At his most lucid, Marx always saw the "ontology" of class in dichotomous terms. People either were or were not members of society's key classes, according to their possession or nonpossession of determinate types of property. All other groups were residual or transitional, and it is perhaps a bit of self-conscious embarrassment about Marx's rigor that has led thoughtful neo-Marxists like Alain de Janvry to sidestep the peasantry by arguing that peasants are "class-fragments," "part-classes," or "classes of low classness."[23] Much neo-Marxist analysis of the countryside is exceptionally rich and

20. Eric Wolf, *Peasant Wars of the Twentieth Century* (New York: Harper and Row, 1969), *Peasants* (Englewood Cliffs, N.J.: Prentice-Hall, 1966); Joel Migdal, *Peasants, Politics, and Revolution: Pressures toward Political and Social Change in the Third World* (Princeton: Princeton University Press, 1974); Shanin, "Defining Peasants."

21. See the new edition of Chayanov's *The Theory of Peasant Economy* and the critical analysis provided in the volume by Daniel Thorner, Basile Kerblay, and R. E. F. Smith. The best application to a case study is Teodor Shanin, *The Awkward Class: Political Sociology of Peasantry in a Developing Society: Russia, 1910–1925* (Oxford: Clarendon Press, 1972).

22. See Eric Wolf, "Types of Latin American Peasantry: A Preliminary Discussion," *American Anthropologist* 57 (1955), 452–71, and Juan Martinez-Alier, *Labourers and Landowners in Southern Spain* (London: Allen and Unwin, 1971).

23. Alain de Janvry and Carmen Diana Deere, "A Conceptual Framework for the Empirical Analysis of Peasants," *American Journal of Agricultural Economics* 61 (Nov. 1979), 606–11; Alain de Janvry, *The Agrarian Question and Reformism*, 106.

provocative, but any openminded comparativist may pause when confronted by a class that turns out not to be a class at all.

If there is no specifiable form of peasant property then one of the chief props of class analysis is simply missing. But what of the other two criteria that a Marxist would use in trying to identify a peasant class? Can we describe a form of life and labor that is uniquely peasant? More important, can we identify a distinctively peasant politics that has a genuinely comparative reference?

The existence of a homogeneous mode of peasant life and labor appears to be unproblematic. Peasants are agriculturalists, and their common fate as victims of the agrarian calendar should give rise to a shared subjective experience of nature. Moreover, that they all work the land ought to indicate deep similarities in the process of production, beneath any surface differences of culture and institutions.

These subjective and objective similarities are important, but it is not obvious that they can be used as a basis for the class analysis of the countryside. A common relationship to nature does not guarantee a common subjective consciousness of the implications of natural rhythms for social life. As Thomas C. Smith has pointed out, the Japanese villagers of the Tokugawa period had a conception of the natural flow of time very different from that of their English counterparts, and Smith's findings can be generalized into a critique of any simple equation of agriculture with a uniquely determined psychology or view of the world.[24] It is worth remarking that American farmers have never regarded themselves as peasants, even though their objective economic circumstances resembled those of European peasants.[25]

A more significant objection to the notion of a peasant way of life is directly related to the question of the nature of rural labor. Involvement in cultivation can mean many things, depending on the time and place. In medieval English villages the abstract category of rural labor could refer to anything from the year-long work of a semiskilled farm servant to the strenuous existence of a yeoman or husbandman, whose labor required both skill and a stock of farm tools.[26] Similarly, rural labor in eighteenth-century Japan, cannot be disaggregated into a homogeneous category. In a single village every member family would probably have a slightly different combination of work routines, specific skills, and work-related equipment.[27]

Marx's notion of the growing homogeneity of factory labor cannot be trans-

24. Thomas C. Smith, "Peasant Time and Factory Time in Japan," *Past and Present* 111 (May 1986), 165–97.

25. Scott G. McNall, *The Road to Rebellion: Class Formation and Kansas Populism, 1865–1900* (Chicago: University of Chicago Press, 1988), 93–184.

26. See the essays in T. H. Aston, ed., *Landlords, Peasants, and Politics in Medieval England* (Cambridge: Cambridge University Press, 1987), esp. Robert A. Didgshon, "The Landholding Foundations of the Open Field System," 6–32, and Zvi Razi, "Family, Land, and the Village Community in Later Medieval England," 360–93.

27. Thomas C. Smith et al., *Nakahara: Family Farming and Population in a Japanese Village, 1717–1830* (Stanford: Stanford University Press, 1977), 105–32.

posed to agriculture without generating a whole series of empirical problems. Agricultural labor, unlike the assembly line, is marked by a high degree of local and national variation. Different soils, crops, and forms of cooperation guarantee a diversity of types of labor not easily reduced to a common core. Agriculturalists may also be involved in a wide range of occupations and modes of labor in addition to cultivation, as we now know from the study of "protoindustrialization." But, in addition to by-employments, cultivators may simultaneously occupy a number of roles in the farmwork process, from owner-farmer to tenant and employee. Perhaps the most that can be said is that peasant farming tends to approximate a system of small-scale, household production; but this is too general a category to be useful as a basis for class analysis.

It is equally difficult to identify a specifically "peasant" politics. During the nineteenth and early twentieth centuries, peasants were regarded as inherently conservative and passive, addicted to small property and reactionary nostalgia. The explosion of rural radicalism in the twentieth century forced a complete revision of this older view, and by the 1970s some scholars had concluded that the peasantry had replaced the proletariat as the world's revolutionary class. Recently, however, James C. Scott has persuasively argued that peasants are not usually the carriers of revolutionary consciousness, even if exceptional periods of crisis may yield rare bursts of radical enthusiasm.[28]

The absence of any consensus about the simple question of peasant political interests and ideology is a certain indication that something is wrong with the way we have approached the issue. We have been so accustomed to thinking of the peasantry as a unitary class with homogeneous political interests that it has become difficult to conceptualize the remarkable political diversity of rural societies. The record of even a single national society presents a complex picture of competing and contrary rural interests and political values—not the stuff from which a precise class analysis is made.

The history of postrevolutionary France is an excellent illustration of the pitfalls that result when we assume that there must be a form of politics characteristic of peasants. After 1789, rural France fractured politically along lines that were related to support for or opposition to the revolutionary legacy. In the west, for example, the anticlericalism of the early revolutionary regimes bred a tradition of hostility to the republic that lasted into the twentieth century.[29] But in parts of the south and center the Revolution was a popular event, and village radicalism

28. Scott, *Weapons of the Weak*, 1–48.

29. T. J. A. Le Goff and D. M. G. Sutherland, "The Social Origins of Counter-Revolution in Western France," *Past and Present* 99 (1983), 65–87; and T. J. A. Le Goff and D. M. G. Sutherland, "Religion and Rural Revolt in the French Revolution: An Overview," in Janos M. Bak and Gerhard Benecke, eds., *Religion and Rural Revolt: Papers Presented to the Fourth Interdisciplinary Workshop on Peasant Studies, University of British Columbia, 1982* (Dover: Manchester University Press, 1984), 123–45.

became a force to be reckoned with in the 1800s, as Maurice Agulhon and Ted Margadant have shown.[30] In between the extremes of reaction and revolutionary radicalism were the other regions of rural France, and in this broad center popular opinion combined guarded acceptance of parts of the revolutionary program with a healthy skepticism about the meaning of the republic. It is therefore illusory to speak categorically about the French peasantry; there were several French peasantries with distinct patterns of political action and ideals.[31]

France is no exception in this regard, and the more rural history we know the less confident we become about our ability to isolate peasant classes at the level of the nation-state. This is why so little rural history is written at the level of regions and localities, a fact that goes some way toward undermining the notion of a uniform peasant political interest or program. Peasant politics, if it means anything, is a shorthand for the rich diversity of local political issues that constitute the public text of rural life.

The point is worth underscoring, because it is easy to assume that peasant politics can be reduced to struggle over land and the conditions of land tenure. As we shall see, the definition of property rights to land has always been important, but it is in no way the only crucial issue. Taxation, religious politics, and the status of cultivators have also been at the root of much rural political mobilization, including periods that have led to rebellion. Marx's understanding of unitary class interests has little relevance to making comparative sense out of this complexity, and it may have been the difficulty of interpreting the countryside according to class logic that led Marx to his famous tirade against peasants in "The Eighteenth Brumaire."[32]

It is anomalous that peasant classes manifest social characteristics that are not part of the logic of class relations. Even more puzzling, peasants are able to engage in collective action even though they lack the structural organization the Marxists associate with class and that is often seen as prerequisite to the effective performance of group action. How can peasants act at all if they do not have an unambiguous class structure and identity, if they are a "class of low classness"? The question is meant to throw into sharp relief the whole problem of the peasant in social theory. If we are to resolve that problem we must move to a new discourse about rural society.

At a minimum, that discourse should build on the rich work already done by historians and social scientists. More important, our rethinking should provide

30. Maurice Agulhon, *The Republic in the Village: The People of the Var from the French Revolution to the Second Republic* (Cambridge: Cambridge University Press, 1982), esp. 273–304; Ted Margadant, *French Peasants in Revolt: The Insurrection of 1851* (Princeton: Princeton University Press, 1979), esp. 231–32, 239–42, 249–50, 257–64.
31. Jones, *The Peasantry in the French Revolution,* esp. 60–123.
32. For an overall analysis of Marx's thinking about rural society, see Athar Hussain and Keith Tribe, *Marxism and the Agrarian Question,* 2 vols. (Atlantic Highlands, N.J.: Humanities Press, 1981).

basic concepts that equal Marx's understanding of class in terms of clarity and fruitfulness. An alternative conceptualization of rural life must also offer a plausible interpretation of the links between material circumstances and political institutions. In short, a new understanding of the countryside ought to enable us to present a more powerful explanation of the issues that are treated in a less satisfactory way by class analysis.

Community against Class

Community is the most obvious alternative to class as a basis for interpreting the logic of rural institutions.[33] Community appears as an organizing category in rural scholarship with awesome frequency, and the ethnographic tradition in anthropology focuses on the meaning of community in local contexts.[34] Historians and social scientists have also spent a great deal of effort in trying to interpret the nature of community institutions. Indeed, a clever content analysis would probably show that references to community outnumber references to class in peasant studies.

There is nothing, therefore, novel or eccentric about the use of community in rural analysis. What is puzzling is the failure of writers to think how community might substitute as an organizing category for class. In this section, I explore the failure to take community seriously as a "foundational" category.

The first and most obvious weakness in traditional discussions of community is the failure to situate the concept in terms of distinct criteria of application. Notions of community are too often vague, and we are left to wonder how to define who is a member and how much social space is included in a given community.[35] At its worst, this imprecision reduces community to a vaguely specified state of mind, a kind of nebulous value or cultural variable that has little connection with the real

33. Scholars who have come close to my meaning of community include Jerome Blum, "The European Village as Community: Origins and Functions," *Agricultural History* 45 (July 1971), 157–78; Eric Wolf, *Sons of the Shaking Earth* (Chicago: University of Chicago Press, 1959); Peter H. Prindle, "Peasant-Worker Households and Community Based Organizations in Rural Japan," *Modern Asian Studies* 19 (April 1985), 279–97; Clifford Geertz, *Agricultural Involution: The Process of Ecological Change in Indonesia* (Berkeley: University of California Press, 1963); R. Stavenhagen, "Changing Functions of the Community in Underdeveloped Countries," *Sociologia Ruralis* 4 (3 and 4) (1964); and Henri Stahl, *Traditional Romanian Village Communities: The Transition from the Communal to the Capitalist Mode of Production in the Danube Region* (Cambridge: Cambridge University Press, 1980).

34. The best example is Clifford Geertz's "Deep Play: Notes on the Balinese Cockfight," in Geertz, *The Interpretation of Cultures* (New York: Basic Books, 1973), 459–90; also see his *Local Knowledge: Further Essays in Interpretive Anthropology* (New York: Basic Books, 1983), esp. 19–35.

35. This is a problem, for example, with Craig Calhoun's brilliant book, *The Question of Class Struggle: Social Foundations of Popular Radicalism during the Industrial Revolution* (Chicago: University of Chicago Press, 1982), esp. 149–82, 204–35.

world of power and production. Even at its best, open-ended analysis of community begs a key question: What is community about; or, more precisely, what are the kinds of problems that provide the organizational principles of community institutions? Legislatures pass laws, and armies wage wars. But what are the conditions and meaning of rural communities, and can we understand them in a way that avoids the cruder forms of functionalism?

One way of addressing the issue is to situate rural community in a material context, beyond questions of cultural identity. This reinterpretation ought to show how community institutions draw the territorial boundaries of social action by defining basic rules of membership. If community is more than sentiment, it must be rooted in substantive issues of power and production.

An illustration will help to illuminate the point. Villagers in medieval and early modern Europe were highly conscious of the importance of maintaining the territorial integrity of their villages.[36] Boundaries were often marked with the precision of a ritual fetish, and local rights to gleaning and alms begging were determined by village membership.[37] The territory that lay within the community was the locus of a whole series of mutually implicated institutions, a fact carefully preserved in the discourse of village elders. In seventeenth-century England, for example, the memory of place was enacted yearly in the festive perambulation of the village at Rogationtide.[38]

Nor was the intimate connection between territory and community simply a historical artifact of the European open-field village. A similar connection can be found in Japan, China, and the complex civilizations of the New World.[39] In every

36. Susan Reynolds, *Kingdoms and Communities in Western Europe, 900–1300* (Oxford: Clarendon Press, 1984), pp. 101–54; Harold J. Berman, *Law and Revolution: The Formation of the Western Legal Tradition* (Cambridge: Harvard University Press, 1983), 316–32.

37. See, for example, Jerome Blum, *The End of the Old Order in Rural Europe* (Princeton: Princeton University Press, 1978), 95–115; Marc Bloch, *French Rural History: An Essay on Its Basic Characteristics* (Berkeley: University of California Press, 1966), 35–48; Carl Dahlman, *The Open Field System and Beyond: A Property Right Analysis of an Economic Institution* (Cambridge: Cambridge University Press, 1980), esp. 1–64.

38. David Underdown, *Revel, Riot, and Rebellion: Popular Politics and Culture in England, 1603–1660* (Oxford: Clarendon Press, 1985), 45–47.

39. For China, see Philip C. C. Huang, *The Peasant Economy and Social Change in North China* (Stanford: Stanford University Press, 1985), esp. 23–32, 219–49; Elizabeth Perry, *Rebels and Revolutionaries in North China, 1845–1945* (Stanford: Stanford University Press, 1980), 1–95; Prasenjit Duara, *Culture, Power, and the State, Rural North China, 1900–1942* (Stanford: Stanford University Press, 1988), 86–193; Richard Madsen, *Morality and Power in a Chinese Village* (Berkeley: University of California Press, 1984), 1–66; and Michio Tanigawa, *Medieval Chinese Society and the Local "Community,"* trans. Joshua A. Fogel (Berkeley: University of California Press, 1985), 100–26. For Japan, see Tadashi Fukutake, *Japanese Rural Society* (Tokyo: Oxford University Press, 1967), 25–27, 81–116; John Embree, *Suye Mura: A Japanese Village* (Chicago: University of Chicago Press, 1946); Thomas C. Smith, *The Agrarian Origins of Modern Japan* (Stanford: Stanford University Press, 1959), 36–37, 208–9; and Ronald P. Dore, *Land Reform in Japan* (London: Oxford University Press, 1959). For the New World, see Karen Spaulding, *Huarochiri: An Andean Society under Inca and Spanish Rule* (Stanford: Stanford University Press, 1984), 1–71; Nancy M. Farriss, *Maya Society under Colonial Rule: The Collective Enterprise of Survival* (Princeton: Princeton

case, spatial boundaries defined the nature and meaning of agrarian social structure. To belong to a rural community was to belong to a specific place with a particular history.

The significance of territorial boundaries for agrarian community should not be surprising. Land is obviously crucial to agricultural life, and this looks like another instance in which theory should start with the obvious. Land is a fixed and finite resource, always subject to demographically induced scarcity. We should expect all civilizations to develop firm rules governing the use and control of lands.

There seems to be a very close association between property rights to land and the nature of community institutions in small-scale agricultural societies. Community institutions have often determined the rules that control who can use land and how. For example, the Russian village land commune was the locus of property rights in the Russian countryside, and periodic redistributions of land rights were made by the assembled members of the village.[40] Even in less corporate societies, community typically forms the matrix of critical decisions that affect the disposition of land. In medieval open-field villages, the village or parish and its associated manor was vital to the operation of both common and household property. It was at this level that conflicts were decided, exchanges were consummated, and routine forms of land use were determined.

It is reasonable, then, to redescribe rural community as the core institutional matrix that controls territorial membership rights, especially rights to landed property. We should expect community members to have a highly developed consciousness of place; and "localism," or attachment to a discrete territory, should serve as one important indicator of the strength of community.

Territorial membership, however, is insufficient as a basis for rethinking rural community. We also need to consider how power is institutionalized in communities and how it is mobilized and maintained in traditional rural societies. Unfortunately, this subject has not received a completely convincing discussion in the literature, and seeing why is important in understanding the confusion that has surrounded the concept of community.

University Press, 1984), 3–56, 131–46; Steve J. Stern, *Peru's Indian Peoples and the Challenge of Spanish Conquest: Huamanga to 1640* (Madison: University of Wisconsin Press, 1982), 3–50; Brooke Larson, *Colonialism and Agrarian Transformation in Bolivia: Cochabamba, 1550–1900* (Princeton: Princeton University Press, 1988), 133–70; Steve J. Stern, ed., *Resistance, Rebellion, and Consciousness in the Andean Peasant World, 18th to 20th Centuries* (Madison: University of Wisconsin Press, 1987), 3–33, 232–79; and Friedrich Katz, ed., *Riot, Rebellion, and Revolution: Rural Social Conflict in Mexico* (Princeton: Princeton University Press, 1988), esp. John Tutino, "Agrarian and Peasant Rebellion in Nineteenth-Century Mexico: The Example of Chalco," 95–140.

40. Dorothy Atkinson, *The End of the Russian Land Commune, 1905–1930* (Stanford: Stanford University Press, 1983), 13–40, and Geroid Tanguary Robinson, *Rural Russia under the Old Regime: A History of the Landlord-Peasant World and a Prologue to the Peasant Revolution of 1917* (Berkeley: University of California Press, 1967), 34–36.

It has been typical to associate community with equality, and the tendency to presume that communities are inherently egalitarian is the second major weakness in our received theories of community. Even a thinker as sophisticated as Michael Taylor defines community as a situation of at least rough equality of rights and resources.[41] Taylor's argument is compelling, but it seems to rest on a subtle misreading of the old notion of gemeinschaft. In classical social theory, gemeinschaft, or community, referred to a sentiment of corporate belonging rooted in tradition, but it did not refer to modern notions of social and political equality.

Rural communities are usually places of hierarchy and inequality in which prestige, power, and privilege are strictly regulated according to entrenched principles of selective distribution. What has made this relatively uncontroversial point so difficult for theorists of community to account for is that many forms of rural hierarchy are not based in property or class. Status, gender, age, and office are just as significant.

An interesting example of community-based hierarchy can be found in the Russian land commune. Land communes did repartition land rights in an effort to level out the disparities of landholding between households. But in all other areas of village life inequality was both the theory and practice of village routine. Men clearly dominated women, and established male householders dominated the rest of the village population. None of this would be evident, however, to someone who saw equality purely as a material problem of property rights. Similarly, illustrations like this one should provide a cautionary tale for anyone who still believes that inequality per se is the fundamental cause of rural protest and political instability.

The existence of hierarchy within rural communities is not difficult to explain. If community institutions are central in the determination of territorial membership, we would expect those institutional practices to be embedded in the enforcement of the rules of community rights and obligations. Thus, the forms of inequality that underpin community cohesion should be interpreted as having deep implications for the maintenance of group order in conditions of scarcity. Some kind of sanctioning is necessary to enforce the local rules of the game, and the kinds of sanctioning mechanisms available in agrarian societies will be closely related to the range of hierarchies that have developed around the rhythms and problems of agriculture. Of these forms of "natural" hierarchy, kinship and ritual prestige are particularly important and seem to characterize much of what we mean by power and politics in rural life.[42]

41. Michael Taylor, *Community, Anarchy, and Liberty* (Cambridge: Cambridge University Press, 1982), esp. 1–38.
42. The classic expression is Louis Dumont, *Homo Hierarchicus: An Essay on the Caste System* (Chicago: University of Chicago Press, 1970). But also see the discussion of "reciprocal hierarchy" in Allen W. Johnson and Timothy Earle, *The Evolution of Human Societies: From Foraging Group to Agrarian State* (Stanford: Stanford University Press, 1987), esp. 1–26, 101–206. These issues are

A striking instance of the interaction of power, hierarchy, and the maintenance of group discipline can be found in the history of the Irish phenomenon of Whiteboyism.[43] Whiteboys were Ireland's most violent and uncompromising popular opponents of the Anglo-Irish landed elite, and the "outrages" committed by Whiteboy secret societies plunged entire counties into chaos during the eighteenth and early nineteenth centuries. But Whiteboys were not revolutionaries, and the fury was as often directed at tenant farmers who violated Whiteboy rules as it was at the real landed elite. Nor were they dispossessed quasi-proletarians, and the evidence indicates that they were bound by ties of kinship and neighborhood that extended to the limits of a village or townland. Local networks constituted the paths of hierarchy that allowed Whiteboy societies to flourish in an atmosphere of community secrecy and solidarity. Indeed, there was no real distinction between groups and the established institutions of local Irish communities; and Whiteboyism can best be described as a militant defense of poor rural communities by the junior members of farming families. The "law" they claimed to enforce was the elite's but the law as understood by popular custom, something that tenant farmers and graziers discovered to their cost when they accepted leases at rates unacceptable to local norms.[44]

The essential point here is that institutional inequalities can be a source of cohesion and solidarity, and the types of hierarchy that facilitate group discipline cannot be reduced to simple class categories. Rural communities almost always display deeply rooted distinctions between the more and less advantaged. Yet those distinctions and divisions allow the community as a whole to mobilize itself for collective action by projecting the advantaged into natural leadership roles.[45]

By emphasizing the inegalitarian dimensions of rural community I do not wish

sometimes lumped under the heading of "patron-client" relations. See, for example, Steffen Schmidt et al., eds., *Friends, Followers, and Factions: A Reader in Political Clientalism* (Berkeley: University of California Press, 1977).

43. See C. H. E. Philpin, ed., *Nationalism and Popular Protest in Ireland* (Cambridge: Cambridge University Press, 1987), 163–263.

44. Samuel Clark, *The Social Origins of the Irish Land War* (Princeton: Princeton University Press, 1979), 65–106.

45. Interesting support for this notion comes from a variety of cultures. See, for example, David Lan, *Guns and Rain: Guerrillas and Spirit Mediums in Zimbabwe* (Berkeley: University of California Press, 1985); Ranger, *Peasant Consciousness and Guerrilla War in Zimbabwe*, 1–53; Johanna Menzel Meskill, *A Chinese Pioneer Family: The Lins of Wu-Feng, Taiwan, 1729–1895* (Princeton: Princeton University Press, 1979), 83–176, 179–232; Hue Tam Ho Tai, *Millenarianism and Peasant Politics in Vietnam* (Cambridge: Harvard University Press, 1983), 3–43, 169–84; Raheja, *The Poison in the Gift*, 1–67; Ward Keeler, *Javanese Shadow Plays, Javanese Selves* (Princeton: Princeton University Press, 1987), 51–108, 261–68; Michael Herzfeld, *The Poetics of Manhood: Contest and Identity in a Cretan Mountain Village* (Princeton: Princeton University Press, 1985), 3–91, 259–74; David Gilmore, *Aggression and Community: Paradoxes of Andalusian Culture* (New Haven: Yale University Press, 1987), 126–53, 171–86. For a more theoretic perspective, see F. G. Bailey, *The Tactical Uses of Passion: An Essay on Power, Reason, and Reality* (Ithaca: Cornell University Press, 1983).

to exaggerate the degree of hierarchy characteristic of rural institutions.[46] All the examples mentioned so far were much less stratified than the larger social wholes that were built on the foundation of local community resources. For example, the disparity in power and wealth between a Russian nobleman and a serf villager was vastly greater than between villagers. More important, the former difference is really a matter of kind rather than degree, because the nobleman could make claims on village resources that were not reciprocated by any flow of resources from lord to serf, whereas within rural communities the advantaged were forced to practice a measure of reciprocity, even if it was done solely as a kind of insurance against the wrath of the envious. Community hierarchy was reciprocal hierarchy, and this marks an important borderline between the institutional logic of community and the division between popular communities and the institutions of elite power. In the latter case, the separation between elites and popular groups is so pronounced that we are justified in speaking of a qualitative gap or discontinuity between groups in terms of resources and advantage. But in the former case the privileges of local rank and position do not translate into the basis of unchecked domination. The local elders may be patriarchs and oligarchs, but they are too dependent on their followers and neighbors to become real despots.[47]

Rural community has been shown by many scholars in diverse disciplines to be a core principle of rural social organization. Yet the full theoretical significance of community cannot be appreciated unless we link the concept with an understanding of how community institutions regulate the conditions of access to land and provide rules for the enforcement of rights and responsibilities attached to community membership. In agrarian societies the key existential problem is how to organize the production and distribution of the means of subsistence, and we can interpret community institutions as the core organizational framework in which that problem is managed across time and space. Rural communities are thus marked by a balance of cooperation and conflict in which cooperation is sufficiently developed to outweigh the range of conflict that is likely to occur in situations of severe scarcity. Rural communities are inegalitarian and hierarchic, but hierarchy is mitigated by reciprocity and by the existence of customary local codes of moral rules that bind people together. Agricultural communities are forms of political order that have at least a limited jurisdiction over their members and the definition of the criteria of membership.

46. For more "egalitarian" perspectives, see E. P. Thompson, "The Moral Economy of the English Crowd in the Eighteenth Century," *Past and Present,* 50 (Feb. 1971), 76–136; Karl Polanyi, *The Great Transformation* (Boston: Beacon Press, 1957); and Eric Wolf, "Aspects of Group Relations in a Complex Society: Mexico," *American Anthropologist* 58 (Dec. 1956), 1065–78.

47. Theoretical underpinning for this perspective was drawn from essays in Taylor, ed., *Rationality and Revolution,* esp. the Introduction, 1–6, Samuel Popkin's "Political Entrepreneurs and Peasant Movements in Vietnam," 9–62, and Michael Taylor's "Rationality and Revolutionary Collective Action," 63–97; and Eli Sagan, *At the Dawn of Tyranny: The Origins of Individualism, Political Oppression, and the State* (New York: Knopf, 1985), esp. 225–300.

Rural institutions that manifest these characteristics will be described hereafter as communities of grain. The name captures two basic features of small-scale agrarian societies. First, it points to the centrality of subsistence issues and the logic of subsistence production throughout most of human history, something that has been restored to importance by the work of Scott.[48] But it also highlights the importance of local, territorially based modes of organizing the ongoing problem of producing *and* distributing the means of life.

Fully developed communities of grain should therefore be identifiable according to three dimensions of institutional variation. To begin with, the rules of membership and the modes of resolving conflicts about the rights and duties of membership ought to fall within the jurisdiction of community institutions. In the limiting case, membership will be hereditary, and the rules governing access to community resources will be ascriptive and limited to those born within a particular locality. The only exception will be for those whose status is changed from outsider to insider through marriage or fictive kinship. Even in more open communities, however, membership is a scarce and jealously guarded resource, because its possession confers access to whatever material and social resources fall within local jurisdictions. The mechanisms through which jurisdiction is exercised are of equal importance; and we should expect the most cohesive communities to manifest strong institutions of local control, although the precise nature of those institutions may vary widely across societies. Councils of village notables, religious confraternities, and agricultural cooperatives are some of the most frequently encountered types of jurisdictional hierarchies.

The second major dimension of rural community has to do with the existence of a local tradition of social identity that shapes the preferences of community members. Strong communities will have a folklore of place that affects the ways in which group members categorize their primary interests and basic loyalties. Historians and anthropologists are familiar with the phenomenon of "local patriotism," a powerful sense of identification with a village or hometown; and at a minimum, rural communities will be able to mobilize the loyalties of their members in defense of community interests. In some cases, community will rank with kinship as a primary focus of loyalty, even if it means direct conflict with external authorities.

Although the empirical identification of a folklore of place is difficult, especially in oral cultures, historians have compiled impressive evidence of the existence of such traditions; and they have also helped us to think about how we can locate and interpret local traditions. One fruitful approach is to look for institutional practices that ritually focus group consciousness at the level of single communities. The English perambulation of the village at Rogationtide is an obvious example.

The final characteristic of rural community that is important concerns the

48. Scott, *The Moral Economy of the Peasant.*

relationship between material production and community institutions. Well-entrenched communities will have well-defined forms of economic cooperation that link households in patterns of work and exchange. At a minimum, cooperation among members involves ongoing practices of mutual aid at crucial periods of the agricultural cycle. In the limiting instance, cooperation may include commonly owned property rights and cooperative labor. The essential issue, however, is the presence or absence of community practices that provide members with a limited guarantee of household survival during periods of subsistence crisis. I shall apply the threefold division of community institutions along economic, political, and ritual lines throughout the case studies, organizing them according to the specific logic of each case.

None of these characteristics should be taken to imply that rural communities are egalitarian, risk-sharing associations; as indicated earlier, agrarian communities are certainly hierarchical. Nor does the presence of material cooperation beyond the level of the nuclear household imply that collective labor and land tenure are statistically typical. But even a very circumscribed arena of economic action subject to community rules should offer potent incentives to abide by community norms, especially in poor societies.

Rural communities, then, can be studied in terms of the institutionalization of basic practices that constitute agrarian social order. The crucial arenas of institutional action are the mechanisms of authoritative control and jurisdiction of membership, the channels of discursive focus that establish a folklore of place, and the forms of economic cooperation that underpin membership claims to local subsistence. The presence of these three forms of institutional action can be thought of as the jointly necessary criteria for the identification of community. Where all three criteria are absent, there is a strong presumption that we are faced with an alternative logic of social action. An even more interesting problem is explaining how and why rural communities vary in terms of institutional cohesiveness and persistence, a problem that will be explored in the case studies. If this approach to community is fruitful it should give us a useful framework for interpreting the dynamics of rural change in comparative perspective.

Community and Its Critics

Before turning to a discussion of community and rebellion, it is useful to consider some characteristic objections to the notion that community is a significant analytic category. One potentially damaging criticism is that I have mistaken an elaborate form of popular false consciousness for the really important material and class issues that give meaning to community. Ordinary people may believe that they are living within a logic of community institutions, but they are really responding to ulterior class forces. Community is just another "primitive" ideology, and like all ideologies it should not be turned into an analytic category.

This is a difficult objection to deal with, but only because false consciousness is sufficiently elastic and imprecise to be resurrected in any debate. James C. Scott, who is otherwise sympathetic to the use of class logic, has gone some way toward demolishing false consciousness as a useful way of understanding rural societies. I can only add that I have gone to considerable lengths to situate my concept of the community of grain in a very real material problematic of territorially based production and exchange. I do not think this can be fairly described as a form of "idealism" or ideological reification.

A more substantive objection to the argument is that it revives an old "structural-functionalism" in which institutions are falsely given the mental and causal properties of real human beings. Community is merely a hypostatized fiction, a kind of miniature Leviathan that has no reality apart from the people who compose it.[49]

My response to this line of attack is straightforward. Teleological and other excessive functionalisms are real problems, and many forms of structural logic have crashed on their shoals. But the world of theory is more complex than some suppose, and a commitment to community is not the same as a commitment to systems theory. When I use the notion of institutional patterns I simply mean that determinate social practices have specific effects. I do not mean that I believe that structure is more real than individual action and that the theoretical parts of this work can be read in the spirit of Weber's methodological individualism. Moreover, the use of community does not entail a speculative anthropology about the ultimate origins of agrarian institutions. I am well aware of the "fallacy of affirming the consequent," and all I have to show is that *if* community is important it should carry a particular logic of motivation, whatever its ultimate genesis might be. My starting point is the commonplace observation that agrarian societies must manage the ongoing problem of producing and distributing the means of subsistence. If this is functionalism then it is a weak variety that seems to be a necessary feature of all social science.

Finally, an observation about irrationality is in order.[50] Some may accuse me of reintroducing irrational motives into the study of rural society. After all, rural community has often been treated as a species of arational action, or a kind of primitive collectivism. Surely the argument would be better served by a crisp reduction of community to self-interested behavior.

Irrationality is an explosive term in social science, and there is no reason to defend some of the bizarre errors that have been committed in its name. In this book I adopt a weak notion that ordinary action is rationally motivated, although I stress the institutional patterns that structure rational behavior. My assumption is that rural people will defend the autonomy and cohesiveness of community practices against external threats, but only because those practices are important

49. See the critique of functionalism in Jon Elster, *Ulysses and the Sirens: Studies in Rationality and Irrationality* (Cambridge: Cambridge University Press, 1985), 28–35.

50. For rationality and irrationality, see Martin Hollis, *The Cunning of Reason* (Cambridge: Cambridge University Press, 1987), 15–46, 173–93.

in protecting popular interests. In this sense, the community of grain can be understood as a protective matrix in which individual and kin-based interests are played out in a context of scarce resources and uncertain outcomes.[51]

Why, then, have I not deployed a microeconomic or choice theoretic explanation of rural behavior? I have no particular objection to these tasks, and to some extent the basic work has already been done by Samuel Popkin and Michael Taylor.[52] Still, I am interested in trying to reconceptualize rural societies in a way that moves beyond the problems of class analysis, and this is a task that is best undertaken in a vocabulary drawn from classical social theory. If my concept of community works well, it ought to be of use to choice theorists who wish to situate politics in a framework of specifiable interpersonal interactions.

But more important, the kinds of issues I address are rather different from the issues that occupy choice theory. Much of the best work in game theory is concerned with the preconditions of collective action, whereas the issues I will deal with already presuppose some type of collective organization. In short, the people called peasants are "preorganized," and the basic problem has always been how we are to interpret the nature of that organization. My own suggestion is that we can understand community as rooted in a series of mutually implicated forms of cooperation in which the successful performance of cooperative action in one problem area (production, for example) depends on the successful performance of cooperation in other arenas (rituals or politics, for instance). A game theoretic perspective might see such cooperation as an instance of "iterated prisoner's dilemma" or "tit-for-tat" conditional cooperation.[53] For my purposes, however, the larger issue is how we are to understand the logic of rural social organization, especially when rebellion is the problem that must be explained, for, whatever else it may be, rebellion is a collective act.

Rebellion as Representative Violence

Rural rebellion is one of the most studied and least clearly thought out concepts in social science. There is little agreement about the causes of rural insurrection, and even less about the relative significance of the phenomenon. Recently, for example, Scott reversed his previous evaluation of the problem by declaring that

51. For a similar logic, see Sahlins, *Stone Age Economics*, 41–100; Jack Goody et al., eds., *Family and Inheritance: Rural Society in Western Europe, 1200–1800* (Cambridge: Cambridge University Press, 1976), esp. Goody, "Inheritance, Property and Women: Some Comparative Considerations," 10–36, and Emmanuel Le Roy Ladurie, "Family Structures and Inheritance Customs in Sixteenth-Century France," 37–70; and Hans Medick and David Warren Sabean, eds., *Interest and Emotion: Essays on the Study of Family and Kinship* (Cambridge: Cambridge University Press, 1984).

52. Popkin, *The Rational Peasant;* Michael Taylor, *Anarchy and Cooperation* (London: John Wiley, 1976).

53. See Michael Taylor, *The Possibility of Cooperation* (Cambridge: Cambridge University Press, 1987), 82–108.

rebellion is too rare and inconsequential to be taken seriously as a focus of inquiry. But Scott's pessimism is not shared by many other scholars, who continue to investigate the episodes of revolt that can be found in an amazing variety of social and historical contexts.[54]

Fortunately, historians have not been as perplexed as social scientists by the complexity of the issues, and they have produced an extraordinary range of studies that investigate the nature of rural revolt in detailed monographs that reconstruct the microcontexts in which insurrection has occurred. What these studies seem to show is that there is no single cause or variable that best explains rebellion. Land tenure is often singled out in theoretical works as the principal problem around which violent struggles take place, but the historical record seems to indicate that tenure is just one source of rural violence. Taxation, religious conflict, colonialism, and political struggles have also been linked to the deep origins of rebellion.[55] The old notion of a monolithic type of behavior lumped under the heading of peasant revolt cannot withstand close scrutiny. The causes and characteristics of the phenomenon are too diverse and too contingent to be reduced to a simple causal model rooted in class forces.

This conclusion begs a very difficult question. How are we to make comparative sense out of the phenomenon, and how can we theoretically locate rebellion in a workable analytic framework that respects the integrity of history without sacrificing comparative scope? To begin with, there is no reason to suppose that rural rebellion needs to be understood as a type of revolution. Revolution involves the conscious and total destruction of an established social order, and measured by this criterion there is little that is revolutionary about rural collective violence.

Much of the violence discussed in this book was limited to a very small territorial area, and the goals and methods at work were not consciously subversive of the whole social order. It is this fact that has led some to dismiss rural

54. See, for example, John Tutino, *From Insurrection to Revolution in Mexico: Social Bases of Agrarian Violence, 1750–1940* (Princeton: Princeton University Press, 1986); Karen Field, *Revival and Rebellion in Colonial Central Africa* (Princeton: Princeton University Press, 1985); William Beinart and Colin Bundy, *Hidden Struggles in Rural South Africa: Politics and Popular Movements in the Transkei and Eastern Cape, 1890–1930* (Berkeley: University of California Press, 1987); and George A. Collier, *Socialists of Rural Andalusia: Unacknowledged Revolutionaries of the Second Republic* (Stanford: Stanford University Press, 1987). The list of monographic studies of rural rebellion could, in fact, be extended almost indefinitely.

55. This reading of the multicausal origins of revolt is indebted to the following works: Michael Adas, *Prophets of Rebellion: Millenarian Protest Movements against the European Colonial Order* (Chapel Hill: University of North Carolina Press, 1979), 43–79; Phil Billingsley, *Bandits in Republican China* (Stanford: Stanford University Press, 1988), 193–286; James B. Rule, *Theories of Civil Violence* (Berkeley: University of California Press, 1988), 1–53; John Walton, *Reluctant Rebels: Comparative Studies of Revolution and Underdevelopment* (New York: Columbia University Press, 1984), 1–36, 141–72; and Charles Tilly, *From Mobilization to Revolution* (Reading, Mass.: Addison-Wesley, 1978), 189–222. Perhaps the most subtle discussions of rural rebellion can be found in Zagorin, *Rebels and Rulers*, 1:3–60, 175–227, and Alan Knight, *The Mexican Revolution*, 2 vols. (Cambridge: Cambridge University Press, 1986), 1:78–170.

rebellion as unimportant, because it can never meet the grand objectives of a truly revolutionary project. Yet unless we are willing to ignore the problem entirely, we should be prepared to rethink rural rebellion in a way that breaks completely with the somewhat sterile debate about whether peasants are the revolutionary class of the twentieth century.

My own suggestion is that we view rural insurrection as an instance of what might be described as representative violence. In situations of representative violence, the escalation to violent struggle is the medium through which fundamental interests are made the object of direct conflict. Violence is therefore a means of representation that specific social actors use to challenge those aspects of an established order that threaten deeply valued practices. Such situations are radical moments, but solely in the old-fashioned sense of being about root-and-branch issues, and there should be no confusion of radical action with a revolutionary design for the complete revision of all institutions. The archetypical cases of representative violence are those moments when popular groups represent themselves through collective violence in order to change elite preferences and behavior. This must be seen as an instant when one or more elements of the deep constitution of society are thrown into question, even though much of the rest of that constitution is never challenged. Thus, violence of this kind is inherently ironic and contradictory. It combines a basic challenge to the status quo with at least a tacit commitment to elements of the same status quo; and it uses the most radical and dangerous of all political mediums, collective violence, to effect a nonrevolutionary break with the past.

The concept of representative violence is necessarily open-ended, and that is precisely its virtue. It is broad enough to encompass the rich diversity of issues and interests that show through the historical record of rural societies, without reducing the problem of rebellion to a futile debate about whether such behavior is best understood as materially or culturally motivated. It therefore avoids arbitrary distinctions and focuses the underlying problems of power and authority that are implicated in the representation of interests.

More important, the concept highlights the distinctive character of collective violence in human life. Violent conflicts are unlike any other kind of politics, because violence vastly magnifies the problem of unintended consequences. When violence occurs it is impossible to predict exactly what will take place; and disastrous outcomes and failed performances are just as likely as outcomes preferred by the actors. For example, assassination was a fairly common form of popular violence during the Whiteboy phase of Irish agrarian history.[56] Assassination attempts could always fail, however; their perpetrators could wind up victims themselves and the innocent could be accidentally killed. In this and similar cases,

---

56. Stanley H. Palmer, *Police and Protest in England and Ireland, 1780–1850* (Cambridge: Cambridge University Press, 1988), 193–236, 548–53.

violent acts had no clear endings and closed plots. No amount of ritual or regulation through conventional rules can eliminate the radical indeterminacy of violent politics.

Some scholars have tried to understand rural collective violence under the rubric of "bargaining by riot."[57] This is too restricted as an interpretation of rural violence, because it forces us to focus on narrowly economic issues, thereby ruling out a whole range of political and social problems that are connected to rebellion. More important, the notion of bargaining seems anachronistic. It implies that rural collective violence can be understood according to the same logic that we use in explaining industrial labor strikes, and this does a large injustice to the historical integrity of the phenomenon. We must try to think through the logic of *rural* violence, and the category of representative violence should be a better aid to doing so.

57. The "bargaining by riot" theme appears implicitly or explicitly in many works. See, for example, Irwin Scheiner's "Benevolent Lords and Honorable Peasants: Rebellion and Peasant Consciousness in Tokugawa Japan," in Tetsuo Najita and Irwin Scheiner, eds., *Japanese Thought in the Tokugawa Period, 1600–1868: Methods and Metaphors* (Chicago: University of Chicago Press, 1978), 39–62. Also see Charles Tilly, Louise Tilly, and Richard Tilly, *The Rebellious Century, 1830–1920* (Cambridge: Harvard University Press, 1975), 1–16, 239–300; E. J. Hobsbawm, *Primitive Rebels: Studies in Archaic Forms of Social Movement in the 19th and 20th Centuries* (Manchester: Manchester University Press, 1959); Edward Shorter and Charles Tilly, *Strikes in France, 1830 to 1968* (Cambridge: Cambridge University Press, 1974); and Henry A. Landsberger, ed., *Latin American Peasant Movements* (Ithaca: Cornell University Press, 1969), esp. Landsberger, "The Role of Peasant Movements and Revolts in Development," 1–61. For a very different logic of social movements and collective action that provides a useful alternative, see Francesco Alberoni, *Movement and Institution* (New York: Columbia University Press, 1984); and Ranajit Guha, *Elementary Aspects of Peasant Insurgency in Colonial India* (Delhi: Oxford University Press, 1983).

CHAPTER 2

The Forces of Constraint
and Community Rebellion

If community is significant it should be possible to establish the kinds of threats to community institutions that are likely to generate collective violence. More important, it should be possible to indicate the types of conflict between elites and popular communities that lead to eruptions of representative violence.

In my discussion of elite forces of constraint I am interested in focusing on three dimensions of the problem. First, and most important, these forces can be understood as threats to the autonomy and cohesion of community institutions that can lead to the dissolution of community institutions. Second, the forces of constraint are *non*reciprocal hierarchies in the sense that they are not subject to continuous control by community institutions. Finally, supralocal elites may or may not provide patronage and other distributive benefits for local communities; but these benefits are revocable and do not necessarily outweigh the potential for conflict between supralocal elites and popular communities.

Community and the Problem of Institutional Survival

Community institutions provide a range of benefits to those who have enforceable claims to the rights and duties of community membership. Those benefits include some minimal protection of household subsistence and the right to an established identity as a member of a particular territorial group. We should expect that the wider the range of benefits, the greater the degree of attachment to community practices; this attachment is the origin of the kinds of localism that historians and anthropologists have taken to be fundamental to the social logic of many agrarian societies.

We may therefore expect any fundamental and long-term external threat to the survival of community institutions to generate conflict that will escalate into a struggle over the issues that are at stake in the threatened institutional arena. For

25

example, any change in the political links between communities and elites that undermine the ability of community institutions to maintain jurisdiction over their members will create the potential for struggle over the extent of community autonomy. Similarly, elite projects that directly undercut community regulations concerning the use of land will likely result in acute conflict about who has the right to define the rights and duties of land tenure.[1]

A large body of empirical literature has been written about the impact of large-scale forms of power and property on the integrity of rural communities. Particularly good case studies exist for Europe, Mexico, and highland Peru and Bolivia.[2] All this material seems to agree that community is important and that community institutions are deeply implicated in characteristic struggles between elites and subordinate groups. Although these studies are rich, they do not provide much in the way of an explicit comparative framework, perhaps in part because of a lingering commitment to a less than appropriate class logic. In any event, we know that community conflicts include an enormous diversity of concrete problems, ranging from taxation and land tenure to religious and ritual authority. What we need is a conceptual language broad enough to highlight critical comparisons and contrasts.

One way of acquiring such a language is to focus on the sorts of ongoing problems that scholars usually associate with the conditions of life in small-scale agrarian societies. I deployed this strategy in establishing the plausibility of the concept of the community of grain, and it is a strategy worth pursuing because of its utility as a way of making comparisons that do not entail teleological commitments. It is equally important as a means of avoiding the use of concepts that liquidate history by assuming that societies characterized by similar problems must have identical patterns of conflict and identical ways of perceiving social reality. Class analysis is especially vulnerable to this weakness, another reason why class is not always a fruitful category.

What, then, are the kinds of problems that are most salient in traditional agrarian societies? The existing literature suggests two basic problem areas that

1. Joel Migdal, *Peasants, Politics, and Revolution: Pressures toward Political and Social Change in the Third World* (Princeton: Princeton University Press, 1974), 33–132; also see Henry Landsberger, ed., *Rural Protest: Peasant Movements and Social Change* (London: Macmillan, 1974), and John Tutino, *From Insurrection to Revolution in Mexico: Social Bases of Agrarian Violence, 1750–1940* (Princeton: Princeton University Press, 1986), 13–40.
2. See Chapter 1, n. 39. Also see B. Porshnev, *Les Soulèvements populaires en France de 1623 à 1648* (Paris: S.Z.U.P.E.N., 1963), 47–131, 303–502; D. Deal, "Peasant Revolts and Resistance in the Modern World," *Journal of Contemporary Asia* 5 (4) (1975), 414–45; Perez Zagorin, *Rebels and Rulers, 1500–1660*, 2 vols. (Cambridge: Cambridge University Press, 1982), 1:175–227; Leon Zamosc, *The Agrarian Question and the Peasant Movement in Colombia: Struggles of the National Peasant Association, 1967–1981* (Cambridge: Cambridge University Press, 1986), 202–14; Henry Kamen, *The Iron Century: Social Change in Europe, 1550–1660* (New York: Praeger, 1971), 307–85; and John L. Keep, *The Russian Revolution: A Study in Mass Mobilization* (New York: Norton, 1976), 153–248.

are associated with community conflicts. First, there are problems that grow out of the demographic instability common in agricultural populations. Second, there are problems that have to do with the tensions between popular communities and elites who claim supralocal authority. The latter sorts of problems deeply affect the ability of community members autonomously to define the rules of community membership, and since this is at the heart of community cohesion, it will receive more attention than demographic forces. Both kinds of problems are important, however, and both deserve attention in any discussion of the causes of rebellion.

Demographic forces and pressures have a long lineage in the study of rural societies. Emmanuel Le Roy Ladurie has made demographic expansion and contraction central to his interpretation of French agrarian life.[3] Although Guy Bois and others have criticized Ladurie for being a "neo-Malthusian," one does not have to accept demographic reductionism in order to appreciate the force of Ladurie's key argument.[4] In small-scale rural societies with fixed or slowly changing technical possibilities, population growth follows a cyclical trajectory in which periods of relative underpopulation are eventually followed by phases of overpopulation. The inevitable result is a period of demographic crisis that reduces an entire society to a population minimum that becomes the starting point for a new cycle of growth and decline. Famines and epidemics are the most historically frequent kinds of crises that characterize agrarian societies.

The implication of demographic forces for the stability of rural institutions is clear. Too few or too many people must strain the ability of established institutional practices to manage scarce resources with a minimum of conflict. For example, during periods of rapid population growth, land will become a more intensely valued and disputed resource, as more younger sons and daughters must be provided for out of a shrinking aggregate supply of land. Societies with partible inheritance customs will soon be characterized by tiny and unusable smallholdings, thereby increasing the potential for struggle over the definition of land rights. But even in societies with primogeniture or impartible inheritance, the growth of numbers will create a potentially dangerous cohort of the dispossessed, who no longer have a clear stake in established communities.[5]

The kinds of demographic pressures that undermine community institutions can best be thought of as a series of forces of erosion that undercut institutional integrity by creating a radical gap between institutional roles and the size of a

3. Emmanuel Le Roy Ladurie, *The Peasants of Languedoc* (Urbana: University of Illinois Press, 1974), 11–83, 289–312. Also see Ester Boserup, *The Conditions of Agricultural Growth: The Economics of Agrarian Change under Population Pressure* (London: Allen and Unwin, 1965), and D. B. Grigg, *Population Growth and Agrarian Change: A Historical Perspective* (Cambridge: Cambridge University Press, 1980), 11–145, 281–95.

4. Guy Bois, *The Crisis of Feudalism: Economy and Society in Eastern Normandy, c. 1300–1550* (Cambridge: Cambridge University Press, 1984), 1–5.

5. See, for example, Jean Louis Flandrin, *Families in Former Times: Kinship, Household, and Sexuality* (Cambridge: Cambridge University Press, 1979), 11–50.

territorial population. As that gap increases, the probability of conflict is enhanced; and at least in the limiting case, violence may erupt over the terms and conditions of community practices. For example, in sixteenth- and seventeenth-century England, common-field villagers occasionally used collective violence to eject vagrants who had built rough dwellings on the edge of the village, thereby encroaching on the common rights of established village families.[6]

The most theoretically interesting cases involved precisely this kind of clash between established communities and the vagrant or wandering poor, because it is in these situations that we can glimpse the ability of communities to act collectively during periods of material crisis. Pauperization and transiency are constant possibilities in rural societies, and the problem becomes one of explaining how local institutional practices are made to adapt in the face of demographic forces of erosion that threaten to dissolve existing patterns of cooperation.

A more significant locus of conflict in rural societies is the division between rural communities and extracommunity elites who claim jurisdiction over one or more realms of community life.[7] These claims can be thought of as a series of social and political forces of constraint that impinge on the autonomy and cohesion of community institutions. The essential problem is the tension between elite and popular interests, and the political question is who will have the power to define the rights and duties of community membership. In both theoretical and case-study literature, the conflicts that develop from this tension have been treated as central in the explanation of rural rebellion. This position has much to recommend it, although it is usually not cast in terms that are sufficiently general to offer much comparative power. Consequently, in the following discussion I redraw the terrain by dividing key forms of conflict into three broad patterns of interaction between community institutions and supralocal elites.

The classic form of contest between elite and community interests is linked to the range of struggles that grow out of the claims to rule that are made by landed aristocracies.[8] Both in Asia and in Europe, after the Bronze Age much of the historical record is of the rise and decline of aristocratic politics.[9] Landed aristoc-

---

6. Roger B. Manning, *Village Revolts: Social Protest and Popular Disturbances in England, 1509–1640* (Oxford: Clarendon Press, 1988), 157–86.

7. The best theoretical expression is Migdal, *Peasants, Politics, and Revolution;* also see Joel Migdal, *Strong Societies and Weak States: State-Society Relations and State Capabilities in the Third World* (Princeton: Princeton University Press, 1988).

8. This is the key argument made by two classics of modern historical sociology, although the claims are made in very different ways. See Barrington Moore, *Social Origins of Dictatorship and Democracy: Lord and Peasant in the Making of the Modern World* (Boston: Beacon Press, 1966), 413–508, and Reinhard Bendix, *Kings or People: Power and the Mandate to Rule* (Berkeley: University of California Press, 1978), 21–127.

9. The only work to have drawn these themes together in any systematic fashion is the excellent study by John H. Kautsky, *The Politics of Aristocratic Empires* (Chapel Hill: University of North Carolina Press, 1982), esp. 3–27, 79–168. Also see Perry Anderson, *Passages from Antiquity to Feudalism* (London: New Left Books, 1974); Marc Bloch, *Feudal Society,* 2 vols. (Chicago: Univer-

racies have developed through a variety of historical routes, including conquest and the "feudalization" of authority. Still, the origins of aristocracy are less interesting than the common logic of power that marks out landed aristocracies as distinctive social forces. Aristocratic elites claim a right to rule on the basis of hereditary principles of blood-right, and to this is attached a potent notion of honor that approximates the exclusiveness of caste.[10] The most highly developed aristocracies project themselves as the holders of an institutionalized charisma that entitles them to the unconditional obedience of their social inferiors. Thus, the logic of aristocratic domination is the logic of absolute hierarchy, in which superiors command subordinates and expect compliance even in the absence of a reciprocal exchange of services. A particularly striking illustration can be found in the legal definition of the rights of a lord over his serfs in medieval Europe.[11] According to the fully elaborated Roman law theory of serfdom, serfs had to obey their lords in all matters, since serfs had no publicly recognized right to compel their lords to do or not to do anything.

Aristocratic power has been rooted in a complex pattern of situations and resources. Aristocratic power has typically been associated with control over land and agricultural labor, however, and it is to the interaction of landed aristocracies and local communities that we must look in order to understand the points of tension that characterize much of rural history.

One obvious point of tension is the clash between popular and aristocratic principles of hierarchy. Historians and anthropologists have shown how the logic of hierarchy in small-scale rural societies is tied to asymmetric exchanges between advantaged and disadvantaged groups.[12] Indeed, reciprocal hierarchy can be

---

sity of Chicago Press, 1961), 2:282–358; Marc Bloch, *The Royal Touch: Sacred Monarchy and Scrofula in England and France* (London: Routledge and Kegan Paul, 1973), 1–50; Ernest Kantorowicz, *The King's Two Bodies: A Study in Medieval Political Theology* (Princeton: Princeton University Press, 1966), 42–86; and Max Weber, *Economy and Society: An Outline of Interpretive Sociology*, 3 vols. (New York: Bedminster Press, 1968), 3:1006–1158.

10. The best working through of this logic is found in the work of Georges Duby. See, in particular, Georges Duby, *The Chivalrous Society* (Berkeley: University of California Press, 1977), 94–111, 178–225. Also see Roland Mousnier, *The Institutions of France under the Absolute Monarchy, 1598–1789*, vol. 1, *Society and the State* (Chicago: University of Chicago Press, 1979), 3–47, 477–562, and Louis Dumont, *Homo Hierarchicus: An Essay on the Caste System* (Chicago: University of Chicago Press, 1970), esp. 212–14.

11. A good starting point for this argument is Marc Bloch, "The Rise of Dependent Cultivation and Seignorial Institutions," in M. M. Postan, ed., *The Agrarian Life of the Middle Ages*, vol. 1 of *The Cambridge Economic History of Europe* (Cambridge: Cambridge University Press, 1966), 235–90. Also see Paul R. Hyams, *Kings, Lords, and Peasants in Medieval England: The Common Law of Villeinage in the Twelfth and Thirteenth Centuries* (Oxford: Clarendon Press, 1980), and the theoretical discussion in Orlando Patterson, *Slavery and Social Death: A Comparative Study* (Cambridge: Harvard University Press, 1982), 25–26.

12. See the essays in Steffen Schmidt et al., eds., *Friends, Followers, and Factions: A Reader in Political Clientalism* (Berkeley: University of California Press, 1977), esp. James C. Scott, "Patron-Client Politics and Political Change in Southeast Asia," 123–46; John Duncan Powell, "Peasant Society and Clientelist Politics," 147–60; L. M. Hanks, "The Corporation and the Entourage: A

understood as a core institutional principle of rural communities. The logic of aristocracy, however, points in a radically different direction. The aristocratic project is imperious in its demand for absolute obedience; and we can expect continual conflict over the definition of authority in societies with powerful landed nobilities. Popular communities will try to define lordship as a social compact in which the duty to obey is balanced by reciprocal obligations on the part of the aristocratic overlord. But aristocracies will resist and will attempt to maximize the range of issues over which they can exercise arbitrary jurisdiction. We should also expect this kind of tension to yield collective violence if neither side to the contest can gain a preponderance of power. For example, the upsurge of local revolts in late-fourteenth-century England was closely related to the breakdown of local power balances that took place in the wake of the Black Plague.[13] Neither lords nor their serf communities had an unambiguous advantage in the struggle for local hegemony, and in this ambiguous context, insurrection became a means of re-negotiating the local social order.

A more subtle but related form of conflict in aristocratic societies has to do with the location of final authority over the rights and rules that determine the conditions of community membership. Aristocratic elites will naturally try to establish captive communities over which they hold ultimate and discretionary authority. But their attempt to do so will open up the potential for direct conflict with the holders of community positions and institutional roles who will resist the subjugation of their communities to the imperious jurisdiction of aristocratic elites. Community members will struggle to reserve to themselves the power to decide what membership will mean and who can exercise it, especially in cases of conflicting claims to scarce resources.

Struggle over the terms of ultimate jurisdiction cannot be reduced to economic issues, although such issues are obviously involved. Authority cuts across the analytic boundaries that are normally employed by social science, and at a general level it implies status and social ranking, as well as more purely material matters. In small-scale rural societies in which social identity is closely related to local institutions, any change in the rights and duties of local membership will entail a change in a whole way of life. Consequently, the problem of who defines these matters is of vital concern; and we should expect violence to accompany the extension of aristocratic domination to include the right of supralocal elites to

Comparison of Thai and American Social Organization," 161–66; and Eric R. Wolf, "Kinship, Friendship, and Patron-Client Relations in Complex Societies," 167–78. For a good case study, see Jan Berman, *Patronage and Exploitation: Changing Agrarian Relations in South Gujarat, India* (Berkeley: University of California Press, 1974), 3–24. And for a rebellion in which a breakdown of patron-client ties occurred, see Benedict J. Kerkvliet, *The Huk Rebellion: A Study of Peasant Revolt in the Philippines* (Berkeley: University of California Press, 1977), 249–69.

13. Rodney Hilton, *Bond Men Made Free: Medieval Peasant Movements and the English Rising of 1381* (New York: Viking Press, 1977), esp. 9–136.

exercise discretionary authority. It should be emphasized that the attempt of elites to capture popular communities, if successful, leads to a world in which the rights of local membership are turned into a precarious form of life defined by the will of an unaccountable outsider.[14]

The best example of such a situation can be seen in the history of European serfdom and the institutions of manorial control through which aristocratic power was exercised. As already indicated, the formal law of serfdom defined most ordinary cultivators as rightless subjects who owed absolute obedience to an unaccountable aristocracy. In practice, the conditions of serfdom varied widely, and it is safe to say that the formal theory of serfdom rarely approximated its realities. This radical gap between theory and practice seems paradoxical only if we fail to understand that serfdom was not a uniform class relationship that can be explained through macrostructural categories. Instead, serfdom was a distinctly *local* relationship between rural communities and particular clusters of aristocratic families whose power resided in supralocal networks of feudal authority. The real history of servile agriculture existed in the customary balance of power that developed over time in the relations of conflict and cooperation that tied communities to their overlords. In some cases that balance favored aristocratic interests, while in other cases the balance favored the interests of the commoners who formed the serf community.[15]

The central institutional arena through which the practice of serfdom was worked out was the manorial court.[16] It was here that local rules were formulated and conflicts of interest were negotiated through a ritual procedure in which custom was the key cognitive referent. Many conjunctural factors influenced the balance of interests and outcomes that emerged in the process of manorial rule making. Demography, marketing opportunities, and the history of previous popular resistance all contributed to the precise local determination of aristocratic and popular power.

Yet, in spite of the complexity of local conjunctures, manorial institutions

14. See, for example, the discussion of serfdom at its worst in Jerome Blum, *Lord and Peasant in Russia from the Ninth to the Nineteenth Century* (Princeton: Princeton University Press, 1961), 106–16, 414–574.

15. Bloch, *Feudal Society* 1:255–81; Georges Duby, *Rural Economy and County Life in the Medieval West* (London: Edward Arnold, 1968), 260–88, 332–60; and Peter Kolchin, *Unfree Labor: American Slavery and Russian Serfdom* (Cambridge: Harvard University Press, Belknap Press, 1987), 195–301.

16. Susan Reynolds, *Kingdoms and Communities in Western Europe, 900–1300* (Oxford: Clarendon Press, 1984), 101–54; Helen M. Cam, *Law Finders and Law Makers in Medieval England: Collected Studies in Legal and Constitutional History* (London: Merlin Press, 1962); Helen M. Cam, *Liberties and Communities in Medieval England: Collected Studies in Local Administration and Topography* (London: Merlin Press, 1968), esp. 53–63, 206, 221; R. C. Hoffmann, "Medieval Origins of the Common Fields," in William N. Parker and Eric L. Jones, eds., *European Peasants and Their Markets: Essays in Agrarian Economic History* (Princeton: Princeton University Press, 1975), 23–71; and Bloch, "The Rise of Dependent Cultivation," 235–90.

always embodied a contradiction that could become a potential flash point in particular situations. In theory, the manorial court and its customs existed at the will of the lord; and higher feudal or royal courts did not recognize any other source of valid manorial law. But in practice the ordinary members of the manorial community recognized manorial law as their law and manorial institutions as subject to their customary control. In this context of divided claims and principles of rule, a determined manor lord could spark enormous conflict with his manorial subjects by asserting in practice the full panoply of rights that were his according to the theory of serfdom. For example, German princes and knights of the early 1500s helped to set off a long series of popular revolts when they tried to reconstruct manorial authority according to the logic of aristocratic domination.[17] German lords wanted to create captive communities, and their subjects were just as dedicated to the maximization of community autonomy.

At stake in this and similar conflicts was the primal question of authority. Who had the ultimate right to control the rules of the manorial community, and would those rules serve the interests of aristocratic price or community cohesion? When seen from below, the old picture of abject and passive serfs groaning under the lash of feudal power dissolves into a more subtle portrait of an ongoing politics of conflict and compromise that had no predetermined outcomes.

We can, therefore, identify with some precision the aspects of aristocratic domination that were most likely to eventuate in local insurrections. First, a determined effort on the part of an aristocratic household to enforce its political claims could trigger violent resistance if that effort threatened to transform secure community rights into precarious rights held at the arbitrary will of the lord. A good example can be found in the violent opposition to aristocratic attempts unilaterally to change the terms of land tenure during Europe's inflationary sixteenth century.[18]

A second and more fundamental source of popular opposition to aristocratic claims has to do with the paradoxical character of servile agriculture. All forms of serfdom and agrarian slavery are marked by a potential contradiction between the theory and practice of lordship. When aristocratic groups seek to turn the realities of an unstable local power balance into a reflection of the theory of absolute domination, they have set the stage for a struggle that is likely to escalate into some form of violence. As we shall see, the history of the West can be partly rewritten as a history of conflict that centers on the institutions of the rural manor.

Much of what we call rural rebellion can be understood as rooted in the ways in which the forces of constraint, expressed in aristocratic rule, have played themselves out against the background of local issues and interests. It is therefore

17. Zagorin, *Rebels and Rulers* 1:186–207; Tom Scott, "The Peasants' War: A Historiographical Review," *Historical Journal* 22 (3 and 4) (1979), 693–720, 953–74.

18. Kamen, *The Iron Century,* 199–230, 331–85; Victor G. Kiernan, *State and Society in Europe, 1550–1650* (Oxford: B. Blackwell, 1980), esp. 162–67, 181–214.

essential to explore the nature of aristocratic rule, because the way we see the problem will have a profound impact on how we theorize rural politics. Other, more "modern" forms of conflict, however, can be found in a variety of historical settings, and those forms of conflict can also be explored from the framework of a theory of the forces of constraint. Bureaucratic domination and what is best described as coercive commercialization are the two types of translocal constraint of local institutions that have the most relevance for a comparative analysis of rural violence.

Bureaucratic domination is an essential dimension of state building.[19] Large-scale patterns of authority must be grounded in stable institutional arrangements that are capable of mobilizing human and material resources necessary for the effective governance of a supralocal realm. The consolidation of the modern state requires a bureaucratic mode of domination that eliminates all forms of administration tied to local customs and fragmented jurisdictions. Bureaucracy is informed by a commitment to impersonal rules and uniform principles that stand in opposition to any form of authority that is not sanctioned by the nation-state. This is especially true of the problem of determining the legitimate boundaries of social violence. The bureaucratic nation-state is a compulsory political association, as Weber recognized; and the holders of bureaucratic positions will attempt to maximize their power by concentrating all forms of coercion in clearly defined state institutions.[20] At some point in the process of state constitution, the monopolistic claims of state elites will come into conflict with competing forms of authority and competing claims to the legitimate use of violence. In particular circumstances, this may result in a kind of "internal war" in which state elites deploy force in order to disarm social groups who stand in the way of the state-building project. In extreme cases, the disarmament of civil society will actually undermine state power by raising the level of violent confrontation between state elites and subject groups to a threshold that endangers the maintenance of minimal stage legitimacy. If this happens the state-building project can collapse into a phase of warlord rule that might permanently block any return to centralized authority, at least to the prewarlord forms and territorial limits of governance. China after 1911 and Mexico in the decade following the 1910 revolution are excellent examples of failed state-building projects.[21]

19. See Charles Tilly, ed., *The Formation of National States in Western Europe* (Princeton: Princeton University Press, 1975), esp. essays by Stein Rokkan, "Dimensions of State Formation and Nation-Building: A Possible Paradigm for Research on Variations within Europe," 562–600, and Charles Tilly, "Western State-Making and Theories of Political Transformation," 601–38. See also Peter Evans et al., eds., *Bringing the State Back In* (Cambridge: Cambridge University Press, 1985), esp. essays by Theda Skocpol, "Bringing the State Back In: Strategies of Analysis in Current Research," 3–43, and Charles Tilly, "War Making and State Making as Organized Crime," 169–91.

20. Weber, *Economy and Society,* 3 vols., 1:212–26, and see Anthony Giddens, *The Nation-State and Violence* (Berkeley: University of California Press, 1985), 61–102.

21. D. A. Brading, ed., *Caudillo and Peasant in the Mexican Revolution* (Cambridge: Cambridge

Discussions of the connection between the extension of bureaucratic domination and the origins of rural rebellion usually focus on the impact of state "surplus extraction" on the institutions of agricultural subsistence production.[22] Taxation, in particular, has been cast in the role of a "super cause" that generates rolling waves of popular rebellion when the inexorable and always increasing demands of the state for resources cut into the ability of rural households to maintain a precarious subsistence-level existence. Although there is no doubt that taxation has been an important cause of rural unrest, as Charles Tilly and James C. Scott among others have shown, the focus is too narrow to provide the basis for a wide-ranging comparative analysis.[23]

To begin with, there is an implicit assumption in much of this literature that taxation is necessarily parasitic and predatory, at least during the early phases of state building. The idea seems to be that taxation and other forms of resource mobilization are not counterbalanced by a corresponding range of benefits and protections that flow from state elites to the countryside. Taxation is simply a flat cost, a kind of dead-weight efficiency loss that produces resistance in direct proportion to the escalating demands of the state.[24]

The picture of a parasitic state devouring the countryside is an appropriate image of a definite range of historical experience, as the discussion of French Croquantry in Chapter 5 will demonstrate.[25] But the image is too mechanical as a causal model, because it fails to account for many anomalies. For example, during the seventeenth and eighteenth centuries the real tax burden on the English countryside was probably quite high; yet it did not lead to the waves of unrest that plagued France and parts of Spain. Rural collective violence certainly did exist in England throughout the early modern period, but it was not typically associated with fiscal issues.[26]

University Press, 1980), esp. D. A. Brading, "Introduction: National Politics and the Populist Tradition," 1–16; Alan Knight, "Peasant and Caudillo in Revolutionary Mexico, 1910–1917," 17–58; and Hans Werner Tobler, "Conclusion: Peasant Mobilization and the Revolution," 245–55. Also see Joseph W. Esherick, *Reform and Revolution in China: The 1911 Revolution in Hunan and Hubei* (Berkeley: University of California Press, 1976), 11–33, 216–60.

22. The most consistent recent statement of this argument is Charles Tilly, *The Contentious French* (Cambridge: Harvard University Press, Belknap Press, 1986), 41–78, 380–406.

23. See ibid., 61–63, and James C. Scott, *The Moral Economy of the Peasant* (New Haven: Yale University Press, 1976), esp. 52–58, 91–113, 120–37, 141–56.

24. Some of the problems with seeing taxation as a problem apart from its implications for authority and institutions are addressed in James B. Collins, *The Fiscal Limits of Absolutism: Direct Taxation in Early-Seventeenth-Century France* (Berkeley: University of California Press, 1988), 1–17, 166–222, and Richard Bonney, *Political Change in France under Richelieu and Mazarin, 1624–1661* (Oxford: Oxford University Press, 1978), 3–56, 214–58.

25. Yves Marie Bercé, *Histoire des Croquants* (Paris: Seuil, 1986); Yves Marie Bercé, *Croquants et Nu-pieds: Les soulèvements paysans en France du XVIe au XIXe siècle* (Paris: Gallimard/Julliard, 1974).

26. I am indebted to Margaret Levi's *Of Rule and Revenue* (Berkeley: University of California Press, 1988), 95–144. Also see C. D. Chandaman, *The English Public Revenue, 1660–1688* (Oxford:

What this suggests is the importance of understanding taxation and other forms of resource extraction as just one dimension of a much more subtle and far-reaching interaction between state building and rural social practices. In some contexts, the geographical extension of bureaucratic domination will involve both costs and countervailing benefits for popular communities, and in these cases we would not expect the growth of state power to generate the sustained forms of opposition that emerged so starkly in seventeenth- and eighteenth-century France. But in those instances in which the hierarchies of state power are established on nonreciprocal principles of absolute command and obedience, we should expect popular resistance to the state-building project, and that resistance may take the form of rebellion if state elites lack an effective monopoly of the means of force.

This analysis is, however, an insufficient basis for rigorous comparisons. We should be able talk about more than abstract costs and benefits, but to do so requires a more substantive analysis of the causes of rural collective violence that links state building with the characteristic problems of small-scale agrarian societies.

One fruitful way of approaching state building is to sketch out the logical implications of bureaucratic domination for the integrity of local institutions. When bureaucratic authority begins to rearrange the terms of politics there is a high potential for conflict with groups who have traditions of self-help and autonomous jurisdiction. Bureaucratic elites claim more than the right to tax; they also claim a monopoly over the means of force and the basis of legitimate rule.[27] Both kinds of claims threaten to eliminate the ability of local communities to manage their affairs according to local rules.

There are consequently two situations in which bureaucratic domination may generate the preconditions of rural rebellion. First, state building projects that undercut the authority of local institutions will provide the occasion for struggle over the question of who has the effective right to determine the rules of group membership. Second, and more interesting for the study of rebellion, are cases in which the claims of the state to a monopoly of violence clash with the customary rights of community leaders to exercise coercive jurisdiction over their members. Both situations may be linked to the assertion of bureaucratic rights over novel forms of resource mobilization, but the implications extend far beyond taxation to include the basis of legitimate politics.

Although the problems of state building will receive greater attention in the case studies, an example will illuminate the point. During the nineteenth and early twentieth centuries, northern China experienced an upsurge of local militarism

---

Clarendon Press, 1975), 138–95; J. F. Bosher, *French Finances, 1770–1795: From Business to Bureaucracy* (Cambridge: Cambridge University Press, 1970), 276–318; and Rudolf Braun, "Taxation, Sociopolitical Structure and State-Building: Great Britain and Brandenburg-Prussia," in Tilly, *The Formation of National States in Western Europe,* 243–327.

27. Joel Migdal, *Strong Societies and Weak States,* 3–34, 33–44.

that was closely tied to the increase in the number of fortified village communities that held wide-ranging jurisdiction over their members. Legitimate violence was widely dispersed, and the most autonomous villages clearly believed in their right to use violence against both insiders and outsiders, as Elizabeth Perry has indicated in her study of the Red Spears of Huai-pei.[28] In Huai-pei, state building had to involve the fundamental recasing of authority relations from the bottom up; and, as Prasenjit Dura has shown, the question of the kinds of authority village institutions would hold was a major point of conflict in rural North China from 1400 right through the 1940s.[29] It does not seem to distort the evidence to suggest that many of the local rebellions that occurred in North China during this period were motivated in part by the defense of an autonomous realm of village jurisdiction against the centralizing claims of state-building elites.

Nor was the situation in North China so extreme or bizarre as to be simply exceptional. The Whiteboy movements in rural Ireland also seem to have been involved in asserting the rights of local authority against the demands of bureaucratic authority; and similar examples of the defense of localism against the state can be found throughout southern Europe.[30] But in order to gain a comparative perspective, it is necessary to see state-building as a process of redrawing the lines of authority, and not merely as a matter of resource extraction.

The final major constraint on the autonomy of community institutions is usually described under the somewhat misleading rubric of commercialization.[31] The impact of commerce on agrarian societies has been the focus of much of the best theoretical writing in the field, including the work of Barrington Moore, Jeffrey Paige, and Robert Brenner.[32] This work is based on the notion that markets subvert premodern forms of redistribution and reciprocity that function outside a commercial logic of comparative advantage and supply and demand. At some point, so the argument goes, the expansion of market relations will generate

28. Elizabeth Perry, *Rebels and Revolutionaries in North China, 1845–1945* (Stanford: Stanford University Press, 1980), 152–207.

29. Prasenjit Duara, *Culture, Power, and the State: Rural North China, 1900–1942* (Stanford: Stanford University Press, 1988), 1–41, 158–216.

30. John Davis, *People of the Mediterranean: An Essay in Comparative Social Anthropology* (London: Routledge and Kegan Paul, 1977).

31. For a general understanding of commerce, markets, and rural societies, see C. Peter Timmer, *Getting Prices Right: The Scope and Limits of Agricultural Price Policy* (Ithaca: Cornell University Press, 1986), 13–58; Andrew Pearse, *Seeds of Plenty, Seeds of Want: Social and Economic Implications of the Green Revolution* (Oxford: Clarendon Press, 1980), 161–82; and John Sheahan, *Patterns of Development in Latin America: Poverty, Repression, and Economic Strategy* (Princeton: Princeton University Press, 1987), 130–54.

32. Moore, *Social Origins of Dictatorship;* Jeffrey Paige, *Agrarian Revolution: Social Movement and Export Agriculture in the Underdeveloped World* (New York: Free Press, 1975), esp. 3–4, 9–71, 334–76; and Robert Brenner, "Agrarian Class Structure and Economic Development in Pre-Industrial Europe," in T. H. Aston and C. H. E. Philpin, eds., *The Brenner Debate: Agrarian Class Structure and Economic Development in Pre-Industrial Europe* (Cambridge: Cambridge University Press, 1985), 10–63.

conflict and social instability; and the consequences of commercialization may yield collective violence when the poor and disadvantaged mobilize to oppose the threatening implications of a world in which land and labor have been reduced to mere factors of production. Behind this image of commercialization is the imposing figure of Karl Polanyi, whose grand theory of the illogic of liberal capitalism is still among the best examples of its genre.

There can be little doubt that commercialization does have profound and transforming consequences for traditional agrarian societies. Markets can mobilize people and resources on a scale matched only by the modern state, and the expansion of market logic has been corrosive of nonmarket practices in some contexts, as much of the work of Scott has shown.[33] But ambiguous evidence has led scholars to disagree about the impact of markets on agrarian institutions. For example, many historians and social scientists have pointed out that markets do not necessarily have uniformly negative consequences for the poor, while others have indicated the ways in which markets may improve the overall quality of life in small-scale rural societies. Indeed, there is impressive evidence to support the view that small cultivators avidly accept the logic of the market, and Samuel Popkin's critique of moral-economy approaches has made a powerful case for the positive effects of commercial development.[34]

All of this conflicting theory and evidence adds up to the need to rethink what we mean by the commercialization of traditional agriculture. We cannot assume that market logic has uniform and universal effects; especially because the process of agricultural commercialization has taken such diverse historical paths. In Europe, much of the development of agricultural markets seems to have occurred from below, partly through the active participation of small-scale cultivators who patiently built the channels of trade in basic commodities. But in the third world, where colonial elites imposed market logic on conquered populations, commercialization was a much more violent and destructive process. Whole populations were forced to enter the market in highly biased terms, often within the life span of a single generation. A particularly useful illustration is the sad history of monopoly commerce in seventeenth- and eighteenth-century Latin America. In Spain's Latin American colonies, traditional agricultural communities were forced to buy and sell a whole range of products at highly disadvantageous terms, which sometimes proved fatal to them.[35]

The best way of facing the challenge of ambiguous evidence is to focus on the politics of the commercialization process, and to think comparatively about the kinds of power relations that underpin the growth of rural markets. For present

33. James C. Scott, *Weapons of the Weak* (New Haven: Yale University Press, 1987).
34. Samuel Popkin, *The Rational Peasant* (Berkeley: University of California Press, 1979).
35. See the discussion of the "coercive" exchange mechanism known as the *repartimiento de mercancías* in Karen Spaulding, *Huarochiri: An Andean Society under Inca and Spanish Rule* (Stanford: Stanford University Press, 1984), 188–204.

purposes, the most useful distinction is between compulsory and voluntary forms of commercialization. In the latter case, trade occurs spontaneously on the basis of a roughly mutual exchange of values. Historically, much of European commerce has been voluntary, and it seems odd to assume that it will have profoundly destructive consequences for established institutional practices. For example, as early as the Middle Ages, village communities were widely tied to the European trade in grain and livestock.[36] But this participation seems more voluntary than forced, and much of it was rooted in local networks of exchange that do not appear to have undermined local customs and practices. On the contrary, one might argue that the gains from the petty commerce strengthened local institutions by providing a wider and more secure resource base on which community members could rely.

The coercive forms of commercialization that took place under the auspices of colonialism, however, have a radically different logic. The use of force as a mechanism for inducing participation in market networks implies an unequal distribution of benefits and risks, and those who are compelled to transfer resources from established routines to rigged or monopolistic markets are unlikely to view such use of force as anything more than parasitism. In addition, the use of compulsion to effect commercialization will threaten to unleash an uncontrollable cycle of conflict and institutional disruption, and it is precisely when this occurs that we should expect commercialization to end in collective violence.

More specifically, we should find plausible links between commercialization and rural rebellion when "modernizing" elites use coercive means as a strategy for rapidly incorporating traditional agricultural communities into supralocal markets. This threatens both household control over the means of subsistence *and* the capacity of local institutions to regulate the production and distribution of scarce resources. Once again, the nature of constraint in this and previous cases has more to do with the locus of authority than any simple material calculus. The essential question is who will rule the marketplace, and the related problem is the social definition of the rights and responsibilities that attach to membership in particular groups. Coercive commercialization throws into sharp relief the kinds of tension points that scholars have identified as central to the relationship of elites and popular communities in agricultural societies.

A particularly destructive instance of coercive commercialization can be lo-

36. See, for example, Rodney H. Hilton, *A Medieval Society: The West Midlands at the End of the Thirteenth Century* (Cambridge: Cambridge University Press, 1983), 167–216; P. D. A. Harvey, "The English Inflation of 1180–1220," in R. H. Hilton, ed., *Peasants, Knights, and Heretics: Studies in Medieval English Social History* (Cambridge: Cambridge University Press, 1976), 57–84; Bois, *The Crisis of Feudalism*, 234–36, 135–214; Fernand Braudel, *Capitalism and Material Life, 1400–1800* (New York: Harper and Row, 1973), 83–87, 127–30; and Lynn White, Jr., *Medieval Technology and Social Change* (Oxford: Oxford University Press, 1962). Also see the interesting theoretical discussion of Europe's medieval economic "revolution" in Randall Collins, *Weberian Sociological Theory* (Cambridge: Cambridge University Press, 1986), 45–76.

cated in the history of hut and poll taxes in colonial Africa and Southeast Asia.[37] Colonial administrators, hard-pressed to make colonialism pay, introduced these taxes as a way of forcing subsistence cultivators into the market. In order to pay their taxes in money, as the colonial elite required, agricultural communities were forced to cultivate crops for which there was an international demand. But, as a result, entire regions lost a significant measure of control over the nature of the crops they were allowed to plant, the conditions of the agricultural work process, and the right to make trade-offs between subsistence and market cultivation. It is not surprising that the abolition of these taxes figured heavily in some of the most savage revolts of the interwar period, including the Saya San uprising in Burma and the Nghe An-Ha Tinh episode in Vietnam.[38] In a subsequent chapter, I will try to show that coercive commercialization can also be applied to an interpretation of European history, particularly in the case of Russia's Stolypin reforms.

Property, Hierarchy, and Community Power

Most theoretical discussions of property and hierarchy treat both phenomena as concrete objects that have a reified existence apart from people.[39] I want to break with this tradition of writing because it forces us to read too much determination and fixity into social logic. As I implied in my analysis of the community of grain, I prefer a discourse that states macroconcepts in a microcontext of institutional interactions or "performances," simply because it forces us to think more rigorously about social reality. Some degree of abstract and reifying theory is necessary, as my own use of concepts should indicate. But we should always try to qualify our concepts through a careful specification of the ways in which structural categories can be redescribed in terms of specific patterns of interaction.

Such qualification is especially important in trying to come to grips with the politics of property relations in small-scale agricultural societies. Usually the issue is understood as an abstract dialectic between capitalism and an amorphous

---

37. Scott, *The Moral Economy of the Peasant*, 93–110; Clifford Geertz, *Agricultural Involution: The Process of Ecological Change in Indonesia* (Berkeley: University of California Press, 1963).

38. Michael Adas, *Prophets of Rebellion: Millenarian Protest Movement against the European Colonial Order* (Chapel Hill: University of North Carolina Press, 1979), 34–39; Tran Huy Lieu, *Les Soviets du Nghe-Tinh de 1930–1931 au Viet Nam* (Hanoi: Éditions en Langues Étrangères, 1960), 27.

39. I am indebted in the following analysis to Keith Tribe, *Land, Labour, and Economic Discourse* (London: Routledge and Kegan Paul, 1978), 159–61; Carl Dahlman, *The Open Field System and Beyond: A Property Rights Analysis of an Economic Institution* (Cambridge: Cambridge University Press, 1980); E. G. Furubotn and S. Pejovich, "Property Rights and Economic Theory: A Survey of Recent Literature," *Journal of Economic Literature* 9 (Dec. 1972), 1137–62; Richard Tuck, *Natural Rights Theories: Their Origin and Development* (Cambridge: Cambridge University Press, 1979); William Reddy, *Money and Liberty in Modern Europe: A Critique of Historical Understanding* (Cambridge: Cambridge University Press, 1987); and Neal Wood, *John Locke and Agrarian Capitalism* (Berkeley: University of California Press, 1984).

collection of practices that are often lumped together under the heading of pre-capitalist modes of production. The assumption seems to be that capitalist property relations have a "thing-like" power to restructure everything that has preceded them. Eventually, all customary forms of property will dissolve under the weight of our capitalist world order.[40]

There is a hard, crude truth in this way of seeing the issue. It forces us to face the fact that capitalist elites have often tried to redraw the map of ordinary life according to principles that have little to do with public needs. But it also begs several questions that cannot be answered by focusing on purely macro categories. What does capitalism look like when it is disaggregated to the level of local institutions? More important, what can we say in a comparative way about the conflicts that develop around contested property relations in rural societies? Must we confine our discussion to the most general and reified categories, or can we provide a more subtle analytic logic? Seeing the march of history as a battle between capital and everything else is too blunt to capture the richness of social history written from below.

One alternative is to rewrite the problem as an exercise in thinking through the ways in which property relations are played out in everyday life. Property, after all, is a relationship between people rather than a material logic thing.[41] To own something is to draw boundaries between people and to establish claims to the core rights and duties that make up the interactions we call property. Property, therefore, is best understood as the performances of people in daily life when they claim rights and enforce responsibilities. In small-scale agricultural societies much of the reality of property involves the institutional playing out of claims to land, labor, and the harvest, and conflict can be seen as the clash of opposing claims to the performances of people in specific situations. For example, a landlord who demands novel and unacceptable services from his tenants is engaging in a performance of property relations that is likely to violate deeply entrenched practices. This kind of violation generates a potential clash of interests. How the clash develops and how it is resolved depend on the institutional resources of the participants, but we must not assume that any specific formal property is guaranteed a hegemonic role by the cunning of history.

Anthropologists and social historians have helped us to see how property relations actually look when examined from the ground up.[42] The challenge for

40. See, for example, Barry Bottindess and Paul Q. Hirst, *Pre-capitalist Modes of Production* (London: Routledge and Kegan Paul, 1975), 260–307.

41. This is an insight drawn from Douglas C. North, *Structure and Change in Economic History* (New York: Norton, 1981), 3–70. Also see M. I. Finley, *Economy and Society in Ancient Greece* (London: Chatto and Windus, 1981), 97–198.

42. See Jack Goody, *The Development of the Family and Marriage in Europe* (Cambridge: Cambridge University Press, 1983), 103–93; Jack Goody et al., eds., *Family and Inheritance: Rural Society in Western Europe, 1200–1800* (Cambridge: Cambridge University Press, 1976), esp. Goody's Introduction, 1–9, and essays by Joan Thirsk, "The European Debate on Customs of Inheritance,

comparativists is to use this work as a foundation for general concepts that avoid the hypostatizing abstractions of the past without sacrificing the ability to compare.

The most interesting way of doing this is to consider the types of performative conflicts that are most apt to originate in the points of tension between elites and popular groups. Much of the best empirical literature is rooted in a close study of the struggles that revolve around the political definition of property rights, and this insight can be expanded into a comparative analysis that embraces the issue of conflict and cooperation.

A good starting point is to focus on two forms of property rights that are logically associated with the power of elites to define a realm of rights and duties that are unaccountable to popular demands. Both forms are best described as claims to a prerogative to dispose of resources according to a logic of individual will, and both forms stand in sharp contrast to a practice of property that links individual rights with a conception of the responsibility of individuals to a wider social context.

The first type of property that seems accurately to reflect a wide range of historical experience can be called privileged property. The European manorial order and its associated rights of entail and elite primogeniture are good examples, and the forms of privileged property that emerge from the historical record seem closely connected with the underpinning of aristocratic authority discussed earlier in this chapter.[43] Property as a privileged mode of ownership entails the right to a recognition of the property holder as a bearer of advantages. Those advantages include the power to compel the labor and resources of a subordinate population in the operation of an economic enterprise. This power was common to agrarian slavery and serfdom, and it can be interpreted as one way in which a landed elite can fortify its status in agrarian societies that lack a developed technological base.

A second form of property that is closely associated with elite power is best captured by the notion of exclusive property.[44] Exclusive property rights involve the ability to make exclusionary claims to scarce resources by preventing third parties from making counterclaims to those resources. Exclusive property rights

---

1500–1700," 177–91, E. P. Thompson, "The Grid of Inheritance: A Comment," 328–60, and V. G. Kiernan, "Private Property in History," 361–98; Hans Medick and David Warren Sabean, *Interest and Emotion: Essays on the Study of Family and Kinship* (Cambridge: Cambridge University Press, 1988), 1–8, 129–86; and Michael Taussig, *The Devil and Commodity Fetishism in South America* (Chapel Hill: University of North Carolina Press, 1980).

43. See J. P. Cooper, "Patterns of Inheritance and Settlement by Great Landowners from the Fifteenth to the Eighteenth Centuries," in Goody et al., *Family and Inheritance*, 192–305. Also see this logic at work in E. P. Thompson, *Whigs and Hunters: The Origin of the Black Act* (New York: Pantheon, 1975).

44. For a discussion of the impact of "exclusive" property rights on one rural society, see Arturo Warman, *"We Come to Object": The Peasants of Morelos and the National State* (Baltimore: Johns Hopkins University Press, 1980), esp. 42–90. A more theoretical discussion of the logic of exclusive property can be found in North, *Structure and Change*, 71–157.

are closely tied to legal notions of property as willful and acquisitive possession, and it is most developed in societies that attach rights to individuals rather than groups. Liberal property rights in Western societies are good examples.

But privileged and exclusive property rights are not tangible things; they are relations of conflict and cooperation that must be performed in ordinary life. Consequently, there is no reason to suppose that they can be successfully enforced, and failed performances may be as likely as outcomes that succeed. In practice, property rights may become attenuated and compromised, depending on the balance of micropower and social interests in which they are embedded. For example, privilege of property claims may fail if they are not backed by sufficient force to compel compliance; and the history of slavery and serfdom proves that even the most institutionalized forms of elite property involve compromises with the interests of subordinate groups.

In small-scale agrarian societies, exclusive and privileged forms of property can be thought of as closely linked to the forces of constraint. Privileged property fits the logic of aristocratic domination; and the rise of aristocratic elites in Europe was marked by the extension of claims to a realm of noble power that included the mass of the unfree population as a servile work force whose role, as Georges Duby shows, was to labor for those who "prayed and fought." Exclusive property rights seem more characteristic of bureaucratic and commercial modes of domination. Both involve the attempt to create "modern" social practices rooted in uniform and individual rights, and elites who are committed to this project must view with hostility any traditional or customary forms of property that involve group rights and ambiguous responsibilities. Exclusive property, with its crisp individualism, will seem to be the most effective means of "rationalizing" traditional societies. It is not surprising that in colonial southern and southeastern Asia, the agents of metropolitan power were deeply interested in introducing liberal conceptions of land and commercial property that were defined by exclusive rights of individual possession.[45]

The extension of exclusive and privileged property need not entail pronounced social conflict unless the process of extension clashes with property relations that involve a conflicting logic of ownership. In agrarian societies, especially those strongly based in local custom, conflict is most probable in situations where elite definitions of proprietorship contradict local practices that situate property in overlapping networks of group cooperation, and that qualify individual rights according to group responsibility. In the empirical studies of rural society, there is an old tradition of seeing property as strongly entrenched in practices by which resources are controlled through group arrangements. Individuals exercise rights in the context of enforceable responsibilities that imply stewardship for a larger

45. David Ludden, *Peasant History in South India* (Princeton: Princeton University Press, 1985), 101–63; Martin J. Murray, *The Development of Capitalism in Colonial Indo China (1870–1940)* (Berkeley: University of California Press, 1980), 45–95.

group. Trusteeship property is compatible with a variety of legal tenures, ranging from freehold to common fields, and the underlying principles are the same if they encapsulate individual rights within an institutional matrix that compels individuals to act in trust for a specific community of neighbors and kin. An excellent example was the practice of "open grazing" in the yeoman communities of the Georgia upcountry that have been reconstructed by Steven Hahn.[46] Land rights were bought and sold by individuals, but these rights were not exclusive because of their institutional limitation by local traditions that made the rights of individuals subject to local control. When farmers were not cultivating their land, they were expected to leave it open for grazing by their neighbors' stock, thereby creating a kind of customary open-field regime in the heart of a competitive society. Yet the comparative significance of this arrangement would be lost if we assumed that property was a fixed structure rather than a negotiable field of interactions that must be performed on an ongoing basis. Open grazing was an institutional practice that involved a constantly redrawn boundary between public and private rights.[47]

Trusteeship property is vulnerable to an elite redefinition of ownership that transforms regulated proprietorship into the prerogative of an individual owner who cannot be held accountable to the institutions of community control. A powerful feudal lord or a rack-renting landlord can try to escape local customary practices by coercively rupturing the cooperative arrangements that protect the integrity of local rights. It is precisely here, in the interplay between elite challenge and popular response, that we should find the most intense struggles over the authoritative definition of what property will mean in ordinary life. At least in the limiting case, the contest can escalate into insurrection when elite challenges become an immediate threat to the survival of community institutions. Property rights are fundamental to the cohesion and autonomy of local communities, and a sudden alteration in their practical meaning can cause chaos. This was, for instance, the result of British efforts to turn India into a land of individual proprietors who held clear and exclusive rights to land. Eventually, the tragicomic conflicts that resulted persuaded even the neo-Benthamites in the India office to grant legal recognition to village and lineage forms of tenure that were explicable only in terms of the logic of trusteeship.[48]

46. Steven Hahn, *The Roots of Southern Populism: Yeoman Farmers and the Transformation of the Georgia Upcountry, 1850–1890* (Oxford: Oxford University Press, 1983), 252–54.

47. Joan Thirsk, "The Common Fields," *Past and Present* 29 (1964), 3–25; and Warren O. Ault, *Open-Field Husbandry and the Village Community: A Study of Agrarian By-laws in Medieval Europe* (Philadelphia: Transactions of the American Philosophical Society, 1965).

48. Thomas R. Metcalf, *Land, Landlords, and the British Raj: Northern India in the Nineteenth Century* (Berkeley: University of California Press, 1979), 47–73; Brian Murton, "Land and Class: Cultural, Social, and Biophysical Integration in Interior Tamil Nadu in the Late 18th Century," in R. E. Frykenberg, ed., *Land Tenure and Peasant in South Asia* (New Delhi: Orient Longman, 1977), 81–99; and Ravinder Kumar, *Western India in the Nineteenth Century: A Study in the Social History of Maharashtra* (London: Routledge and Kegan Paul, 1968), 84–127.

The potential clash between the logic of prerogative property and the logic of trusteeship helps us to understand how the macro problems concerning the forces of constraint can be given a precise territorial focus at the level of single communities. Such an understanding is essential if we are to gain a comparative grasp of the rich details presented in the literature. It also facilitates a much clearer interpretation of the problem of land and land tenure in rural societies. Usually the problem is discussed as a dichotomy between peasant collectivism and bourgeois individualism. But, like most of our cherished dichotomies, it is too static and abstract to survive a microanalysis. There are too many forms of "peasant" land tenure and too much individualism in rural societies, and this complexity cannot be reduced to a simple dualism between capitalism and the rest of history. Our thinking must be reoriented toward a more concrete comparative focus that looks at small-scale institutional interactions. When we "deconstruct" the great abstractions about property what we find are ongoing conflict, compromise, and cooperation.

A related but more important point has to do with the interconnection of property rights and hierarchy in rural social formations. In recent years, a sophisticated literature has grown out of the effort to use property rights and transaction costs as a way of situating discussions of property in a microeconomic history. But the empty category in this enterprise is power and the kinds of power relations that inform property. To build on the insights of property-rights analysis, power and political conflict must be explicitly introduced into the argument. The kinds of property relations I have considered are hierarchical arrangements, and the potential struggles that grow out of them are political contests over the right to define claims and appropriate resources. In small-scale rural settings there is no good reason to separate power and property into neat compartments, and much of the historical data indicate that hierarchy and its enactment are central to the ordinary practice of property rights. Indeed, one might argue that in many contexts, property rights were finely graded into tenurial chains that linked the most with the least advantaged in a compact of reciprocal obligations. This, I think, is one way of interpreting the notion of a "moral economy," and it also underpins my description of privileged and trustee forms of proprietorship. In any case, we must situate property in the hierarchical institutions that transform claims into rights by grounding them in a practice of enforcement.

Yet, as we have seen, hierarchy is not a thing with physical or "organismic" dimensions. It is an interrelationship among people that is subject to failure, renegotiation, and transformation. The most we can do is to construct concepts that capture the ambiguities and tensions at work in the world without sacrificing comparative purchase on the issues. I have suggested that we can do this by reemphasizing the ordinary performances that constitute institutions.

Social scientists may find this notion unsettling, because they typically see hierarchy as a fixed organization with neatly arranged roles and compartments.

This is a mechanical way of seeing, however, at least with respect to rural societies. In agrarian social formations, hierarchy is often overlapping and intermittent. Hierarchies of status and property overlap with hierarchies of age and gender in a complex pattern that is not easily comprehended by the dualisms of state and society, public and private. Moreover, the patterns of hierarchy are not always embedded in permanent organizations that have clear boundaries and full-time staff. Hierarchy emerges occasionally in particular contexts of power and dispute. Patriarchy, one of the oldest types of domination, is a relationship of power that is enacted in specific situations in which ordinary routines have become sufficiently ambiguous to require an assertion of male power. In rural communities, violence too is an intermittent performance of actors locked in conflict; and it would be futile to reduce this to a clear-cut organization chart. As David Warren Sabean argues in his analysis of Herrschaft, or domination, the "secrets" of village power can be unlocked only by focusing on the real actions and exchanges of everyday life.[49]

The intermittent and performative quality of rural hierarchy is most amenable to an analysis that focuses on the small scale and the mundane. This is one reason that I have tried to break with macro conceptions of peasantry and to relocate the study of rebellion at the level of communities. But in attempting this I have also tried to keep the analysis rooted in the patterns of tension and interaction that link strategic elites with popular communities. My consideration of property relations and the forces of erosion and constraint was designed as a bridge between macro power and micro problems, and its utility should emerge in the case studies.

The Peasant as Elite Project

Many readers will have concluded that I have washed away the concept of the peasant in my search for a microanalysis of rural power and politics; and this surely seems odd given the powerful attachment to the concept in much work on the countryside. In following chapters I will use the concept of peasant very sparingly, partly in order to conduct an experiment in analytic writing that tries to make sense without constant invocations of the peasant. I do not, however, presume that "peasant" is a meaningless category, nor does the argument imply that people who use it are talking nonsense. There is a use for the concept of peasant, but it is not the use that most social scientists have clearly understood. The peasantry is perhaps best understood not as a class but as a determinate relation of power that binds supralocal elites to local communities. Throughout

49. David Warren Sabean, *Power in the Blood: Popular Culture and Village Discourse in Early Modern Germany* (Cambridge: Cambridge University Press, 1984), 1–36, and Sabean, *Landbesitz und Gesellschaft am Vorabend des Bauernkrieges: Eine Studie der sozialen Verhältnisse im sudlichen Oberschwaben in den Jahren vor 1525* (Stuttgart: Gustav Fischer, 1972).

much of human history powerful elites have attempted to capture the countryside through institutions of subjugation and surveillance, and those institutions comprise a strategy of control that rests on a maximization of the hierarchical distance between elites and popular groups. Servile agriculture is the most vivid example, but, as Goran Hyden argues, the struggle to capture rural people and resources is also characteristic of the grand development projects of third-world leaders.[50] Agriculture is too important to be abandoned to fortune, and throughout history we can find instances of an elite project that denies popular autonomy in the name of privilege and power.

What I propose, therefore, is that we see the peasantry as a mode of domination that is always contested and incomplete. Peasants do not exist in some "natural" state; they are created through mechanisms of political subordination that lie at the interface of popular institutions and translocal authority. This is an idea that many scholars have tried to employ when, like Redfield or Shanin, they have pointed to the "low-status," "underdog" or "part culture" features of ordinary cultivators.[51] But the insistence on using a class logic has stood in the way of a more perspicuous understanding. By focusing on elite strategies of domination, or what I have called the forces of constraint, we can push our concepts toward a more bounded and precise specification.

The shift from class to community also helps to provide a richer analysis of the institutional motivations and incentives that explain collective violence. In most theories of rebellion the underlying incentives are either cultural or psychological, and this begs the question of what kinds of mechanisms exist to compel participation in collective violence even when doing so may not be in the short-run in the self-interest of any particular individual. Rebellion is a dangerous deed, and there is good reason to suppose that many individuals would prefer to be free riders if they cannot predict that they will not be killed in the process.[52] More important, there is no reason to believe that the benefits of successful revolts will be equally shared by the actors, even if the outcome in some sense approximates a "public good." At least at the level of perception, there may be a range of winners and losers, and we should be able to explain rebellion in a way that accounts for the willingness of losers as well as winners to take part. (One illustration of this is the appearance of women and other low-status people in collective violence, even though they may have risked more in the way of life and limb than they could have gained in the way of material payoffs.)

50. Goran Hyden, *Beyond Ujamaa in Tanzania: Underdevelopment and an Uncaptured Peasantry* (Berkeley: University of California Press, 1980), 9–37, 237–60.

51. Robert Redfield, *Peasant Society and Culture: An Anthropological Approach to Civilization* (Chicago: University of Chicago Press, 1965), e.g., 68–69; Teodor Shanin, "Peasantry: Delineation of a Sociological Concept and a Field of Study," *European Journal of Sociology* 12 (1971).

52. For discussions of free riders and moral norms, see Russell Hardin, *Collective Action* (Baltimore: Johns Hopkins University Press, 1982), 212–13; Russell Hardin, *Morality within the Limits of Reason* (Chicago: University of Chicago Press, 1988), 147–51.

One approach to understanding the logic of rebellion is to see it as one among many forms of cooperation that are mutually interconnected across time. Individuals who gain less from participation in revolt than others may nevertheless need the cooperation of those individuals in other arenas of community practice in which they have a stake. For example, a small cultivator who has the Hobbesian fears of death may not be anxious to storm the local manor in heroic fashion.[53] But he may nonetheless follow his less timid fellows because he knows that his failure to perform may result in his exclusion from a local labor-sharing agreement in which his subsistence opportunities are deeply implicated. This kind of mutual implication makes sense only if we can link it to a discrete and territorially defined community that binds people in complex networks of action; and I take this to be a potent *theoretical* reason in favor of the plausibility of my concept of the community of grain. If people could escape the implications of community by fleeing into the anonymity of Simmel's city, or if they could dispense with the rights and duties of territorial membership, it would be difficult to understand even the possibility of rural rebellion.

53. The best recent explication of Hobbes and Hobbesian logic is Gregory S. Kavka, *Hobbesian Moral and Political Theory* (Princeton: Princeton University Press, 1986), 315–84.

CHAPTER 3

Between Manor and State: The
Agrarian Histories of the West

The long and powerful sweep of Western history can be written from as many perspectives as there are generational viewpoints. As Max Weber argued, relevant values inform the problems that we find interesting, although this connection to value positions should not undermine the possibility of objectivity.[1] The rural history of the West, for example, has been reconstructed from a range of perspectives that run the gamut from simple antiquarianism to theories of modernization and development. For political scientists, rural history has been especially interesting as a baseline against which the possibilities of transformation in the postcolonial third world can be measured. The Western agrarian record has been used as a complex standard that has served as a model of what can occur and a mirror of what will occur in specific conditions. For example, England's "agrarian revolution" has been used as an exemplary case of rural modernization, and several major theories of rural development have used the English experience as an implicit criterion of successful economic and political change.[2] It is important, therefore, continually to enrich our theoretical understanding by integrating the findings of historians into the discourse of political and social theory. Barrington Moore's classic study of dictatorship and democracy is only one example of a major argument that is framed in terms of a critical dialogue with Western rural history.[3]

1. Susan Hekman, *Weber: The Ideal Type and Contemporary Social Theory* (Notre Dame: University of Notre Dame Press, 1983), 153–60; Thomas Burger, *Max Weber's Theory of Concept Formation: History, Laws, and Ideal Types* (Durham: Duke University Press, 1976), 94–114.
2. See, for example, David Landes, *The Unbound Prometheus* (Cambridge: Cambridge University Press, 1969). For a less sophisticated treatment, see Simon Kuznets, "Underdeveloped Countries and the Pre-Industrial Phase in the Advanced Countries," in Amar Narain Agarwala and S. P. Singh, eds., *The Economics of Underdevelopment: A Series of Articles and Papers* (New York: Oxford University Press, 1963), 135–53.
3. Barrington Moore, *Social Origins of Dictatorship and Democracy: Lord and Peasant in the Making of the Modern World* (Boston: Beacon Press, 1966).

But if our understanding of the West must be revised in light of the unfolding of historical scholarship we should be prepared to undertake the task in order to construct better theory. At a minimum, the process will show us what we *cannot* do with the Western record. It will, for example, show us what features of the Western past are simply irrelevant to the comparative interpretation of the third world. By highlighting the decisive contrasts between the Western past and the non-Western present we can develop theory free from an implicit ethnocentrism that sees all history as the teleological march of social forces invented in the West. More important, we can gain a more fruitful starting point for analyzing the features of the West shared by contemporary developing societies. This type of theorizing takes history seriously.

Locating the Game

The obvious starting point is to ask whether the European record can be read in a way that supports the analysis of Western agrarian institutions as exemplifying the community of grain. In Chapter 1, I argued that a reasonably stringent test of the significance of community could be worked out by identifying the core institutions that must be present if a strong theoretical case is to be made for community as a framework of social identity. Those institutions should, at a minimum, encompass a set of interlocking practices that control the rights and duties of community membership, regulate the routines of production and consumption, and focus the social action of members on a tradition of community consciousness. How well does the long sweep of Western rural history meet the requirements of these three identifying characteristics?

First, it is evident that at least a weak notion of community has provided a kind of "basic unit of analysis" for most of the classic works in agrarian history. Scholars with such diverse interests and values as Marc Bloch, Eugenii A. Kosminsky, P. G. Vinogradoff, and Ladurie have turned to the concept of community as an almost "natural" framework for the ongoing flow of rural life.[4] Even Marxists such as Guy Bois and Georges Lefebvre and "eclectics" such as Maurice Agulhon and Georges Duby, who are often skeptical of community, return to a

4. Marc Bloch, *French Rural History: An Essay on Its Basic Characteristics* (Berkeley: University of California Press, 1966), 1–63; Marc Bloch, *Feudal Society*, 2 vols. (Chicago: University of Chicago Press, 1961); Eugenii A. Kosminskii, *Studies in the Agrarian History of England in the Thirteenth Century* (Oxford: Blackwell Press, 1956); P. G. Vinogradoff, *The Growth of the Manor:* (London: Allen and Unwin, 1911); P. G. Vinogradoff, *The Collected Papers of P. G. Vinogradoff,* with a memoir by H. A. L. Fisher, 2 vols. (Oxford: Clarendon Press, 1928); Emmanuel Le Roy Ladurie, *The French Peasantry, 1450–1660* (Berkeley: University of California Press, 1987), esp. 359–420. Also see T. H. Aston, ed., *Landlords, Peasants, and Politics in Medieval England* (Cambridge: Cambridge University Press, 1987), esp. Zvi Razi, "Family, Land, and the Village Community in Later Medieval England," 360–93, and Peter Gatrell, "Historians and Peasants: Studies of Medieval English Society in a Russian Context," 394–422.

community focus with surprising regularity.[5] Indeed, Susan Reynolds, in her synthetic treatment of the Middle Ages, dedicated an entire chapter to rural communities; and her work suggests that rural communities have a much older genealogy than the skeptics may have realized.[6] It is not surprising, then, to discover that pioneering efforts at uniting microhistory and popular history use community institutions as an essential backdrop.[7]

But how can we account for the pervasiveness of the concept of community in the historiography of the rural West? The most parsimonious answer is that this is just the way the primary sources present themselves to the researcher. Almost all our understanding of the rural West is locked in the records of villages, estates, parishes, and other local institutions, and those records treat local communities as basic reference points for purposes of apportioning fundamental rights and duties. For example, until well into the twentieth century many European nations based taxation on hearths or households grouped into territorial communities, and it is clear that the menial scribblers who compiled the records regarded this way of viewing the world as so natural as to be beyond comment.[8] Similarly, the European landed aristocracies did not address their demands to an abstract peasantry or a mass of disconnected individuals. They addressed the collectivity of people who

5. Guy Bois, *The Crisis of Feudalism: Economy and Society in Eastern Normandy, c. 1300–1550* (Cambridge: Cambridge University Press, 1984), esp. 1–77, 137–214; Georges LeFebvre, *The Great Fear of 1789* (Princeton: Princeton University Press, 1982), esp. 7–58, 148–97; Georges Lefebvre, *Les paysans du Nord pendant la Revolution française* (Bari: Editori Laterza, 1959); Maurice Agulhon, *The Republic in the Village: The People of Var from the French Revolution to the Second Republic* (Cambridge: Cambridge University Press, 1982), 21–56; and Georges Duby, *The Chivalrous Society* (Berkeley: University of California Press, 1977), 186–215.

6. Susan Reynolds, *Kingdoms and Communities in Western Europe, 900–1300* (Oxford: Oxford University Press, 1984), 79–154. See also Jerome Blum, "The European Village as Community: Origins and Functions," *Agricultural History* 45 (1971), 157–78; Jerome Blum, "The Internal Structure and Polity of the European Village Community from the Fifteenth to the Nineteenth Century," *Journal of Modern History* 43 (4) (1971), 541–76.

7. See Carlo Ginzburg, *The Night Battles: Witchcraft and Agrarian Cults in the Sixteenth and Seventeenth Centuries* (Baltimore: Johns Hopkins University Press, 1983), 33–68; Carlo Ginzburg, *The Cheese and the Worms: The Cosmos of a Sixteenth-Century Miller* (New York: Penguin Press, 1982); Natalie Z. Davis, *Society and Culture in Early Modern France: Eight Essays* (Stanford: Stanford University Press, 1975), esp. 152–87; David Warren Sabean, *Power in the Blood: Popular Culture and Village Discourse in Early Modern Germany* (Cambridge: Cambridge University Press, 1984); and Margaret Spufford, *Contrasting Communities: English Villagers in the Sixteenth and Seventeenth Centuries* (Cambridge: Cambridge University Press, 1974).

8. This is the clearest in France. See, for example, Pierre Goubert, *The French Peasantry in the Seventeenth Century* (Cambridge: Cambridge University Press, 1986), 6–21, 179–86; Ladurie, *The French Peasantry*, 100–101, 188–89; and Hilton Root, *Peasants and King in Burgundy: Agrarian Foundations of French Absolutism* (Berkeley: University of California Press, 1987), 1–65. For Europe as a whole, see Jerome Blum, *The End of the Old Order in Rural Europe* (Princeton: Princeton University Press, 1978), esp. 65–68, 77–78, 414–17. A similar principle of collective responsibility seems to have been at work in imperial China. See, for example, Brian E. McKnight, *Village and Bureaucracy in Southern Sung China* (Chicago: University of Chicago Press, 1971), 1–72; Madeleine Zelin, *The Magistrate's Tael: Rationalizing Fiscal Reform in Eighteenth Century Ch'ing China* (Berkeley: University of California Press, 1984), 1–24, 238–63.

were identified with particular named places, and they evidently assumed that the people they ruled were organized around a logic of community cohesion and action. Even in the records of the church, the most nonterritorial of European supralocal forms of domination, the parish early on became the basic unit of administration and cognitive modeling, and at least in parts of Europe, the parish had precisely the dimensions of territorial identity and mutually implicated networks of cooperation that I have identified as constitutive of the community of grain.[9]

The source material used in writing rural history thus forces us to organize our data in a way that emphasizes the salience of territory and small-scale institutions. This is a good reason to be suspicious of arguments that are framed along class lines, because class logic does not seem to mesh with the way the source materials were written. Naturally, the source materials may themselves be the product of a false consciousness about social reality. If the sources are in some sense false, however, there is no other court of appeal to which we can turn to establish the facts of the case. Archaeology, a possible if oblique alternative to written data, actually supports the idea that spatially defined communities have been important in organizing rural societies in the West. One need only read Bloch's discussion of the importance of walking the local boundaries of fields and forests in order to gain an understanding of how salient highly localized village and hamlet organizations have been to the archaeological enterprise.[10]

A true skeptic will reply that the preceding argument is really beside the point and proves nothing. The "records" of rural history are elite artifacts created for purposes of control and exploitation. They tell us next to nothing about popular realities, and they cannot be trusted as a foundation for reconstructing the lives of people long dead. Moreover, so this argument goes, the salience of community was something elites imposed on subject populations; left to their own devices, rural people would have organized themselves according to a completely different logic.

My response to this line of attack is twofold. First, it is not at all clear that it makes any sense to argue that community institutions are best seen as elite constructions, especially if those institutions increase rather than reduce the ability of ordinary people to resist elite demands. One of the purposes of the first two chapters was to show that there are good theoretical reasons for supposing that communities provide a focus for popular organizations that can limit elite power. But, even if the theoretical argument is rejected, it does not follow that territorial communities exist only in the presence of powerful elites who use community as a

9. For the origins and importance of the parish, see Harold J. Berman, *Law and Revolution* (Cambridge: Harvard University Press, 1983), 320–31; Jack Goody, *The Development of the Family and Marriage in Europe* (Cambridge: Cambridge University Press, 1983), 83–102; and esp., Reynolds, *Kingdoms and Communities*, 79–100.

10. Bloch, *French Rural History*, xvii–56.

framework of exploitation. For example, Switzerland after the defeat of the knights of the Holy Roman Empire and Russia after the 1917 Revolution both exhibited strong popular currents that reaffirmed the integrity of community institutions.[11]

More important, the assertion that rural community is merely a reflex of elite power begs too many key questions. It forces us to ask why landed and commercial elites would choose this form of social organization as a basis for exercising domination, rather than "creating" even more atomized forms of popular life that would leave those to be dominated much more defenseless. In addition, we would want to ask how elites amassed the power necessary to transform popular groups into communities, especially if we define elite power as the ability to create rural communities out of the flux of history. There is obviously more than a touch of circularity and tautology in this way of seeing things, and it cannot be evaded without returning to the records that historians have used as a means of reconstructing rural history. But this brings us full circle, and it will be of no more than cold comfort to the critics of the historical record to recognize that the "facts" speak to community as an important mode of social life in the rural West.

In any event, my argument does not hinge on demonstrating that community forms emerged spontaneously or naturally in the transition from hunting and gathering to settled agriculture. What I must show is that community was a major and long-lasting framework of *popular* politics and society, and in the illumination of this problem the question of ultimate origins is of decidedly secondary importance. The interesting issue is whether the traditions of Western rural scholarship can be read as supporting a social and political theory that takes community as primary in describing and explaining agrarian history.

In addressing this question, I will focus on two "units" of historical analysis and narrative that have been commonly deployed in the relevant literatures: the village and the parish. So central are these to historical writing that they seem to play the role of key cognitive models described by George Lakoff.[12]

Village institutions are the easiest to evaluate, because they are geographically ubiquitous from an early date. By A.D. 900, villages could be found throughout Europe, from the shores of the Mediterranean to the far forests of northern Europe.[13] In central and eastern Europe, nucleated villages were well established

11. For the continuing importance of community in Switzerland as late as 1525, see Peter Blickle, *The Revolution of 1525: The German Peasants' War from a New Perspective* (Baltimore: Johns Hopkins University Press, 1981), 65–67, 128–29. For Russia, see Donald J. Male, *Russian Peasant Organisation before Collectivization: A Study of Commune and Gathering, 1925–1930* (Cambridge: Cambridge University Press, 1971).

12. George Lakoff, *Women, Fire, and Dangerous Things: What Categories Reveal about the Mind* (Chicago: University of Chicago Press, 1987), 5–12, 77–118.

13. The widespread occurrence of villages in medieval times is discussed in depth in M. M. Postan, ed., *The Agrarian Life of the Middle Ages* (Cambridge: Cambridge University Press, 1971). For evidence of premedieval communities in Greek and Roman times, see Geoffrey E. M. de Ste. Croix, *The Class Struggle in the Ancient Greek World: From the Archaic Age to the Arab Conquest* (Ithaca: Cornell University Press, 1981), 10–11, 221–25, 157–58. For Scandinavia, see Øyvind Østerud,

by the later Middle Ages, although in forest regions there may have been a more dispersed form of habitat.[14] There is no doubt, however, that villages have constituted a basic political and economic building block of rural life from medieval times through the twentieth century.[15]

The archetypical village was, of course, the open-field village of the medieval and early modern periods. In open-field villages the core of daily life revolved around a complex of cooperative practices that integrated arable farming and animal husbandry. In open-field villages the property rights of individuals, households, and communities were intermixed in a pyramid of tenurial rights and duties that defy any reduction to a simple dichotomy between private and public property. Households, or "hearths," were the usual bearers of ultimate property rights to land in the common fields and forests, but the whole membership of the village had rights of control over what specific households could do with their property.[16] Individual proprietors were bound by what I call rules of property as trusteeship, and householders could be held accountable for violating their role as trustees of the village. For example, excessive grazing of animals, chopping of wood, or enclosure without the consent of neighbors and kin could result in penalties ranging from stiff fines to violent reprisals.[17] The very architecture and physical organization of the village must have reinforced the ties of material cooperation, because the combination of nucleated dwelling spaces and intermixed strips of arable in the common fields generated a context of interaction in which household rights were contingent on the behavior of neighbors. Rights of access to a household's arable strips, for instance, were crucially molded lby the patterns of exchange and coordination that existed among all village members. Even the decision about when and what to plant was shaped by the group practices of the village, and a cultivator who was foolish enough to plant when his neighbors grazed ran the risk of having his crops eaten by the village flock.[18]

But the open-field village was much more than miniature economic enterprise. It was also an arena of politics and ritual that exercised a large degree of authority

---

Agrarian Structure and Peasant Politics in Scandinavia: A Comparative Study of Rural Response to Economic Change (Oslo: Universitets forlaget/Scandanavian University Books, 1978), 68–194.

14. Alfons Dopsch, "Agrarian Institutions of the Germanic Kingdoms from the Fifth to the Ninth Century," in Postan, *The Agrarian Life,* 180–204.

15. Blum, *The End of the Old Order,* 123–25, 414–17.

16. For the political economy of the open-field village, see Carl Dahlman, *The Open Field System and Beyond: A Property Right Analysis of an Economic Institution* (Cambridge: Cambridge University Press, 1980), 16–64, 93–145; T. A. M. Bishop, "Assarting and the Growth of the Open Fields," *Economic History Review* 6 (1935–36), 13–29; H. M. Cam, "The Community of the Vill," in Frederic L. Cheyett, ed., *Lordship and Community in Medieval Europe: Selected Readings* (New York: Holt, Rinehart and Winston, 1968); G. C. Homans, *English Villagers of the Thirteenth Century* (New York: Norton, 1970); and J. Z. Titow, "Medieval England and the Open-field System," *Past and Present* 32 (1965).

17. Roger B. Manning, *Village Revolts: Social Protest and Popular Disturbances in England, 1509–1640* (Oxford: Clarendon Press, 1988), 31–131.

18. K. J. Allison, "Flock Management in the Sixteenth and Seventeenth Centuries," *Economic History Review,* 2d ser., 11 (1958–59), 98–111.

over everyone who claimed membership. There is good evidence that village institutions could be used to exert substantial jurisdiction over the key issues and conflicts that emerged in the course of local life. Manor courts, councils of householders, and political authorities like the village mayor or Schultheiss could compel the performance of duties and adjudicate disputes about the meaning of village rights. Outsiders with no local kin ties were unwelcome in this world in which surnames may have been less important as a source of identity than the name of the village in which one was born.[19]

Intersecting the political and economic practices of the village were the numerous holidays and ritual occasions that obligated village members to a local folklore of place that would have pleased Durkheim. Rooted both in pagan antiquity and Christian doctrine, the ritual of the village marked off a space in the flux of time that was shared with a wider culture and yet specific to the people who made up the village.[20] Weddings and funerals, holy days and holidays, were important manifestations of the routine festivals of the village. These were occasions for at least a modicum of conspicuous consumption, and they may also have offered a pretext for a limited redistribution of excess consumption resources from the better off to the less advantaged.[21] Yet prestations and exchanges should not blind us to the importance of ritual events as moments of performed cohesion that made visible all the underlying forms of cooperation that made an open-field village a place with a history.

The European open-field village was not an egalitarian brotherhood, nor was it cut off from supralocal networks of power and exchange. Village institutions were hierarchical, at least to the extent of being patriarchal. Village members were also involved in relations of politics and market exchange that stretched beyond local boundaries. But most important, the open-field village was a community. It was rooted in territorial membership, and its institutional practices were closely connected to the problems of producing and distributing the means of life. Open-field institutions exercised control over village members, organized the material routines of agriculture, and constituted a solid ritual focus for local customs and identities. In this sense, the open-field village closely matches the conditions and practices that I have identified as central to the community of grain.[22]

Yet not all European villages were characterized by the tight routines of the

19. This is my reading of Sabean, *Power in the Blood*, 1–36; Victor G. Kiernan, *State and Society in Europe, 1550–1650* (Oxford: B. Blackwell, 1980), 7; Perez Zagorin, *Rebels and Rulers* 2 vols. (Cambridge: Cambridge University Press, 1982), 1:85–86, chap. 7; and Henry Kamen, *European Society, 1500–1700* (London: Hutchinson, 1984), 17.

20. Sabean, *Power in the Blood*, 37–60.

21. See, for example, Emmanuel Le Roy Ladurie, *Carnival in Romans* (New York: George Braziller, 1979); David Underdown, *Revel, Riot, and Rebellion: Popular Politics and Culture in England, 1603–1660* (Oxford: Clarendon Press, 1985), 44–73; and James Obelkevich, *Religion and Rural Society: South Lindsey, 1825–1875* (Oxford: Clarendon Press, 1976), 143–82.

22. For a case study, see Homans, *English Villagers of the Thirteenth Century*.

open-field regime. Many villages, especially after the eighteenth century, displayed nucleated patterns of habitation without joining those patterns to common-field agriculture. For example, the disestablishment of church property and communal land in nineteenth-century Spain and Italy vastly reduced the extent of collective proprietorship; and in parts of western France, the Low Countries, and Scandinavia, open-field agriculture was never highly developed.[23] Did villages without open fields exhibit clear indicators of community cohesion, or did they resemble mere residential neighborhoods that lacked substantial institutional integrity?

First, it is not true that villages without common fields did not have rights of collective proprietorship over other resources necessary for agrarian life. Forests, for example, were often subject to strict local regulation, and village use rights were jealously guarded against outside interference, even if it meant a direct clash with the manor land or forest police.[24] Furthermore, it is not always the case that de jure changes in communal land tenure were matched by de facto change in the way land rights were institutionalized at the local level. During the eighteenth and nineteenth centuries, reforming elites had a habit of decreeing changes in popular life that they had neither the power nor the will to enforce, and it appears that the abolition of common fields and use rights often failed to effect any deep changes in popular practices.[25] A particularly striking illustration comes from Ruth Behar's lucid study of a Spanish community, *Santa María del Monte.*[26] In Behar's Leonese village, common and interspersed land rights were found as late as the end of the Franco regime, even though such rights had been technically rendered illegal by modernizing Spanish regimes. Other data from the Mediterranean confirms the notion that local property institutions may be more widespread than commonly thought, and the history of modern Greece could partly be written as the story of the ways in which local communities have evaded and resisted the right of the state to define local property rights.[27] We will be oblivious to the survival of local institutions if we go on drawing on a false picture of property as solely defined and enforced by elite interests backed by state power.

23. For disestablishment in Italy, see Christopher Seton-Watson, *Italy: From Liberalism to Fascism, 1870–1925* (London: Methuen, 1967), 24–25. The limits of the open-, or common-field, system are more conjectural. But see Charles Darain, "The Evolution of Agricultural Technique," in Postan, *The Agrarian Life,* 126–79. For Spain, see Edward E. Malefakis, *Agrarian Reform and Peasant Revolution in Spain: Origins of the Civil War* (New Haven: Yale University Press, 1970), 61–64, 135–36.

24. P. M. Jones, *The Peasantry in the French Revolution* (Cambridge: Cambridge University Press, 1988), 15–29; Agulhon, *The Republic in the Village,* 226–35.

25. Blum, *The End of the Old Order,* 216–40, 357–417.

26. Ruth Behar, *Santa María del Monte: The Presence of the Past in a Spanish Village* (Princeton: Princeton University Press, 1986), 193, 228–29, 255–56.

27. William N. McGrew, *Land and Revolution in Modern Greece, 1800–1881: The Transition in the Tenure and Exploitation of Land from Ottoman Rule to Independence* (Kent: Kent State University Press, 1985), 41–79, 111–49.

In any event, the larger issue has to do with the existence of networks of community cooperation beyond the common-field system. Many scholars have noted the persistence of cooperative exchanges of labor and agricultural resources in societies that are otherwise characterized by either individualized modes of tenure or acute land shortages that have led to the fragmentation and enclosure of holdings. Ireland, for example, was a society of smallholders and laborers throughout much of the eighteenth century, and Irish common fields were gradually eroded by demographic pressures and elite enclosures.[28] Yet Irish agriculture was marked by a whole series of cooperative practices that included mutual aid in adverse times and a strong commitment to reserving the local market for tenancy leases to community members.[29] Here again we can glimpse a local and customary practice of property rights that did not depend on the state for definition and enforcement. Local hierarchies that emerged from village or town social networks offered a popular alternative to the courts and laws of the Anglo-Irish gentry, and that alternative jurisdiction also created the possibility of local opposition to the landed elite.

Villages without open fields also developed institutions of group regulation and ritual that controlled membership and reinforced local ties. In medieval forest villages, established under the auspices of the Cistercians on the German frontier common fields were not much in evidence until fairly late in the Middle Ages. But from the beginning they were organized along clearly demarcated territorial principles; and village rights and duties were under the scrutiny of village headmen, who were often drawn from the households of community founders.[30] Similar examples can be found in the villages of militiamen who guarded the Byzantine Empire, as well as in the group solidarities that appear in the sketchy histories of the free villages of the Roman imperium.[31]

It is clear that villages could generate strong community institutions with or without open-field agriculture. Admittedly, the latter kinds of villages are less frequently dealt with in the historical literatures, largely because open-field systems have been a major puzzle for economic historians. Nevertheless, we should not try to reduce community to one particular pattern of legal or customary land

28. Kerby A. Miller, *Emigrants and Exiles: Ireland and the Irish Exodus to North America* (New York: Oxford University Press, 1985), 54–56, 220–39.

29. See "Introduction: The Tradition of Violence"; David Dickson, "Taxation and Disaffection in Late Eighteenth-Century Ireland"; Paul E. W. Roberto, "Caravats and Shanavests: Whiteboyism and Faction Fighting in East Minster, 1802–1811"; and William L. Feingold, "Land League Power: The Tralee Poor-Law Election of 1881," all in Samuel Clark and James S. Donnelly, Jr., eds., *Irish Peasants: Violence and Political Unrest, 1780–1914* (Madison: University of Wisconsin Press, 1983), 25–101, 285–310. Also see Samuel Clark, *The Social Origins of the Irish Land War* (Princeton: Princeton University Press, 1979), 65–106, 246–304.

30. Dopsch, "Agrarian Institutions of the Germanic Kingdoms"; Herman Aubin, "The Lands East of the Elbe," in Postan, *The Agrarian Life*, 449–86.

31. George Ostrogorsky, "Agrarian Conditions in the Byzantine Empire in the Middle Ages," in Postan, *The Agrarian Life*, 205–34; de Ste. Croix, *The Class Struggle*, 10–11, 157–58, 221–25.

tenure. The European experience shows that a variety of tenure relations can be compatible with powerful local institutions tied to the problems of territorial organization and agricultural production. The concept of the community of grain seems best able to capture this variety without forgoing comparative perspective.

Villages, however, were not the exclusive mode of community life in the European West. Parishes can also be found throughout Europe; in some cases, parish boundaries had a significance beyond their role in organizing religious observance and clerical taxation. Especially in areas of dispersed habitation and pastoral farming, parishes formed a basic unit of economic and political cooperation, as Susan Reynolds has shown. At the center of the parish community were the institutional rituals that grew up around the parish church and its cycle of masses and festivals. It was through the mediation of parish life that families developed ties of co-godparenthood, ties that could be central in arranging political alliances and networks of economic exchange.[32]

Parishes seem to have been important in western France; parts of Spain, including the Basque provinces; and regions of light population, especially certain "frontier" areas where animal husbandry was as important as arable in providing the means of subsistence. The underlying correlation, however, seems to be between dispersed habitats or enclosed farms and the parish as a meaningful unit of action.

The parish has not received sufficient attention from social scientists, partly because of an assumption that nucleated villages form the only real locus of community in rural societies. Still, historians have long recognized the existence of fairly cohesive parishes; and it should be difficult to understand the patterns of popular mobilization in events like the French Vendée or Spanish Carlism without first understanding the logic of parish cooperation.[33]

In some cases, of course, parishes were coterminous with the boundaries of nucleated villages, and in this sort of situation it seems best to locate community in the wider context of village life. Nonetheless, the case that can be made for the existence of parish communities in parts of Europe should alert us to the futility of trying to reduce community to one particular pattern of habitation. Territory and territorially based rules of local membership are more salient criteria, and they are general enough to allow us to make broad comparisons across cases.

That village and parish communities were central to the logic of popular organization in rural Europe, at least from roughly the early Middle Ages (c. A.D. 800–900) through the early twentieth century, is a bold generalization. One must,

32. Reynolds, *Kingdoms and Communities in Western Europe,* 79–100.
33. For the Vendée, see T. J. A. Le Goff and D. M. G. Sutherland, "The Social Origins of Counter Revolution in Western France," *Past and Present* 99 (May 1983), 65–87; D. M. G. Sutherland, *The Chouans: The Social Origins of Popular Counter-Revolution in Upper Brittany, 1770–1796* (Oxford: Oxford University Press, 1982); and Charles Tilly, *The Vendée* (Cambridge: Harvard University Press, 1976). For Carlism, see Raymond Carr, *Spain, 1808–1939* (Oxford: Clarendon Press, 1966), 185–88.

however, be impressed by the importance of villages and parishes in rural studies, and the constant organization of the data in terms of village and parish units provides a crude cross-verification of my claim that these forms of social life were basic modes of local community in the West.

Aristocratic Domination, Manorial Power, and Rural Localism in the West, c. 900–1800

From the end of the Roman imperium to the French Revolution, aristocratic elites were the most powerful political actors in the West. Whatever their origins, aristocracies held the commanding heights of sacred and secular power from England to Russia and were at the core of the social forces that gave rise to the modern world. The fact of aristocratic hegemony is so well known as to appear uncontroversial, yet the implications for comparative rural history are often unclearly thought through. By unlocking the nature of aristocratic power we can build a more rigorous framework for interpreting rural politics and rebellion, especially because so much of the history of collective violence in the West grew out of the clash of aristocrats and "commoners."[34]

First, aristocracies were not economic classes in any recognizable sense. They based their claims to rule on hereditary privilege and control of the means of political power, particularly the means of supralocal military violence that emerged out of the feudal fragmentation of royal authority. Still, aristocracies in many areas did develop typical relations of hierarchy and subordination that attached aristocratic privilege to the kinds of village and parish communities discussed earlier.

One way of understanding this phenomenon is to think of aristocratic power not as a class structure but as a complex of institutional positions that were marked by ambiguity and tension.[35] Aristocrats demanded obedience as a matter of right, yet that right was justified as a function of the protective role that noble power played in ordinary life. It was the tension between pretensions of the nobles to arbitrary power and their claim to perform vital functions of order and defense that made the position of aristocracies inherently ambiguous. Neither autocrats nor representatives of the people, European aristocracies combined privilege and function in an uncertain balance. That balance was uncertain because of the possibility that, by playing out one or the other pole of the tension, the basis of aristocratic power would collapse. By emphasizing their functional and protective role, aristocrats

34. The following argument is heavily indebted to three key works by Georges Duby: *The Three Orders: Feudal Society Imagined* (Chicago: University of Chicago Press, 1980), esp. 271–357; *The Age of the Cathedrals: Art and Society, 980–1420* (Chicago: University of Chicago Press, 1981), esp. 10–96; and *The Chivalrous Society*, esp. 1–80, 158–85. For aristocratic power in Europe, also see Eleanor Searle, *Predatory Kinship and the Creation of Norman Power, 840–1066* (Berkeley: University of California Press, 1988).

35. See essays in Cheyette, ed., *Lordship and Community in Medieval Europe*.

risked undermining their status as power holders who ruled according to prerogative rather than consent. But if they emphasized the arbitrary and unaccountable
features of their role, they risked becoming "parasites" whose privileges could
not be justified. In the latter situation, the end result could be popular rebellion.
Aristocracy, then, was neither a class nor a thing; it was an ambiguous institutional performance in which privileged rulers struggled to maintain a precarious
balance between conflicting interests.

Evidence for this reading of European aristocracy comes from a wide variety of
standard sources.[36] Duby's analysis of the origins of the tripartite social schema
that came to inflect elite discourse after the tenth century is particularly useful,
because it indicates the paradoxes and ironies that underlay the European conception of nobility.[37] Aristocrats were always poised at the intersection of diverging
principles of action. At once sacred and secular, good and evil, without being
simply one or the other, Western nobilities tried to project an image of charisma
that could never be entirely successful.

In order to establish a link between aristocratic ambition and rural collective
violence, we must concentrate on the ways in which aristocratic power affected
the politics of popular communities. Specifically, we must show how aristocratic
domination was played out at the level of the manor, because the manor was the
most important unit of elite power and production in the West for some ten
centuries. During this period there were few if any national institutions in which
elite and popular interests could be articulated; and political life was a politics of
local needs and institutions. It does no good to talk of abstract lords confronting
abstract peasants; we must situate our analysis in a comparative framework that
explains the local contexts in which these confrontations occurred. Such a framework ought to offer at least a plausible explanation of an apparent paradox: Why
did manorial institutions lead to violent conflict in some cases but not others, and
can we make generalizations about the character of manorial power that help us to
understand both its longevity and ultimate decline?

The literature dealing with manorial power is exhaustive; and it is clear that,
whatever their differences, most authoritative studies agree about the following
points.[38] First, the manor evolved out of the general crisis of authority that

---

36. Bloch, *Feudal Society;* Blum, *The End of the Old Order,* 80–94; D. A. Bullough, "Early
Medieval Social Groupings: The Terminology of Kinship," *Past and Present* 45 (1969), 3; Constance
Bouchard, "The Origins of the French Nobility: A Reassessment," *American Historical Review* 86
(1981), 501–32; John Le Patourel, *The Norman Empire* (Oxford: Clarendon Press, 1976); Karl
Leyser, *Rule and Conflict in an Early Medieval Society: Ottonian Saxony* (Bloomington: Indiana
University Press, 1979); Timothy Reuter, "Plunder and Tribute in the Carolingian Empire," *Transac-
tions of the Royal Historical Society,* 5th ser., 35 (1985); and R. H. Hilton, ed., *Peasants, Knights, and
Heretics: Studies in Medieval English Social History* (Cambridge: Cambridge University Press, 1976).

37. Duby, *The Three Orders.*

38. The following discussion draws heavily on Bloch, *Feudal Society,* 241–79; Duby, *The Chivalrous Society,* 186–215; Hilton, *Peasants, Knights, and Heretics,* esp. essays by Sally Harvey, "The
Knight and the Knight's Fee in England," 133–73, Rodney H. Hilton, "Freedom and Villeinage in

accompanied the death of centralized kingship in the West. In this context, warrior bands inserted themselves in the local networks of power that became the basis for feudal overlordship. Part of the process of rebuilding elite power involved the assertion of elite claims of jurisdiction over land and labor, and the equally crucial division of the population into aristocrats and commoners. Manorial institutions took shape as supralocal overlords parceled out benefices over which their followers began to claim sweeping rights of economic and political jurisdiction. This was the beginning of the kinds of privileged property relations discussed in chapter 2; and by the twelfth century much of the rural population of Europe was formally considered to be a servile extension of the patrimony of the manor lord, compelled by law to labor at the will of an aristocratic elite. Serfdom was inseparable from the logic of manorial power, and manorial power was central to noble identity.

Nevertheless, the formal rules of the manor rarely matched daily realities, as Paul R. Hyams has shown quite clearly in his study of England.[39] From the standpoint of aristocratic manor lords the problem was to constrain their "subjects" in a tight net of daily rules and orders that would maximize the flow of resources and deference on which noble privilege depended. At the heart of this enterprise was the manorial court, the institutional locus of politics for the manor lord and his subjects. If the lord relaxed his vigilance over the manor court he stood to lose his effective control over the daily routines of agricultural life. But if he pressed too hard, he risked having to use force to establish his power, and this was not an easy exercise in societies that lacked even the rudiments of a modern transportation system.[40]

The "constitution" of manorial domination might have been unproblematic if it had been imposed on an atomized mass of cultivators. Yet such was *not* the case, as I have already indicated. Manors were associated with relatively cohesive popular communities, and the boundaries of village and manor overlapped often enough to suggest that manorial institutions were imposed on existing communities.[41] In any event, the successful manor depended on the effective cooperation of member households; indeed, the surplus produced by members' cooperation was the tributary base of manorial power.

But how could service institutions be effectively consolidated in societies in

England," 174–91, and Christopher Dyer, "A Redistribution of Incomes in Fifteenth-Century England," 192–215; Rodney H. Hilton, *The English Peasantry in the Later Middle Ages: The Ford Lectures for 1973 and Related Studies* (Oxford: Clarendon Press, 1975), 54–75; and Bryce Lyon, *A Constitutional and Legal History of Medieval England* (New York: Norton, 1980), 59–103, 166–79, 391–407.

39. Paul R. Hyams, *Kings, Lords, and Peasants in Medieval England: The Common Law of Villeinage in the Twelfth and Thirteenth Centuries* (Oxford: Clarendon Press, 1980), 3–81, 221–68.

40. Douglas C. North, *Structure and Change in Economic History* (New York: Norton, 1981), 124–42.

41. Reynolds, *Kingdoms and Communities*, 101–54.

which popular groups had enough cohesiveness to cooperate above the level of the household? Would this not have led to continuous popular opposition that would eventually undermine the whole manorial project? The answer cannot be found in an ad hoc appeal to the ability of local aristocracies to exercise violence in order to effect their will. Violence was part of the manorial order, but it is impossible to credit the notion that a relatively small aristocratic elite could have exercised violence everywhere and at all times. Yet that is precisely what we must suppose if we eliminate the tension between aristocratic claims and practical realities, something that proponents of a "pure coercion" theory of the manor have a tendency to do. In addition, we will be left with the uncomfortable fact that the means of violence were widely dispersed rather than concentrated in elite hands, and anyone who disputes this will have a hard time explaining how the great popular revolts of the medieval and early modern periods could have occurred at all.

The puzzle of the European manor becomes tractable if we rethink it in terms of the theoretical discussion of the forces of constraint presented in chapter 2. Manorial institutions did threaten the integrity of popular institutions, particularly if the former impinged on the subsistence security of subject households. But this threat was realized only when the manor lord attempted to create "captive" communities in which all aspects of community life were bent to the will of the lord. It is precisely in this context that we would expect popular opposition to manorial demands to escalate into open opposition to the pretensions of aristocracy. Yet this was probably the limiting case; in more normal times manorial power is best thought of as an unstable compromise that was negotiated through the manorial court.

It would seem, then, that manorial serfdom was almost always an incomplete and contested form of domination. The customs of the manor could represent either the interest of the rulers or the ruled, and they probably represented both in most cases. The particular balance cannot be predicted according to a general theory because the precise mixture depended on a whole range of contingent factors. What theory can do is to reconstruct the logic of political conflict and cooperation that underpinned the manor as a political type. That logic was connected with an aristocracy that claimed to rule without popular consent yet also needed at least minimal consent in order to provide its rule with real material foundations. The radical gap between aristocratic theory and popular practice opened an institutional space in which popular communities could exercise substantial if precarious autonomy.

The larger implication is that the most stable and long-lived forms of aristocratic power were to be found in situations characterized by aristocracies who offered a real margin of protection in exchange for the contingent deference of popular communities. As I pointed out, the role of protector was one component of the aristocratic code, and it was a political resource that could be used to stabilize a local manorial order. Providing defense against "barbarous" enemies was a point of potential cooperation between lords and commoners, as the history of Europe during the Viking invasions plainly indicates.[42] It is important, of course, to underscore the *non*representative quality of this protection, and it is clear that nobles did not see themselves as the "elected" agents of the communities they ruled. Still, the survival of a viable manorial regime must have been aided by a careful calculation of how far aristocratic prerogatives could be pushed before the whole game collapsed in recrimination and violence. Underlying the long history of aristocracy was a protective division of labor between "those who fought and those who labored," and when this division of labor came to an end the nobility became a collection of privileged individuals without a natural institutional home.

Support for this reading of aristocratic power and the manorial order can be found in a wide range of historical studies that have reconstructed the European manor from the ground up. For example, several generations of English scholars have helped us to understand how manorial institutions grew out of a slow accumulation of customs that owed as much to the ruled as to their rulers. Building on the classic constitutional work of historians like F. W. Maitland, more sociologically oriented scholars have exploded any lingering myths about a passive peasantry that unthinkingly obeyed its masters.[43] The work of Aston, John Hatcher, Zvi Razi, and Christopher Dyer stands out as exemplary in this regard. French scholars, working in the Annales tradition, have also helped to show how much manorial custom was rooted in popular customs and institutions.[44] Even the history of central and eastern European serfdom has been rewritten from below, and the results do not support the picture of serfdom as simply imposed from above on a helpless rural population. As the work of William W. Hagen on Prussia shows, serfdom was a negotiated set of institutional practices that worked through, rather than against, existing village solidarities.[45] A similar case can probably be made

42. Peter Sawyer, *The Age of the Vikings* (London: Edward Arnold, 1971); and see William E. Kapelle, *The Norman Conquest of the North: The Region and Its Transformation, 1000–1135* (Chapel Hill: University of North Carolina Press, 1979), 50–85.

43. See, for example, R. H. Hilton, "Peasant Movements before 1381," *Economic History Review*, 2d ser., 2 (1949); R. H. Hilton and T. H. Aston, eds., *The English Rising of 1381* (Cambridge: Cambridge University Press, 1984).

44. See the essays in Aston, *Landlords, Peasants, and Politics;* Zvi Razi, *Life, Marriage, and Death in a Medieval Parish: Economy, Society, and Demography in Halesowen, 1270–1400* (Cambridge: Cambridge University Press, 1980); Christopher Dyer, *Lords and Peasants in a Changing Society: The Estates of the Bishopric of Worcester, 680–1540* (Cambridge: Cambridge University Press, 1980). For French scholarship, see Michel Mollat and Philippe Wolff, *Ongles bleus, Jacques et Ciompi: Les révolutions populaires en Europe au XIV et XVe siècles* (Paris: Calmann-Lévy, 1970).

45. William W. Hagen, "How Mighty the Junkers: Peasant Rents and Seigneurial Profits in Sixteenth-Century Brandenburg," *Past and Present* 108 (1985), 80–116; Richard J. Evans and W. R. Lee, eds., *The German Peasantry: Conflict and Community in Rural Society from the Eighteenth to the Twentieth Centuries* (London: Croom Helm, 1986), esp. contributions from Hartmut Harnisch, "Peasants and Markets: The Background to the Agrarian Reforms in Feudal Prussia East of the Elbe, 1760–1807," 37–70, and William W. Hagen, "The Junkers' Faithless Servants: Peasant Insubordination and the Breakdown of Serfdom in Brandenburg-Prussia, 1763–1811," 71–101.

for Russian serfdom, although here the picture is somewhat clouded by the shadows of Marx and Lenin, who have continued to shape Soviet thinking on the subject. Yet, as Peter Kolchin has pointed out in his comparison of Russian serfdom and American slavery, the Russian serf village was not simply the passive object of elite demands, and serf owners who pushed too far could easily become the objects of popular wrath.[46]

None of this, of course, will be considered conclusive by those who are skeptical of the idea that European manorialism was anything other than unbridled exploitation. But the rich literature dealing with the subject does force us at least to reconsider the problem from the standpoint of the weaknesses of aristocratic power.

A different sort of support for my reading of manorial and aristocratic domination can be found in the many studies of rural insurrection during the medieval and early modern periods. The work of Rodney Hilton and his students for England and that of Ladurie and Goubert for France goes some way toward dispelling the notion that manorial communities were simply automatic machines that produced a surplus according to unquestioned rules of exploitation.[47] Rural communities did question elite demands, and they were capable of directly opposing aristocratic domination. Numerous small-scale revolts clutter the medieval record, and they show that commoners could act collectively to defend their interests. Often confined to a single village or parish, these "uprisings from below" were marked by the imposition of a savage justice on those who demanded too much or who went too far in transgressing community rights. Never revolutionary, the miniature revolts of the age of aristocracy focused on the rights and duties of the particular manorial orders. As Hilton has argued, the key issue of contention was the practical definition of serfdom and the local rights of the manor lord to control community life.[48] When local lords tried to rule arbitrarily, or when they displayed the "parasitic" rather than the protective face of nobility, they could find themselves besieged by an armed community.

The English Risings of 1381 illustrate well the paths that led from manorial order to community rebellion.[49] In 1381, a wave of insurrection, partly urban but largely rural, spread through several English counties. Villages leagued together

---

46. Peter Kolchin, *Unfree Labor: American Slavery and Russian Serfdom* (Cambridge: Harvard University Press, Belknap Press, 1987), 195–358.

47. Hilton and Aston, *The English Rising of 1381;* Emmanuel Le Roy Ladurie, *Peasants of Languedoc* (Urbana: University of Illinois Press, 1974), 265–86, and Ladurie, *The French Peasantry,* 359–420; Goubert, *The French Peasantry,* 178–220; Y. M. Bercé, *Fête et révolte: Des mentalités populaires du XVIe au XVIIIe siècle* (Paris: Hachette, 1976); Pierre Goubert, *The Ancien Régime* (New York: Harper and Row, 1973); and Georges Duby and Amand Wallon, eds., *Histoire de la France rurale,* 4 vols. (Paris: Sevil, 1975–76).

48. Rodney H. Hilton, *The English Peasantry,* 54–75.

49. Rodney Hilton, *Bond Men Made Free: Medieval Peasant Movements and the English Rising of 1381* (New York: Viking Press, 1977); Edgar Powell, *The Rising in East Anglia in 1381* (Cambridge: Cambridge University Press, 1896); Charles Oman, *The Great Revolt of 1381* (Oxford: Clarendon Press, 1969); and Hilton and Aston, *The English Rising of 1381.*

to attack noblemen, destroy the visible manifestations of manorial power, and challenge the prerogatives of aristocracy. At their high point, the insurrections of 1381 even threatened the basis of English kingship, a threat that was symbolized by the capture of the king near London.

Two facts about the events of 1381 stand out. First, it was not a rising of the peasantry, and there was simply no national or English peasant class that could have acted collectively. The events of 1381 are best thought of as an aggregation of many smaller revolts. Second, the revolts that made up the incident cannot be reduced to a single economic or social cause. The particular mix of factors varied across regions and localities. The common factor that gives thematic unity to 1381 was the attempted resurrection of an increasingly archaic form of aristocratic power and the response this produced at the level of the manorial village.[50]

The year 1381 followed the Black Death, a pandemic that reduced local population pressures and tipped the demographic balance in favor of commoners who, for the first time in a century, were able to bargain more effectively in manorial courts over the conditions of domination.[51] The aristocratic reaction, typified by the Statute of Laborers, was to attempt to restore manorial discipline, aristocratic prerogatives, and the full subjection of the rural population to the will of the manor lord. Consequently, the insurrections of 1381 should be interpreted as fundamentally about politics and more specifically about the political relations of local manorial communities. Ordinary villagers struggled to assert autonomy in the face of local lords who were just as determined to assert their right to rule arbitrarily and "at their pleasure." The second face of lordship, discussed earlier as part of the ambiguity of aristocracy, was imperious and capable of escalating the level of conflict to the breaking point.[52]

The revolts of 1381 help to put in perspective the long history of aristocratic domination in Europe. They show how significant the politics of lordship and manorial power were in shaping the conditions of community autonomy and rebellion, and they remind us of the importance of understanding the struggle of "lord and peasant" as a local one.

Bureaucracy, Markets, and Community

The reintroduction of a discourse about the state into comparative politics has had wide-reaching implications for the analysis of agrarian politics and social

---

50. Alan Harding, "The Revolt against the Justices," in Hilton and Aston, *The English Rising in 1381,* 165–93.

51. Rodney H. Hilton, *Bond Men Made Free,* 28–62, 63–134.

52. J. A. Tuck, "Nobles, Commons, and the Great Revolt of 1381," in Hilton and Aston, *The English Rising of 1381,* 194–212; and see the translations in Richard B. Dobson, ed., *The Peasant's Revolt of 1381* (London: Macmillan, 1983).

change. Theda Skocpol's study of state power and revolution indicated the impact of expansive state authority on the causes of rural insurrection, and Skocpol's suggestive interpretation added an important dimension to the study of rural violence by complementing Barrington Moore's more economic focus on social forces. Working from a somewhat different direction, Charles Tilly has highlighted the consequences of state power for the changing patterns of rural violence. Tilly and his students have made much of the interplay between changing forms of elite coercion and the logic of popular mobilization, and Tilly's various analytic frameworks have gained a wide currency in social science.[53]

Much of this work stands in sharp contrast to an older interpretive tradition that saw the causes of rural insurrection in the penetration of market forces and the consequent commodification of agrarian social relations. Although Moore and, to some extent, Tilly are exceptions in this regard, the revived interest in the origins of the modern state has signaled a refocusing of perspective that sees macro authority structures as determinative of the logic of rural collective violence. Yet earlier generations of scholars, including R. H. Tawney, Hobsbawm, and Karl Polanyi, saw state power as secondary to the corrosive consequences of the market. Commercialization was thought of as so disruptive of precommercial agrarian routines as to make unrest and violence likely if not inevitable, at least during the early phases of economic growth. This position still has powerful defenders, including Robert Brenner and his supporters.[54]

The problem with both approaches has to do with the largely macro, or top-down, focus that has been used as a framework for analysis. Both perspectives have much to say about elite choices, elite power, and elite institutions. But they have much less to say about the ways in which popular groups have responded to and shaped the forces that have supposedly transformed the contours of everyday life. We are, consequently, often unclear about the causal dynamics that lead from state building and commercialization to rural rebellion. More important, it is difficult to draw broad comparisons that can serve as the basis for more substantive concepts, because the popular institutional networks that form the basis for

53. Theda Skocpol, *States and Social Revolutions: A Comprehensive Analysis of France, Russia, and China* (Cambridge: Cambridge University Press, 1979), 3–46, 284–93; Theda Skocpol, "What Makes Peasants Revolutionary?" in Robert E. Weller and Scott E. Guggenheim, eds., *Power and Protest in the Countryside: Studies of Rural Unrest in Asia, Europe, and Latin America* (Durham: Duke University Press, 1982), 157–79; Charles Tilly, *From Mobilization to Revolution* (Reading, Mass.: Addison-Wesley, 1978), 189–221. For a case study of the impact of war on rural society, see Myron P. Gutman, *War and Rural Life in the Early Modern Low Countries* (Princeton: Princeton University Press, 1980), esp. 3–30, 196–210.

54. R. H. Tawney, *The Agrarian Problem in the Sixteenth Century* (New York: Harper and Row, 1967); Eric Hobsbawm, *Primitive Rebels: Studies in Archaic Forms of Social Movement in the 19th and 20th Centuries* (New York: Norton, 1959); and Karl Polanyi, *The Great Transformation* (Boston: Beacon Press, 1957), esp. 163–64; also see Eric Hobsbawm and George Rudé, *Captain Swing* (New York: Pantheon Press, 1968); Robert Brenner, "The Origins of Capitalist Development: A Critique of Neo-Smithian Marxism," *New Left Review* 104 (July–Aug. 1977), 25–92.

collective action are only vaguely conceptualized. We know that people act and react, but it is not always obvious how or why they do so.

It should be clear that the debate about commercialization and agrarian violence is simply inconclusive.[55] The expansion of market forces has been shown to have been linked to popular unrest, especially in early modern England and France. The struggle over the rights and duties associated with the grain trade was a perennial source of riot in much of Europe, and it has justly received enormous attention. The problem is neither so simple or straightforward, however, as many economic historians have shown. In some parts of Europe, markets were not feared by ordinary rural people, and market forces did not simply come from the outside, like some inexorable force of nature.[56] As Jan de Vries has pointed out for the Low Countries, agrarian commercialization was a complex and ambiguous process.[57] In many cases, markets offered a welcome support for household subsistence opportunities, as well as a way of building important networks of credit and cooperation.

An inconclusive debate of this kind demands a reconceptualization of the basic issues. Earlier I argued that the link between commercialization and rural violence can be understood in terms of the impact of elite coercion on popular practices. Coercively enforced commercialization seems more likely to result in popular resistance, especially if the imposition of market logic is sudden and subversive of established institutions.

The advantage of this approach is that it helps us to think about commercialization as an inherently ambiguous process that had different effects in specific regions and local contexts. Much depended on the political context in which market development took place, as the history of European agriculture indicates.[58] For example, in southern Spain the commercialization of agriculture was a very coercive and conflict-ridden process that saw the growth of commercial

55. See William N. Parker and Eric L. Jones, eds., *European Peasants and Their Markets: Essays in Agrarian Economic History* (Princeton: Princeton University Press, 1975); T. H. Aston and C. H. E. Philpin, *The Brenner Debate: Agrarian Class Structure and Economic Development in Pre-Industrial Europe* (Cambridge: Cambridge University Press, 1985). For the origins of markets in Europe, see R. Hodges, "Trade and Market Origins in the Ninth Century," in M. Gibson and Janet Nelson, eds., *Charles the Bald: Court and Kingdom,* Papers presented at a colloquium held in London in April 1979 (Oxford: British Archaeological Reports, 1981).

56. This has been shown in magnificent detail for England. See Joan Thirsk, "Enclosing and Engrossing," and Alan Everitt, "The Marketing of Agricultural Produce," in Joan Thirsk, ed., *The Agrarian History of England and Wales* (hereafter *AHEW*), vol. 4, *1500–1640* (Cambridge: Cambridge University Press, 1967), 200–255, 466–592; Peter J. Bowden, "Agricultural Prices, Wages, Farm Profits, and Rents," Christopher Clay, "Landlords and Estate Management in England," and J. A. Charters, "The Marketing of Agricultural Produce," in Joan Thirsk, ed. *AHEW*, vol. 5, *1640–1750,* part 2, "Agrarian Change" (Cambridge: Cambridge University Press, 1985), 1–61, 83–118, 170–97, 406–502; and Joan Thirsk, ed., *AHEW*, vol. 5, *1640–1750,* part 1, "Regional Farming Systems" (Cambridge: Cambridge University Press, 1984), xix–xxxi.

57. Jan de Vries, *The Dutch Rural Economy in the Golden Age, 1500–1700* (New Haven: Yale University Press, 1974).

58. This is also the logic in North, *Structure and Change,* 3–70, 199–209.

latifundia at the expense of community land and institutions.[59] The end result was a fractured social order in which a very radical form of popular anarchism became the institutional matrix that laid the basis for a long cycle of violent opposition to the great estates of the elite.

Similarly, late nineteenth- and early twentieth-century Russia saw the rise of novel and coercively enforced market networks that linked Russian agriculture to the trans-European grain trade.[60] As a result, village communities were hard pressed by grasping estate owners, whose commitment to the constant expansion of trade clashed with the land hunger of the village. By 1902 the level of violence in parts of Russian had escalated, and by 1905 the survival of a market-oriented and progressive agriculture was jeopardized by an explosion of rural insurrection.

What is interesting about the Spanish and Russian situations is the sharp light they throw on the links between popular resistance and forms of commercialization that are driven by elite violence and forcible transformation of the conditions of agricultural production. But this was not the only route to the market, as the history of Scandinavia shows. In Scandinavia, commercial networks were built horizontally, by the efforts of small farmers and dairymen, who voluntarily entered the market and played it against the interests of established elites.[61] Like the small farmers, market gardeners, and village artisans of nineteenth-century England and France, these people used the market to enhance self-sufficiency; and they were interested in controlling the terms of the market rather than destroying the basis of commercialization.

The concept of coercive commercialization helps to make sense out of all this diversity by forcing us to focus on the local and institutional context in which markets developed. But it also can be seen as building on one of the keenest insights of E. P. Thompson, whose work has had a decisive impact on the writing of social history. In a remarkable article, Thompson reconstructed the logic of the crowd in eighteenth-century England in terms of a moral economy of economic exchange. He argued that market riots and other forms of popular opposition to the new commercial practices of merchants and middlemen reflected a popular commitment to a precise code of commercial fairness and justice that had been violated by the targets of the crowd's wrath.[62] For example, millers and other large-scale traders who were seen as grinding the faces of the poor through hoarding or price gouging were subject to attack, and their stores of grain or flour were often redistributed at fixed, popular prices. In the background was a gentry elite of justices and parish officials who viewed popular self-help with ambiva-

59. Temma Kaplan, *Anarchists of Andalusia, 1868–1903* (Princeton: Princeton University Press, 1977), 3–60; and Nicolás Sánchez-Albornoz, *Las crisis de subsistencia de España en el siglo XIX* (Rosario, Argentina: Instituto de Investigaciones Historicas, 1963).

60. A good synthesis of this argument can be found in Robert Edelman, *Proletarian Peasants: The Revolution of 1905 in Russia's Southwest* (Ithaca: Cornell University Press, 1987), 1–34.

61. Østerud, *Agrarian Structure and Peasant Politics,* 152–94.

62. E. P. Thompson, "The Moral Economy of the English Crowd in the Eighteenth Century," *Past and Present* 50 (Feb. 1971), 76–136.

lence. They feared riotous behavior, but they were also suspicious of the behavior of middlemen who seemed avaricious. In this situation, magistrates were unwilling to invoke the rigors of the riot act, unless the level of violence seemed about to escalate into a threat to the social order. As a result, the willingness of the authorities to forgo coercive enforcement of the commercial property rights of middlemen helped to reduce the scale and intensity of popular hostility to the status quo. English food riots became ritualized affairs, and they disappeared altogether when markets became stable and efficient enough that they no longer threatened popular subsistence.[63]

Thompson's argument is usually glossed by social scientists to mean that popular values were completely opposed to the logic of the market.[64] But this is not a result we must accept in order to see the force of Thompson's point. Ordinary people resisted markets that compromised their lives by forcing them to enter commercial networks over which they had no routine mechanisms of control. Coercion could take a variety of forms, ranging from boarding and price gouging to the forcible extinction of common rights and the commodification of land. But in all these cases the target of popular wrath was the imposition of compulsion in market transactions, rather than market exchange in some abstract sense.

Politics were crucial to the quality of commercialization, and political institutions were central in determining the local social balance of power through which conflicting market principles were played out. Theories of agrarian society that treat commercialization as a purely material process, or as the unfolding of capital, miss the political dimensions that add a necessary component to our understanding of the diverse consequences of commercialization.

In contrast to the study of markets, the study of state building has necessarily focused on politics and the impact of political forces on agrarian institutions. Tilly, Skocpol, and others, however, have tended to view the problem in narrowly material terms. State building is usually seen as the extraction of some notionally sufficient level of resources through the penetration of traditional agricultural societies. As a result, the impact of state authority on rural institutions is treated as an economic problem that implicates the subsistence security of small-scale agriculturalists. The link between agrarian unrest and state power is reduced to a clear-cut struggle over the agricultural surplus, and taxation becomes the central variable that explains rural rebellion.

There is no doubt that taxation has been intimately related to agrarian unrest,

---

63. John Walter and Keith Wrightson, "Dearth and the Social Order in Early Modern England," *Past and Present* 71 (May 1976), 22–42; John Walter, "Grain Riots and Popular Attitudes for the Law: Maldon and the Crisis of 1629," in John Brewer and John Styles, eds., *An Ungovernable People: The English and Their Law in the Seventeenth and Eighteenth Centuries* (New Brunswick: Rutgers University Press, 1980), 47–84.

64. James C. Scott, *The Moral Economy of the Peasant* (New Haven: Yale University Press, 1976), 1–12, 33–34.

especially in France.[65] Yet the focus is too restricted, and it leads to a mechanical cause-and-effect relation between rising tax levels and increasing levels of popular opposition to the state-building process. The result is an inability to explain puzzling or deviant cases like that of eighteenth-century England, where high real tax rates on land and agricultural commerce were not associated with rural collective violence. More important, the exclusive focus on taxation limits the analysis of the effects of state building to questions of economic security and subsistence. But the rise of state authority affected a much broader range of interests, and the monopolistic claims of state elites challenged the basis of established authority relations in every arena of popular life; the right to define property, kinship networks, acceptable forms of violence, and the balance of sacred and secular authority were all redefined by the imposition of state power. State elites demanded nothing less than the transfer of all forms of rule making from nonstate to state institutions. By advancing claims of exclusive authority, the officials of the state directly threatened every association or community that stood outside of the official institutions of governance. It should not be surprising that popular opposition would develop in the wake of state building, particularly if popular practices were the target of the state-building enterprise. In this context, popular revolt was certainly a possibility, and taxation was perhaps as much a pretext as a cause. Ordinary rural people, who resisted the claim of state elites to control everything from the marriage contract to the property role of sacred authority, could rally around the problem of taxation as a point of symbolic consensus capable of mobilizing broad popular opposition. Taxation was a grievance; yet it was also a symbol of the totalistic demands of modern state elites.[66]

A good example of the broad, politically motivated issues that swirled around European state building can be found in the strange history of Spanish Carlism.[67] Carlism was, strictly defined, a royalist movement that sought to overthrow the Spanish king in favor of the pretender Don Carlos. Carlism drew its supporters from a wide social coalition, although its chief support came from the largely rural districts that formed Basque Spain. Between 1833 and the 1880s, the Carlists fielded substantial irregular military forces that posed a direct threat to the stability of the post-Napoleonic Spanish state, a threat that did not diminish until both sides were politically exhausted.

65. The following discussion of bureaucratic logic draws heavily from Robert R. Alford and Roger Friedland, *Powers of Theory: Capitalism, the State, and Democracy* (Cambridge: Cambridge University Press, 1985), 387–443; Kenneth Dyson, *The State Tradition in Western Europe* (Oxford: Oxford University Press, 1980), 25–80; Gianfranco Poggi, *The Development of the Modern State: A Sociological Introduction* (Stanford: Stanford University Press, 1978), 16–85; Norbert Elias, *Power and Civility* (New York: Pantheon, 1982), 104–16, 149–225, and Norbert Elias, *The Court Society* (New York: Pantheon, 1983), 268–75. A good synthetic overview of France can be found in Zagorin, *Rebels and Rulers.*

66. Zagorin, *Rebels and Rulers* 1:87–121, 2:1–50.

67. The best account in English is John F. Coverdale, *The Basque Phase of Spain's First Carlist War* (Princeton: Princeton University Press, 1984), esp. 11–55, 56–119.

At one time, the Carlists were seen as atavistic reactionaries, and the peculiar mix of traditionalism and radicalism that was at the heart of the good old cause of Don Carlos was reduced to a dialectic between Basque antimodernism and the "progressive" Spanish state. Historians have shown that rural Carlism had a real logic, however, one that is best interpreted as a completely comprehensible response on the part of Basque cultivators and artisans to the intrusive demands of the Spanish state. The post-Napoleonic phase of Spanish history was a period of feverish state building that led to a frontal assault on popular rural institutions. In the Basque region, this assault focused on the role of the church as a corporate landowner and on the institutional regulation of popular life. Spanish elites wanted nothing less than the capitulation of the church to secular authority, and in the Basque region this was symbolized by the disentailment of church property.

For Basque cultivators the onslaught of the secular state was a direct threat to the autonomy and integrity of community institutions. The church was a source of popular identity, a mediating and conciliating presence in everyday life, and a relatively benevolent landowner and protector of local interests. The effort radically to restrict the role of sacred institutions was bound to produce opposition. Carlism was not a tax revolt, although taxation was one among many other issues. The larger theme was the defense of community against an intrusive state. The Carlists were fighting to preserve local autonomy from the authoritarian demands of the state, and the fight cut across issues and arenas to embrace the conditions of life that made a popular tradition.

Similar violent responses to the state-building project's assault on community autonomy can be found in Italy, France, and Greece. In Italy, for example, the postindependence state attempted to "civilize" the countryside by imposing restrictive regulations that disestablished church and communal property rights. In addition, new taxes, like the hated macinato, or grist tax, and novel forms of rural police further undercut the ability of local communities to manage their own affairs.[68] The result was a series of local revolts in the nineteenth and twentieth centuries that defended localism and civic pride against the construction of bureaucratic power.

Bureaucratic domination, therefore, can be seen as a major source of violent conflict in the European countryside, at least from the seventeenth century on. In order to understand it we have to broaden our focus to include the broad range of issues and interests that were at stake. As Joel Migdal has argued, state building is always a violent process, because the creation of the state's monopoly of legitimate violence calls into question every social or political practice not sanctioned by state elites.[69]

68. Seton-Watson, *Italy*, 20–64.

69. Joel Migdal, *Strong Societies and Weak States: State-Society Relations and State Capabilities in the Third World* (Princeton: Princeton University Press, 1988), 259–78.

The Bauernkrieg: Manors, Lords, and Bureaucratic Authority

On the edge of the Black Forest, sometime in 1524, the villagers who lived and worked on the estate of the court of Lupfen rose in revolt against the lord.[70] The events of that year were scarcely without precedent. As far back as 1476, serious rural disturbances had broken out in the Tauber valley, and by the 1490s the standard of insurrection had been raised in much of the Upper Rhine, a problem that aristocratic and princely authorities would face until at least 1517. The insurrections that began in the 1490s took as their symbol the Bundschuh, or heavy rustic boot; a clear indication that the rebels saw themselves as defending a sphere of popular rural autonomy through armed self-help.[71] The rustic boot, displayed for the whole world to see, showed that the rebels were denying the power of aristocrats to rule them through the usual symbols of lordly power.

The events at Lupfen, however, are often regarded as the proximate beginning of the Bauernkrieg, the so-called Peasants War of 1525. Within less than a year, rural rebellion had spread throughout several regions of the decaying Holy Roman Empire, including the Upper Rhine, Upper Swabia, Franconia, Thuringia, Salzburg, and the Tyrol.[72] At their peak, the insurrections of 1525 saw the mobilization of local insurgent armies of anywhere between 5,000 to 10,000 men, and pitched battles combined with the sacking of castles and estates left a broad swath of destruction. In some cases, the revolts were crushed with the ruthless ferocity of an aristocratic counterrevolt, but in others, especially the Tyrol and Upper Rhine, the rebels were able to gain real concessions from the feudal and princely authorities.[73] For example, the lords of the margrave of Baden signed a pact with their rural subjects that enacted parts of the famous Twelve Articles, the most important rebel manifesto of 1525.

The Bauernkrieg, however, was not a peasant revolution, at least not in the sense of a class war centered on the relations of production. The goals of the rebels were diverse, ranging from religious freedom to a reduction of manorial tithes and taxes.[74] More important, the insurrections of 1525 lacked any basis in a "national" or transregional political organization, and from beginning to end the Bauernkrieg was played out in terms of highly localized solidarities that were rooted in ties of kinship and village community. This fact, as historians going back to Günther Franz have shown, was a source of both strength and weakness for the

70. Blickle, *The Revolution of 1525*, xiv.
71. Peter Blickle, "Peasant Revolts in the German Empire in the Late Middle Ages," *Social History* 4 (May 1979), 223–39; David W. Sabean, "The Communal Basis of Pre-1800 Uprisings in Western Europe," *Comparative Politics* 8 (3) (1976), 355–64; and H. Zins, "Aspects of the Peasant Rising in East Prussia in 1525," *Slavonic and East European Review* 38 (1959), 178–88.
72. Blickle, *The Revolution of 1525*, xi–xxiii, 3–17; and Zagorin, *Rebels and Rulers* 1:186–207.
73. See Blickle, *The Revolution of 1525*, 176–80.
74. David Sabean, "The Social Background of the Peasants' War of 1525 in Southern Upper Swabia" (Ph.D. diss., University of Wisconsin, 1969), esp. 36, 58–59, 90–94, 131–35, 186–95; Blickle, *The Revolution of 1525*, 97–161, 195–205.

insurgents.[75] It meant that the rebels could mobilize entire manors for a direct confrontation with their overlords. But it also meant that the complex local uprising that made up the heart of the events could never gain sufficient translocal cohesion to be regarded as a revolutionary challenge to the whole late-medieval order.

Indeed, we should be suspicious of viewing the Bauernkrieg as a protorevolution that failed to restructure fully the contours of German society.[76] The notion of revolution as a complete break with the past is anachronistic when applied to the sixteenth century, as Perez Zagorin has argued at length.[77] The participants in the events of 1525 could not have been motivated by a desire to create a socialist utopia; nor could they have built a vanguard party to lead them into a classless society. In the Germany of the sixteenth century the most important issues were played out at local and regional levels. Those issues cannot be reduced to a simple recitation of class conflict as the motor of history. They must be understood as the unfolding logic of a local balance of conflict and cooperation. Yet this local balance will remain obscure unless we focus on the institutional terrain in which the events of 1525 were carried out. The many separate struggles that occurred in 1525 had to do with the authoritative institutional arrangements that organized social order and economic production. Conflict took its most violent form when manor lords and territorial princes attempted radically to restrict the autonomy of village institutions. The issues at stake involved the right of manor lords to determine unilaterally the benefits and burdens of village life and the right of territorial lords to control all aspects of local justice and social custom.[78]

In some parts of Germany, the late fifteenth and early sixteenth centuries saw the intensification of aristocratic power, including the power to be able arbitrarily to increase the complex of dues and labor services that were at the heart of serfdom. Much of the German countryside was still legally enserfed, and the decades before 1525 saw a heightening of tensions concerning the terms and conditions of servile agriculture. Manor lords were interested in reasserting their rights to land and labor, which had been undermined during the 1300s by a combination of political anarchy and demographic decline. At stake was the reconstitution of aristocratic domination, and the German nobility can be aptly characterized as engaged in a project of rebuilding the kind of aristocratic imperium discussed previously. German manor lords wanted captive communities that would serve as extensions of the political power and privileged property of the

75. Günther Franz, *Der deutsche Bauernkrieg* (Darmstadt: Wissenschaftliche Buchgesellschaft, 1972).

76. Adolf Laube, "Precursors of the Peasant War: Bundschuh and Armer Konrad—Movements at the Eve of the Reformation," *Journal of Peasant Studies* 3 (1975), 49–53, shows the relative continuity of goals.

77. Zagorin, *Rebels and Rulers* 1:3–60.

78. Blickle, *The Revolution of 1525*, 44–57.

aristocracy. Ordinary villagers were confronted with a combination of legal subjugation and interlocking material demands that included servile rents and taxes, judicial fines and monopolies, and aristocratic rights to regulate all matters touching inheritance and marriage.[79]

But the kinds of issues that led to the Bauernkrieg went beyond the question of the nature of aristocratic domination. Another set of issues centered on the creation of novel forms of supralocal politics that followed from the gradual extension of princely power and jurisdiction. As the Holy Roman Empire disintegrated, local and regional rulers were able to develop bureaucratic institutions of domination that penetrated the countryside much more effectively than the older modes of feudal power. Territorial rulers began to increase their intake of rural production through the imposition of money taxes, something that was a necessary precondition for the mobilization of the new mercenary armies of Landknechte (knights) that underpinned princely power. More significant, however, was the attempted reconfiguration of the law and the institutions of justice. Princely power was used quite ruthlessly to impose the will of the ruler as the sole source of ultimate justice in the prince's territories. Local custom, the good old law of the village and manor court, was overridden by codes of Roman law and jurisprudence that transferred control over the political management of daily life to the institutions of bureaucratic domination that served the territorial ruler. The key issue was whether popular communities or the prince's officials would have the power to make and coercively enforce the norms governing every aspect of behavior from property rights to moral conduct.[80]

At the point of intersection between aristocratic and bureaucratic forms of domination was the German village community. In the sixteenth century the village was still a fairly cohesive institutional framework, at the heart of which were the typical open- and common-field agricultural systems. Households held property rights to arable land, either in the form of allod or, more frequently, heritable tenancies, but they were regulated in their use of property by the village officers or manor court. The combination of open-field farming and open commons is a good indicator of the existence of a political economy of trust in which households exercised property rights as trustees of the whole village. As David Sabean has pointed out, the early modern German village was marked by subtle tensions and conflicts that nonetheless were situated in wider networks fo kinship and cooperation. For example, in the villages of Württemberg all people within a village territory had *Bürgerrecht,* or rights of local membership.[81] Those rights, interestingly, could be gained by birth or by the special permission of the village

<hr />

79. Ibid., 25–57, and Thomas Brady, *Ruling Class, Regime, and Reformation at Strasbourg: 1520–1555* (Leiden: E. J. Brill, 1978).

80. See Gerald Strauss, *Law, Resistance, and the State: The Opposition to Roman Law in Reformation Germany* (Princeton: Princeton University Press, 1986), 3–30, 96–135.

81. Sabean, *Power in the Blood,* 13–15.

magistrates, which underscores the importance of territorial community as a core social framework in the German countryside. It was the village as a whole collectivity, or gemeinde, that apportioned taxes, controlled access to markets and fairs, and mediated disputes between neighbors and kin.

The reconstruction of aristocratic authority and the early growth of bureaucratic domination threatened the autonomy of the village in two ways. First, both forms of domination exaggerated the arbitrary claims of supralocal elites to supersede local custom in the interests of elite privilege. Second, the reduction of village autonomy undermined the integrity of community institutions, directly threatening the material security of established village households. Both points are important and will be treated in turn.

The creation of more rigorous forms of serfdom, and the concurrent rise of more effective bureaucratic power, could be effected only through the circumvention of popular institutions. New and old elites alike wanted greater direct control over the land, labor, and daily behavior of rural commoners. Yet this enhanced constraint was impossible as long as village institutions retained wide-ranging powers of resistance. Moreover, the demands of the German elite could not be met through the mobilization of popular consent based on an appeal to custom, because the logic of much of the customary legal order protected the autonomy of local institutions and community resources against outsiders. As Gerald Strauss has argued, the customs of manors and villages in early modern Germany were protective webs of jealously guarded "particularism" that were highly resistant to a consideration of any but local interests.[82] In this context, elite interests were always in potential conflict with popular demands, especially if elite power required more than intermittent popular support. As a result, aristocratic and bureaucratic elites could achieve their ends only if they could arbitrarily change the customary social constitution of rural life. Old customs and local laws that severely restricted the ability of outsiders to control village resources had to be swept away. The resulting assertion of the arbitrary face of noble and state power was almost designed to lead in the end to a violent confrontation between elite demands and community opposition.

The rise of a more imperious and demanding elite also tended to upset the institutional arrangements that provided at least a margin of material security for the more advantaged village householders. During the 1400s the demographic contraction of the previous century allowed many families with full village rights to expand their scale of operations and raise their level of subsistence. Some may have even begun to enter local markets on a small scale, although Peter Blickle maintains that active market involvement was still quite limited at the time of the Bauernkrieg.[83] In any event, the early sixteenth century was not a period of

---

82. Strauss, *Law, Resistance, and the State,* 117–19.
83. Blickle, *The Revolution of 1525,* xi–xxvi, 3–17, 25–57.

extraordinary rural hardship, and many villagers must have achieved a degree of solid material comfort and social respectability.

This must also have allowed full landowning households to maintain the reciprocal if hierarchical relations with less advantaged villagers that held the community together during periods of adversity. Those relations included the provision of year-long work for household servants and laborers, as well as the creation of solidarities that were rooted in community religious practices. To be sure, the modest material successes of the 1400s would ultimately be eroded by the population increase and inflationary spiral of the "long" sixteenth century. But at the time of the Bauernkrieg the chief material threat to village well-being did not come from the forces of erosion. It came instead from the intensification of servile agriculture and the appearance of a tax-hungry officialdom.[84] Manor lords began unilaterally to claim a share of the village product that was much greater than custom had allowed, Similarly, the agents of territorial state building became much more insistent on the right of the prince to tax everything from land and labor to the profits of local courts. It should not be surprising that entire villages resisted this kind of material constraint, because the well-being, and perhaps the very survival, of both well-off and less-well-off villagers depended on maintaining local control of the production and distribution of agricultural resources.

It is worth noting that the material context in which the Bauernkrieg occurred cannot be adequately portrayed as a classic subsistence crisis, at least not in the way that concept has been used by Perez Zagorin or Roland Mousnier.[85] The problem was not immediate dearth or famine. Rather, the problem was a political question of who had the right to control the disposition of the agricultural surplus. Local communities and supralocal elites advanced contradictory and conflicting political claims to be the ultimate sources of authoritative control. In a more prosperous world, this clash might have been resolved through a broadly defined compromise. But in sixteenth-century conditions, where the basis of everyday life was still quite precarious, the politics of material authority was always shot through with deep tension and the possibility of violence.

The origins and events of the Bauernkrieg are clearly linked to the defense of community autonomy against the kinds of elite constraints discussed in chapters 1 and 2. Moreover, community defense was possible because of the overlapping networks of village cooperation that I have referred to as mutually implicated forms of cooperation. Individual villagers may or may not have been anxious to respond to the tocsin of revolt. But their choices were not made in a vacuum; they were formed in a context of village institutions that shaped the life chances of village members. To deny the call of revolt once the village as a collectivity had

84. See, for example, Herman Rebel, *Peasant Classes: The Bureaucratization of Property and Family Relations under Early Habsburg Absolutism, 1511–1636* (Princeton: Princeton University Press, 1983), 230–84.

85. Zagorin, *Rebels and Rulers* 1:186–207.

decided to fight was a risky decision, because the failure to defend community power could lead to a withdrawal of vital support from kin and neighbors. Conflict within the village was real; yet it was always balanced by the reciprocal hierarchies and cooperative relations that made the village a gemeinde.[86]

When the conditions of 1525 led to an upsurge of local violence, it was the village as an armed collectivity that became the essential cell of insurrection. As mentioned earlier, villagers then confederated at local and regional levels, sometimes forming rural "parliaments" or estates that claimed a kind of constitutional authority over local political relations. Nevertheless, there was no national "peasant" association, and the character of violence in 1525 remained highly local and intensely focused on manorial and territorial politics. This fact has been emphasized by Peter Blickle among others, even though Blickle tends to see 1525 as much more radical than many other historians who have treated the subject.[87]

How, then, should we interpret the kinds of violence that shook regions like Upper Swabia in 1525? Should we follow Blickle and view those events not as a class war but as a revolution of the common man? Or, following Tilly and others, should we see the Bauernkrieg as an instance of reactive violence that struggled vainly against the tides of modernization?

Perhaps the best way of addressing these issues is to focus on the Twelve Articles, the widely circulated manifesto that became an archetypical symbol and statement of rebel demands in 1525. Moreover, as Blickle has shown, the demands in the Twelve Articles were reflective of the kinds of grievances listed in the hundreds of locally produced manifestos that were written by villagers during the Bauernkrieg. Thus, the Twelve Articles can be read as an authentic statement of rebel goals and ideals. The conspirational notion that the Twelve Articles caused rather than symbolized the violence of 1525 has been discredited by serious historical research.

The Twelve Articles

To the Christian reader, the peace and grace of God through Jesus Christ.

There are many antichrists who, now that the peasants are assembled together, seize the chance to mock the gospel, saying, "Is this the fruit of the new gospel: to band together in great numbers and plot conspiracies to reform and even topple the spiritual and temporal powers—yes, even to murder them?" The following articles answer all these godless, blasphemous critics. We want two things: first, to make them stop mocking the word of God; and second, to establish the Christian justice of the current disobedience and rebellion of all the peasants.

First of all, the gospel does not cause rebellions and uproars, because it tells of Christ, the promised Messiah, whose words and life teach nothing but love, peace,

86. Sabean, *Power in the Blood*, 1–60.
87. Blickle, *The Revolution of 1525*, 97–154.

patience, and unity. And all who believe in this Christ become loving, peaceful, patient, and one in spirit. This is the basis of all the articles of the peasants (as we will clearly show): to hear the gospel and to live accordingly. How can the antichrists call the gospel a cause of rebellion and disobedience? It is not the gospel that drives some antichrists and foes of the gospel to resist and reject these demands and requirements, but the devil, the deadliest foe of the gospel, who arouses through unbelief such opposition in his own followers. His aim is to suppress and abolish the word of God, which teaches love, peace, and unity.

Second, it surely follows that the peasants, whose articles demand this gospel as their doctrine and rule of life, cannot be called disobedient or rebellious. For if God deigns to hear the peasants' earnest plea that they may be permitted to live according to his word, who will dare deny his will? Who indeed will dare question his judgment? Who will dare oppose his majesty? Did he not hear the children of Israel crying to him and deliver them out of Pharaoh's land? And can he not save his own today as well? Yes, he will save them, and soon! Therefore, Christian reader, read these articles diligently, and then judge for yourself.

The First Article

First of all, we humbly ask and beg—and we all agree on this—that henceforth we ought to have the authority and power for the whole community to elect and appoint its own pastor. We also want authority to depose a pastor who behaves improperly. This elected pastor should preach to us the holy gospel purely and clearly, without human additions or human doctrines or precepts. For constant preaching of the true faith impels us to beg God for his grace, that he may instill in us and confirm in us that same true faith. Unless we have his grace in us, we remain mere, useless flesh and blood. For the Scripture clearly teaches that we may come to God only through true faith and can be saved only through His mercy. This is why we need such a guide and pastor; and thus our demand is grounded in Scripture.

The Second Article

Second, although the obligation to pay a just tithe prescribed in the Old Testament is fulfilled in the New, yet we will gladly pay the large tithe on grain, but only in just measure. Since the tithe should be given to God and distributed among his servants, so the pastor who clearly preaches the word of God deserves to receive it. From now on we want to have our church wardens, appointed by the community, collect and receive this tithe and have our elected pastor draw from it, with the whole community's consent, a decent and adequate living for himself and his. The remainder should be distributed to the village's own poor, again with the community's consent and according to need. What then remains should be kept in case some need to be called up to defend the country; and then the costs can be met from this reserve, so that no general territorial tax will be laid upon the poor folk.

Wherever one or more villages have sold off the tithe to meet some emergency, those purchasers who can show that they bought the tithe with the consent of the whole village shall not be simply expropriated. Indeed we hope to reach fair compromises with such persons, according to the facts of the case, and to redeem the tithe in installments. But wherever the tithe holder—be he clergyman or layman—did not buy the tithe from the whole village but has it from ancestors who simply seized it from the village, we will not, ought not, and do not intend to pay it any longer, except (as we said above) to support our elected pastor. And we will reserve the rest or distribute it to the poor, as the Bible commands. As for the small tithe, we will not pay it at all, for the Lord God created cattle for man's free use; and it is an unjust tithe invented by men alone. Therefore, we won't pay it anymore.

The Third Article

Third, it has until now been the custom for the lords to own us as their property. This is deplorable, for Christ redeemed and bought us all with his precious blood, the lowliest shepherd as well as the greatest lord, with no exceptions. Thus the Bible proves that we are free and want to be free. Not that we want to be utterly free and subject to no authority at all; God does not teach that. We ought to live according to the commandments, not according to the lusts of the flesh. But we should love God, recognize him as our Lord in our neighbor, and willingly do all things God commanded us at his Last Supper. This means we would live according to his commandment, which does not teach us to obey only the rulers, but to humble ourselves before everyone. Thus we should willingly obey our elected and rightful ruler, set over above us by God, in all proper Christian matters. Nor do we doubt that you, as true and just Christians, will gladly release us from bondage or prove to us from the gospel that we must be your property.

The Fourth Article

Fourth, until now it has been custom that no commoner might catch wild game, wild fowl, or fish in the running waters, which seems to us improper, unbrotherly, selfish, and contrary to God's Word. In some places the rulers protect the game to our distress and great loss, for we must suffer silently while the dumb beasts gobble up the crops God gave for man's use, although this offends both God and neighbor. When the Lord God created man, he gave him dominion over all animals, over the birds of the air, and the fish in the waters. Thus we demand that if someone owns a stream, lake, or pond, he should have to produce documentary proof of ownership and show that it was sold to him with the consent of the whole village. In that case we do not want to seize it from him with force, but only to review the matter in a Christian way for the sake of brotherly love. But who even cannot produce adequate proof of ownership and sale should surrender the waters to the community, as is just.

The Fifth Article

Fifth, we have another grievance about woodcutting, for our lords have seized the woods for themselves alone; and when the poor commoner needs some wood, he has to pay twice the price for it. We think that those woods whose lords, be they clergymen or laymen, cannot prove ownership by purchase should revert to the whole community. And the community should be able to allow in an orderly way each man to gather firewood for his home and building timber free, though only with permission of the community's elected officials. If all the woods have been fairly purchased, then a neighborly and Christian agreement should be reached with their owners about their use. Where the woods were simply seized and then sold to a third party, however, a compromise should be reached according to the facts of the case and the norms of brotherly love and Holy Writ.

The Sixth Article

Sixth, there is our grievous burden of labor services, which the lords daily increase in number and kind. We demand that these obligations be properly investigated and lessened. And we should be allowed, graciously, to serve as our forefathers did, according to God's word alone.

The Seventh Article

Seventh, in the future we will not allow the lords to oppress us any more. Rather, a man shall have his holding on proper terms on which it has been leased, that is by agreement between lord and peasant. The lord should not force or press the tenant to perform labor or any other service without pay, so that the peasant may use and enjoy his land unburdened and in peace. When the lord needs labor services, however, the peasant should willingly serve his own lord before others; yet a peasant should serve only at a time when his own affairs do not suffer and only for a just wage.

The Eighth Article

Eighth, we have a grievance that many of us hold lands that are overburdened with rents higher than the land's yield. Thus the peasants lose their property and are ruined. The lords should have honorable men inspect these farms and adjust the rents fairly, so that the peasant does not work for nothing. For every laborer is worthy of his hire.

The Ninth Article

Ninth, we have a grievance against the way serious crimes are punished, for they are constantly making new laws. We are not punished according to the severity of the case but sometimes out of great ill will and sometimes out of favoritism. We think that punishments should be dealt out among us accordingly to the ancient written law and the circumstances of the case, and not according to the judge's bias.

The Tenth Article

Tenth, we have a grievance that some people have seized meadows and fields belonging to the community. We shall restore these to the community unless a proper sale can be proved. If they were improperly [obtained], however, then a friendly and brotherly compromise should be reached, based on the facts,

The Eleventh Article

Eleventh, we want the custom called death taxes totally abolished. We will not tolerate it or allow widows and orphans to be so shamefully robbed of their goods, as so often happens in various ways, against God and all that is honorable. The very ones who should be guarding and protecting our goods have skinned and trimmed us of them instead. Had they the slightest legal pretext, they would have grabbed everything. God will suffer this no longer but will wipe it all out. Henceforth, no one shall have to pay death taxes, whether large or small.

Conclusion

Twelfth, we believe and have decided that if any one or more of these articles is not in agreement with God's Word (which we doubt), then this should be so proved to us from Holy Writ. We will abandon it, when this is proved by the Bible. If some of our articles should be approved and later found to be unjust, they shall be dead, null and void from that moment on. Likewise, if Scripture truly reveals further grievances as offensive to God and a burden to our neighbor, we will reserve a place for them and declare them included in our list. We, for our part, will live and exercise ourselves in all Christian teachings, for which we will pray to the Lord God. For He alone, and no other, can give us truth. The peace of Christ be with us all.[88]

The Twelve Articles can be divided into three broad themes, although the document as a whole focuses on aristocratic power and its abuses, exactly what we would expect in an era of heightened manorial and princely power. The manifesto is not what we would expect of a revolutionary treatise, however. It does not advance a single, sustained argument. Nor, more significantly, does it propose a comprehensive blueprint for the reconstruction of German society. The goals and issues are limited to a highly specific list of problems that were evidently seen as typical of rural society; yet the message of the Twelve Articles mixes radical and reformist themes in a disjunctive list that strikes the modern reader as strangely fragmentary and disconnected. Still, the Twelve Articles do make sense when placed against the backdrop of village politics discussed earlier.

One set of issues deals with the right of local communities to control the terms of religious authority and observance within their customary jurisdictions. Article 1 proclaims the right of "the whole community" to elect its own pastor, and article 2 insists on the return of the tithe, the key religious tax in early modern Europe, to the control of the local community. The "large tithe" on grain was to be reserved for the exclusive use of local ministers and the local poor, while the "small tithe" on cattle was to be simply abolished. Finally, the conclusion of the manifesto calls on the protection of God and states flatly that any of the previous articles will be abandoned if it can be shown that they are not in accord with divine laws as revealed by Scripture.

Given the extraordinary religious ferment of the Reformation, it is not at all unusual for the Twelve Articles to be inflected by a heavy concern with religious issues. Nor can there be any doubt that the message of a reformed church, preached so eloquently by Luther, had a deep impact on popular rural and urban politics during the events of 1525. But it would be a mistake to view the Twelve Articles, or more generally the Bauernkrieg, as a simple effect of the Reformation.[89] The issues at stake were much broader, and the call for the communal

88. Reprinted by permission of the publisher, Johns Hopkins University Press, from Blickle, *The Revolution of 1525: The German Peasants' War from a New Perspective*, 195–201.

89. See Sabean, "The Social Background of the Peasants' War."

selection of pastors and reform of the tithe should be seen as intimately connected to the expansion of princely authority. Part of the process of state building involved the subordination of sacred to secular authority, and the rise of bureaucratic domination meant the transformation of religious institutions into official agencies of the prince. By focusing on the relationship between community institutions and religious authority the authors of the Twelve Articles were doing more than calling for the reform of the church. They were challenging the state-building pretensions of the territorial prince and calling into question the right of the prince to make binding rules for his subjects.

Moreover, the heart of the Twelve Articles deals with more purely secular concerns that touch on the conditions of manorial governance and legal jurisdiction. One set of issues (article 9 and the preamble) attacks the legal claims of the territorial ruler to create a sphere of justice controlled by princely will rather than customary norms. The most radical articles, however, challenge the right of manor lords to reassert power over the institutions of the village community. Article 3 questions the morality of serfdom and argues that Christ's law somehow forbids the literal ownership of men. Yet article 3 does not completely deny the need for just lordship, and the implication seems to be that the rebels were willing to accept aristocratic privilege if it is bounded by clear rules of justice and accountability. Perhaps this can be read as another instance of the popular belief that aristocracies were legitimate as long as they exercised protective functions on behalf of their communities.

In any event, the remaining seven articles draw up a detailed indictment of contemporary manorial practice. Articles 4, 5, and 10 call for the return of common right to fish and hunt, cut wood, and control the terms of access to meadows and fields. Articles 6 through 8 attack unjust and abusive manorial obligations, especially unfair labor services; while article 11 rejects the presumed right of the manor lord to collect death "taxes" or dues when hereditary tenements are inherited. The clear meaning of this set of antimanorial complaints is that villagers were not willing to accept the arbitrary and unilateral imposition of a stiffened form of servile tenure. It was the village community rather than the lord that was regarded as the legitimate owner of land and labor. Aristocratic claims were judged by this standard, and elite demands were not accepted unless they could be held accountable to village institutions.

Taken as a whole, the document calls for an end to aristocratic and princely arbitrariness, both in the government of the manor and the governance of the emerging territorial state. Market relations and commercialization figure hardly at all, either as specific grievances or as implicit objects of popular unrest. The overarching theme was the need to return to a partly apocryphal age of village "freedom" when local institutions had the largest possible measure of autonomy from outside interference. There was nothing inherently egalitarian in any of this, and the articles were mute when it came to the internal hierarchies of power and patriarchy that held the village together. Nevertheless, the Twelve Articles remains one of the most remarkable statements of the goals of rural rebels to have survived the ravages of time, and this alone justifies a close examination of its meaning.

The Twelve Articles can also be used as a key or coda that allows us to interpret the logic of collective violence in the Bauernkrieg. As the document shows, the rebels of 1525 were not responding blindly or irrationally to the "inevitable" forces of historical change. They had clear goals, and the targets of their anger were carefully selected because of their obvious centrality to the village community. Nor were the rebels of 1525 simply the hopeless victims of "peasant" misery. Indeed, the fact that many of the rebels wore armor and came from the ranks of established householders should caution us against viewing the Bauernkrieg as a "peasant" rebellion. On the contrary, the evidence indicates that the rebels were trying to prevent the consolidation of elite institutions that would have led to the reduction of semiautonomous communities to the kind of low-status, vulnerable groups that social scientists associate with peasant classes. In short, the Bauernkrieg can be read as a war against the "peasantization" of early modern German society.

Some readers of the Twelve Articles may still wish to see the Bauernkrieg as a class war. After all, this was a large-scale revolt, or, more properly, series of revolts, that had a common focus.

But how should we territorially delimit the class that was supposed to have been acting? Was it defined by the Holy Roman Empire or Saxony or merely by one or another economic region?

To be sure, the articles use the word *Bauern* (farmer), but this was as much a political and social category as it was a material structure. Indeed, I would argue that it referred primarily to the institutional relations of local domination. In any case, the reader of the articles should be struck by their emphasis on local autonomy. As I indicated, this is seen most clearly in the call for the local selection of pastors. This was not a question of class; it was a question of the right of a local community to define the basic rules of institutionalized power. That, however, is not something that can be easily understood in terms of a German peasantry bent on seizing the means of production or carrying out a bourgeois revolution. The very same point applied to the demands issued in England by Kett's followers.

The localized and highly specific nature of rebellion in 1525 is a striking illustration of what I have called representative violence. The performance of violence was the medium through which popular interests were articulated in a direct confrontation with the agents of aristocratic domination. The moments of violence literally represented communities by making present the grievances and goals of the whole village. At its most radical, a local uprising could create a political space in which the tacit political and social constitution of the community could be redrawn. During 1525, for example, some of the most radical insurrectionary violence saw the destruction of manorial institutions from the bottom up. At least in cases of this kind, the rebels tried to create a completely autonomous realm of popular power, free from any involuntary links to elite authorities. This tendency toward a spontaneous and nonideological rural anarchism based on popular communities can be found in many social contexts. But even in the less radical phases of the Bauernkrieg the logic of collective violence was political and representative. The enactment of violence challenged basic elements of the relations of power and authority that formed the core of rural institutions.

It is important to remember that in 1525 there were few mechanisms of negotiation and reconciliation short of confrontation through which elites and popular groups could resolve fundamental differences. In much of the Holy Roman Empire, rural commoners were excluded from the territorial estates in which the prince bargained with his privileged subjects for taxes and support.[90] At a local level, the manorial court did offer a forum in which popular interests found a voice. But the manorial court was an ambiguous institution, always drawn uncomfortably between popular custom and the will of the lord, and during periods of crisis the manorial court could simply break down. In 1525 one of the major points of conflict had to do with the question of whether elite or popular interests would prevail in the manorial courts. Not even the royal and princely courts offered a secure institutional arena for the expression of popular grievances. Whole categories of the servile or unfree were denied any access at all; and even those commoners who could litigate against their lords found the experience uncertain, expensive, and arbitrary. In this situation of weakly institutionalized forms of negotiation the possibility of violent confrontation was very real, especially when popular groups had enough cohesion to act collectively.

The events of the Bauernkrieg may surprise those social scientists who view rural insurrection through the prism of capitalism and commercialization. The Bauernkrieg had very little to do with capitalism, and the expansion of agrarian market relations was not one of the targets of the rebels.[91] Of course, markets of any kind were weakly developed in sixteenth-century central Europe, even when viewed by the standards of the 1500s. Yet, where markets did exist, they may have strengthened rather than weakened popular institutions. Market networks provided an alternative to the rigid channels of manorial domination, and markets could offer a way of transferring resources outside of the institutions of elite power. This was probably one of the reasons that motivated manor lords to create the maze of tolls and monopolies that cluttered the late medieval landscape. They realized that markets were lucrative, and they were determined to prevent their subjects from benefiting at the expense of aristocratic pretensions.

A more significant point is that market relations allowed rural people to build

90. Kiernan, *State and Society in Europe, 1550–1650*, 162–200.
91. This is my reading of the Twelve Articles and Blickle's *The Revolution of 1525*.

networks of exchange and alliance that could be turned against landed elites during periods of crisis and confrontation. For example, village wage labor could bind cultivators and laborers together in relations of mutual obligation, and those ties could reinforce the nonmarket institutions of village solidarity. In addition, markets could constitute a kind of horizontal bridge between rural communities and urban groups. We know that the rural rebels of 1525 did have urban supporters and imitators, and it seems reasonable to suppose that the ties between city and countryside were partly shaped through the many local agrarian markets that serviced urban populations. This would have been true in areas like the Rhine, where village market gardeners and wine growers were in fairly frequent contact with townsmen. In short, if commercialization was a cause of the Bauernkrieg, it must have been more a product of the elite's coercive interference with the market than a result of commercialization as such. The tolls, taxes, and monopolies of the aristocracy were much more threatening and disruptive than the petty, largely voluntary market exchanges that escaped manorial control.

Still, the central issue that motivated the rebels of 1525 was the struggle over the conditions of authority in the German countryside. The Bauernkrieg was a *political* event, and the villagers who compiled grievances and rallied to the Twelve Articles were attempting to redefine lordship and political power. For decades the German aristocracy had become increasingly distant from the management and defense of village agriculture. Yet this same aristocracy had become more imperious in its demands and less willing to abide by local custom. This was the deteriorating context in which village revolts, like the uprising at Lupfen, began to escalate into a representative confrontation between elites and popular communities. The rebels of 1525 upheld a notion of good lordship that was best expressed by the Schwabenspiegel. According to this old legal code of the thirteenth century, "We ought to serve the lords because they protect us."[92] It was the withering of the protective dimensions of aristocratic power that led to the crisis of central European feudalism, a crisis that would not be resolved until well into the modern period.

92. Cited in ibid., 44.

CHAPTER 4

The English Model and the Compromise of Community

During the early 1900s, English politics stood poised between the collectivism of the welfare state and the fading individualism of the Victorian past. New ideas and novel political issues struggled for control of a political agenda that was still dominated by the old clash of Liberal and Tory. The stakes of the game were high, and the urgency of the issues was matched by a remarkable flowering of politically motivated journalism and scholarship. English history was rethought and rewritten by all those who were concerned to show the ways in which the English experience could be connected to the current politics of the "modern" age. Conservatives turned to the historical record as a source of stability and validation, while liberals and socialists read English history as an indictment of current problems.[1]

It was this context that provided the inspiration for a thorough rethinking of the agrarian history of England. R. H. Tawney, the Hammonds, and the Webbs were among the many politically active scholars who turned to rural England as a key to the understanding of the present. Agrarian history became a permanent source of inspiration and debate; a mirror by which the strengths and weaknesses of industrial society could be evaluated. For liberals and social democrats, the rural experience was seen as embodying lost values of collectivism and communalism that could be emulated in the present. But for Conservatives, English rural history was a peculiar blend of economic rationality and enlightened elitism that led to the stable prosperity of the Victorian apogee.[2]

---

1. See Michael Freeden, *The New Liberalism: An Ideology of Social Reform* (Oxford: Clarendon Press, 1978), 25–75, and Avner Offer, *Property and Politics, 1870–1914: Landownership, Law, Ideology, and Urban Development in England* (Cambridge: Cambridge University Press, 1981), esp. 1–10, 317–406.

2. R. H. Tawney, *The Agrarian Problem in the Sixteenth Century* (New York: Harper and Row, 1967); John L. Hammond and Barbara Hammond, *The Village Labourerund* (New York: Longmans, 1978); and Sidney Webb and Beatrice Webb, *English Poor Law History,* 3 vols. (London: Longmans, Green, 1927–29). Gertrude Himmelfarb explores the "conservative" and "radical" positions in *The Idea of Poverty: England in the Early Industrial Age* (New York: Knopf, 1984).

Since the pioneering efforts of the early twentieth century, the field of English rural studies has become a rich and subtle enterprise, a kind of luxuriant landscape that is constantly renewed through new approaches and the patient discovery of new materials. It is no exaggeration to claim that we know as much, if not more, about the long sweep of English rural life than we do about any other society. As a result, England's agrarian past has become a major case for historical and sociological theories that claim to explain the dynamics of change in rural societies. England has become a model of how a successful transition can be made from a "peasant" past to an industrial future. Even critical thinkers, such as Karl Polanyi and Barrington Moore, have seen England as somehow paradigmatic of at least one route to modernity, and the histories of other societies have been studied in order to show how they have deviated from the English standard.[3]

The problem with this kind of theory is that it exaggerates the uniqueness of the English case. The question that dominates research is why England made an early and successful transition to agrarian capitalism.[4] There is no doubt that this is a major issue, but it can easily divert our attention from the deep patterns that England shared with other rural societies in the West. The result is a depreciation of the value of the English case as a basis for comparative theorizing, particularly unfortunate given the remarkable quality of the English source materials.

This following chapter starts from a fundamentally different point. It asks the reader to think comparatively about English rural history, and it poses the question whether the broad sweep of England's agrarian past can be understood in terms of the theoretical issues addressed in Chapter 3. The accent is on continuity and comparison, rather than change and contrast. The first section develops a case for the long-term importance of community institutions in the English countryside, while the second explores enclosure and enclosure rioting in the context of aristocratic power and rural commerce. The third section focuses on two major episodes of rural insurrection, Kett's rebellion in Norfolk and the Midlands uprisings of 1607. Both incidents illuminate the character of community and violence with special clarity, and their logic can be easily reconstructed from the detailed studies carried out by R. B. Manning, Charlesworth and others.[5] Finally, I reexamine the logic of

3. Alexander Gershenkron, *Economic Backwardness in Comparative Perspective: A Book of Essays* (Cambridge: Harvard University Press, Belknap Press, 1962); Mancur Olson, *The Rise and Decline of Nations: Economic Growth, Stagflation, and Social Rigidities* (New Haven: Yale University Press, 1982). These are just two of many works that deploy this theme implicitly or explicitly.

4. The most recent example of the debate about agrarian development is the "Brenner debate." See T. E. Aston and C. H. E. Philpin, *The Brenner Debate: Agrarian Class Structure and Economic Development in Pre-Industrial Europe* (Cambridge: Cambridge University Press, 1985).

5. Among the best monographic studies are Barrett L. Beer, *Rebellion and Riot: Popular Disorder in England during the Reign of Edward VI* (Kent: Kent State University Press, 1982); John Bohstedt, *Riots and Community Politics in England and Wales, 1790–1810* (Cambridge: Harvard University Press, 1983); Andrew Charlesworth, ed., *An Atlas of Rural Protest in Britain, 1548–1900* (Philadelphia: University of Pennsylvania Press, 1983); John Brewer and John Styles, eds., *An Ungovernable People: The English and Their Law in the Seventeenth and Eighteenth Centuries* (New Brunswick: Rutgers University Press, 1980); Frederick G. Emmison, *Elizabethan Life*, Essex Record

power and politics in rural England and offer a political explanation for the phenomenon that other theories have understood as the economic "demise" of the English peasantry. The core argument is that the relative strength of community institutions in rural England must be given much greater weight in our reading of the transitions that led to England's "agrarian equipoise."[6]

It is worth stressing that much of the argument diverges sharply from the work of theorists like Barrington Moore, who have read English history as the unfolding of a class logic that somehow abolished the English peasantry long before a similar logic unfolded on the European continent. It also diverges from the analysis of those who, like Alan Macfarlane, believe that a robust individualism has always been the dominant theme in English rural life. The very fact that there is little theoretical agreement about these issues means that we need to rethink the English situation from the bottom up. It also means that England is an intriguing case, because established theoretical discourses would lead us to expect that the concept of community would be the least likely analytic framework for understanding English rural life. If the community of grain is a plausible interpretive device in the English case, it can only strengthen its plausibility where community has long been recognized as a central institutional feature of rural history.[7]

My concept of unilateral or elite enclosure is meant to show elite constraint at work. It is not tautological, because it does not depend on defining enclosure riots as automatic or necessary responses to elite enclosure; nor do I assume that all enclosures were of this kind or that all of them fitting this category had identical consequences.

Community in the English Rural Landscape, 1500–1800

During the furious parliamentary debates that accompanied what J. C. D. Clark has called the end of the ancien régime in nineteenth-century England, the

---

Office Publications, no. 56 (Chelmsford: Essex County Council, 1970–80); Douglas Hay et al., eds., *Albion's Fatal Tree: Crime and Society in Eighteenth Century England* (New York: Pantheon, 1975); Brian Stuart Manning, *The English People and the English Revolution, 1640–1649* (London: Heineman, 1976); Roger B. Manning, *Village Revolts: Social Protest and Popular Disturbances in England, 1509–1640* (Oxford: Clarendon Press, 1988); Paul Slack, ed., *Rebellion, Popular Protest, and the Social Order in Early Modern England* (Cambridge: Cambridge University Press, 1984); Buchanan Sharp, *In Contempt of All Authority: Rural Artisans and Riot in the West of England, 1586–1660* (Berkeley: University of California Press, 1980); E. P. Thompson, *Whigs and Hunters: The Origin of the Black Act* (New York: Pantheon, 1975); and Anthony Fletcher and John Stevenson, eds., *Order and Disorder in Early Modern England* (Cambridge: Cambridge University Press, 1985).

6. The term is from Bohstedt, *Riots and Community Politics,* 165.

7. For a full statement of Alan Macfarlane's position, see Alan Macfarlane, *Reconstructing Historical Communities* (Cambridge: Cambridge University Press, 1977), and his *The Origins of English Individualism: The Family, Property, and Social Transition* (New York: Cambridge University Press, 1979). For good critiques, see C. J. Calhoun, "History, Anthropology, and the Study of Communities," *Social History* 2 (May 1977), 631–52, and his "Community: Towards a Variable Conceptualization for Comparative Research," *Social History,* 5 (Jan. 1980), 105–29.

discussion often turned on how the members were going to interpret the lessons of English agrarian development.[8] Issues as diverse as suffrage reform, disestablishment, and the poor laws were seen through the lens of a political consciousness still closely tied to agriculture. Mainstream Whigs and Liberals could find in the English countryside an exemplary sanity and stability, a reflection of the moderate reformism they advocated for politics. But for radical and reactionary critics, and for men like Disraeli, who combined both strains of critique in an unstable synthesis, the rural history of modern England was a sad spectacle of betrayal and disaster. Enclosure, market values, and the creeping industrialization of a once-pastoral landscape were taken as indicators of the debasement of the English soul.

These were large and potent issues, and the failure to resolve them was indicative of the clash of ultimate values that has always accompanied moments of fundamental social change. Yet all the participants in the debate do seem to have agreed on at least one point: at some time in English history, community was a basic principle of rural life, and the character of community was understood as a metaphor for all of English history. Authors, polemicists, and politicians had a familiarity with notions of community that seems strange or quaint to twentieth-century readers, whose cognitive map has been shaped by the logic of class. Yet one cannot read the work of a Cobbett or an Arthur Young without being struck by how much weight they gave to considerations of locality, place, and space; exactly what one would expect of a society in which community was more than a rhetorical flourish. William Cobbett, for example, could wax truly eloquent about the virtues of a social order in which farmers and farm servants shared a common interest in local cooperation.[9]

Naturally, the mental images of early-nineteenth-century Englishmen cannot be used as decisive proof of anything. But those images do alert us to the need at least to entertain the possibility that community was significant in the English countryside. We need to follow Cobbett and Young and pose the question anew: What is the evidence for community in English rural history, especially during the critical centuries that saw the enclosure of common fields and wastes? In coming to grips with this question, I will focus on the forms of economic, political, and ritual cooperation that I have identified as central to the theoretical understanding of rural community. The time frame will center on the years from 1500 to 1700, because this was the period that many authors have considered decisive in changing rural society forever. Much of the debate between Robert Brenner and his critics has hinged on the presence or absence of a capitalist reconstruction of

8. J. C. D. Clark, *English Society, 1688–1832: Ideology, Social Structure, and Political Practice during the Ancien Régime* (Cambridge: Cambridge University Press, 1985), esp. 8–41, 349–407. For enclosure debates, see K. D. M. Snell, *Annals of the Labouring Poor: Social Change and Agrarian England, 1660–1900* (Cambridge: Cambridge University Press, 1985), esp. 104–227.

9. William Cobbett (speeches against the New Poor Law), *Hansard Parliamentary Debates,* 3d. ser., xxiii (1834), 1335–37; *Hansard,* 3d ser., xxiv (1834), 386–87; and William Cobbett, *Cottage Economy* (London: Peter Davies, 1926).

English society sometime in the early modern era.[10] Continuity of community institutions should, therefore, be less visible between 1500 and 1700 than at other, more "stable" periods; and this allows us at least to approximate a hard test of the hypothesis that community institutions help to explain collective action in rural England.

It is clear that the centuries *before* 1500 do show strong signs of rural community, and both Marxist and non-Marxist historians seem to converge on a kind of consensus about the salience of community institutions prior to the rise of the Tudors. Rodney Hilton, for example, can be read as linking his analysis of antiservile rebellion to the mechanisms of parish and village fellowship, and his classic work has been greatly expanded by the contributors to journals like *Past and Present,* which have continued the investigation of medieval and early modern social history. Economic historians have also used English estate records to think through the logic of common-field agriculture, and the work of D. N. McCloskey, Christopher Dyer, and Joan Thirsk leaves little doubt about the widespread existence of community practices in the manorial villages of medieval England.[11] Dyer, for instance, has used the estate records of the Bishopric of Worcester over the period 680 to 1540 to reconstruct the rural fabric of medieval society in detail. According to Dyer, "The evidence examined so far suggests that the village community performed many different functions through a variety of organizations. It was both a unit of government, with some coercive power, and a focal point of social cooperation."[12] Dyer's analysis has also been echoed by the work of Zvi Razi, who has shown that the notion of a weakening of rural communities after the Black Death must be severely qualified and, for certain parts of England perhaps rejected.[13]

10. Robert Brenner, "The Agrarian Roots of European Capitalism," in Aston and Philipin, *The Brenner Debate,* 213–327.

11. For example, see Martin Ingram, "Ridings, Rough Music, and Popular Culture," *Past and Present* 105 (1984); J. M. Neeson, "The Opponents of Enclosure in Eighteenth Century Northamptonshire," *Past and Present* 105 (1984); Rodney Hilton, *Bond Men Made Free: Medieval Peasant Movements and the English Rising of 1381* (New York: Viking, 1977), 28–62, and his *Medieval Society: The West Midlands at the End of the Thirteenth Century* (Cambridge: Cambridge University Press, 1983), esp. 15–22; Joan Thirsk, "The Common Fields," in R. H. Hilton, ed., *Peasants, Knights, and Heretics: Studies in Medieval English Social History* (Cambridge: Cambridge University Press, 1976), 10–32; Joan Thirsk, *English Peasant Farming: The Agrarian History of Lincolnshire from Tudor to Recent Times* (London: Routledge and Kegan Paul, 1957); D. G. Hey, *An English Rural Community: Myddle under the Tudors and Stuarts* (Leicester: Leicester University Press, 1974); William G. Hoskins, *The Midland Peasant: The Economic and Social History of a Leicestershire Village* (London: Macmillan, 1957); D. N. McCloskey, "The Persistence of English Common Fields," in William N. Parker and Eric L. Jones, *European Peasants and Their Markets: Essays in Agrarian Economic History* (Princeton: Princeton University Press, 1975), 73–119.

12. Christopher Dyer, *Lords and Peasants in a Changing Society: The Estates of the Bishopric of Worcester, 680–1540* (Cambridge: Cambridge University Press, 1980), 365–66. (Dyer qualifies this by pointing to forces that weakened the community, but his logic is clear.)

13. Zvi Razi, "Family, Land, and the Village Community in Later Medieval England," in T. H. Aston, ed., *Landlords, Peasants, and Politics in Medieval England* (Cambridge: Cambridge University Press, 1987), 360–93.

At the center of this consensus is the English common-field arable village. Much of lowland England practiced common-field arable and animal husbandry by 1300, and, as I argued, earlier common-field villages were closely knit networks of social cooperation that bound member households into overlapping relations of affection and exchange. The presence of a complex two- or three-field regimen of alternating phases of cultivation and fallow demanded what the English called "good neighborhood," and the intermixing of arable strips in the common fields underpinned and enhanced the ties of kinship and religious observance. As Joan Thirsk has observed, the true common-field economy was a highly institutionalized affair, something that a focus on class relations will tend to underestimate. It is not surprising that the great regional revolts of the medieval era, especially the insurrections associated with the names Wat Tyler and Jack Cade, were made possible by the legacies of cooperation that grew out of the economy of common cultivation.[14]

But what are we to make of the centuries after 1500? Did economic cooperation disappear with the growth of population and the transition to enclosed fields held in severalty? Or is it possible to identify the traces of a material practice of community even after the change identified by Robert Brenner had begun to transform the rural landscape?

There are two significant points to be made in response to these sorts of issues, and both deserve to be considered at some length. First, it is simply not true that common-field agriculture disappeared as an important element of English agrarian society prior to 1800. As the patient research that fills the pages of the Cambridge agrarian history project shows, the death of common-field England was a very slow process, even if we use the stringent criteria between open and common fields proposed by Joan Thirsk.[15] For example, in the Midlands, one of the earliest sites of enclosure, common-arable farming can be found in the late seventeenth century, and the Midlands region was not exceptional in this regard.[16] Of course,

14. The best exposition of the logic of common-field agriculture is Carl Dahlman, *The Open Field System and Beyond: A Property Rights Analysis of an Economic Institution* (Cambridge: Cambridge University Press, 1980). Also see L. Dudley Stamp and William G. Hoskins, *The Common Lands of England and Wales* (London: Collins, 1963); Eric L. Jones, ed., *Agriculture and Economic Growth in England, 1650–1815* (New York: Barnes and Noble, 1967); J. D. Chambers and G. E. Mingay, *The Agricultural Revolution, 1750–1880* (London: Batsford, 1966); J. Z. Titow, "Medieval England and the Open-Field System," *Past and Present* 32 (1965); Frederic Seebohm, *The English Village Community, Examined in Its Relations to the Menorial and Tribal Systems and to the Common or Open-Field Systems of Husbandry: An Essay in Economic History* (London: Longmans, Green, 1915); C. S. Orwin and C. S. Orwin, *The Open Fields* (Oxford: Clarendon Press, 1967); and J. A. Yelling, *Common Field and Enclosure in England, 1450–1850* (London: Macmillan, 1977). For regional revolts of the Wat Tyler and Jack Cade variety, see E. B. Fryde, *The Great Revolt of 1381* (London: Historical Association, 1981). Also see Roger Manning, "Violence and Social Conflict in Mid-Tudor Rebellions," *Journal of British Studies* 16 (1977), 18–40.

15. Thirsk, "The Common Fields," esp. 10–11, and her preface to the third edition of Orwin and Orwin, *The Open Fields*, v–xv.

16. Joan Thirsk, ed., *The Agrarian History of England and Wales* (hereafter *AHEW*), vol. 5,

no absolutely precise statistical claims can be made, but the work of local historians clearly indicates that the period 1500–1700 involved much more continuity with medieval practices than some, including Barrington Moore, once believed. Indeed, it can be argued that the demographic pressures of the sixteenth and seventeenth centuries led in some cases to an enhancement of community solidarities in the face of the sorts of forces of erosion that I identified in chapter 2. For example, the 1500s saw an intensification of the rationing of grazing or pasture rights according to the rules of "stinting," a practice that limited pasturage rights to local community members who held hereditary copyhold or freehold arable property. Similarly, the work of Margaret Spufford has shown how community control of local moral practices increased in the same period that saw a tightening of access rights to the commons for stinting and gleaning.[17] The implication is that village cohesion remained strong wherever the methods of common agriculture persisted, even if cooperation often overlapped with a very real struggle over the power and privileges of village membership.

But there is a second and perhaps more significant point that can be made about the logic of economic cooperation in rural England. Even in regions without common-field agriculture it is possible to identify deep patterns of material exchange and mutuality that were simultaneously hierarchical and reciprocal. For example, in both pastoral and sylvan England, common arable fields were apparently of little importance, and enclosed arable fields had an ancient history. Yet other kinds of common property rights were important, especially with regard to the control of local pastures, wastes, and forests.[18] Local membership in a manor, village, or township was apparently prerequisite to full enjoyment of these various use rights. Territorial communities could actually take shape in the absence of a strong manorial order, as shown in the case of the forest communities of "wild and masterless men" studied by Buchanan Sharp.[19] As Sharp has demonstrated for the royal forests of Dean, Gillingham, and Braydon, occupationally mixed commu-

1640–1750, part 1, "Regional Farming Systems" (Cambridge: Cambridge University Press, 1984), esp. G. E. Mingay, "The East Midlands: Northamptonshire, Leicestershire, Rutland, Nottinghamshire, and Lincolnshire (excluding the Midlands)," 89–128; David Hey, "The North-West Midlands: Derbyshire, Stafordshire, Cheshire, and Shropshire," 129–58; and Joan Thirsk, "The South-West Midlands: Warwickshire, Worcestershire, Gloucestershire, and Herefordshire," 159–96. See also Joan Thirsk, ed., AHEW, vol. 5, 1640–1750, part 2, "Agrarian Change" (Cambridge: Cambridge University Press, 1985), esp. Christopher Clay, "Landlords and Estate Management in England," 119–251 (esp. 198–244), and Joan Thirsk, "Agricultural Policy: Public Debate and Legislation," 298–388.

17. Margaret Spufford, "Puritanism and Social Control?" in Fletcher and Stevenson, Order and Disorder in Early Modern England, 41–57; Margaret Spufford, Contrasting Communities: English Villages in the Sixteenth and Seventeenth Centuries (Cambridge: Cambridge University Press, 1974), 34–45, 319–53.

18. Joan Thirsk, "Farming Techniques," and "Enclosing and Engrossing," in Joan Thirsk, ed., AHEW, vol. 4, 1500–1640 (Cambridge: Cambridge University Press, 1967), 161–255; Snell, Annals of the Labouring Poor, 138–227.

19. Sharp, In Contempt of All Authority, 82–125, 220–56.

nities of artisans and cultivators were quite capable of defending local use rights, with or without the manipulative assistance of the gentry.[20]

We can also identify a pattern of material cooperation that cuts across the usual distinction that has been made between pastoral, arable, and sylvan communities. The practices of the old poor laws, and the related institutions of long-term farm service, can be understood as a powerful source of community cohesion that lasted in some instances well into the 1800s.[21] The subtle interplay of hierarchical deference and obligatory mutual assistance that lay at the core of both sets of practices throws a sharp light on the logic of rural community in England.

The Tudor poor laws developed in response to the dissolution of English monasticism, the decline of elite private charity, and the concurrent growth of population that so frightened Tudor and Stuart officials.[22] The purpose of English poor-relief legislation was to combine a minimal subsistence guarantee for the poor with a comprehensive code of moral regulation designed to prevent the destitute from falling into a life of unregenerate vice. In practice, however, the poor laws became a way of transferring maximum responsibility for the poor from royal officials to local communities. Every parish in the realm was required to levy a poor rate on local property holders, establish a board or vestry of poor law officials, and provide for the needs of the local indigent through a complicated range of indoor and outdoor relief. The range of benefits was often much more than a mere handout, and, as K. D. M. Snell has pointed out, as late as the end of the eighteenth century many parishes offered their poor a wide array of transfers in cash and kind, including bedding, firewood, and subsidized funerals.[23] Combined with a right to pasture on the commons and access to a garden plot, the poor law meant more than insurance against starvation. It meant the difference between abject degradation and a respectable life as a member of a particular community. As Gertrude Himmelfarb suggests in her analysis of English ideas of poverty, polemicists like Cobbett understand that the poor saw the old poor laws as a kind of common property right that gave them a stake in the social order.[24]

What is most important about the old poor laws is that they were based on a

20. For the institutional patterns of the forests and fens, see Thirsk, *English Peasant Farming;* E. Kerridge, *The Farmers of Old England* (Totowa, N.J.: Rowman and Littlefield, 1973), 59–61; Keith Lindley, *Fenland Riots and the English Revolution* (London: Heinemann Educational Books, 1982), esp. 57–67; Joan Thirsk, "Horn and Thorn in Staffordshire: The Economy of a Pastoral County," *North Staffordshire Journal of Field Studies* 9 (1969), 1–16; and C. Holmes, "Drainers and Fenmen: The Problem of Popular Political Consciousness in the Seventeenth Century," in Fletcher and Stevenson, *Order and Disorder,* 166–95.

21. The best discussion of these issues is in Snell, *Annals of the Labouring Poor,* 67–137. Also see the clever discussion of poor-law reform in Himmelfarb, *The Idea of Poverty,* 133–90, 207–29.

22. For the origins of Tudor and Stuart "paternalism," see Penry Williams, *The Tudor Regime* (Oxford: Clarendon Press, 1979), 196–252. Also see John Pound, *Poverty and Vagrancy in Tudor England* (London: Longman, 1971), 25–26; E. M. Leonard, *The Early History of English Poor Relief* (New York: Barnes and Noble, 1965), 11–21, 61–66; and Keith Wrightson and David Levine, *Poverty and Piety in an English Village: Terling, 1525–1700* (New York: Academic Press, 1979), 174–83.

23. Snell, *Annals of the Labouring Poor,* 105–9.

24. Himmelfarb, *The Idea of Poverty,* 218–20.

view of England as naturally divided into local rural communities that were responsible for the support of the "deserving" poor. Until the 1830s, the poor rate was a strictly local levy assessed on the freeholders, yeomen, and better-off tenants who were the foundation of the parish or village community. The gentry elite naturally played a role in administering the parish vestry, but the chief responsibility for the poor laws fell on the advantaged commoners who were clearly set apart from the world of court and parliament in which elites moved with no difficulty. Moreover, the farming community seems to have shown little overt opposition to the assumption of poor-law responsibilities, and I have been unable to find examples of violent resistance to the old poor laws that parallel the often riotous struggles against enclosure.[25]

The right to receive poor-law relief was not, however, granted freely to any who applied. It was a jealously guarded privilege given primarily to the residents of local communities who could prove entitlement on the basis of birth or long-term employment. During the seventeenth and eighteenth centuries the growth of a landless and semilandless rural population put increasing strain on the poor laws, because these were the groups most likely to require parish assistance.[26] Yet, until the post-1815 collapse of agricultural prices, relief was given on a large scale to those who could make some claim to membership in the local community. Strangers and wanderers, the "sturdy rogues" of Tudor legend, could be whipped out of the parish through the application of the practice known as warning out. Once again, local, territorial rules of membership were crucial in determining who could claim rights of material aid and cooperation. Established and better-off householders were evidently willing to bear the burden of poor relief, but only for their poorer neighbors to whom they were linked by ties of community.

The poor law should not be seen simply as a primitive form of welfare, nor should it be idealized as part of the myth of "merry old England." It was a deeply rooted material practice that shaped the political economy of villages and parishes well into the 1800s. The poor were entitled to limited support in exchange for submitting to the paternalistic oversight of their neighbors. Here we see clearly the principle of reciprocal hierarchy that informs so many traditional rural societies. The poor laws reinforced local solidarity and order by linking families together in a distributive economy of clearly circumscribed scope.

Closely related to the poor laws were complex forms of farm service and apprenticeship, which have been investigated by K. D. M. Snell.[27] In many regions of England, young men and women were bound out for farm labor, often

---

25. See, for example, Manning, *Village Revolts*, 157–86; Joan R. Kent, *The English Village Constable, 1580–1642: A Social and Administrative Study* (Oxford: Clarendon Press, 1986), 186–204.

26. Paul Slack, "Vagrants and Vagrancy in England, 1598–1664," *Economic History Review* 17 (Aug. 1974), 360–79; Snell, *Annals of the Labouring Poor*, 149–87.

27. Snell, *Annals of the Labouring Poor*, 67–103. Also see Ann S. Kussmaul, *Servants in Husbandry in Early Modern England* (Cambridge: Cambridge University Press, 1981), 121–30.

for a year or more. Poorer families with numerous children indentured sons and daughters to established farming families in order to reduce the material strain on weak household budgets. Farm service of this kind was doubly important. It allowed poor laborers and husbandmen to gain a stake in the local agricultural economy, and it helped to establish a right to poor-law relief. Qualifications for poor relief could be gained either by birth or by proof of local apprenticeship or service for a period of at least one year. By taking on a farm servant for the statutory period, local farmers committed themselves to paying relief to their servants during periods of unemployment, because it was the farming population that paid the poor rate. As Snell has shown, this practice lasted into the eighteenth century, and its demise signaled a fundamental reorientation of rural social relations. Farm service was not uniquely English, and Herman Rebel made a subtle argument about the importance of similar practices in central Europe.[28] In the English context, however, farm service can be seen as an important form of economic cooperation and reciprocal hierarchy that linked advantaged and disadvantaged families in networks of local community. Farm service underpinned production by providing a large reserve of labor that cultivating households could tap when the demands of the agrarian cycle exceeded the available household labor supply. But traditional forms of service also affected the relations of distribution and consumption. Poor households could obtain a larger measure of what James C. Scott would call "subsistence security" by gaining access to the resources of their advantaged neighbors. Farm servants and apprentices not only received a consumption wage in cash and kind; they also obtained what the English called a "stake" in the local social order.[29]

This sketch of the logic of farm service and the poor laws indicates the plausibility of locating community economic cooperation at the center of English rural history, even in periods and areas that lacked common-field agriculture. We should, of course, expect community cohesion to be strongest in common-field villages, especially those located in the lowland rustic regions of England. The central argument is not undermined by this kind of qualification, however. Institutions of material cooperation can be found throughout rural England, which seems to support Henry Kamen's contention that territorial networks of neighborliness may have been as important as kinship throughout northern Europe.[30] Indeed, we can go one step further and argue that property relations in rural England can be understood in terms of the logic of trusteeship that was explained in earlier chapters. The established householders of the English village and parish acted

28. Herman Rebel, *Peasant Classes: The Bureaucratization of Property and Family Relations under Early Habsburg Absolutism, 1511–1636* (Princeton: Princeton University Press, 1983), 93–119.
29. Snell, *Annals of the Labouring Poor,* 67–103; Keith Wrightson, *English Society, 1580–1680* (New Brunswick: Rutgers University Press, 1982), 39–65.
30. Henry Kamen, *European Society, 1500–1700* (London: Hutchinson, 1984), 17.

within a framework of social relations that made them the trustees and benefactors of their communities. It is certainly true, as Alan Macfarlane has argued, that English rural society was not encumbered with the complex web of collective property rights that characterized eastern Europe.[31] Yet, as the examples of the poor laws and farm service show, farming households were bound by relations of obligation that forced them to exercise proprietary rights on behalf of their kin and neighbors. This idea emerges clearly into view only when we understand property rights as social practices or "performances," rather than as objective facts or notions that can be abstracted from the context in which they are embedded.

None of these ideas are incompatible with the tradition of scholarship that sees rural England as highly commercial and market oriented.[32] It is clear, for example, that property rights were bought and sold at the local level as early as the medieval period, and even the smallest copyholders and tenants were involved in marketing grain and livestock. Nevertheless, we must be skeptical of drawing a simplistic dichotomy between the logic of the market and the institutions of community cohesion. The fact that there has been a century-long debate about the weight of "collectivism" and "individualism" in the English countryside, with both sides capable of mobilizing important and persuasive arguments, indicates the need to reconceptualize the issues. One way of doing this is to understand both markets and communities as complex patterns of institutional action that are not necessarily incompatible. In England, networks of commerce and economic cooperation were intertwined at the level of the village and parish through the medium of kinship and neighborhood.

The forms of politics and ritual that were characteristic of the ordinary routines of agrarian life prior to the 1800s further strengthen the argument for community in rural England. Massive and richly documented research concerning these issues has accumulated during the last century; and the work of David Underdown, Christopher Hill, and Joan Kent has been especially successful in synthesizing the scholarship of local historians and regional specialists.[33]

---

31. Macfarlane, *The Origins of English Individualism*, 7–61.

32. The most lucid statement of the mix of "individualism and collectivism" in rural England is Wrightson, *English Society*, 51–57. Also see B. A. Holderness, "Credit in English Rural Society before the Nineteenth Century, with Special Reference to the Period 1650–1720," *Agricultural History Review* 24, part 2 (1976), 97–109; Mildred Campbell, *The English Yeoman under Elizabeth and the Early Stuarts* (New Haven: Yale University Press, 1942), 64–155; Hey, *An English Rural Community*, esp. 117, 141, 170–76.

33. David Underdown, *Revel, Riot, and Rebellion: Popular Politics and Culture in England, 1603–1660* (Oxford: Clarendon Press, 1985); David Underdown, "The Chalk and the Cheese: Contrasts among the English Clubmen," in Slack, *Rebellion, Popular Protest, and the Social Order*, 162–85; Christopher Hill, *The World Turned Upside Down: Radical Ideas during the English Revolution* (New York: Harper and Row, 1972); Christopher Hill, *Puritanism and Revolution: Studies in Interpretation of the English Revolution of the Seventeenth Century* (New York: Schocken, 1967); Kent, *The English Village Constable;* Joan Kent, "The English Village Constable, 1580–1642: The Nature and Dilemmas of the Office," *Journal of British Studies* 20 (1981), 26–49. Also see, for a synthesis of local studies, Peter Clark, *English Provincial Society from the Reformation to the*

At the heart of local rural politics was the existence of an institutional order through which local conflicts and local interests were mediated.[34] In both villages and parishes, there were strong notions of good order and neighborliness, and transgressors were subject to coercive sanctioning by all or part of the local community. Many disputes between members, or between community members and outsiders, were probably never brought before official institutions of the crown and the landed elite but were instead handled through local and customary procedures that ranged from informal mediation to group violence against male-factors. It is this local and customary face of politics in rural England that has led Keith Wrightson to postulate the existence of "two concepts of order" in early modern England, one elite and official, the other popular and conventional.[35]

In many parts of England prior to the end of the 1600s, the institutional locus of popular rural politics was focused on the manor court, especially in arable regions with common fields and mixed sheep-corn husbandry.[36] The English manor court was probably much like its counterparts in the rest of Europe, and a good deal of manorial business was taken up with negotiations between the manor lord and his "subjects" over the terms of rent, fines, and manorial privileges. The court of the manor also provided a forum for the limited self-government of local communities. For the good order of the manorial community, regulations were made that specified the rights and duties of local householders. Wherever they existed, manorial rules controlled access to wastes and commons, regulated the farming cycle, and worked out the terms of temporary and permanent enclosure. In addition, the manor court probably helped shape local moral practices, including the procedures governing lewdness, bastardy, and premarital sex. Although these were issues also claimed by the jurisdiction of the church courts, there is good reason to suppose that matters of such grave local importance would be handled by manorial justice rather than by outsiders whenever possible.[37]

Enforcement of the decisions of manorial courts was relatively easy, given the large number of manorial officials who managed community issues and interests.

Revolution: Religion, Politics, and Society in Kent, 1558–1640 (Hassocks, Sussex: Harvester Press, 1977), and John S. Morrill, *The Revolt of the Provinces: Conservatives and Radicals in the English Civil War, 1630–1650* (New York: Barnes and Noble, 1976).

34. Kent, *The English Village Constable*, esp. 15–18, 41–44, 190–215.

35. Keith Wrightson, "Two Concepts of Order: Justices, Constables, and Jurymen in Seventeenth Century England," in Brewer and Styles, *An Ungovernable People*, 21–46.

36. For the manor court see Joan Thirsk, "The Farming Regions of England," and Alan Everitt, "Farm Labourers," in Thirsk, *AHEW*, vol. 4, *1500–1640* (Cambridge: Cambridge University Press, 1967), 1–112, 396–465, esp. 8–9, 33, 63–69, 459–61; Manning, *Village Revolts*, esp. 44, 70, 136–42. For the range of manorial actions and decisions, see John Parsons Earwaker, ed., *The Court Leet Records of the Manor of Manchester, 1552–1686 and 1731–1846*, 12 vols. (Manchester: H. Blackwell, 1884–90).

37. For the strongest statement of the role of the church, see Richard Lachman, *From Manor to Market: Structural Change in England, 1536–1640* (Madison: University of Wisconsin Press, 1987), 3–19, but this should be balanced by reading Kent, *The English Village Constable*, 24–79.

Drawn from local community members, the officials of the manor court included the many reeves, bailiffs, overseers, and beadles, whose strange titles belie their importance to the ordinary routines of agrarian life.[38] For example, manorial "officials" were responsible for observing and reporting infractions of community rules, and it is unlikely that the level of surveillance in a well-ordered manor would have been too low to permit ongoing correction of petty conflicts and abuses.

Nor would it be correct to argue that the absence of manorial courts meant the absence of effective institutions of local community governance.[39] As Joan Kent has observed, many agencies of village and parish politics were involved with the lives and disputes of English commoners.[40] Parish vestries administered the poor law, regulated popular morality, and maintained the religious focus of local life, while the militia bands offered a forum for solidarity and community defense. In some parts of the countryside, rural communities were actually organized as townships, and David Allen has shown how township government offered a powerful model of community that was transplanted to America in the 1600s. For example, in Hingham, Norfolk, the institutions of the rural town regulated property sales and the use of commons and wastes, and these practices were transferred to the New World town called Hingham, Massachusetts.[41]

In areas without strong manors, however, the most significant agency of popular government was the village constable.[42] Long considered a figure of fun or a corrupt incompetent, the village constable was actually an important source of community self-regulation. The petty and parish constables both represented popular interests before the elite of justices and landlords and enforced law and order according to the accepted norms of community life. Village constables arrested criminals, proclaimed royal laws, guarded the community against vagrants and troublemakers, and generally oversaw all aspects of local administration. Above all, they served as the natural leaders of their communities, composing differences and articulating the "sense" or opinion of their community members.

---

38. See, for example, David Grayson Allen, *In English Ways: The Movement of Societies and the Transferal of English Local Law and Custom to Massachusetts Bay in the Seventeenth Century* (Chapel Hill: University of North Carolina Press, 1981), esp. 47–54, 83–84, 116. Also see four studies by Warren O. Ault: "Some Early Village By-Laws," *English Historical Review* 45 (1930), 208–31; *Open-Field Farming in Medieval England: A Study of Village By-Laws* (London: Allen and Unwin, 1972); "Village By-Laws by Common Consent," *Speculum* 29 (1954), 378–94; and *Open-Field Husbandry and the Village Community: A Study of Agrarian By-Laws in Medieval England* (Philadelphia: American Philosophical Society, 1965). Finally, see M. W. Barley, "East Yorkshire Manorial By-laws," *Yorkshire Archaeological Journal* 25 (1943), 35–60.

39. For the role of the parish, see Sedley L. Ware, "The Elizabethan Parish in Its Ecclesiastical and Financial Aspects," *Johns Hopkins University Studies in Historical and Political Science*, ser. 26, nos. 7–8 (Baltimore: J. H. Press, 1908), 5–93; Carl Bridenbaugh, *Vexed and Troubled Englishmen, 1590–1642* (New York: Oxford University Press, 1968), 243–47.

40. Kent, *The English Village Constable*, 24–56, 186–221.

41. Allen, *In English Ways*, 55–81.

42. See Kent, *The English Village Constable*.

This was a role the local constable played fairly effectively; although it was a role that made sense only in a world in which local communities rather than the state were responsible for the routine coercive enforcement of political order.[43]

A striking illustration of community politics and self-regulation can be found in the practice of the "skimmington," or what historians have sometimes called the English charivari.[44] As Martin Ingram has pointed out, many English rural communities were quite sensitive to the violation of traditional patriarchal ideals, particularly when "scandalous" women threatened to upset the local social order by cuckolding their husbands or committing adultery.[45] Men and women who were particularly flagrant in this regard could become the targets of collective humiliation that included noisy jeering and pot banging, mild violence, and an occasional stay in the stocks or dunking in a pond or stream. The playing out of this ritual of humiliation was what contemporaries meant by the term "skimmington" or "riding skimmington"; and, like the French charivari, it was both an expression of local solidarity in the face of transgression and a performance of hierarchy in which malefactors were openly subordinated to the coercive power of the community. Just as the Anglican church was in some sense the Tory party at prayer, so the charivari was the enactment of community through the drawing of moral and territorial boundaries between good and evil. It was a form of politics no less real than the spectacle of Parliament, because it involved the assertion of power in the context of conflicting interests and contested passions.

In order to show what was at stake in the skimmington it is useful to quote the testimony of a charivari victim cited in the interesting study of popular culture by Martin Ingram. Thomas Mills, a cutler, and his wife, Agnes, were the objects of a particularly violent charivari in 1618, and according to Mills the action reached its peak when a whole community mobilized against him. According to Mills, "about noon came again from Calne to Quemerford another drummer named William Wiatt, and with him three or four hundred men, some like soldiers armed with pieces and other weapons, and a man riding upon a horse, having a white night cap upon his head, two shoeing horns hanging by his ears, a counterfeit beard upon his chin made of a deer's tail, . . . and he and all his company made a stand when they came just against this examinate's house, and then the gunners shot off their pieces, pipes and horns were sounded, together with low bells and other smaller bells which the company had amongst them, and rams' horns and bucks' horns, carried upon forks, were then and there lifted up and shown."[46]

Mills and his wife were unfortunate, but their travails clearly illuminate the ability of popular communities to regulate their own definitions of order, even if it meant using extralegal or illegal violence. Technically, the shaming of Mills could

43. See Stanley Palmer, *Police and Protest in England and Ireland, 1780–1850* (Cambridge: Cambridge University Press, 1988), esp. 70–74, 420–24.
44. The best discussion is Underdown's *Revel, Riot, and Rebellion,* 100–111.
45. Ingram, "Ridings, Rough Music, and Popular Culture," 79–113.
46. Ibid., 82.

have been construed as a riotous assembly and prosecuted as at least a misdemeanor. Yet fear of prosecution obviously did not deter the participants from assaulting Mills and his wife after they had forcibly dragged the wife from her house.

With the charivari we have reached the boundary between community politics and the more purely ritual practices of leisure and ceremony that provided a focus of identity and a folklore of place. Thanks to research into the nature of popular culture, we know a great deal about the local ceremonies and festivals of rural England, and what we know points to the importance of local ritual as a medium of expressive action that reinforced the cooperative relations of the village or parish.[47] For example, David Underdown has helped us to understand the ways in which local festivals, underpinned by commensality and pageantry, helped to focus popular identity, and, in a previous chapter, I argued that the ritual perambulation of the village or manorial boundaries at the Rogationtide ceremony clearly enacted a sense of territorial identity.[48] When all the householders of a village circled its boundaries together, under a banner or crucifix, they were performing community in the most direct and literal way. Indeed, in a society still largely oral, we should expect folklore to be performative and centered on the enactment of drama and symbolism.

At the center of a community ritual stood the alehouse and the church, two institutions that formed popular identity and focused local discourse, in spite of being sometimes at odds in the opinion of the magistracy. The village alehouse was more than a source of commercial insobriety or a welcome supplement to the incomes of smallholder proprietors. The alehouse also offered a natural forum for the articulation of local opinion and a meeting place for the making of decisions. This was one reason for the hostility that many magistrates expressed toward the alehouse, and it also explains the Tudor and Stuart obsession with licensing all alehouses, a task that proved beyond the limited powers of early modern English governments. It was obvious that the alehouse was an important source of seditious rumors and potential plots against elite power. More important, alehouse discourse reinforced the boundaries of community by articulating a folklore of place that encompassed a collective memory of key events and personalities.[49] This was not gossip in the modern sense; it was the kind of language of power and place that James W. Fernandez discovered in Asturian deep song.[50]

Church observances were just as important as the alehouse in drawing together

47. See Robert W. Malcolmson, *Popular Recreations in English Society, 1700–1850* (Cambridge: Cambridge University Press, 1973), esp. 52–74.

48. Underdown, *Revel, Riot, and Rebellion*, 45–47, 90–97.

49. Keith Wrightson, "Alehouses, Order, and Reformation in Rural England, 1590–1660," in Eileen Yeo and Stephen Yeo, eds., *Popular Culture and Class Conflict, 1590–1914: Explorations in the History of Labor and Leisure* (Atlantic Highlands, N.J.: Humanities Press, 1981), 1–27; S. K. Roberts, "Alehouses, Brewing, and Government under the Early Stuarts," *Southern History* 2 (1980), 58.

50. James W. Fernandez, *Persuasions and Performances: The Play of Tropes in Culture* (Bloomington: Indiana University Press, 1986), 73–102, 103–27.

the threads of community life.[51] In sabbath services the community was enacted in the hierarchical seating arrangements of the congregation and in the various ritual performances that gave meaning to the seasons of the agricultural calendar. Even in communities that experienced some measure of division over the terms of the Protestant Reformation, the church remained a core element in the experience of ordinary men and women. Church practices cemented kinship alliances through the ceremonies of marriage, and the sermons and pageants of the pastor focused group values on a common and easily understood set of moral principles. Any attempt on the part of elite outsiders to manipulate the integrity of community control of the religious experience could produce widespread hostility, and, as C. S. L. Davies has shown for the Pilgrimage of Grace of 1536, in limiting cases elite interference with popular religion could lead to open rebellion.[52]

Community rituals linked the patterns of economic and political cooperation into a coherent whole, and they should not be underestimated in any explanation of rural community in England. Ritual life implicated its participants in mutual relations of hierarchy and reciprocity that cut across occupational and social division. Ritual was also the medium that invested mundane life with a sense of purpose and meaning by demonstrating and dramatizing the need for solidarity in the face of adversity. More important, the persistence of local ritual underscores the analytic fruitfulness of interpreting English rural history in terms of community institutions.

Enclosure Riots and the Defense of Community, 1500–1800

The publication of R. H. Tawney's classic, *The Agrarian Problem in the Sixteenth Century,* began a long debate about the meaning of enclosure in English history.[53] Tawney believed enclosure, especially enclosure that shifted land from arable to sheep pasture, had gradually undermined English peasant society. Enclosure extinguished secure copyhold tenures, depopulated the countryside, and led to the eventual domination of the landlord and the large-scale farmer. Although Tawney gave considerable attention to popular resistance to enclosure, he

---

51. See Geoffrey R. Elton, *Policy and Police: The Enforcement of the Reformation in the Age of Thomas Cromwell* (Cambridge: Cambridge University Press, 1972), 170; Keith Thomas, *Religion and the Decline of Magic* (New York: Scribners', 1971), 151–59; Spufford, *Contrasting Communities,* esp. 233–351; James Obelkevich, *Religion and Rural Society: South Lindsey, 1825–1875* (Oxford: Clarendon Press, 1976), esp. 103–82, 259–312; and David Underdown, *Revel, Riot, and Rebellion,* 48–55.

52. C. S. L. Davies, "The Pilgrimage of Grace Reconsidered," in Slack, *Rebellion, Popular Protest, and the Social Order,* 16–38; C. S. L. Davies, "Popular Religion and the Pilgrimage of Grace," in Fletcher and Stevenson, *Order and Disorder in Early Modern England,* 58–91.

53. Tawney, *The Agrarian Problem in the Sixteenth Century,* esp. 231–313. Also see the useful discussion of Tawney and E. Kerridge in Charlesworth, "The Geography of Land Protests, 1548–1860: Lowland England 1520–95," in Charlesworth, *An Atlas of Rural Protest in Britain,* 8–15.

ultimately found the history of agrarian change in England to be negative, and he seems to have believed that enclosure represented a catastrophe for smallholders and laborers.

Tawney's argument was subjected to searching criticism from the time of its publication, but it was Eric Kerridge who became Tawney's most persuasive opponent.[54] Kerridge showed that, even in areas where enclosure was most advanced, it did not result in the social disaster that Tawney assumed. Indeed, Kerridge gave an extremely optimistic gloss to the process of enclosure, and he argued that enclosure led to increased economic well-being for both smallholders and large farmers. Moreover, he saw enclosure as a patient and rational process of mutual negotiation, rather than as a brutal imposition of class power by an avaricious landlord elite.[55]

Neither Tawney's pessimism nor Kerridge's optimism has been completely accepted by social historians who have written the agrarian history of England from the standpoint of local society. Tawney definitely exaggerated the consequences and timing of enclosure, and he tended to underestimate the extent to which enclosure was supported by smallholders, especially in the period 1500–1700. Kerridge, however, denied the reality of popular opposition to certain kinds of enclosure, and he underestimated the extent of depopulation that often occurred when marginal cultivators and laboring cottagers were pushed off the land following an enclosure agreement.[56] Finally, both Tawney and Kerridge failed to recognize the possibility that enclosure was not an inexorable process driven by the logic of capitalism or economic efficiency. As the work of M. Havinden, Hoskins, and Thirsk has shown, enclosure was not an absolutely necessary precondition for agricultural improvement, and considerable increases in productivity and output were possible in open-field agriculture.[57] This is an important finding, because it

54. Eric Kerridge, *The Agricultural Revolution* (London: Allen and Unwin, 1967), *Agrarian Problems in the Sixteenth Century and After* (London: Allen and Unwin, 1969), and "The Revolts in Wiltshire against Charles I," *Wiltshire Archaeological and Natural History Magazine* 57 (1958–59).

55. Kerridge, *Agrarian Problems*, 94–111, 119–33. For enclosure generally, see A. B. Appleby, "Agrarian Capitalism or Seigneurial Reaction? The North West of England, 1500–1700," *American Historical Review* 80 (1975), 574–94; A. B. Appleby, "Common Land and Peasant Unrest in Sixteenth Century England: A Comparative Note," *Peasant Studies Newsletter* 4 (July 1975), 20–23; P. Croot and D. Parker, "Agrarian Class Structure and Economic Development," *Past and Present* 78 (1978); B. A. Holderness, "Open and Closed Parishes in England in the Eighteenth and Nineteenth Centuries," *Agricultural History Review* 20 (1972), 126–39; Thirsk, "Enclosing and Engrossing," in Thirsk, *AHEW*, 4: 200–255; W. E. Tate, "Opposition to Parliamentary Enclosure in Eighteenth Century England," *Agricultural History* 19 (1945), 137–42; Michael E. Turner, *English Parliamentary Enclosure: Its Historical Geography and Economic History* (London: Folkestone, 1980); and S. J. Watts, "Tenant Right in Early Seventeenth Century Northumberland," *Northern History* 6 (1971), 64–87.

56. Charlesworth, *An Atlas of Rural Protest in Britain*, esp. Introduction, 1–7, and "The Geography of Land Protests, 1548–1860," 8–62. "The Geography of Land Protests" includes sections by John Martin ("The Midland Revolt of 1607," 33–36), John W. Leopold ("The Levellers' Revolt in Galloway 1724," 44–48), and Jeanette M. Neeson ("Opposition to Enclosure in Northamptonshire, c. 1760–1800," 60–62).

57. M. Havinden, "Agricultural Progress in Open-Field Oxfordshire," *Agricultural History*

forces us to see enclosure in political and social rather than purely economic terms. Whether enclosure occurred early or late had as much to do with the local balance of political power as it did with the "iron laws" of the capitalist market.

Part of the endless debate about enclosure can be attributed to the fact that enclosure was not a uniform process with a simple, invariant meaning. Enclosure is a capacious term that masks broad local, regional, and chronological differences.[58] At a minimum, enclosure involved the transfer of land use from scattered parcels held jointly to hedged or fenced farms held in severalty. But beyond this simple minimum, enclosure had multiple meanings and widely divergent social implications. To begin with, we must distinguish between the "private" enclosures of the sixteenth and seventeenth centuries and the "parliamentary" enclosures of the late eighteenth and early nineteenth centuries. In the earlier period, enclosure occurred in the context of a long-term squeeze on prices and profits that put considerable pressure on landlords to raise rents through enclosure. In the latter period, enclosure took place against a backdrop of very rapid urban and industrial growth that made technical improvements attractive investments and that led to enclosure acts that were designed to clear away institutional obstacles to innovation. As Snell has pointed out, it was enclosure in the later period that had perhaps the worst social consequences in terms of underemployment and dispossession, something that may be partly explained by a change in the nature of community institutions.[59]

For our purposes, however, the most interesting variation in the patterns of enclosure has to do with the different kinds of popular political responses that occurred in the wake of enclosure. Especially in the period 1500–1700, violent opposition, called enclosure rioting, met the enclosing projects of the landed elite with sufficient regularity to become a well-recognized problem. How can we account for the presence or absence of enclosure rioting, and how does it relate to the institutions of popular community discussed in the previous section?

At the outset, it is useful to provide at least a crude quantitative overview of the dimensions of the problem. According to Roger B. Manning, perhaps the most careful student of the subject, there were 30 to 35 regional rebellions in England between 1381 and 1685.[60] If we subtract *all* these from the total we are still left

---

Review 9 (1961), 73–83; Hoskins, *The Midland Peasant,* 164; Joan Thirsk, "Agrarian History, 1540–1950," in *Victoria County History of Leicestershire* (Oxford, 1954), 2:212, 221.

58. See, for instance, Thirsk's "Enclosing and Engrossing."

59. Snell, *Annals of the Labouring Poor,* 138–227, 334–43.

60. Manning, *Village Revolts,* 1. Also see Fryde, *The Great Revolt of 1381;* Charlesworth, *An Atlas of Rural Protest in Britain;* and, for a sense of the methodological issues and problems, R. A. E. Wells, "Counting Riots in Eighteenth Century England," *Bulletin of the Society for the Study of Labour History* 37 (1978). The whole question of popular collective violence in rural England gains perspective when placed in the context of English crime and violence. See J. M. Beattie, "The Pattern of Crime in England, 1660–1800," *Past and Present* 62 (1974); J. S. Cockburn, ed., *Crime in England, 1550–1800* (Princeton: Princeton University Press, 1977); Douglas Hay, "War, Dearth, and

with 298 known cases of enclosure rioting between the accession of Henry VIII and the end of the reign of James I, a period of roughly 140 years.[61] Although even this level of precision is difficult for the period after 1640, it is evident that enclosure rioting continued into the 1700s, albeit at a reduced level after the 1680s.[62] Obviously, enclosure rioting had visibility and persistence in the English landscape that gives the phenomenon more than antiquarian interest. Yet it is equally true that enclosure did not automatically provoke violent resistance, and the "optimistic" historians who have followed Kerridge have been able to show many cases of enclosure based on amicable agreements between manor lords and commoners.

What accounts for this difference? Any number of demographic and economic factors have been used to explain the presence or absence of concerted popular opposition to enclosure. For example, population pressure on a fixed supply of land has been employed as a key factor by Roger Manning, who argues that the sixteenth-century upswing of the demographic curve made common rights increasingly significant for smallholders, precisely the group that would be most resistant to any loss of use rights.[63] Similarly, the landed elite's decision to enclose has been linked to the strategy of using enclosure as a means of extinguishing copyhold tenures that were resistant to market forces. The logic here is that customary tenancies had become so encrusted with legal and conventional protections that landlords found it impossible to respond flexibly to the price inflation of the 1500s; enclosure was therefore useful as a means of abolishing the smallholders who stood between landed privilege and enhanced rent rolls.[64]

It would be foolish to deny the significance of economic or "structural" factors in any explanation of the origins and consequences of enclosure. But these kinds of approaches tend to underestimate the importance of politics and institutions. Specifically, we must try to think through the ways in which power affected the course of enclosure in the context of local communities. We must address the question of why enclosure turned into a politics of violent confrontation with sufficient frequency to have become a matter both for government concern and later historical scholarship.

Theft in the Eighteenth Century: The Record of the English Courts," *Past and Present* 95 (May 1982), 117–60; Cynthia B. Herrup, "Law and Morality in Seventeenth Century England," *Past and Present* 106 (1985), 102–23; John H. Langbein, "Albion's Fatal Flaws," *Past and Present* 98 (1983), 96–120; and Lawrence Stone, "Interpersonal Violence in English Society, 1300–1980," *Past and Present* 101 (1983), 22–33.

61. This is my estimate based on the data in Manning, *Village Revolts*, 322–27.

62. See Charlesworth, *An Atlas of Rural Protest in Britain*, 41–62. But also see Bohstedt, *Riots and Community Politics*, 165–201.

63. Manning, *Village Revolts*, 9–30, and "Violence and Social Conflict in Mid-Tudor Rebellions."

64. The best short and incisive statement of this, which discusses early enclosure as an example of aristocratic domination and "seigneurial reaction," is Charlesworth, *An Atlas of Rural Protest In Britain*, 1–22.

One plausible suggestion is that enclosure generated violent opposition when it threatened to destroy the autonomy and cohesion of the kinds of community institutions discussed earlier. If a powerful elite interest, determined to carry out enclosure as a unilateral act, undermined the institutional basis of popular life, we would expect revolt to be a possible response. For example, if enclosure put at risk the whole complex of use rights and procedural protections that were part of the early modern manor, we could expect the intensity of the threat to result in the self-mobilization of the village against the extinction of the manor. Similarly, an attempted enclosure that failed to gain widespread consent in a closely knit community would end in a situation conducive of a direct clash between the "encloser" and the community as a whole. To put the matter as bluntly as possible, there were two political paths to enclosure with very different implications for local political order. In cases in which enclosure occurred as a unilateral transformation of local practices of property and authority, the state was set for a violent clash of interests. But in cases in which enclosure occurred through a compromise of interests that gained community consent, the way was clear for an orderly settlement. The distinction between enclosure as a unilateral act of (typically) elite will and enclosure as a compromise of mutually negotiated interests is meant to show the *necessary* preconditions for enclosure rioting. In order to draw the *sufficient* conditions, we would have to introduce contextual factors that were highly specific to regions and localities. For example, we should expect unilateral enclosure to have generated maximum opposition in densely populated manorial villages that had strong institutional solidarity.

How well does this argument stand up against the historical record? Although it is not yet possible to provide an aggregate statistical survey of ecological correlations that might prove or disprove the case, my statement of the issues at least provides a testable analysis that future scholars may pursue. More important, the reintroduction of politics into our understanding of enclosure helps to resolve an apparent anomaly in the historical literatures. As pointed out earlier, "optimists" and "pessimists" have never been able to agree about the nature of enclosure. Pessimists have seen enclosure as a violent and disruptive event, while optimists have interpreted enclosure as a beneficent and amicable process.[65] Both positions, I believe, are plausible, because each focuses on a distinct political pattern of enclosure. The enclosure process involved a political conflict over the question of who had the authority to define the terms and timing of the institutional changes that enclosure brought to popular communities throughout England. It is important to remember that enclosure could be much more than a shift from open fields to closes. Enclosure could affect everything from rent levels to the ability of cottagers to keep a cow or a garden.[66]

---

65. The strongest statement of the optimists is Chambers and Mingay, *The Agricultural Revolution*. For the pessimists see Hammond and Hammond, *The Village Labourer*.
66. See Manning, *Village Revolts,* 9–30.

We can gain a clearer understanding of the politics of enclosure by sketching the logic of a typical enclosure riot. This involves a stylization of complex events, but it has the advantage of highlighting the kinds of issues that were at stake when enclosure turned violent.

Enclosure rioting usually began when an elite landowner, either a member of the gentry or aristocracy or a landed merchant, tried to undercut local custom by arbitrarily enclosing arable or wasteland. The decision to enclose was made easier by the ambiguities of the common law that gave some degree of discretion to royal and manorial landlords. In the background of the enclosure decision was a process of agricultural "improvement" that had not resulted in a sufficient enhancement of rent or the other prerogatives of estate ownership.[67]

Rioting began when the tenants and freeholders of an enclosing landlord mobilized for a direct assault on the hedges and fences that symbolized the physical loss of common rights and community control. The numbers of rioters could reach several hundred, and in some cases, women as well as men took an active role.[68] Usually, riotous communities were solicitous of human life, most of the violence that occurred having as its target the property of the offending proprietor. Enclosure was expensive, and the destruction of fences and hedges was both a substantial property loss and a physical mark of ritual humiliation.

Once the riot had occurred the proprietor was on the defensive, forced to react to the sudden disruption of his plans. If a victim of rioting did nothing, the disputed property would revert to commons or open fields under the control of his tenants. But if he chose to fight back he had a wide variety of courses of action, all of which were expensive, time consuming, and uncertain. Prior to the mid-seventeenth century, he could bring an action for riot in the Court of Star Chamber, or he could sue at common law for trespass or assault.[69] The most certain course, however, was to get the crown to establish an enclosure commission that would arbitrate a mutually acceptable outcome. During the 1500s and early 1600s, many enclosure riots were ended in just this way.[70]

Nevertheless, there was no guarantee that even a royal commission could resolve the problem, and some enclosure disputes smoldered on for anything from ten to forty years. Much depended on the willingness of the lord or proprietor to reach an acceptable agreement with at least the bulk of freeholders and copyholders affected by enclosure. In the absence of an accord, the opposition to an unpopular enclosure could evidently become part of local folklore, capable of

---

67. For these points see ibid., 1–54, and Thompson, *Whigs and Hunters*, 108, 133–34, 171–79, 219–69.

68. Manning, *Village Revolts*, 96–98, 114–15.

69. Ibid., 26–27. For a fuller description of the legal aspects, see Association of American Law Schools, *Select Essays in Anglo-American Legal History*, 3 vols. (Boston: Little, Brown, 1907–9), ii, 589; Michael Dalton, *The Country Justice: Containing the Practice, Duty, and Power of the Justices of the Peace, in as well as out of Their Session* (London: William Rawlins and Samuel Roycroft, 1690), esp. 177.

70. Manning, *Village Revolts*, 108–31.

erupting at any time. For example, an enclosure project initiated by the earl of Pembroke in the 1560s resulted in a violent encounter some fifty years later.[71]

It would be false to exaggerate the "seditious" nature or "revolutionary" potential of enclosure riots. Most were small-scale affairs, usually involving no more than a single village or parish, and this fact was recognized at law by the distinction between a mere misdemeanor riot that affected only a single village and a treasonous riot that involved a general attack on the principle of enclosure. English elites evidently regarded the former event as somehow a "natural" response to local problems.[72]

Yet the small-scale nature of the enclosure riot is exactly what we should expect. Enclosure rioting is an excellent illustration of the defense of community autonomy and integrity through the act of representative violence. Rioting was a representation of community power exhibited to protect the communities against the loss of authoritative control over the conditions of landholding. The act of destroying hedges, for example, challenged the basis of elite power and questioned the tacit social constitution on which enclosure rested. The destruction of offending hedges and fences drew a clear moral boundary around acceptable and unacceptable behavior and challenged the encloser to negotiate an acceptable settlement. Ironically, it was the encloser who had acted in an unbounded manner by violating the institutional boundaries of local community power.

We might also speculate that enclosure rioting reached its greatest intensity and duration when enclosure brought in its wake the elimination of secure hereditary tenures.[73] By the 1500s, originally servile tenures had become secure property rights that resembled freehold or allodial property, a fact that was respected by manorial and common law.[74] This was "copyhold" tenure, and, as mentioned earlier, it was extremely important to the enclosure debate. Copyholders were immune to most forms of rapid rent increases, although large fines could be imposed when the heir of a copyholder assumed the tenement or estate.[75] By the sixteenth century, however, even the right of manor lords to exact fines at will had begun to disappear, and certain fines ascertainable through the manorial rolls had replaced the arbitrary fines, or heriots, that had once marked the limits of lordly privilege. Finally, copyholders could sell and bequeath their land and chattels with minimal elite interference, as indicated by the inability of manor lords to extract the traditional dues and labor services that had once attached to servile tenures. As

71. Ibid., 272–76.

72. Ibid., 55–56. Also see Sir William Holdsworth, *A History of English Law,* 13 vols. (Boston: Little, Brown, 1922–52), 8:327–38; Sir Matthew Hale, *Historia Placitorum Coronae: The History of the Pleas of the Crown,* 2 vols. (London: T. Payne, 1800), 1:145.

73. This was perhaps the key insight of Tawney, *The Agrarian Problem in the Sixteenth Century,* 19–54.

74. See Peter Bowden, "Agricultural Prices, Farm Profits, and Rents," in Thirsk, *AHEW* 4:593–695, esp. 681–86.

75. The most lucid discussion of this is found in Lawrence Stone, *The Crisis of the Aristocracy, 1558–1641* (Oxford: Clarendon Press, 1979), 303–23.

Tawney recognized, copyhold was a profound block to the power and pretensions of engrossing landlords and large-scale merchant farmers.[76]

Enclosure offered an obvious means of breaking copyholder power, but only if enclosure led to the complete transformation of copyhold into leases for lives, years, or terms that could be rack-rented, or adjusted periodically to take advantage of market forces. In order to effect this happy result, however, the landlord had to link enclosure to an extinction of all customary tenancies and common rights.[77] This was both legally difficult and subject to the kind of riotous opposition that could drag disputes on for decades. It is not surprising that copyholders and other secure customary tenants show up in the historical record as leaders and fomenters of enclosure rights, especially when their stake as community leaders was put at risk by an "engrossing" landlord.

It would be tempting to view the problem of the copyholder as a pure essay in class politics. But this is a temptation worth resisting, because enclosure riots display too much social complexity to be reduced to the work of a specific class, no matter how broadly class is defined. For example, in Tudor and Stuart enclosure riots we can find a wide range of occupational categories and types of property holders involved on the side of the rioters. Smallholders and large farmers, part-time artisans and laborers, and even members of the village gentry were all caught up in the defense of community institutions.[78] English social categories were relatively fluid, and the membership of a local community could stretch from the petty farming gentry to the landless and land poor.[79] What bound all of them together were the mutually implicated forms of cooperation that made a village or parish an ongoing institutional enterprise. More important, it was the defense of that community against unacceptable forms of outside interference that bound the poor and the prosperous together in times of crisis. The unilateral imposition of an enclosure project by a powerful outsider was precisely a moment of crisis during which community solidarity became most important.

If we understand the enclosure riot in terms of the logic of community, we can

76. Tawney, *The Agrarian Problem in the Sixteenth Century*, 19–54.

77. Thirsk, "Enclosing and Engrossing," 240–55; M. Beresford, "Habitation versus Improvement: The Debate on Enclosure by Agreement," in F. J. Fisher, ed., *Essays in the Economic and Social History of Tudor and Stuart England, in Honour of R. H. Tawney* (Cambridge: Cambridge University Press, 1961), 46–69; and R. W. Hoyle, "Lords, Tenants, and Tenant Rights in the Sixteenth Century: Four Studies," *Northern History* 20 (1984), 38–63.

78. See the social breakdowns and profiles in Manning, *Village Revolts*, 322–24.

79. See, for example, the evidence in Sharp, *In Contempt of All Authority*, 126–74. The fluidity of English social categories and its importance for both "vertical" solidarity and social mobility is a much-discussed subject. See Harold Perkin, *The Origins of Modern English Society, 1780–1880* (London: Routledge and Kegan Paul, 1969), 17–38, 56–62. For an approach that recognizes the importance of "fluid" but vertical and deferential social relations, consult the following essays by E. P. Thompson: "The Peculiarities of the English," in R. Miliband and J. Saville, eds., *The Socialist Register, 1974* (London: Merlin Press, 1974); "The Moral Economy of the English Crowd in the Eighteenth Century," *Past and Present* 50 (1971), 76–136; "Rough Music: Le charivari anglais," *Annales: Economies, Sociétés, Civilisations* 27 (1972), 285–313; and "Patrician Society, Plebian Culture," *Journal of Social History* 7 (4) (1974), 382–405.

also gain a more perspicuous understanding of the vexing problem of gentry participation in English popular violence. Some historians have made much of the fact that members of the gentry were sometimes involved in promoting enclosure riots.[80] This has led to much discussion of whether enclosure riots were manipulated by the gentry for their own ends. We do not have to deny the possibility of manipulation in order to see that this way of posing the issue is too simple. After all, enclosure riots occurred in the absence of gentry participation, which indicates the danger of seeing the English gentry as a rigid class category that must always be defined in terms of objective economic relations. Like all European nobilities, the English aristocracy was as much a social and political as an economic group, and the definition of who fit into its lowest rung, the local gentry, was as much a function of reputation as it was of occupation.[81]

Gentry participation loses its strange and manipulative character if we place it in the context of community politics. In many instances, the gentry were ordinary members of their communities, bound by the same reciprocal hierarchies that linked copyholders and laborers. This was particularly true of the farming gentry, whose economic position was little different from that of well-off tenants, and whose social world was strongly bounded by the village or parish. These were people who could be regarded as local leaders or protectors, and their willingness to support community action was closely tied to their own interest in the survival of community institutions.

But, in contrast to the community gentry, there were also gentry and peers who had little stake in the survival of community practices, and whose power and prestige lay in the supralocal networks of authority that resided in the court and the institutions of county government.[82] These were the powerful outsiders who were behind the unilateral enclosure of arable and waste, and their interests were often best served by reducing the autonomy of community institutions. Strong local community networks could only stand in the way of their ability to assert dominion over the land, as well as standing in the way of an enhancement of their wealth and status.

In earlier chapters I argued that aristocratic domination and coercive commercialization can be interpreted as forces of elite constraint that both threaten community autonomy and help to explain the origins of community revolt. This

80. See the discussion in Manning, *Village Revolts,* 31–54, 309–19.

81. This point is clearly made in Mark A. Kishlansky, *Parliamentary Selection: Social and Political Choice in Early Modern England* (Cambridge: Cambridge University Press, 1986), ix–xiii, 3–21. Also see Gordon Batho, "Landlords in England: Noblemen, Gentlemen, and Yeomen," in Thirsk, *AHEW,* 4:276–305.

82. Stone, *The Crisis of the Aristocracy,* 21–64; Perez Zagorin, *Rebels and Rulers: 1500–1660,* 2 vols. (Cambridge: Cambridge University Press, 1982), 1:61–86; Conrad Russell, *Parliaments and English Politics, 1621–1629* (Oxford: Clarendon Press, 1979), esp. chaps. 1 and 2; and Perez Zagorin, *The Court and the Country: The Beginning of the English Revolution* (New York: Atheneum, 1970), 19–32.

model seems to fit the problem of enclosure fairly well. In some cases, enclosure was undertaken unilaterally by the aristocracy to destroy agrarian communities in order to make way for deer parks and forests, the two great emblems of English lordship.[83] In other instances, enclosure was used to force people and property literally into the market, as Snell has shown for the late eighteenth century.[84]

An entire monograph would be necessary to untangle the precise chronology and social meaning of enclosure in the various regions of England. By focusing on enclosure as a problem of elite power and popular politics, however, we can begin to make sense out of the puzzles that have been at the heart of the enclosure debate since the days of Tawney. We must think of enclosure as a political process of conflict and compromise that should be situated in a local context of negotiated power.

The logic of seeing the enclosure riot as a community revolt against the constraining impact of elite power can be usefully illustrated by focusing on two specific cases of enclosure that resulted in violence. The first, drawn from early-seventeenth-century Bedfordshire, is a good example of the exercise of arbitrary aristocratic power and its close association with unilateral enclosure. The second comes from eighteenth-century Staffordshire; and it neatly illustrates the consequences of coercive commercialization in a compact community that could still resist the unilateral use of elite power.

The Bedfordshire incident occurred during the early Stuart period when the earl of Kent, a titled member of the high nobility, tried to enclose nine acres of waste by fiat. Wasteland was essential for both smallholders and large farmers, who used it to pasture the cows and draft animals that were essential for arable farming. The earl, however, was more interested in turning the disputed land into a horse pasture, probably because horse breeding was a mark of aristocratic privilege. In any event, the earl had not negotiated any settlement satisfactory to the tenants who were dispossessed, and he soon faced a well-organized riot that lasted for two days. Interestingly, the riot was organized by the village constable, which shows that the riot was not simply the work of the village poor, since village constables were usually drawn from the moderately well off householders of the neighborhood. In this case, the constable, a man named Robert Ball, gathered the villagers in the local church and collected forty shillings from every tenant for a "common purse" that was to be used when the tenants prosecuted the earl at law.[85]

83. The issues of game laws, forests, and emparkment are treated in P. B. Munsche, *Gentlemen and Poachers, The English Game Laws, 1671–1831* (Cambridge: Cambridge University Press, 1981); Chester Kirby and Ethyn Kirby, "The Stuart Game Prerogative," *English History Review* 46 (Apr. 1931), 239–54; and Thompson, *Whigs and Hunters*, esp. 27–54.

84. Snell, *Annals of the Labouring Poor*, 138–227. Also see the remarks of some contemporaries that seem to show the logic of coercive commercialization: Arthur Young, *An Inquiry into the Propriety of Applying Wastes to the Better Maintenance and Support of the Poor* (Bury: J. Rackham, 1801), 51; and T. Stone, *Suggestions for Rendering the Inclosure of Common Fields and Waste Lands, a Source of Population and of Riches* (London: J. Nichols, 1787).

85. Manning, *Village Revolts*, 100–102.

Ball was evidently a rather cautious figure, however, and he managed to absent himself from the actual riot. Before leaving the scene, Ball appointed an informal deputy, one Thomas Reyner, who may have been an alehouse keeper or a seller of what Americans would call moonshine.

Along with a deputy constable, Reyner led the village against the earl's enclosures; and the tenants themselves grouped into two paramilitary companies that numbered some sixty persons and included wives and female farm servants. According to the testimony cited in Roger Manning's *Village Revolts*, when this riotous assembly had gathered they marched to the enclosure where "one Thomas Reyner, a dissolute fellow, a rogue and one who wandered about the country selling of acquavite, whom they used as captain of their riotous and rebellious assembly, while they, all weaponed . . . came marching in warlike and rebellious manner to the said close. . . . And the saide Thomas Reyner . . . in most riotous and rebellious manner, flourishing his staff which he then had above his head, cried out with a loud voice: Now for King James and for the commons of Blunham."[86]

Here we see a community mobilized through the institutions of ordinary life. The assembly that plotted the riot met in the church, a potent focus of identity in rural England. Appropriately, the leader of the riot was the village constable, the man most responsible for enforcing daily order. The common purse that he exacted was both an insurance against future needs and a symbol of the collective identity of the village. Like religious oaths, the collection of a common fund was a statement of commitment and obligation, a drawing of boundaries between insiders and outsiders. Finally, the military demeanor of the rioters shows both the influence of militia training and a determination to enforce the village's conception of authority in the face of an imperious aristocrat. Indeed, it is tempting to read the events at Blunham as a kind of enactment or performance of the community's customary sense of law and justice.

The second example of enclosure rioting, drawn from the sensitive account of Douglas Hay, pierces the shadows that often surround the analysis of English agricultural modernization and helps to clarify the logic of coercion and commerce in the English countryside.[87] The trouble began about 1690, when the seventh earl of Uxbridge decided to turn his properties at Cannock Chase into a profitable enterprise by granting a lease to a "warrener," or rabbit keeper, who was charged with turning a large chunk of the local property into a commercial rabbit farm. The warrener dug up part of the waste and began to dig burrows. It was a classic instance of enclosure, because it involved a sudden and unilateral destruction of use rights. Moreover, the attempt to create a rabbit farm doubly

86. Ibid., 101.
87. Douglas Hay, "Poaching and the Game Laws on Cannock Chase," in Hay et al., *Albion's Fatal Tree*, 189–254.

burdened the local community. It left the commoners insufficient common, and it threatened to deluge the whole neighborhood with rabbits, whose voracious appetites were the scourge of farmers. Even worse, commoners were forbidden from killing rabbits by the game laws, and rabbits formed a species of privileged property reserved for the aristocracy, along with entails and game parks. In fact, it was the aristocratic mark of rabbits and other wild game that made rabbits a valuable commercial investment, because rabbit meat had a high prestige value in polite society.[88]

What the earl was trying to do was patently obvious to the community of laborers, farmers, and artisans who inhabited the chase. He was trying coercively to commercialize his estate, regardless of the consequences for his tenants. Unfortunately for the lord of the manor, his plans went sour when a riot occurred that, according to the testimony provided by Hay, began when "the freeholders came and dug the Burroughs and trod them in as he made them, and catched the rabbits what they could, at which . . . Ellis (the warrener) was very much dissatisfied, and upon that took his horse and went to London to Mr. Peter Walters who was then my Lords Stewart to acquaint him there with, the said Mr. Walters replied, that he would have him go and kill the rabbits, and go back into his country again . . . for neither my Lord nor could help him, for if the freeholders etc. had a mind to come and destroy them they might."[89]

The last line in this passage is especially suggestive. It hints at the tenuous nature of lordly power in the face of concerted community opposition, and it also indicates that the manor lord may have been uncertain about his legal position. Even at the end of the seventeenth century it was possible for commoner communities to prosecute their lords; an outcome that may have been easier in a case that could be construed as a public nuisance caused by the presence of hordes of otherwise protected rabbits.

In any event, the trouble did not stop here. In 1710 the lord tried to "warren" his land again, and again his tenants destroyed the burrows. This rhythm of challenge and popular response extended on into 1713 and the rule of the eighth baron, in spite of a stirring harangue by the lord's steward, who informed the commoners that their common rights to pasture were "totally subservient to his Lordship's Paramount or original right."[90] This excellent example of the pretensions of aristocratic domination evidently failed to move the populace, and they managed to extract a promise from the estate's heir that he would eventually destroy the rabbits.

Finally, in 1753, matters came to a head. The rabbits had not been eliminated, and the villagers at Cannock Chase still coveted their common rights. Some of the

88. Ibid., 189–220.
89. Ibid., 221–22.
90. Ibid., 222.

more prosperous villagers took the case to court. When this maneuver failed, the community mobilized for an elaborate riot that lasted for two weeks and saw the participation of between two hundred and three hundred men. The rioters actually sent messages into Leicestershire calling for help, and the town crier of Walsall was paid to announce that any man who joined the "Free Company" on Cannock Chase would be given meat, drink, and 156 pence a day. Although this call for help was probably done for ritual effect, the actual riot was a well-planned effort. The rioters practiced a paramilitary discipline, following the leadership of a "Charlie" or Charles Marshall. On the day of the affair, the rioters, with brooms and rushes in their hats, marched in military style past the manor house and gave three cheers. Then, after the blowing of a trumpet, they hoisted a hat on a stick for colors and marched to the rabbit warrens where they killed ten to fifteen thousand rabbits worth £3,000, a phenomenal sum by eighteenth-century standards.[91]

It should be clear that whatever its ultimate outcome the events at Cannock cannot be described as the work of a wretched or hopeless people. The rioters were willing to pursue a course of violent action that stretched over the course of some fifty years, and they were able to use both "legal" and extralegal strategies in order to preserve the autonomy and integrity of their community. More important, their behavior was neither primitive nor purely reactive. They had clear goals, solid organization, and a commitment to their version of justice. They were undoubtedly responding to a real threat, but their persistence, like their manipulation of the law, shows that they were able to seize the initiative from their lord. In the end, one wonders exactly who the victim was in this miniature political contest. At the core of the dispute was a struggle for local social hegemony: Would the lord or the community have ultimate authority over Cannock Chase? There was no clear answer to this question, because in the clash of interests we see a clash of what Keith Wrightson has called "two concepts of order."[92] One order was the world of high status and aristocratic dominion represented by the earl. The other was the order of the village, with its reciprocal hierarchies of obligation and consent. It was this clash, rather than some abstract class struggle, that gave meaning to the seemingly bizarre war against the privileged rabbits of a market-oriented aristocrat and his heirs.

Neither Cannock Chase nor Blunham, Bedfordshire, can be seen as absolutely typical or representative in any rigid sense, but neither were they atypical or extraneous to the dynamics of English rural history.[93] Still, incidents like these

91. Ibid., 226–29.
92. Wrightson, "Two Concepts of Order." Also see Walter J. King, "Vagrancy and Local Law Enforcement: Why Be a Constable in Stuart Lancashire?" *Historian* 42 (Feb. 1980), 264–83; Cynthia Herrup, "New Shoes and Mutton Pies: Investigative Responses to Theft in Seventeenth Century East Sussex," *Historical Journal* 27 (4) (1984), 811–30; and, for the role of justices of the peace in the local and county power structures, Norma Landau, *The Justices of the Peace, 1679–1760* (Berkeley: University of California Press, 1984), esp. 1–68, 173–268.
93. Charlesworth, "The Geography of Land Protests."

two help us to understand the importance of paying attention to the local context in which grand "macro" forces, like enclosure, must be placed. When we take the view from below we see the need to attend to politics and community.

The enclosure riot is also important as a marker of community violence in England. It was a rebellion in miniature, a radical challenge to elite definitions of property and authority that could change the local balance of social power. But radicalism must not be confused with revolution, and the radicalism of the enclosure riot was confined to a direct and fundamental challenge to the *local* forces of constraint that impinged on community life. This was representative rather than revolutionary violence, as the rioters at Blunham demonstrated when they prefaced their action with a shout for the king. The rioters remained loyal to the traditions of monarchy and magistracy, even as they represented their community in a show of force that aimed at redrawing the local constitution of power. Their enemies were particular members of the local and supralocal elite who had used hedges to violate the boundaries of community institutions.

From Norfolk to the Midlands Rising: Regional Rebellion in Early Modern England

Sometime in June of 1549, the villagers of Attleborough, Norfolk, destroyed the enclosures of a certain John Green, Gentleman of Wilby.[94] The villagers charged Green with enclosing part of their common pasture; and up to this point, there is little to distinguish the events of 1549 from a typical enclosure riot. The events at Attleborough, however, were somehow carried to Wymondham, another village with a local market where, on July 6, a crowd had gathered to celebrate a play called Wymondham Game. At some point, another enclosure riot ensued, and during its course the rioters destroyed the enclosures of another member of the elite, John Flowerdew, a substantial lawyer and estate owner. It was at this juncture that an enraged Flowerdew called for the crowd to attack the enclosures of a commoner named Robert Kett. Kett, perhaps taken aback by this turn of events, agreed that his enclosures should be "thrown down and made even with the ground," and he proceeded to help the rioters demolish his enclosures.[95]

According to the standard narrative, Kett then delivered an oration in which he promised to join the rebels and lead them in a rebellion against the power of aristocratic "great men." Thus was born the odd legend of Robert Kett, the tanner and husbandman whose name would be attached to the great revolt of 1549.[96]

94. Beer, *Rebellion and Riot*, 82.
95. Ibid., 83–84.
96. For the long and complex history and historiography of Kett's Rebellion, see S. T. Bindoff, *Kett's Rebellion, 1549* (London: Historical Association, 1949); Julian Cornwall, *The Revolt of the Peasantry, 1549* (London: Routledge and Kegan Paul, 1977), esp. 8–63, 137–59; C. S. L. Davies,

It was unlikely that Kett "caused" the revolt, although the personal charisma of the man cannot be entirely discounted. But there can be no doubt that the incidents associated with his name rapidly escalated into a regional insurrection that frontally challenged the power of the gentry and peerage throughout the county of Norfolk, as well as parts of Suffolk.[97] By July 9 the rebels had amassed an army of several thousand, armed with cannon and armor. Apart from destroying enclosures and capturing members of the landed elite, Kett's followers created fortified encampments, called "parks," on the area known as Mousehold Heath. The peak of the revolt came when the rebels captured Norwich, the second city of the realm with a population of some thirteen thousand. Eventually, the forces of elite power countermobilized and defeated the rebels, although not without first suffering a serious loss of prestige.

Before the final showdown, however, the rebels inflicted a stinging series of ritual humiliations on captured members of the landed elite. On Mousehold Heath, under a great oak called the Tree of Reformation, Kett and his "governors" passed judicial sentences on captive gentlemen, who were subjected to insults and degradation by the crowds. Most of these men were eventually released, but their rough handling, so reminiscent of the treatment meted out in village charivari rituals, was a permanent reminder of the fragile character of landed power.[98]

How should we explain the logic of Kett's Rebellion? Was it a failed peasant revolution? Or do we need a very different framework in order to make sense out of the events of 1549? It does seem very useful to see Kett's Rebellion as a peasant revolution. The goals of the rebels do not add up to a comprehensive blueprint for the total transformation of English society, as shown both by their residual royalism and the cautious particularistic nature of their manifesto, the document called Kett's Demands Being in Rebellion. Moreover, the social composition of the movement was quite diverse, and the rebels were drawn from a variety of social and occupational categories. Kett himself was a multioccupational man, with a limited degree of wealth by the standards of the time. Yet he volunteered the destruction of his own enclosures, surely something that cannot be explained by a theory that links class and political behavior in mechanical fashion. On the

---

"Peasant Revolt in France and England: A Comparison," *Agricultural History Review* 21 (1973), 122–34; Anthony Fletcher, *Tudor Rebellions* (London: Longman, 1973), esp. 64–77; Stephen K. Land, *Kett's Rebellion: The Norfolk Rising of 1549* (Ipswich: Boydell Press, 1977); Roger B. Manning, "Review Article: The Rebellions of 1549 in England," *Sixteenth Century Journal* 10 (1979), 93–99; J. R. Ravensdale, "Landbeach in 1549: Kett's Rebellion in Miniature," in Lionel M. Munby, ed., *East Anglian Studies: Essays by J. C. Barringer (and Others)* (Cambridge: W. Heffer and Sons, 1968), 94–116, and Diarmaid MacCulloch, "Kett's Rebellion in Context," in Slack, *Rebellion, Popular Protest, and the Social Order*, 39–62.

97. See Diarmaid MacCulloch, "Kett's Rebellion in Context"; Julian Cornwall, "Kett's Rebellion in Context: A Comment"; and Diarmaid MacCulloch, "Kett's Rebellion in Context: A Rejoinder," all in Slack, *Rebellion, Popular Protest, and the Social Order*, 39–62, 68–72, 63–67.

98. Beer, *Rebellion and Riot*, 93–96.

contrary, Kett's action makes sense only if we see him as deeply situated in a local institutional network that made his leadership an involuntary obligation rather than a freely chosen commitment.

If we reject the notion that Kett's Rebellion was a peasant revolution, we can focus on the complex local dynamics that wound from Wymondham to Mousehold Heath. Those dynamics are better described from the standpoint of community defense than from the framework of class analysis.

To begin with, it is simply not the case that the revolt was a single, unified movement, as historians have long recognized. Much of the violence in Norfolk and Suffolk counties was independent of Kett's encampments on Mousehold Heath, and it included village or parish enclosure riots that were quite limited in scope. Kett did not lead a vanguard party that controlled all the action from a common center. It is more correct to visualize the events of 1549 as a series of circles of revolt, with Kett's group at the center and a number of simultaneous but distinct revolts stretching out from this center to the periphery. Toward the periphery, local enclosure revolts may have occurred in response to the news from Norfolk, but they were neither controlled nor consciously promoted by Kett's followers.

How, then, should we explain the encampments that took place at Mousehold Heath? This was more than enclosure rioting, and Kett's ritual trials of aristocrats under the Tree of Reformation displays a willingness to call into question the foundations of landed power on a massive scale. Fortunately, in answering the problem of Kett's motives we can draw on the brief manifesto Kett's Demands Being in Rebellion.[99] Historians agree that this is as close as we can come to an authentic voice of the Norfolk revolt, and I have reproduced it in full in order to give the reader a clear sense of the logic of Kett and his supporters. The document reads as follows:

ONE. We pray your grace that where it is enacted for enclosing that it be not hurtful to such as have enclosed saffron grounds for they be greatly chargeable to them, and that from henceforth woman shall enclose any more.

2. We certify your grace that whereas the lords at the manors have been charged with certain free rent, the same lords have sought means to charge the freeholders to pay the same rent, contrary to right.

3. We pray your grace that no lord of no manor shall common upon the common.

4. We pray that priests from henceforth shall purchase no lands neither free nor bond, and the lands that they have in possession may be letten to temporal men, as they were in the first year of King Henry VII.

5. We pray that reed ground and meadow ground may be at such price as they were in the first year of the reign of King Henry VII.

6. We pray that all the marshes that are held of the King's majesty by free rent or of

99. Reproduced in ibid., 105–7.

any other, may be again at the price that they were in the first year of the reign of King Henry VII.

7. We pray that all bushels within your realm be of one stice, that is to say, to be in measure viii gallons.

8. We pray that priests or vicars that be not able to preach and set forth the word of God to his parishoners may be thereby put from his benefice, and the parishoners there to choose another or else the patron as lord of the town.

9. We pray that the payments of castleward rent, and blanch farm, and office lands, which hath been accustomed to be gathered of the tenements, whereas we suppose the lords ought to pay the same to their bailiffs for their rents gathering, and not the tenants.

10. We pray that no man under the degree of a knight or esquire keep a dove house, except it hath been of an old ancient custom.

11. We pray that all freeholders and copyholders may take the profits of all commons, and there to common, and the lords not to common nor take profits of the same.

12. We pray that no feodary within your shores shall be a counsellor to any man in his office making, whereby the king may be truly served, so that a man being of good conscience may be yearly chosen to the same office by the commons of the same shire.

13. We pray your grace to take all liberty of leet into your own hands whereby all men may quietly enjoy their commons with all profits.

14. We pray that copyhold land that is unreasonably rented may go as it did in the first year of King Henry VII and that at the death of a tenant or of a sale the same lands to be charged with an easy fine as a capon or a reasonable sum of money for a remembrance.

15. We pray that no priest [shall be a chaplain] nor no other officer to any man of honour or worship but only to be resident upon their benefices whereby their parishoners may be instructed with the laws of God.

16. We pray that all bondmen may be made free for God made all free with his precious blood shedding.

17. We pray that rivers may be free and common to all men for fishing and passage.

18. We pray that no man shall be put by your escheator and feodary to find any office unless he holdeth of your grace in chief or capite above £10 a year.

19. We pray that the poor mariners and fishermen may have the whole profits of their fishings as porpoises, grampuses, whales, or any great fish so it be not prejudicial to your grace.

20. We pray that every proprietary parson or vicar having benefice of £10 or more by year shall either by themselves or by some other person teach poor men's children of their parish the book called the catechism and the primer.

21. We pray that it be not lawful to the lords of any manor to purchase lands freely and to let them out again by copy of court roll to their great disadvantage and to the undoing of your poor subjects.

22. We pray that no proprietary parson or vicar in consideration of avoiding trouble and suit between them and their poor neighbors, which they daily do proceed and

attempt, shall from henceforth take for their contentation of all the tenths which now they do receive but viii d. of the noble in full discharge of all other tithes.

23. [We pray that no man] under the degree of [esquire] shall keep any conies [rabbits] upon any of their own freehold or copyhold unless he pale them in so that it shall not be to the commons' nuisance.

24. We pray that no person of what estate, degree, or condition he be shall from henceforth sell the wardship of any child but that the same child if he live to his full age shall be at his own chosing concerning his marriage [the king's wards only except].

25. We pray that no manner of person having a manor of his own shall be no other lord's bailiff but only his own.

26. We pray that no lord, knight, nor gentleman shall have or take in farm any spiritual promotion.

27. We pray your grace to give license and authority by your gracious commission under your great seal to such commissioners as your poor commons hath chosen, or to as many of them as your majesty and your council shall appoint and think meet, for to redress and reform all such good laws, statutes, proclamations, and all your other proceedings, which hath been bidden by your justices of your peace, sheriffs, escheators, and others your officers, from your poor commons, since the first year of the reign of your noble grandfather, Henry VII.

28. We pray that those your officers that hath offended your grace and your commons and so proved by the complaint of your poor commons do give unto these poor men so assembled iv d. every day so long as they have remained there.

29. We pray that no lord, knight, esquire, nor gentleman do graze nor feed any bullocks or sheep if he may spend £40 a year by his lands but only for the provision of his house.

The modern reader will find this manifesto quite strange, even confused; I have included the full text partly to shock the reader into recognizing of the need to see Kett's Rebellion in context. More important, however, Kett's Demands shows the subtle blend of radicalism and traditionalism that is characteristic of agrarian societies. The demands are addressed to the king, and the language is deferential and formal whenever the throne is mentioned. Yet the document does present a radical critique of the aristocratic and authoritarian institutions of the middle period of Tudor England. Articles 4, 8, 15, 20, 22, and 26 call for the complete transformation of authority relations in the English church; and, like the Twelve Articles of 1575, they demand a transfer of control over the wealth and supervision of pastors from the nobility to popular communities. A second set of articles (12, 13, 18, 24, 27, and 28) demands a fundamental reform of the king's local government through the purge of all aristocratic abuses of the king's offices. Had this set of demands been enacted it would have effectively transferred power over county magistrates to commoners, a result that would have undercut aristocratic manipulation of royal justice.

But the heart of Kett's Demands lies in the remaining articles, all of which challenge the basis of local aristocratic domination of land and men, and it is this, I believe, that provides the explantory key to the Norfolk uprising. The document attacks enclosure, arbitrary rent increases, the extinction of copyhold, and the survival of servile tenures. As we have seen, all these issues were central to the enclosure riots of the early modern period, and they point to a deeply anti-aristocratic theme in Kett's revolt. For example, several articles (2, 5, 7, 11, 14, 21, 23) deal with the forms of aristocratic domination that were most liable to undercut the viability of community institutions, while articles 7, 9, and 10 treat abuses attendant upon the lordship of manors. Finally, article 16 calls for the final abolition of all forms of residual servility, a demand that still had some significance in regions where weak forms of serfdom survived. Taken as a whole, the articles that concern the limits of manorial and lordly power can be read as demanding the end of all abusive enclosures and the radical limitation of the power of lords unilaterally to dominate the countryside.

Kett's Rebellion did not represent a class war in rural England. It is best understood as a confederation of aggrieved local communities that rallied around Kett's Demands in order to break the power of a predatory aristocracy. Norfolk and Suffolk had long known the abuses of lordly irresponsibility, and both counties had experienced what I have called unilateral enclosures carried out by an avaricious elite. Moreover, the unchecked power of the elite was abetted by the corruption of local and county administration in the years prior to 1549. As Barrett Beer and Diarmaid MacCulloch have shown, the years leading up to Kett's revolt had seen a weakening of royal control over the counties, and it was in this context of political confusion that the men who followed Kett were able to translate local enclosure rioting into a translocal or regional event.[100] The political corruption and uncertainty of the times provided both a pretext for revolt and an occasion for villages to confederate on Mousehold Heath.

Yet, as a careful reader of Kett's Demands will admit, the rebels did not call for the abolition of lordship or manorial government. What they did demand was a "reformation" of lordship that would make it institutionally accountable to the communities of commoners whose interests figured so prominently in the Demands. This indicates, however weakly, that the rebels adhered to a "protective" standard of aristocracy that saw lordship as legitimate only if it protected local interests. Although this was a radical vision for 1549, it was not without precedent, and the rebels could appeal to an ethic of paternalism and obligation that was widely shared by all levels of English society.[101]

If this analysis is correct, it means that we must understand Kett's Rebellion as a political crisis in which established authority relations were challenged and recast.

100. MacCulloch, "Kett's Rebellion in Context," and Beer, *Rebellion and Riot,* 82–139. Also see the excellent analysis of Kett's revolt in Zagorin, *Rebels and Rulers,* 1:208–14.

101. Lawrence Stone, "Patriarchy and Paternalism in Tudor England: The Earl of Arundel and the Peasants' Revolt of 1549," *Journal of British Studies* 13 (1974), 19–23.

Under the great Tree of Reformation, Kett and his supporters attempted to enforce a standard of justice that was deeply rooted in the practices of local communities throughout rural England. The violence of 1549 provided a means of representing community interests against the interests of an irresponsible aristocracy. Traditional theories of rebellion that fail to take politics seriously must be revised to take account of the deep logic of power and authority that moved the rebels of Norfolk to follow Robert Kett.

The logic of community politics and popular rebellion can also be seen in the Midlands Revolt of 1607. Like Kett's revolt, the Midlands uprising occurred through the horizontal confederation of communities on a regional scale. Also like Kett's Rebellion, the Midlands insurrection demonstrates the deep popular hostility to aristocratic domination that lay beneath the surface of enclosure rioting.[102]

The Midlands Revolt began in April 1607 and spread from Northamptonshire to Warwickshire and Leicestershire. Crowds of up to one thousand people, including women and children, leveled enclosure hedges and ditches, and, as in 1549, this initial burst of enclosure rioting was followed by attacks on the clergy and gentry. According to one of the contemporaries, Robert Wilkinson, the rebels passed rumors to the effect that "they will accompt [i.e., settle accounts] with clergymen, and counsel is given to kill up Gentlemen, and they will level all states [i.e., estates, or social distinctions] as they levelled bankes and ditches."[103]

In Northampton, village rebels rallied to the charismatic leadership of John Reynolds, a man called Captain Pouch because of the supposedly magical contents of a pouch he carried at his side. Pouch led his followers in massive enclosure riots that were aimed at restoring community control of land and property rights, especially to the commons and wastes that had been unilaterally enclosed. Edmund Howes testified that Reynolds told his supporters that he had royal approval for his attack on landed power: "He told them also, that he had authority from his majesty to throw down enclosures, and that he was sent of God to satisfy all degrees whatsoever; and thereupon they generally inclined to his direction, so as he kept them in good order; he commanded them not to swear, nor to offer violence to any person, but to ply their business, and to make fair work, extending to continue this work, so long as God should put them in mind."[104]

The strange combination of deference and defiance that shows through Howes's testimony should be read as a statement of the rioters' belief that they were acting "legally," or in terms of a practice of order rooted in community custom and sanctioned by religious truth. The rioters also were sparing in their use of violence against persons, although they were more than willing to challenge the principles

---

102. Manning, *Village Revolts*, 220–52. Also see Charlesworth, *An Atlas of Rural Protest in Britain*, 33–39.
103. Manning, *Village Revolts*, 235.
104. Ibid., 233.

of aristocratic domination through the use of threatening and seditious speech and ritual.

For example, in Leicestershire, some five thousand individuals assembled at Cotesbach, where they proceeded to level hedges and ditches. This particular group also claimed that the king had failed to enforce the law against illegal and depopulating enclosures, and they began to call themselves "levellers," a title that symbolized their determination to destroy the practices of irresponsible lordship.[105] The levellers were evidently not opposed to hierarchy or privilege as such, but they rejected the arbitrary pretensions of a landed elite who refused to abide by the rules of community practices.

The kinds of issues that led to the Midlands Revolt can be usefully illustrated by the events in Haselbach, the site of one of the leveller demonstrations of 1607. During the 1570s, Sir Thomas Tresham, a man charitably described as a greedy or "engrossing" landlord, had increased his rents fivefold while trying to force his copyholders to accept precarious leases. In addition, he enclosed enough common land to be able to pasture seven thousand sheep. His tenants resisted this exercise of imperious lordship, and Tresham's servant informed him as early as 1596 that "the common people exclaim exceedingly . . . upon enclosures and you are not forgotten for Haselbach, although it be beforehand." Tresham ignored this advice, perhaps because he spent much of his time in prison. In any case, Tresham suffered the consequence in 1607, when his tenants wrecked his estate and proclaimed themselves the masters of his property.[106]

Scenes like those in Haselbach occurred throughout the Midlands prior to 1607, as Roger Manning has demonstrated.[107] At the root of the trouble was what historians have called "fiscal seigniorialism," or what I have called the problem of aristocratic domination. Lords throughout the Midlands had begun to use enclosure as a weapon against community autonomy and power. Behind this strategy was the economic pressure that was once described by Lawrence Stone as the crisis of the English aristocracy, and there can be little doubt that enclosing landlords had a material interest in enhancing the revenues of their estates through all possible means.[108] Yet, from the standpoint of the commons, the enhancement of lordship meant a political struggle over the constitution of authority in the countryside. Who would have the ultimate authority to regulate the conditions of power and the meaning of property, and how much authority would reside in the institutions of community life? These were the deep issues that gave the Midlands uprising a logic and coherence that simple materialist explanations tend to ignore.

Although the political struggle over enclosure and lordship explains the underlying causes of the Midlands events, it does not explain the timing and scale of the disturbance. For this we must look to the supralocal or "national" politics of the

105. Ibid., 231.
106. Ibid., 239–40.
107. Ibid., 229–46.
108. Stone, *The Crisis of the Aristocracy*, 129–98, 273–334.

early 1600s and especially to the weakening of royal authority that followed the death of Elizabeth I. Her successor, James I, soon found himself locked in a struggle over the nature of royal power; in this atmosphere of uncertainty and corruption the politics of enclosure rioting could erupt into a regional confrontation with landed power.[109] Like the Norfolk uprising in 1549, the Midlands Revolt must be understood as a confederation of community revolts that gained minimal organizational coherence through the medium of popular leaders like Captain Pouch.

Kett's Rebellion and the Midlands insurrection were just two of the many regional revolts that occurred in early modern England; the uprisings in Kent in 1549, in Oxfordshire in 1596, and the so-called "Clubmen" uprisings of the civil war period (1642–48) were very similar. In addition, regional antienclosure risings occurred in several royal forests during the reign of Charles I.[110] Finally, a number of other types of rural collective violence took place into the early 1800s, including food riots and anti-impressment disturbances.[111] The events in Norfolk and the Midlands, however, nicely illustrate the tenuous nature of lordship in rural England. Indeed, we can argue that the basis of landed power was constantly subject to challenges from below, and the struggle over aristocratic domination seems to have been the chief cause of popular unrest and collective violence during much of the period surveyed in this chapter. In contrast to the European continent, problems growing out of state building and commercialization were relatively less significant in the generation of popular revolt, although coercive commercialization does have something to do with some of the incidents of enclosure rioting that I have discussed.[112] Yet, in spite of its apparent weaknesses the English aristocracy did not experience a revolution, as the French did in 1789, and aristocratic power survived into the twentieth century.

Politics and the Strange Demise of Peasant England

Historians have long been in agreement about the relatively early and thorough demise of the English peasant. By the 1850s, England had become a modern society, and English agriculture was characterized by large-scale farming and an

109. Manning, *The English People and the English Revolution*, 292–94; David O. Pam, *The Hungry Years: The Struggle for Survival in Edmonton and Enfield before 1400*, Occasional Papers, n.s. 42 (Enfield: Edmonton Hundred Historical Society, 1980); and J. S. Morrill and J. D. Walter, "Order and Disorder in the English Revolution," in Fletcher and Stevenson, *Order and Disorder in Early Modern England*, 137–65.

110. For the period from the reign of Charles I through the revolution, see Henry N. Brailsford, *The Levellers and the English Revolution* (London: Cresset Press, 1961), esp. 426–33; J. D. Hughes, "The Drainage Disputes in the Isle of Axholme and Their Connection with the Leveller Movement: A Re-examination," *Lincolnshire Historian* 2 (1954), 13–45; Brian Stuart Manning, *The English People and the English Revolution*, esp. 292–93; C. Holmes, "Drainers and Fenmen," in Fletcher and Stevenson, *Order and Disorder in Early Modern England*, 166–95; Underdown, "The Chalk and the Cheese"; and Sharp, *In Contempt of All Authority*.

111. Manning, *Village Revolts*, 132–54; for a later period, see Bohstedt, *Riots and Community Politics*, 165–223.

112. My argument finds support in Davies, "Peasant Revolt in France and England."

efficient, market-oriented agriculture.[113] How did this change come about, particularly in a society with a long tradition of popular protest? It will not do to argue that the English peasants were powerless to resist the transformation of English agriculture. After all, the equally "powerless" rural people of France were capable of widespread opposition to the ancient régime, and their struggles helped to produce the French Revolution.[114] More important, the historical evidence reviewed in this chapter does not support the view of English rural society that sees ordinary rural people as the passive objects of history. They were more than capable of defending their interests, and the process and politics of community defense lasted well into the nineteenth century.

I argued earlier that the concept of peasantry should be understood as referring to the institutions of domination that elites have used as a basis for capturing rural communities. This definition, I think, is the key to understanding the paradox of English rural history. The "peasantry" disappeared in England because of the relative weakness of elite institutions rather than as a result of the weakness of popular society.[115] Serfdom began to disappear in the fifteenth and sixteenth centuries, and the absence of servile institutions by the early modern period resulted in balanced social power in which landed elites and rural commoners could negotiate the terms of the economic and social order. Enclosure rioting, for example, was a medium of representation that allowed rural communities to draw moral and political boundaries. It is difficult to believe that enclosure revolts could have been so widespread and persistent if they were simply futile exercises or mere acts of desperation.[116] On the contrary, the evidence from incidents like that at Cannock Chase indicates the significance of enclosure rioting as a block to elite arbitrariness and elite power. In short, the English experience can be read as a continual renegotiation between elite power and popular institutions and the eventual redrawing of community life through a tacit social compromise that left English agriculture inflected by the deep patterns of the past. This compromise of community was not an unmixed story of success. The landless and land poor lost much in the process, and we can view the period from 1500 to 1800 as a long wave of institutional change that led to the bifurcation of rural communities into established villages of farmers and marginal communities of laborers.[117] The

113. G. E. Mingay, *English Landed Society in the Eighteenth Century* (Toronto: University of Toronto Press, 1963), 268–69; G. E. Mingay, ed., *The Victorian Countryside*, 2 vols. (London: Routledge and Kegan Paul, 1981), esp. 1:3–17, 177–272.

114. Georges Lefebvre, *The Great Fear of 1789: Rural Panic in Revolutionary France* (Princeton: Princeton University Press, 1982), esp. ix–6, 202–11.

115. For the end of serfdom, see Hilton, *Bond Men Made Free*, and Brenner, "The Agrarian Roots of European Capitalism," esp. 275–84.

116. This seems to be the conclusion reached in Thompson's "The Peculiarities of the English." Also see his classic *The Making of the English Working Class* (New York: Pantheon, 1964), esp. 77–101, 213–33, 401–28.

117. See, for example, Obelkevich, *Religion and Rural Society*, 23–102. For a strong defense of the importance of community quite different from my own, see Craig Calhoun, *The Question of Class*

latter were hard pressed by the commercial society of the nineteenth century, and, as the Captain Swing revolt proves, they were far from the passive and contented people of legend.[118] Yet the bifurcation of rural community in England was not the result of a unilateral exercise of elite power. It was the consequence of a deeply rooted social compromise that had developed out of the political logic of the sixteenth and seventeenth centuries. The English landed elite was simply not powerful enough to establish authoritarian and arbitrary rule of the countryside. As a result, economic change could occur through a long-term process of adaptation to market and social forces in which both elites and commoners participated.

In the background were the political and legal institutions that made England a society in which political compromise was possible. From a relatively early date, English commoners had access to institutional forums that could be used to check elite power.[119] For example, the royal common law and equity courts provided a complex set of procedures that could be used to blunt aristocratic power in the countryside. We have seen on several occasions that popular rural violence against enclosure was often accompanied by community lawsuits that were not invariably decided against popular interest; royal law was ambivalent, and the royal government did not uniformly favor aristocratic interests. As early as 1235, the Statute of Merton had been enacted in an attempt to limit the right of lords unilaterally to enclose their lands, and this was followed in the Tudor and Stuart periods by a whole series of laws against depopulating enclosures, the engrossing of land, and the transfer of arable to pasture.[120] The famous Stuart Books of Orders and Book of Sports, the first attempts at social regulation on a sweeping scale, can be read as deeply ambiguous documents that could be used against aristocratic interests.[121] Similarly, the old poor laws offered an opportunity for ordinary rural people to maintain a stake in their communities that could not be simply denied by the local elite. Finally, Parliament became an increasingly representative body in the early

---

Struggle: Social Foundations of Popular Radicalism in the Industrial Revolution (Chicago: University of Chicago Press, 1982), esp. 149–82.

118. Eric J. Hobsbawm and George Rudé, *Captain Swing* (New York: Pantheon Books, 1968), 35–36.

119. A good source of support for this argument is found in Langbein, "Albion's Fatal Flaws," 115–20. Also see Bryce Lyon, *A Constitutional and Legal History of Medieval England* (New York: Norton, 1980), 613–49; Palmer, *Police and Protest in England and Ireland*, 1–82; Richard Ashcraft, *Revolutionary Politics and Locke's Two Treatises of Government* (Princeton: Princeton University Press, 1986), 228–85. There is also a vast literature that shows how ordinary Englishmen viewed themselves as uniquely privileged by a polity of rights that protected their interests. For a good (if strong) statement of this popular "constitutionalism," see John Phillip Reid, *Constitutional History of the American Revolution: The Authority of Rights* (Madison: University of Wisconsin Press, 1986), 9–81.

120. See Thirsk, "Enclosing and Engrossing," 213–38.

121. See Williams, *The Tudor Regime*, 139–215; Underdown, *Revel, Riot, and Rebellion*, 65–68. For the Book of Orders, see Alfred E. Bland et al., eds., *English Economic History: Select Documents* (London: G. Bell and Sons, 1915), 374–80; for the statute of Merton, see Tawney, *The Agrarian Problem in the Sixteenth Century*, 87, 180, 248, 371–72 (also see his list of similar statutes, 437).

modern period, and ordinary rural people had at least a limited chance to make their will known in the periodic rituals of election.[122]

The evidence, of course, certainly does not support the notion that English society was peculiarly egalitarian or responsive to popular demands. Violence, after all, was a tacit indication of a society in which elite interests were strongly favored in the ordinary course of politics and justice. Indeed, the landed elite was favored with laws that permitted entail and primogeniture and that allowed titled landowners a monopoly of game hunting. Yet the *reality* of landed power stopped at the boundaries of the manor or village, and what the privileged property of the elite really meant in practice was largely determined by the local balance of social and political power. Popular communities were able to affect that balance through a variety of strategies, of which collective violence was long a key component.

We can, then, argue that community rather than class is the most parsimonious and powerful analytic framework for understanding English rural history. The concept of rural community helps us to explain both the organization of rural collective violence and the goals that were at stake in the violent episodes discussed in this chapter. The defense of community was the object of popular action, and that defense was potent enough to limit the pretensions of the English landed elite. In this sense, the English peasantry dissolved because of the ability of ordinary rural people to defeat the logic of servility and aristocratic domination. England's experience was not unique and its history was never providential, but it must be seen as distinctive when we shift our attention from grand issues like the rise of capitalism to the local terrain in which the day-by-day politics of rural life took place.

England and the Irish Entanglement

The situation in Ireland demonstrates quite clearly that English elites had no particular cultural propensity to engage in a "civilized" politics of compromise. Ireland was, in effect, an English colonial province for some four centuries.[123] By 1700 the Anglo-Irish aristocracy had become a powerful and entrenched elite, its property privileged by the firm protection of an Irish legal order that barred Catholics, the vast majority of Irish rural people, from owning land.[124] Moreover, the landed elite was little constrained by the complex of manorial, legal, and

122. Kishlansky, *Parliamentary Selection,* 73–101, 192–230; Derek Hirst, *The Representative of the People? Votes and Voting in England under the Early Stuarts* (Cambridge: Cambridge University Press, 1975); J. E. C. Hill, "Parliament and the People in Seventeenth Century England," *Past and Present* 93 (1981), 100–125.

123. Kerby A. Miller, *Emigrants and Exiles: Ireland and the Irish Exodus to North America* (New York: Oxford University Press, 1985), 9–101.

124. Samuel Clark, *Social Origins of the Irish Land War* (Princeton: Princeton University Press, 1979), 24; Maureen Wall, *The Penal Laws, 1691–1760* (Dundalk: Dundalgan Press, 1967).

parliamentary institutions that offered at least the possibility for English commoners to defend their interests before the royal law.[125] English landlordship in Ireland was authoritarian and uncompromising, and the ultimate protection for the landlord was the presence in Ireland of a large standing army that was regularly used against popular protest. For example, in the 1770s Ireland had a resident English army of 15,000 men while England itself had a standing force of only 17,000, even though Ireland was only about half as populous as England and Wales.[126]

It was in this context of unchecked aristocratic power, backed by the centralized coercive power of an alien bureaucracy, that Ireland became infamous as one of Europe's most violent rural societies. According to Stanley Palmer, an enormous gulf separated collective violence in England and Ireland. In Ireland, collective violence was more widespread, persistent, and brutal than in England, and murder was a favorite tactic of popular groups during periods of agrarian conflict. For example, in the year 1835 alone there were 6,175 committals for assault in Ireland, and Palmer sees this as a fairly typical year before the famine of 1846–51, with much of the violence directed against the agents and supporters of the landed elite.[127]

Irish rural violence was not simply mindless and formless rioting. Its victims were well chosen, and it gained its organizational cohesion through its close connection with the networks of popular community life, something that shows clearly through the research of historians like M. R. Beames and Tom Garvin.[128] It was their rootedness in local institutions that allowed Irish rural secret societies to flourish in the eighteenth and nineteenth centuries. Groups with colorful names, like the Ribbonmen, Defenders, Shanavests, and Whiteboys, kept up an almost constant wave of violent opposition to the agrarian order.[129]

How do we explain the stark contrast between England and Ireland? I suggest that the greater relative frequency and intensity of rural violence in Ireland must be explained in terms of the comparative weakness of institutional "mediations" between elite and popular interests. In contrast to England, Ireland did not

125. Clark, *Social Origins*, 21–64.

126. Stanley H. Palmer, *Police and Protest*, 62.

127. Ibid., 40–56, 548.

128. The best introduction to the work of scholars who specialize in this area is C. H. E. Philpin, ed., *Nationalism and Popular Protest in Ireland* (Cambridge: Cambridge University Press, 1987), esp. 219–83.

129. Samuel Clark and James S. Donnelly, Jr., "Introduction: The Tradition of Violence"; David Cickson, "Taxation and Disaffection in Late Eighteenth-Century Ireland"; Paul E. W. Robert, "Caravats and Shanavests: Whiteboyism and Faction Fighting in East Munster, 1802–1811"; James S. Donnelly, Jr., "Pastorini and Captain Rock: Millenarianism and Sectarianism in the Rockite Movement of 1821–1824"; "Introduction II: Land and Religion in Ulster"; David Miller, "The Armagh Troubles, 1784–1795"; and Paul Bew and Frank Wright, "The Agrarian Opposition in Ulster Politics, 1848–1887," all in Samuel Clark and James S. Donnelly, Jr., eds., *Irish Peasants: Violence and Political Unrest, 1780–1914* (Madison: University of Wisconsin Press, 1983), 25–191.

develop the political and ritual linkages that allowed rural commoners some room for compromise and negotiation short of rebellion.[130] The Irish legal order was seen, quite rationally, as an alien and unilaterally imposed order of force and fraud that was fundamentally biased in favor of the landed elite.[131] Yet, in spite of their legal and political disabilities, Irish communities retained enough autonomy and cohesion to be able to resist Anglo-Irish power, at least until the great famine swept away the fabric of Irish society for a generation.[132] Although the contrast should not be overdrawn, the comparison of England and Ireland does indicate the disastrous implications of a society in which strong communities and irresponsible landed elites struggled for local social hegemony in the absence of clear rules of representation and negotiation. In Ireland, institutions of unchecked domination—institutions that I have described as forming the basic logic of the concept of the peasantry—made possible a long social civil war that ultimately led to the collapse of Anglo-Irish elite power.

130. This is the logic explicated in Clark, *Social Origins,* 21–64. For a similar but more Marxist logic, see Michael Beames, *Peasants and Power: The Whiteboy Movements and Their Control in Pre-Famine Ireland* (New York: St. Martin's Press, 1983), esp. 42–153.

131. Miller, *Emigrants and Exiles,* 9–101.

132. Clark, *Social Origins,* 107–52. The contrast with the English case is striking. See Dale Edward Williams, "Morals, Markets, and the English Crowd in 1766," *Past and Present* 104 (1984), 56–73.

CHAPTER 5

France and the Politics of
Controlled Community, 1500–1900

From 1823 to 1826, a rural bandit, Louis Roque, known to his supporters as "L'homme à moustache," was one of the most wanted men in the department of the Gard.[1] Supported by many of the rural Protestant communities in the Cévennes, Roque led a kind of low-level insurrection against the forces of the restored Bourbon monarchy. Although scrupulous about his conduct in most respects, Roque infuriated local officials through his seditious flouting of the status quo, and his dangerous ability to circumvent the official rules of the game was symbolized by his routine appearance in front of isolated police stations where he would cheerfully wave at the guards before disappearing into his rural hideouts. For the forces of order, Roque was intolerable because he represented a tradition of local republican and Protestant dissent, indicated by his prominent mustache, a symbol of political radicalism in early-nineteenth-century France. But above all, L'homme à moustache stood for the autonomy and integrity of local rural communities, and no French administration could view Roque's politics as anything less than an insidious challenge to the transcendent claims of the French state.[2]

Louis Roque was in no sense a statistically representative sample of French rebels, but his career was typical of many of the movements of local resistance that occurred in rural France between 1500 and the opening of the Third Republic in 1871. Historians of agrarian France have long been fascinated by the interplay of local institutions and national politics that gave meaning to the glacially slow transformation of France's rural economy, and their work has proven how important it is to put the grand issues of historical analysis into local and regional context.[3] Here I place special emphasis on the years of revolutionary turmoil,

1. Gwynne Lewis, "A Cévenol Community in Crisis: The Mystery of 'L'Homme à Moustache,'" *Past and Present* 109 (1985), 144–75. The best accessible study of popular community in early modern France is Robin Briggs, *Communities of Belief* (Oxford: Clarendon Press, 1988).
2. Lewis, "A Cévenol Community in Crisis," 151–65.
3. I have drawn heavily on the following works for this chapter: Maurice Agulhon, *The Republic*

because this was the period of maximum strain for rural communities throughout France. Consequently, even if the concept of community is a significant analytic device, it should be *least* likely to appear as an important social framework during the years of revolutionary upheaval when all institutions were subject to radical change. This way of approaching the issue provides a kind of mental test as "thought experiment" that can only strengthen the case if rural community can be shown to have been central in the years of revolutionary struggle.

Mapping Community in Rural France, 1500–1789

Anyone who seriously reads the enormous scholarly literature that treats rural France will be struck by the constant invocation of the concept of community. Scholars with otherwise quite diverse political and methodological agendas seem to agree about the saleince of local community institutions throughout the long sweep of French agrarian history. For example, Ladurie, whose primary thrust has been demographic and structural, nonetheless admits that community was primary in shaping the behavior and mentality of rural life. Similarly, Roland Mousnier, whose emphasis on the French ancien régime as a society of status orders has provoked heated debate, has pointed to the significance of territorial community in his monumental study of the institutions of the absolute monarch. Finally, even historians who work with class categories and Marxist viewpoints, including the great rural historian Georges Lefebvre, have often indicated the significance of community institutions, even during periods of economic and political crisis. Indeed, it was probably France that inspired Perez Zagorin, in his magisterial study of what he calls "early modern revolutions," to argue that it was the village community that formed the institutional cellule of revolt in the sixteenth and seventeenth centuries. We are, therefore, on fairly firm ground when we analyze rural France in terms of the concept of community, at least prior to the nineteenth century.[4]

---

in the Village: The People of the Var from the French Revolution to the Second Republic (Cambridge: Cambridge University Press, 1982); Yves Marie Bercé, *Histoire des croquants* (Paris: Seuil, 1986); Guy Bois, *The Crisis of Feudalism: Economy and Society in Eastern Normandy, c. 1300–1550* (Cambridge: Cambridge University Press, 1984); T. J. A. Le Goff, *Vannes and Its Region: A Study of Town and Country in Eighteenth Century France* (Oxford: Clarendon Press, 1981); Pierre Goubert, *The French Peasantry in the Seventeenth Century* (Cambridge: Cambridge University Press, 1986); Georges Duby and A. Wallon, eds., *Histoire de la France rurale*, 4 vols. (Paris: Seuil, 1975–76); Emmanuel Le Roy Ladurie, *The Peasants of Languedoc* (Urbana: University of Illinois Press, 1974); and Emmanuel Le Roy Ladurie, *The French Peasantry, 1450–1660* (Berkeley: University of California Press, 1987).

4. Ladurie, *The French Peasantry*, esp. 359–99; Roland Mousnier, *The Institutions of France under the Absolute Monarchy, 1598–1789* (Chicago: University of Chicago Press, 1979), vol. 1 *Society and the State*, 551–62; Georges Lefebvre, *The Great Fear of 1789: Rural Panic in Revolutionary France* (Princeton: Princeton University Press, 1982), esp. 91–121, 170–211, and see Georges

But can we use the work of French rural history to support the analysis of French rural politics in terms of the concept of the community of grain presented in Chapter 1? More specifically, can we identify institutional networks of hierarchical cooperation that shaped the contours of economic, political, and ritual life in rural France across the period under review?

It is quite clear that institutions of local and territorial cooperation underpinned rural production and distribution throughout France. In many regions, especially the north and northeast, common-field agriculture with its characteristic scattering of strips and intermingling of use rights, survived well into the 1800s.[5] But, even in regions of "dispersed" habitation and enclosed fields like the west, cooperative practices were evident in the daily and seasonal rhythms of agriculture. For example, in areas of dispersed habitat with important livestock economies, hamlet or parish institutions maintained control of pasture rights and collectively held commons and wastes.[6] Even in the south, where Roman law made for a more "individualistic" set of property relations, local custom drew sharp limits of community regulation with regard to what proprietors could and could not do with their holdings.[7] In the south, the *droit de compascuité,* a form of common or collective right to pasture on unenclosed fields, developed in the interstices of Roman law through the accretion of private, local agreements known as servitudes. Over time these servitudes developed into a body of village and manorial custom that often ran counter to the individualist logic of the written law.[8]

Indeed, the importance of community economic institutions can be seen most vividly in the complex pattern of property rights that characterized rural France in the seventeenth and eighteenth centuries.[9] France in 1789 was scarcely a society in which "bourgeois" notions of property had become ascendant in the countryside, and the notion that rural France was undergoing a process of creeping capitalism has not stood up too well to historical scrutiny.[10] Instead, property rights to land and labor were extraordinarily diverse, and almost every region showed peculiarities of custom and law that makes a shambles of any attempt to

---

Lefebvre, *Les paysans du Nord pendant la Révolution française* (Bari: Laterza, 1959); Perez Zagorin, *Rebels and Rulers, 1500–1660,* 2 vols. (Cambridge: Cambridge University Press, 1982), 1:85–86.

5. P. M. Jones, *The Peasantry in the French Revolution* (Cambridge: Cambridge University Press, 1988), 7–29. Also see Marc Bloch, *French Rural History: An Essay on Its Basic Characteristics* (Berkeley: University of California Press, 1966), esp. 35–55; Ladurie, *The French Peasantry,* esp. 66–154.

7. See, for example, the detailed discussion carried out at the micro level in Le Goff's *Vannes and Its Region,* 151–75. *Parcours* (common rights) was evidently the most typical form of collective-use right in the bocage.

7. Jones, *The Peasantry in the French Revolution,* 19–21. Also see Ladurie, *The French Peasantry,* 137–38, 153–56.

8. Jones, *The Peasantry in the French Revolution,* 18–21. Also see Goubert, *The French Peasantry in the Seventeenth Century,* esp. 23–34, 122–34.

9. Bloch, *French Rural History,* 102–49.

10. Jones, *The Peasantry in the French Revolution,* 1–59.

isolate a unitary or national French peasantry defined in terms of an invariant class structure.[11] Within a single village or parish, property could be held under a variety of tenures, some of which were regulated by manorial customs and some of which were more closely responsive to local market demand for land.[12] In contrast to England, France never knew a genuinely national equivalent of English enclosure, and even as late as the twentieth century there were real differences of tenurial conditions between the north and south of the country.[13]

Beneath this tremendous regional variety, however, we can identify certain basic principles of proprietorship that underscore the salience of community institutions. First, as late as 1789, individual rights to property were intermixed with principles of household and community regulation that circumscribed the ability of individual owners to make unilateral decisions about the use of their holdings.[14] For example, in the north and northeast, the eighteenth century saw the development of commercial grain farming and the rise of market-oriented farmers, called *laboureurs* or *fermiers,* who were actively involved in producing food grain for the urban market.[15] Yet even in these regions the rights of owners and large tenants were controlled by forms of common-property rights that attached to a village or manorial territory. Those rights included gleaning (*glanage*) of harvested fields, grazing of stock on unenclosed fields (*droit de vaine pature*), reciprocal grazing between adjacent villages (*droit de parcours*), common-use rights to local forests (*affouages*), and common access to meadows (*droit au regain*).[16] Nor were these rights confined to the Ile-de-France and the east, and common-use rights under community control were evidently so widespread as to be an accepted part of the social fabric, although the *precise* nature and extent of those rights differed widely between regions. In addition, in some parts of the west, including the areas of lower Brittany studied by T. J. A. Le Goff and D. M. G. Sutherland, tenants had hereditary rights of proprietorship, known as *domaine congéable,* a system of secure tenure that resembled English copyhold.[17] Property rights of this kind display a chain of rights and responsibilities that linked owners and tenants in relations of conflict and cooperation that show no clear boundaries between ownership and its absence.

Second, and more important, the definition and regulation of property rights were closely linked to the specific institutions of local communities. Although

11. Note the wide regional and economic differences that have already been noted. See, in addition, Duby and Wallon, eds., *Histoire de la France rurale.*

12. Bloch, *French Rural History,* 64–149.

13. Ibid., 197–248.

14. Jones, *The Peasantry in the French Revolution,* 1–29.

15. Ibid., 9–15.

16. Ibid., 19–21. Also see Hilton Root, *Peasants and King in Burgundy: Agrarian Foundations of French Absolutism* (Berkeley: University of California Press, 1987), 66–154.

17. T. J. A. Le Goff and D. M. G. Sutherland, "The Social Origins of Counter-Revolution in Western France," *Past and Present* 99 (1983), 65–87.

manorial courts had become increasingly unimportant in many regions of France, except for purposes of rent collection, this was not universally true, and in areas like the Franche-Comté, where seigneurial institutions remained powerful, the manor count continued to serve as the ultimate source of proprietary norms and rules.[18] Moreover, in areas where seigneurial justice had decayed there is no reason to suppose that community institutions were no longer of consequence in defining property rights and managing conflicts over the use and abuse of land and labor. A clear indication that they remained important can be found in the tremendous diversity of language and law respecting the nature of property, and that they did so shows that property had not yet been "nationalized" in the sense of being subject to the decisive control of the formal institutions of royal or bureaucratic administration. On the contrary, in regions of subsistence agriculture and in regions of commercial farming much of the real "practice" of property was still embedded in a local political economy that was centered on the village, hamlet, or parish. The influence of the local economy was most clearly reflected in areas where strip farming and common fields persisted, because it was in areas of this type that the basic routines of agriculture depended on collective decisions about crops and the timing of the agricultural cycle.[19] Yet in more dispersed regions the decisions of local householders were bound up with customary practices that were situated in rules of neighborhood and community as shown by the traditions of domaine congéable in the west.[20]

We can, therefore, argue that at a popular level at least, the theory and practice of property were deeply interconnected with networks of overlapping obligations between neighbors and kin. This notion corresponds quite closely to the concept of property as trusteeship. Individual French proprietors exercised rights of proprietorship within a set of institutional practices that enforced a principle of accountability in which property holders were required to act as the trustees of their communities. Common rights, like the coveted right of vaine pature, fit neatly into this category, as does the survival of gleaning in the commercialized regions of the center and north.[21] These sorts of rights were not open to any who claimed them, however; rights of territorial membership in the local community were rooted in birth, marriage, and long residence. Strangers and the wandering or homeless poor were unwelcome.[22]

It would also be a mistake to assume that French rural communities were internally egalitarian. By the seventeenth century there were large differences of wealth and status between advantaged villagers and the marginal poor, who often disappeared from the community altogether according to the research undertaken

18. Bloch, *French Rural History*, 104–6; Jones, *The Peasantry in the French Revolution*, 83.
19. Bloch, *French Rural History*, 35–56.
20. Le Goff, *Vannes and Its Region*, 151–75.
21. Jones, *The Peasantry in the French Revolution*, 19–21.
22. See Lefebvre, *The Great Fear of 1789*, 7–23.

by James Collins.[23] For example, in commercially active regions there was a large difference between laboureurs, or fermiers, who made a good living from commercial tenant farming, and the petty *haricotiers* and *journaliers,* who supplemented inadequate landholdings with wage labor and artisan production. Finally, we should not underestimate the importance of patriarchy as a source of hierarchy, particularly in the areas affected by Roman law traditions.

Yet it would be a mistake to read into this an incipient class division that outweighed the significance of community institutions. Economic fortunes were mutable, and one generation's prosperous family could become quite poor in the next if holdings were subdivided through inheritance or the accidents of nature. More important, the survival of collective controls over property meant that the more and the less advantaged were linked by reciprocal hierarchies that may have been more salient in the course of ordinary life than mere disparities of wealth. As Hilton Root has shown in some detail for Burgundy, community institutions could often be manipulated by the better off, but, as Root's own research indicates, community was no less real or important as a result.[24]

Thus, economic differentiation, it seems, must be seen within the context of material institutions that ordered everyday life. Gleaning, for instance, provided both a form of institutionalized subsistence for the local poor and a means by which the established members of the community could maintain social peace. Similarly, the practices of wage labor and farm service can be interpreted as complex networks of conflict *and* cooperation that implicated ordinary people in ongoing performances of power and asymmetrical reciprocity. Even the ability of French villagers jointly to expand and contract common pastures and arable in the face of demographic changes should be linked to the durability of economic institutions of community. In this context, popular anger was likely to take as its target not the prosperous as such but, rather, well-off farmers and merchants who refused to be bound by community rules.

An interesting illustration of the latter point comes from the opening years of the French Revolution. As J. Boutier has demonstrated for the southwest, well-off farmers and proprietors were rarely the victims of popular violence during the period 1788–90; instead, whole communities turned their fury against powerful outsiders, who were probably least likely to have been bound by local institutional conventions.[25] In some cases, however, well-off "commoners" as well as noblemen and urban landowners were the targets of local violence; and the fact that

23. James B. Collins, *The Fiscal Limits of Absolutism: Direct Taxation in Early Seventeenth Century France* (Berkeley: University of California Press, 1987), 166–222, and see Paul Bois, *Paysans de l'Ouest: Des structures économiques et sociales aux options politiques depuis l'époque révolutionnaire dans la Sarthe* (Paris: Mouton, 1960), esp. 436–48.

24. Root, *Peasants and King in Burgundy,* 66–104, 205–33.

25. J. Boutier, "Jacqueries en pays croquant: Les révoltes paysannes en Aquitaine (décembre 1789–mars 1790)," *Annales: Economies, Sociétés, Civilisations* 34 (1979), 760–86.

some but by no means all of the members of a particular economic stratum were targeted forces us to rethink simple models of class polarization. Could it be that the difference between a prosperous *gros fermier* (big farmer), or *laboureur,* who fell afoul of popular violence and one who did not had more to do with their respective positions in local institutions than with their class backgrounds?

In any event, it is clear that the economic institutions of village or parish life were strongly reinforced by community networks of politics and ritual. Local communities were used as the basis for taxation and judicial administration, and collective solidarity was strengthened by the levying of taxes on whole communities rather than on individuals, thereby placing the burden of apportioning the levy on community institutions.[26] In addition, territorial communities were recognized at law as corporations that could sue, own common property, and be held collectively responsible. As a corporate body, one of many in the ancien régime, the rural community was known as the *communauté d'habitants;* and underneath the legal rubric one can glimpse a vibrant political life that cannot be reduced to a mere reflection of elite power. For example, the communauté d'habitants varied in terms of its precise territorial boundaries, and the monarchy never succeeded in implanting a uniform grid of local administration in the French countryside. In the north and center, the institutions of the communauté corresponded to the village or seigneurie, while in the west, the formal institutions of local governance were largely indistinguishable from the parish, and the post of syndic or mayor developed out of the medieval posts of vestry clerk (*fabricien*) or church warden (*marguiller*). On the other hand, in the south the formal communauté was underpinned by councils of village householders known jointly as the *conseil politique.*[27]

Thus the institutions of royal power were absorbed and transformed through a process of mutual adjustment. Far from undermining the integrity of local politics, this process of adjustment may have strengthened the ability of community members jointly to regulate their affairs through the local enforcement of coercively binding norms. Local syndics and other executive officers must have had enough authority to maintain at least a semblance of local order in a world that was still innocent of anything resembling a professional police force. In this context, community self-help was the rule rather than the exception, although it seems odd that communities could have taxed and policed themselves in the absence of deeply rooted institutional practices. The "ultimate" origins of community politics is a question that is irrelevant to the main point: in the seventeenth and eighteenth centuries French rural communities were capable of acting politically.[28]

26. This practice was often called *contrainte solidaire.* See Root, *Peasants and King in Burgundy,* 40–42.
27. Jones, *The Peasantry in the French Revolution,* 21–29.
28. For the seventeenth century, see Goubert, *The French Peasantry in the Seventeenth Century,*

Popular culture and ritual were closely linked to the forms of politics that underlay the communauté d'habitants. We now know a great deal about rural festival and ritual, thanks to the pathbreaking work of Davis, Ladurie, and Mona Ozouf. In addition, Lynn Hunt, following the lead provided by François Furet, has provided us with a much more cogent understanding of the role of culture during the French revolutionary period.[29] All this work demonstrates the complex ways in which what I have called the "folklore of place" shaped popular consciousness in rural France. At the center of local identity was the church, especially in dispersed bocage regions in the west. But throughout France, the many holidays and feast days of the church provided a template through which agrarian life was ordered. Much of village routine centered on the rituals of the seasons and the rhythms of birth and death, and, whatever the orthodox elites may have thought, the doctrines of the faith were popularly reconstituted to take account of the local dimensions of agrarian experience. After all, the French kingdom on the eve of 1789 was a multilingual society in which the survival of many local patois can be understood as an indicator of the extraordinary fragmentation and local particularism of French life. Spoken through local dialects and transformed to meet very particular needs, the high doctrines of Catholicism became part of the myth and magic of rural communities.[30] Like the parishoners who demanded that their priests ring the church bells to ward off lightning, the rural people of ancien-régime France drew selectively on church doctrine as a source of identity and community focus.

An excellent illustration of rural ritual and community folklore can be found in the charivari.[31] Like its English counterpart, the French charivari blended enter-

---

180, 205–19, and Ladurie, *The French Peasantry*, 359–400. For the eighteenth century, see Root, *Peasants and King in Burgundy*, 155–204.

29. Natalie Z. Davis, *Society and Culture in Early Modern France: Eight Essays* (Stanford: Stanford University Press, 1975), esp. 152–87; Emmanuel Le Roy Ladurie, *Montaillou: The Promised Land of Error* (New York: Vintage Books, 1979); Mona Ozouf, *Festivals and the French Revolution* (Cambridge: Harvard University Press, 1987); Lynn Hunt, *Politics, Culture, and Class in the French Revolution* (Berkeley: University of California Press, 1984), esp. 19–122, 213–36; François Furet, *Interpreting the French Revolution* (Cambridge: Cambridge University Press, 1981). For a fuller treatment of rural community, see *Les communautés rurales/Rural Communities*, Recueils de la Société Jean Bodin pour l'histoire comparative des institutions, vol. 43 (Paris: Dessain et Tolra, 1984).

30. For the role of the church and the survival of multilingualism into the nineteenth century, see Eugen Weber, *Peasants into Frenchmen: The Modernization of Rural France, 1870–1914* (Stanford: Stanford University Press, 1976), 339–74, 455–57, and, for patois, 6, 56, 67–94, 249–66. For the church and rural France, see Timothy Tackett and Claude Langlois, "Ecclesiastical Structures and Clerical Geography on the Eve of the French Revolution," *French Historical Studies* 11 (1980), 352–70; J. McManners, "Tithe in Eighteenth Century France: A Focus for Rural Anticlericalism," in Derek Beales and Geoffrey Best, eds., *History, Society, and the Churches: Essays in Honour of Owen Chadwick* (Cambridge: Cambridge University Press, 1985), 147–68; and Ladurie, *The Peasants of Languedoc*, 191–216, 265–86.

31. See in particular Jacques Le Goff and Jean Claude Schmitt, eds., *Le charivari*, Actes de la table ronde organisée à Paris (25–27 avril 1977) par l'Ecole des Hautes Études en Sciences Sociales et le Centre National de la Recherche Scientifique (Paris: Mouton, 1981).

tainment and symbolic performance in a ritual of humiliation. The targets were those who had violated community rules of propriety and hierarchy, and probably the most likely victims were men and women who transgressed local norms of kinship and property holding. But the charivari was not a mindless upsurge of brute violence. It was carefully staged, and at least in some parts of France, there were specific rules about who could participate. For example, in the west, next-door neighbors of the victims were supposed to lead the "festivities." In sum, the charivari was a form of rough justice that involved the performance of community in terms of a powerful code of morality.[32]

We are, therefore, on fairly solid ground if we argue that popular politics in rural France can be understood in terms of the logic of the community of grain. We see strong evidence of the kinds of mutually implicated forms of cooperation that I believe account for the persistence of territorial principles of social action in rural societies. Politics, ritual, and economic production overlapped in terms of participants and principles of performance. Ordinary rural people were tied together in many ways, for many purposes, and on many occasions. This was a world of hierarchy and conflict, yet it was also a world of membership and fellowship. The worst kind of situation in this world was literally to lack a "place," or a secure right to membership in local institutions. The alternative was to become a beggar or a vagabond with no real claim to any rights, save the occasional charity of the pious. France had no equivalent of the English poor laws, and the poor were either provided for by local institutions or abandoned to a sad fate.[33]

French rural communities, however, were never fully autonomous, either in the management of their internal affairs or in their relations with supralocal elites. They were tied to the same forces of constraint that were characteristic of much of the European order during the medieval and early modern periods. First, France was a land of aristocratic power, and the various ranks of the French nobility were among the most tenacious and powerful of all the European aristocracies. Their property was privileged by tax exemptions; they enjoyed the right to own various judicial and seigneurial offices; and hunting and forest rights were theirs alone.[34] In addition, they were the largest rent collectors in the kingdom apart from the church, and there were few villages and parishes that were not involved in transferring a portion of their crops to the nobility in the form of manorial rents

32. Davis, *Society and Culture in Early Modern France*, chaps. 4–5; E. P. Thompson, "Rough Music: Le charivari anglais," *Annales: Economies, Sociétés, Civilisations* 27 (1972), 285–312.

33. Olwen H. Hufton, *The Poor of Eighteenth Century France, 1750–1789* (Oxford: Clarendon Press, 1974), 131–216; Lefebvre, *The Great Fear of 1789*, 7–23.

34. Good discussions of the French aristocracy include Mousnier, *The Institutions of France* 1:112–213; David D. Bien, "La réaction aristocratique avant 1784: L'exemple de l'armée," *Annales: Economies, Sociétés, Civilisations* 29 (1974); Guy Chaussinard-Nogaret, *La noblesse au XVIIIe siècle: De la féodalité aux lumières* (Paris: Hachette, 1976); Zagorin, *Rebels and Rulers* 2:51–86; and Michel Vovelle, *The Fall of the French Monarchy, 1787–1792* (Cambridge: Cambridge University Press, 1984), 1–37.

and tithes for the church. By the 1700s much of the protective and administrative past of the French aristocracy had faded away, and nobles were largely rent receivers who no longer paid attention to purely local issues. Their demand for the deference and support of commoners nonetheless, however, would eventually undermine aristocratic power. Seigneurial privilege would ultimately collapse as a result of the growing gap between aristocratic pretensions and the reality of noble weakness.[35]

Lurking behind the long-term decline of the French aristocracy was the development of the forces of bureaucratic domination associated with the growth of French absolutism.[36] By the seventeenth century, French kings had created the most centralized and effective administrative and military machine in Europe. The economic sinews of French absolutism were naturally provided by the mountain of taxes paid from the French countryside. Between the end of the sixteenth century and 1789, French direct and indirect taxes increased many times over, although the precise quantities at stake are still widely debated.[37] Much of this tax burden was borne by rural communities in the form of excises and direct taxes on wealth and property, of which the taille is the best-known example. In clear contrast to England, taxation in France was imposed from above, and the arbitrary and nonnegotiable nature of the royal fisc was a source of general controversy until the fall of the monarchy.[38] For ordinary rural people, who were assigned collective responsibility for levying and apportioning taxes, the royal bureaucracy was a deeply ambivalent and often a threatening force. The king's agents were numerous and demanding, and even in times of peace they could undermine community peace through their constant interference with village or parish finances. Backed by a large standing army, the officers of the crown provided a constant point of conflict between rural communities and royal authority.[39]

Neither the king nor the aristocracy regarded ordinary rural people as anything more than a source of revenue and passive compliance with elite commands. The active consent of rural people was not considered to be part of the normal logic of seigneurial or royal government, and although allowed access to the royal courts,

35. Jones, *The Peasantry in the French Revolution,* 42–59.

36. For the logic of French absolutism, see Richard Bonney, *Political Change in France under Richelieu and Mazarin, 1624–1661* (Oxford: Oxford University Press, 1978), esp. 3–134; J. F. Bosher, *French Finances, 1770–1795: From Business to Bureaucracy* (Cambridge: Cambridge University Press, 1970). Also, see Alexis de Tocqueville, *The Old Regime and the French Revolution* (New York: Doubleday, 1955), esp. 32–107, 108–37.

37. The best discussion is in Collins, *Fiscal Limits of Absolutism,* 1–17, 65–107, 108–13, 214–22.

38. See, for example, Bonney, *Political Change in France,* 214–36; Goubert, *The French Peasantry,* 188–204; Charles Tilly, *The Contentious French* (Cambridge: Harvard University Press, Belknap Press, 1986), 380–404; and Bosher, *French Finances.*

39. Yves Marie Bercé, *Croquants et Nu-pieds: Les soulèvements paysans en France du XVIe au XIXe siècle* (Paris: Gallimard/Julliard, 1974), and Jones, *The Peasantry in the French Revolution,* 34–42.

rural communities were often excluded from the assemblies of estates and notables that survived the centralizing project of Louis XIV.[40] Rural commoners were
treated as "peasants" whose interests were less important than the prerogatives of
nobles and royal officials. In this context rural communities struggled to maintain
autonomy and cohesion against an entrenched elite who attempted to reduce the
rural population to a subordinate mass that would diligently obey orders. At least
in certain circumstances, the clash between community autonomy and elite privilege could take a violent turn, and in these moments of rebellion the institutions
of elite power were called in question by the violent representations of ordinary
people.

An excellent illustration of this conflict of institutional principles can be found
in the tax revolts of the sixteenth and seventeenth centuries. Between 1548 and the
1630s the French kingdom experienced a wave of local and regional insurrections
that were aimed at halting the escalating fiscal demands of the royal bureaucracy.[41] The revolts included that of the Pitauts in Angoumois, the Croquant and
Gautiers uprisings of the late 1500s, and the so-called Nouveaux Croquants and
Nu-pieds insurrections of the 1630s.[42] Although regionally confined largely to the
west, south, and parts of the center, these episodes reveal a common logic that
throws into sharp relief the dynamics of community politics and bureaucratic
domination in rural France. In all the regional tax revolts of this long period we
can identify two themes that underlie what otherwise might appear to be mindless
acts of savagery. First, these were genuine community revolts, and entire communities participated in the violence, regardless of economic background or class
position.[43] Second, the revolts were not simply generated by economic crisis;
instead, they involved nothing less than a violent contest over the conditions of
authority in rural France.

The first point has been recognized by many historians, including Ladurie,
Boris Porchnev, Yves Marie Bercé, and Pierre Goubert; its starkest expression can
be found in the Pitauts uprising of 1548.[44] The Pitauts referred to the armed
villagers that, as Ladurie writes, "marched parish by parish, under the banner of
each village" in order to resist the imposition of the salt tax, one of the chief
symbols of royal absolutism. At its peak, the revolt mobilized some ten thousand

40. Mousnier, *The Institutions of France*, 1:606–42; James Russell Major, *Representative Government in Early Modern France* (New Haven: Yale University Press, 1980), 160–77.

41. For the antifiscal revolts of this period, see Bercé, *Histoire des croquants*, esp. 129–276; René
Pillorget, *Les mouvements insurrectionnels de Provence entre 1596 et 1715* (Paris: A. Pedore, 1975),
esp. book 1, pp. 169–79, 242–300, and cases in book 2, pp. 313–76; and Bonney, *Political Change in
France*, 214–37.

42. Ladurie, *The French Peasantry*, 359–99.

43. Zagorin, *Rebels and Rulers* 1:214–27.

44. Ladurie, *The French Peasantry*, 359–400; Porchnev, *Les soulèvements populaires en France
de 1623 à 1648* (Paris: S.E.V.P.E.N., 1963); Yves Marie Bercé, *Fête et révolte: Des mentalités
populaires du XVIe au XVIIIe siècle* (Paris: Hachette, 1976); and Goubert, *The French Peasantry*,
205–19.

men in a direct clash with bureaucratic power. Armed with crossbows and farm tools, the Pitauts were led by parish priests, themselves fairly humble members of their communities. Before the revolt ended, the Pitaut bands killed tax collectors, assaulted merchants who engaged in the financing of the royal salt monopoly, and carried the revolt to the gates of Bordeaux. The demands of the rebels, preserved in the *Réclamations des communes d'Angoumois au Roi,* called for an end to the salt tax, the corruption of royal officials, and the institution of *gabeleur,* or salt-tax collectors. In short, the confederated communities of the region claimed jurisdiction over the range and nature of royal authority in the French countryside. Although ultimately subject to heavy repression, the Pitauts were not simply acting out of a rage of desperation that was doomed to defeat. According to Ladurie, "The aim of the rebels was perfectly clear in the reduction or abolition of the salt tax. Despite repression, which was heavy in Bordeaux and relatively light in Angoumois, this aim was achieved. The salt tax was finally abolished after 1550 (after payment of a heavy fine) in the provinces that had opposed it—proof, if proof were needed, of the effectiveness and rationality of the popular revolts."[45]

The relationship between community self-defense and the political logic of France's tradition of rural tax revolt also shows through the uproarious violence that occurred during the "new," or neo-Croquant, uprisings of 1636 and 1637. In 1636, once again the Angoumois, local "seditious" assemblies, gathered in order to discuss grievances and select leaders, like the petty judge Simon Estancheau, who was broken on the wheel for his participation. As more and more villages confederated around the common issue of royal taxes and official arbitrariness, the rebels proclaimed the "commune," or association of rebel communities, and laid siege to the towns that were the seats of royal power. In addition, they attacked tax collectors, who in some cases were chopped into pieces that were passed around and stuck to the doors of the rebels. The rebels' demands included an end to fiscal exemptions for the privileged and a reform of the tithe that would have transferred control of the church from the hierarchy to the ordinary parishoners, who had to pay the costs of the church. Above all, the rebels rejected the right of the crown to exact arbitrary taxes on land and wine, one of the staples of the local market economy.[46]

An even larger regional insurrection took place in 1637 in the area called Périgord. At its height the rebellion involved some four hundred parishes that confederated under the leadership of one La Mothe la Forët, a mystical former soldier. The rebels called for the abolition of locally unpopular taxes and beseeched the king to rule with mercy and justice. This display of deference, however, did not prevent the insurgents from "punishing" royal tax officials, nor did it stop the revolt from spreading out of its original base into Quercy, Sain-

45. Ladurie, *The French Peasantry,* 367–71, quotation from 365.
46. Ibid., 391–97.

tonge, Marche, and the Limousin.[47] In its original base area the revolt actually managed to last for roughly three years under the leadership of a man described as a "peasant soldier." What is striking about the revolts of 1636 and 1637 is that they continued a kind of tradition of local rebellion against royal authority, which seems to indicate that open revolt had become routinized, at least in some regions. For example, the uprisings of 1636 began in the same areas of Angoumois that had experienced the Pitaut incidents of the sixteenth century, and we are probably justified in believing that tax violence had become rooted in the folklore of villages throughout the region.[48] Evidently, collective violence had become legitimate in the discourse of local communities; moreover, violent resistance must have been seen as a plausible and effective means of dealing with royal power. If not, why did the sixteenth and seventeenth centuries witness so many tax revolts that assumed the character of ritual performances, something that Ladurie recognized when he referred to this period as the "peak of a sort of colorful communalism"?[49]

The obvious explanation for the tenacity and frequency of rural tax revolts is that taxation threatened the subsistence security of small cultivators who were already pressured by the population explosion of the 1500s.[50] But this explanation is incomplete, although it is certainly true that royal taxes pressed hard on the economy of rural France. It must be remembered that the tax revolts of the sixteenth and seventeenth centuries were not simply uprisings of the poor. They were community uprisings, and the prosperous as well as the poor actively took part. How can we explain the revolts as "subsistence rebellions" if they so often mobilized the well-off in defiance of royal power? Is it not likely that simple class models of popular behavior and collective violence must be replaced by a more nuanced interpretation that focuses on the *politics* of taxation and its implications for the authority of community institutions? This, I think, is the best way to understand the work of historians who have studied Croquandage in detail. French tax revolts should be understood as the playing out of a logic of community defense in which the principle of arbitrary royal taxation was the object of popular violence. The rebels were demanding nothing less than the right of local communities to exercise ultimate and final authority over the kinds of taxes that would be paid to the royal fisc. This was a direct challenge to the principles of bureaucratic domination that lay at the heart of French absolutism. The agents of the king demanded absolute dominion over the countryside, and it is not surprising that they viewed tax revolts with the greatest concern.[51]

Does this mean that Croquandage should be seen as failed protorevolutions?

47. Ibid., 396–97.
48. See, for example, the discussion in Bercé, *Croquants et Nu-pieds*.
49. Ladurie, *The French Peasantry*, 359–97.
50. Goubert, *The French Peasantry*, 188–219.
51. Zagorin, *Rebels and Rulers* 1:214–27.

The answer is certainly not. As Goubert and others have demonstrated, the tax revolts of the period did not call for a total transformation of French society, nor did they completely reject the authority of the crown, although they did look back to a kind of royal myth of benevolent kingship.[52] More important, the rebels were quite specific in their aims, and they focused on the abuses of bureaucratic domination rather than on the whole set of institutions associated with aristocratic power. Indeed, the absence of a frontal attack on the principle of nobility led Mousnier to conclude that Croquandage was manipulated by nobles for their own purposes. As Ladurie points out, this conclusion is too extreme, and tax revolts occurred with or without aristocratic support.[53] Croquandage and similar forms of tax protest were performances through which local communities represented themselves and their understanding of authority. These protests were much more than bargaining by riot; they were representative violence that created a space in which basic problems of politics and power were debated, disputed, and transformed. The tax revolts of the sixteenth and seventeenth centuries were radical challenges to the claim of royal bureaucrats to rule without community consent, and in this sense they were not simply mechanical responses to material deprivation.

The logic of representative violence at work in Croquandage can be clarified by focusing on one final episode of large-scale tax rebellion, the Nu-pieds revolt of 1639. The uprising began in lower Normandy, in the area of Avranches, and took its name from the rebel leader Jean Nu-pieds.[54] The immediate occasion for the revolt was the imposition of a new set of salt taxes that threatened to wipe out the political exemption from the salt tax that had previously been enjoyed by this part of Normandy. The rebels' opposition to the principle of royal arbitrariness that underlay the unilateral imposition of the salt tax is at least indirectly evident in their wide-ranging attacks on tax offices and officials and in their claim that a charter of Louis X from 1315 gave the Normans the right to consent to royal taxes. This invocation of lost rights and local privileges shows that the rebels saw themselves as engaged in a struggle over the terms of authority in the Norman countryside. Rallying around the myth of the charter also provided a means for horizontal federation among parish communities that, in the dispersed habitat of the bocage, needed a symbolic focus that cut across parish boundaries.[55]

But the rising of the Nu-pieds cannot be reduced to a simple material struggle over the salt tax. It was not a class struggle between rich and poor, or between the "peasantry" and the towns. Social participation in the rebellion was very broadly

52. Goubert, *The French Peasantry*, 188–219; Zagorin, *Rebels and Rulers* 1:214–27.
53. Ladurie, *The French Peasantry*, 366–70.
54. Ibid., 386–91; Madeleine Foisil, *La révolte des Nu-pieds et les révoltes normandes de 1639* (Paris: Presses universitaires de France, 1970), 171–79.
55. Bercé, *Croquants et Nu-pieds*, 82.

based, and leaders and followers came from the ranks of cultivators, artisans, salt workers, parish priests, and even some members of the petty nobility. This was a political rising of the bocage, the land of the hedgerow, against the unilateral imposition of novel forms of royal power that were unaccountable to community institutions.

The Nu-pied rebels, like those involved in the other Croquandage risings discussed here, were not necessarily interested in power for its own sake.[56] They were certainly motivated by a sense that the integrity of local institutional practices had been placed in jeopardy by the sudden and sweeping assertion of bureaucratic power. Who could predict how far the tax officials would go or how much of the community's harvest and labor they would claim? It was important to draw a boundary around community autonomy that royal officials would fear to violate, and rebellion was a way of placing that boundary before royal demands escalated into a massive assault on community resources.

Yet there was more to the politics of tax revolt than a simple effort to protect community authority over local resources. Taxation could also become a threat to the relative harmony of community life. French communities were collectively responsible for apportioning the tax bill presented to them by outside authorities. In this situation it is easy to imagine that ever more burdensome taxes could lead to escalating *intra* community conflicts as households argued with each other and with village leaders about who owed how much of the collective tax bill. Even worse, high taxes could impoverish weaker households, thereby heightening community tensions as the poor sought exemptions and the rich began to face the prospect of paying a larger share of the total tax. In small communities, where conflict as well as cooperation was a fact of life, the threat of new taxes could be met only with a mixture of fear and outrage, as was expressed by groups like the Nu-pieds.[57]

Those who are critical of the concept of community may concede that the tax revolts of the sixteenth and seventeenth centuries display a marked defense of community autonomy against outside interference. Yet they may argue that this was merely because Croquandage never escalated into a genuinely revolutionary challenge to the ancien régime. According to this logic, rural community was somehow an artifact of the world of status and privilege that characterized absolutist France. If that is true, once that world had dissolved after 1709, rural communities should have disappeared as effective units of power and production, and if community is less important than class, rural violence in the revolutionary years should have displayed a logic that differed in kind from the violence of early modern tax rebellions.

56. Zagorin, *Rebels and Rulers* 1:214–27.
57. Ladurie, *The French Peasantry*, 386–99.

The Rebellion within the Revolution, 1789–1815

The history of the French Revolution can be written from as many viewpoints as there are scholarly generations and political perspectives. But for our purposes the most salient viewpoint is the world of villages and parishes that defined the rural landscape of France on the eve of the great revolution. What happened to that world after 1789? Did community institutions disintegrate in the wake of a rural class war spearheaded by an agrarian bourgeoisie? More specifically, did the logic of rural politics between 1789 and 1815 correspond to a model of class conflict? Or did community continue to constitute the key logic of collective action in the countryside? Fortunately, all these questions can be addressed, thanks to the voluminous local and regional histories that have accumulated since the appearance of the pioneering studies of Georges Lefebvre.[58] Indeed, the problem is to find a way of synthesizing a vast literature that does justice to the complexity of the case. As a result, I have chosen to focus fairly closely on rural France, and I will make only intermittent forays into national and urban politics. Readers who are unfamiliar with the period may wish to consult one of the standard narrative histories that deal with the Revolution from the standpoint of national politics.[59]

It is worth noting that historians agree that the French Revolution led to very important changes in the countryside. Usually these changes have been understood within the rubric of the "crisis of feudalism," a crisis that led to the destruction of the institutions of seigneurial power in many regions of France. There is little doubt that, between 1789 and 1793, popular uprisings led to the forcible dismantling of aristocratic domination in a broad swath of territory stretching from the Atlantic coast to the eastern frontiers.[60] Yet, apart from this very general agreement, there is a great deal of debate about how we should conceptualize rural politics during the years of revolution. For example, Lefebvre and his students tended to see the events of 1789 and after through the prism of a simple model of peasant revolution in which the countryside struggled against the

58. Lefebvre, *Les paysans du Nord*. For overviews of the rural phase of the Revolution, see D. Hunt, "Peasant Politics in the French Revolution," *Social History* 9 (Oct. 1984), 277–99; G. Lemarchand, "La féodalité et la Révolution française: Seigneurie et communauté paysanne (1780–1799)," *Annales Historiques de la Révolution Française* 52 (4) (1980), 536–58; Emmanuel Le Roy Ladurie, "Révoltes et contestations rurales en France de 1675 à 1788," *Annales: Economies, Sociétés, Civilisations* 29 (1974), 6–22; R. B. Rose, "Tax Revolt and Popular Organization in Picardy, 1789–1791," *Past and Present* 43 (1969), 92–108; D. M. G. Sutherland, *The Chouans: The Social Origins of Popular Counter-Revolution in Upper Brittany, 1770–1796* (Oxford: Oxford University Press, 1982); and Jones, *The Peasantry in the French Revolution* (in my opinion the best synthesis in English or French).

59. For histories that deal more with provincial and social issues and less with high politics in Paris, see Donald M. G. Sutherland, *France, 1789–1815: Revolution and Counterrevolution* (New York: Oxford University Press, 1986); and Hunt, *Politics, Culture, and Class*.

60. Jones, *The Peasantry in the French Revolution*, 67–85, 103–9.

aristocratic and bourgeois forces of the towns.[61] "Revisionist" historians, however, have disputed the existence of any overarching ideological or social unity to
the rural phase of the Revolution; instead, they have shown how diverse and
locally specific rural politics became after 1789.[62]

This sort of debate can be resolved only by specialists, but a comparative and
theoretical perspective does help to clarify the issues. To begin with, there is no
reason to suppose that there must have been something like a "national" peasantry, and it is worth remembering that there were no national peasant parties or
associations in France during the revolutionary period. If class forces were
important they will show through the record only at local and regional levels.
Moreover, there is no reason to assume that commonly shared problems and
grievances necessarily led to identical responses throughout France, and scholars
should beware of generalizing from a single case to the whole of French agrarian
society.

What, then, can we say in a general way about the factors that led to the
breakdown of agrarian order after 1789? First, it is clear that the pressures of
aristocratic domination, often referred to as the seigneurial "reaction" of the
1700s, contributed to rural revolt in several regions of the countryside. The first
major waves of insurrection took place in 1789–90 in eight well-defined regions:
the Franche Comte, Dauphine, Provence, Hainaut and Cambresis, Lower Normandy, Maconnais, Alsace, and the southwest. According to P. M. Jones, all
these cases can be described as popular uprisings against the decaying manorial
order, and this fits with Georges Lefebvre's massive synthesis of case materials in
the *Great Fear*.[63] When news of the dramatic events in Paris reached the countryside, often in the form of wildly garbled rumors, it worked as a kind of signal
that the seigneurial regime was at an end. Entire villages marched on local
chateaux, seized or destroyed land deeds or feudal court rolls owned by the
aristocracy, and refused to pay manorial dues and tithes.[64]

In order to account for the antiseigneurial dimensions of the events in rural
France, we can use the concept of aristocratic domination. I have argued that one
dimension of nobility in the West was the tendency to assert unilateral, non-

61. Lefebvre, *The Great Fear of 1789*, 79–121.
62. Sutherland, *France, 1789–1815*, 126–60.
63. Jones, *The Peasantry in the French Revolution*, 67–85, 103–9; Lefebvre, *The Great Fear of 1789*, 99–121. Also see S. Aberdam, "La Révolution et la lutte des métagers," *Etudes Rurales* 59 (1975), 73–91; Boutier, "Jacqueries en pays croquant"; J. Dalby, "L'influence de la Révolution sur la société paysanne dans le Cantal, 1789–1794," *Revue de la Haute-Auvergne*, 49 (1983), 113–33; M. Edelstein, "La Feuille Villageoise, the Revolutionary Press, and the Question of Rural Political Participation," *French Historical Studies* 7 (1971), 175–203; Hunt, "Peasant Politics in the French Revolution," 277–97; H. C. Johnson, *The Midi in Revolution: A Study of Regional Political Diversity, 1789–1793* (Princeton: Princeton University Press, 1986), 100, 175–76.
64. Jones, *The Peasantry in the French Revolution*, 86–123.

reciprocal domination over land and labor. This sort of aristocratic imperium can be found in many parts of France prior to 1789, as seigneurs tried to tighten control of their estates through the unilateral imposition of increased dues and rents.[65] The symbol of this attempt to reassert manorial power in the face of popular opposition was the rise of a new professional group, the *feudistes,* experts in ancient manorial law who were hired by manor lords to discover and restore manorial dues that had fallen into disuse.[66] This imposition of lordly power was possible only because manor lords had the prerogative to control the renewal of the terriers, the estate registers that contained the list of manorial obligations owed by the lord's subjects. The ability of manor lords unilaterally to increase seigneurial obligations, *without* providing anything in return, neatly illustrates the logic of privileged property. It was the legal privilege of the lord to override the will of his subjects; this privilege was obliquely recognized in the statement by the municipality of Arpajon that there was no source of income more solid, more assured, than that of ground rent and that it involved no danger and no expense.[67] In practice, of course, the miracle of ground rent was constrained by the ability and willingness of rural people to resist aristocratic power, and by 1791 that resistance had escalated in many areas into a direct confrontation with the whole landed elite.

The exact range of obligations associated with aristocratic property varied across regions, but certain common forms of manorial dues can be singled out as exemplary. Leaving aside the survival of serfdom in a few areas, we can identify harvest dues as the most burdensome and unpopular form of manorial property. Known variously as *champart, terrage, agrier,* or *cens,* harvest dues were usually paid in kind at or near the time of the harvest, and the source of their unpopularity is not difficult to explain. In some areas, especially the southwest, they represented a large absolute burden on the subsistence opportunities of ordinary cultivators, and in the areas subject to the laws called the Custom of Poitou, harvest dues could take as much as 25 percent of gross production.[68] Even worse, harvest dues taken in kind reduced the ability of farmers, large and small alike, to take advantage of the expanding eighteenth-century market for grain and wine. Since they were inflexible, dues in kind interfered with the capacity of small producers to play the market by balancing the amount of grain sold and consumed in line with price fluctuations. Harvest dues constituted a kind of compulsory opportunity cost that weighed heavily on the right of local communities autonomously to control the process of production and distribution. Finally, harvest dues

65. Ibid., 30–59. Also see William Doyle, *Origins of the French Revolution* (Oxford: Oxford University Press, 1980), 195–98.

66. Jones, *The Peasantry in the French Revolution,* 42–59. Also see Lemarchand, "La féodalité et la Révolution française."

67. Jones, *The Peasantry in the French Revolution,* 55–56.

68. Ibid., 44–51.

represented the "parasitic" face of lordship in eighteenth-century France, because such dues were not paid in recognition of any real functions performed by the lord. Increasingly, French nobles who claimed manorial privileges were simply rent receivers with no real role in the communities they ruled. The protective functions of French lordship had largely disappeared by 1789, and it is not surprising that popular irritation with manorial power grew in step with the efforts of lords to revive and force seigneurial customs.[69]

In addition to harvest dues, French seigneurs extracted a range of other obligations, including transfer taxes on property (*lods et ventes*), death dues (*mainmorte*), and fines for the violation of lordly rights to hunt game. In some areas, aristocratic monopolies (*banalités*) required seigneurial subjects to use the lord's mills and wine presses, and, like harvest dues, banalités restricted the ability of rural commoners autonomously to control the terms and conditions of the marketplace. Even the tithe, the notional tenth paid to the local church, was in some cases appropriated by seigneurs, who thereby added the tithe in kind to the rent roll.[70]

By the last decades of the eighteenth century this whole complex of ancient obligations had become the subject of controversy throughout France, and rural communities had begun to resist seigneurial pretensions even before 1789 changed the logic and balance of power in the countryside. As the *cahiers de doléances,* or statements of grievances written for the convocation of the States General, reveal, rural communities were willing to launch a frontal assault on aristocratic power, whether or not local manor lords had tried to heighten seigneurial jurisdiction in the decades preceding the revolution. As the research of P. M. Jones has demonstrated, there was little doubt that ordinary rural people would seize the political opportunity of the Revolution to dismantle aristocratic domination. Jones investigated 389 parish cahiers, and he concluded that, in the area of Troyes, 40 percent of rural cahiers criticized seigneurial dues and monopoly rights, while the cahiers from Auxerre and Sens listed these sorts of grievances in 36 and 27 percent of all cases, respectively. Interestingly, the cahiers were written by small-town lawyers and notaries who often had an interest in preserving feudal privileges, and the fact that the figures are as high as they are shows how powerful rural pressure must have been to include them in grievance lists that otherwise would have omitted them entirely.[71]

Seigneurial power was an issue that united entire communities in opposition to

69. Lefebvre, *The Great Fear of 1789,* 7–46, 101–21. Also see Hunt, "Peasant Politics in the French Revolution."

70. Jones, *The Peasantry in the French Revolution,* 42–59; Duby and Wallon, eds., *Histoire de la France rurale,* 2:562, 583.

71. Jones, *The Peasantry in the French Revolution,* 60–85, 103–23, 59; and see P. M. Jones, *Politics and Rural Society: The Southern Massif Central, c. 1750–1880* (Cambridge: Cambridge University Press, 1985). For a more "revisionist" view, see George V. Taylor, "Noncapitalist Wealth and the Origins of the French Revolution," *American Historical Review* 72 (2) (1967), 469–96.

noble authority. Every community member, from the most prosperous farmer to the lowliest cottager, had an interest in eliminating the forms of manorial power that restricted and, in some cases, undermined the autonomy of community institutions. When local revolts broke out against aristocratic power they could draw on the more or less unified collectivity of the village or parish, and the issues at stake were less questions of class than issues of authority. Who would have the ultimate right to determine the politics of the community, and would this right reside in the lord or the assembled householders who formed the communauté d'habitants? These were the questions that led to violence and to the forcible destruction of the symbols and substance of manorial power.

Indeed, the violence studied so meticulously by Jones, Boutier, Lefebvre, and Bois was highly localized, often encompassing the territory of only a single village or manor.[72] It took the form of a more or less well organized outburst of arson, looting and, in some instances, murder. But, in contrast to the supralocal community confederations of the sixteenth and seventeenth centuries, there seems to be no evidence of regional movements or associations that bound together these many simultaneous but separate acts of revolt. This lack demonstrates that local political struggles rather than translocal class conflict defined collective violence in France during much of the revolutionary upheaval.

Still, the struggle to abolish aristocratic domination did not exhaust the range of factors that generated insurrection in the countryside. Two related sets of problems grew out of coercive commercialization and bureaucratic domination. Some parts of France had undergone a kind of analogue to English enclosure prior to 1789, particularly in the cereal-growing regions near major urban centers.[73] Landlords, whether aristocratic or bourgeois, gave license to large-scale farmers to extinguish common rights in order to transform estates into profitable commercial enterprises. This led to local struggles between commercial middlemen and local communities that refused to relinquish local rights of common pasture and collective control of wastes and forests.[74] As I pointed out earlier, this kind of struggle could end in violent attacks on the offending enclosers when, during the revolutionary upheaval, the chance for communities to settle old scores presented itself. For example, in the Mâconnais, tensions had been mounting for some time before 1789 as a result of the enclosure of local commons by absentee magnates and ecclesiastical landowners. Local flocks were excluded from the commons, and nonresident proprietors (forains) introduced commercial livestock in their place.[75] Villagers responded by destroying ditches and hedges in a French version

---

72. Jones, *The Peasantry in the French Revolution*, 67–80, 103–23; Bois, *Paysans de l'Ouest*, 190–219, 577–678; Boutier, "Jacqueries en pays croquant"; Ladurie, "Révoltes et contestations."

73. Jones, *The Peasantry in the French Revolution*, 67, 74–76, 121–29; F. Evrard, "Les paysans du Mâconnais et les brigandages de juillet 1789," *Annales de Bourgogne* 19 (1947), 7–39, 97–121.

74. Jones, *The Peasantry in the French Revolution*, 67–81, 121–34, 143–44.

75. Evrard, "Les paysans du Mâconnais."

of the enclosure riot, and by 1789 a local revolt against both manorial power and coercive entrepreneurship broke out at Igé. Violence then spread to Verzé, Cluny, and Senozan, where the enclosing steward of the Talleyrand Perigord family was held to account for his usurpation of the commons. As F. Evrard has shown, the crisis in the Mâconnais was a complex affair with roots in the collapse of wine prices in the mid-1780s and the savage winter of 1788–89. But running through the whole of the period was the struggle to defend community-property rights against the thrusting large-scale middlemen, who were trying to use the willingness of royal officials to enforce the "superior" rights of lords and entrepreneurs as a weapon against the common rights of local communities. As Jones argues, in regions like the Mâconnais the period beginning in 1789 saw a mixture of local antiseigneurialism and a popular assault on anyone who threatened common rights, especially the rights associated with vaine pature.[76]

Admittedly, these quarrels look like old-fashioned class conflict, and readers who cannot imagine a theoretical world without class struggle will view this sort of evidence as proof of a war between peasants and emerging bourgeois farmers over the future of rural France. However appealing the conclusion might be, it should be qualified in two respects. First, the kinds of "antienclosure" violence that occurred in the Mâconnais were probably much less pervasive than the local conflicts that erupted over the survival of aristocratic power. Lefebvre was certainly right to stress the bonds of communal solidarity that marked the revolutionary period; in the absence of those bonds, which cut across social and occupational divisions, it would be difficult to explain how rural collective action could have occurred at all.[77]

More important, it seems just as reasonable to see the events in regions like the Mâconnais as expressions of political conflict and community self-defense.[78] As I already pointed out, commercial farmers were never universal targets of popular wrath after 1789; indeed, they sometimes led their villages into revolt against the forces of aristocracy and bourgeois power. A defender of strict class logic must find this deeply puzzling, even anomalous, and the problem suggests the need to look more closely at the political dimensions of the problem.

What is striking about the Mâconnais case is that popular anger was directed against powerful outsiders, called *forains*, whose economic behavior was not subject to the regulative control of community institutions. The forains used the protective shield of seigneurial power unilaterally to challenge common-property rights, and they could be held accountable through the reciprocal hierarchies of village life.[79] In short, they threatened to overturn community life through a process of dispossession. It was in this context that they became a target of

76. Jones, *The Peasantry in the French Revolution*, 71–81.
77. Ibid., 77–78; Lefebvre, *The Great Fear of 1789*, 91–121.
78. See in this regard *Les communautés rurales/Rural Communities*.
79. Jones, *The Peasantry in the French Revolution*, 7–29, 75, 30–34.

popular violence, and we may feel justified in believing that it was their political status as "irresponsible" outsiders, rather than their class backgrounds, that made them both visible and hated.

A simple class logic that posits an inevitable conflict between precommercial peasants and commercial farmers will also have difficulty explaining the social composition of the forces of insurrection in areas like the Mâconnais. As Evrard has shown, the Mâconnais on the eve of 1789 was deeply involved in the commercial wine economy, and many of the rebels who attacked enclosures were sharecroppers and laborers whose own livelihood depended on market forces.[80] They did not rise in revolt against the market as an abstract principle; instead, they turned their anger against those who had violated the autonomy and integrity of community institutions. It seems best to understand this as a political contest between local communities and the forces of elite constraint that undercut local practices. The struggle to maintain common rights like vaine pature was more than a question of subsistence; it was a struggle to determine who would rule the countryside.[81]

A good illustration of the tenacious defense of community institutions can be found in the history of the various pieces of land-reform legislation passed by the succession of revolutionary regimes that governed France prior to the rise of Napoleon.[82] Most of these regimes were resolute defenders of what I have called "exclusive" or bourgeois property rights. They believed that all forms of property should be vested in individual owners who should have the prerogative to control their property without any corporate or communal controls. As a result, they enacted a whole series of decrees that sought to abolish common-land and use rights, disestablish corporate landholders like the church, and enhance the ability of landowners freely to buy, sell, and enclose land. For example, the decree of August 14, 1792, mandated the division of all nonwooded commons, although the precise mode of division was left uncertain. More significant was the legislation of June 10, 1793, which provided for the division of commons into freehold plots on a per capita basis if at least one-third of the inhabitants of a given community voted in favor of the plan.[83]

In theory, legislation of this kind would have created a nation of yeoman

80. Evrard, "Les paysans du Mâconnais," 7–39, 97–121.

81. For some "micro" studies of rural insurrection and "counterrevolution" that show its political character, see Le Goff and Sutherland, "The Social Origins of Counter-Revolution"; Sutherland, *The Chouans;* Gwynne Lewis, *The Second Vendée: The Continuity of Counter-Revolution in the Department of the Gard, 1789–1815* (Oxford: Clarendon Press, 1978), esp. 1–79; Charles Tilly, *The Vendée* (Cambridge: Harvard University Press, 1976), esp. 58–99; and H. L. Root, "En Bourgogne: L'état et la communauté rurale, 1661–1789," *Annales: Economies, Sociétés, Civilisations* 37 (1982), 288–302.

82. R. B. Rose, "The 'Red Scare' of the 1790's: The French Revolution and the Agrarian Law," *Past and Present* 103 (1984), 113–30; Jones, *The Peasantry in the French Revolution,* 86–103.

83. Jones, *The Peasantry in the French Revolution,* 144–54.

proprietors if it had been fully implemented. But, in fact, the mountain of revolutionary land-reform laws failed to be fully effective. Some laws died at the legislative stage; others were thoroughly redrafted or rescinded by subsequent statutes.[84] More important, however, the attack on common-property rights failed because of widespread popular opposition. It is true that in areas of land shortage and demographic pressure, the reform decrees offered a useful pretext for expanding arable production at the expense of stock raising, and some scholars have argued that they thereby benefited small and land-poor cultivators, who could use them to transform themselves into secure proprietors.[85]

Yet, in many regions the reform laws remained a dead letter well into the nineteenth century, and rural communities stoutly defended collective-use rights, especially common grazing. What explains the tenacious defense of common rights in some cases but not others? I would suggest that whether or not communities opposed the reform legislation depended on its implications for the autonomy and cohesion of local institutions. In regions of acute land shortage, the division of common lands actually might have enhanced the survival of community institutions by broadening the base of property-owning households that could afford to support the life of the village or parish.[86] But in regions lacking such demographic erosion, the reform laws may have seemed a threat to community autonomy akin to the threat presented by coercive enclosures. French rural communities had a long history of authoritatively controlling the use of land and labor through village and parish institutions, and the reform decrees promised to eliminate community autonomy by transferring political control of property relations to the new supralocal institutions of the revolutionary regime.[87] Consequently, the resistance to the abolition of use rights was as much a political as an economic matter, and the community decision to support or oppose the reforms was made in response to the logic of the local political economy.

This point has been made quite forcefully by Jones, who, in answer to scholars who have seen an expression of class conflict in the response to the reform laws, has argued, "The reality is altogether less complicated. By and large the commons were not partitioned because it suited nobody's interest to do so. Most peasants shared a customary conception of property and they found the decree of 10 June 1793 a source of frustration rather than inspiration."[88] The most important term here is "customary," because it shows how significant local practices of property were in defining the logic of rural politics in revolutionary France. The

84. Ibid. 124–54.
85. Lefebvre, *Les paysans du Nord*, 549–51; Jones, *The Peasantry in the French Revolution*, 154–66.
86. J. J. Clàre, *Les paysans de la Haute-Marne et la Révolution française: Recherches sur les structures de la communauté villageoise*, 2 vols. (Ph.D. diss., University of Dijon, 1979), 2:456–561; Jones, *The Peasantry in the French Revolution*, 137–66.
87. Jones, *The Peasantry in the French Revolution*, 167–205.
88. Ibid., 148.

key issue was not an abstract clash between precommercial and commercial or bourgeois classes, nor was it a struggle between tradition and modernity. The problem was how the events of 1789 and after would affect local institutions of politics and production. Historically, those institutions had mediated between elite power and the subsistence needs of ordinary rural people. Any threat to dispossess those institutions endangered the ability of ordinary people to defend themselves in a world that had always pressed hard against their interests; as a result, the opportunities and threats of the revolutionary era were evaluated in terms of their implications for community survival.[89]

The logic of community defense in the revolutionary period can also be seen in the response of rural people to the forces of bureaucratic domination, both before and after the fall of French absolutism. Along with aristocratic power and coercive commercialization, the problem of bureaucratic power constituted a major focus of popular violence from 1789 through the end of the 1790s, and the local revolts that defied the authority of both pre- and postrevolutionary governments clearly reveal the deep politics of the French Revolution in the countryside.

The decision to elect a national assembly of estates according to a broad franchise was a response to the fiscal crisis of French absolutism, and the king and his ministers, who chose to convoke this assembly in 1789, probably never believed that it would provide the occasion for a massive outpouring of popular opposition to the monarchy.[90] But for ordinary rural people, whose encounters with the bureaucratic agents of absolutism had long been difficult, the events of 1789 offered an opportunity to dismantle the local structure of bureaucratic power. Local cahiers of grievances called for the elimination of the taille and other direct and indirect taxes, the reform of the General Farm, which collected indirect taxes; and the thorough overhaul of royal justice. More significant, however, was the willingness of rural communities to back up words with deeds, and in areas like Picardy that were heavily taxed, the news of July 14 led to collective attacks on the tax bureaucracy.[91] Tollgates and customhouses were smashed, and many tax officials fled for their lives. By 1790 the whole northeast was in open opposition to the tax on alcoholic drinks, a tax that was particularly irksome to small-scale cultivators who sold wine and grapes to local markets. Meanwhile, in Languedoc

89. The importance of local interests and institutions in determining "revolutionary" or "counter-revolutionary" popular attitudes emerges in many studies. See, for example, Richard Cobb, *The People's Armies: The Armées Révolutionnaires, Instrument of the Terror in the Departments, April 1793 to Floréal Year II* (New Haven: Yale University Press, 1987), 249–512; Marc Bouloiseau, *The Jacobin Republic, 1792–1794* (Cambridge: Cambridge University Press, 1983), 83–118, 155–90; Le Goff and Sutherland, "The Social Origins of Counter-Revolution," 65–87; Timothy Tackett, *Religion, Revolution, and Regional Culture in Eighteenth Century France: The Ecclesiastical Oath of 1791* (Princeton: Princeton University Press, 1986), esp. 34–58, 159–204.

90. Sutherland, *France, 1789–1815*, esp. 15–87.

91. Jones, *The Peasantry and the French Revolution*, 34–42, 62–67, 180–91, and Rose, "Tax Revolt," 92–108.

and Rousillon, violent episodes occurred with sufficient frequency and ferocity to alarm the national authorities. At Béziers, a crowd infuriated by the confiscations of untaxed wine drove fifty-two tax officials to seek refuge in the hôtel de ville.[92] Indeed, throughout France, the years from 1789 to 1791 resemble a vast but uncoordinated tax strike that combined passive noncompliance with collective violence.[93]

The immediate background to this upsurge of popular antitax and antibureaucratic behavior is fairly easy to understand. Tax rates were high in the 1770s and 1780s, although there was probably nothing like the tripling of royal tax rates that took place between the 1630s and 1660s.[94] Nevertheless, taxes could take a substantial share of the cash income of rural households, and in a region like the lower Auvergne, direct taxation actually shot up by 60 percent between 1730–39 and 1780–90. Obviously, royal taxation was a real and visible burden for ordinary rural people, particularly for those who, under the regime of collective taxation, had to pay for their poorer neighbors.[95]

It would be a mistake, however, to assume that popular hostility to the agents of royal bureaucracy was simply motivated by material hardship. Opposition was also generated by the extraordinary intrusiveness and complex inequities that were characteristic of taxation during the ancien régime. Tax officials formed a huge and corrupt bureaucracy that was constantly pressuring rural communities to pay their taxes, and the "legal" tax bill was often inflated by illegal surcharges and outright bribes.[96] Moreover, tax defaulters and resisters could be subjected to a whole range of degrading and brutal punishments, including the forcible quartering of troops on delinquent communities. Finally, the tax system was a jumble of exemptions, special jurisdictions, and outrageous inequities. Whole groups of the population, especially nobles and the clergy, were exempt from most taxes, which left rural people with the clear impression that only they were forced to pay for a bureaucracy that gave them little in return.[97] It should not be forgotten that royal justice meant little in the countryside because of its expense and its physical and social distance from the world of the village. To be sure, some royal officials, like the intendants of the late eighteenth century, did support local communities against rapacious lords, and Hilton Root has argued that rural communities in Burgundy were quite able to sue the seigneurs in the royal courts.[98] But litigation should not blind us to the fact that most rural communities were not represented in

92. Jones, *The Peasantry in the French Revolution*, 181–83.

93. Rose, "Tax Revolt," 92–108.

94. Jones, *The Peasantry in the French Revolution*, 34–41.

95. A. Poitrineau, *La vie rurale en Basse Auvergne au XVIIIe siècle* (Paris, 1965); see Duby and Wallon, *Histoire de la France rurale* 2:423.

96. Tilly, *The Contentious French*, 119–61, 201–44; see Collins, *Fiscal Limits of Absolutism*, 166–222.

97. Jones, *The Peasantry in the French Revolution*, 181–91.

98. Root, *Peasants and King in Burgundy*, 156–93.

the royal government, and soldiers and tax collectors were probably the only representatives of the regime with whom many rural people came into contact.[99] After all, the logic of absolutism was to minimize all forms of popular and corporate control over the decisions of royal officials. This logic applied with special force to the countryside, which was seen largely as a source of taxes and cannon fodder.[100]

Even worse, the exact rationale for the tax system was almost impossible to justify or explain, and enormous disparities in tax rates between localities and groups were a constant source of irritation to rural communities. For example, the village of Belmont overlapped the border of the provinces of Guyenne and Languedoc, but because tax rates and methods of assessment varied radically in the two provinces, the villagers in Languedoc paid one-third less for their holdings than those in Guyenne did for equivalent holdings. Not surprisingly, the people of Belmont treated a provincial tax "reform" commission to a tirade against the "horrors of capriciousness" that governed their lives.[101]

Naturally, ordinary rural people were not inherently egalitarian—far from it. But they did resent and resist the constraints imposed on them by an alien officialdom that could not be controlled or held accountable through the routine institutional practices of community politics. Royal taxes and tax officials affected every aspect of local life. They drained away scarce resources in the form of an endless stream of money, thereby reducing the capacity of communities to mobilize land and labor in a way that would maximize their ability to survive periodic episodes of dearth. They also impinged on the few items of popular consumption, like wine and spirits, by increasing the price and interfering with popular control of the market.[102] In addition, communities that failed to pay on time or in the right amounts could find themselves forced to borrow from urban money lenders and tax officials, and debts accumulated in this way added little to the productive economy of local communities.[103]

Given the parasitic and arbitrary nature of the royal bureaucracy, and the long traditions of tax protest in regions like the southwest, the reaction of rural people to the crisis of royal power in 1789 is perfectly understandable. Local communities sought to destroy the most onerous and visible forms of royal taxation, and they sought to turn bureaucratic power into an agency accountable to community institutions. Bureaucratic domination had long been part of the forces of constraint that impinged on the autonomy and cohesion of local institutions, and 1789

---

99. Tilly, *The Contentious French,* esp. 201–44.

100. For a similar argument, see Theda Skocpol, *States and Social Revolutions: A Comprehensive Analysis of France, Russia, and China* (Cambridge: Cambridge University Press, 1979), 46–66, 118–27.

101. Jones, *The Peasantry in the French Revolution,* 39.

102. Rose, "Tax Revolt," 92–108.

103. Root, *Peasants and King in Burgundy,* 34–40.

opened up the possibility of transforming the basis of royal power. The tax revolts of 1789 and after signaled an end to rural absolutism and the rise of a new popular consciousness of the power of ordinary men and women to make history.[104] This was the most radical implication of 1789 and the hard years that followed.

Yet we should not confuse rural radicalism with revolution; nor should we believe in some inherent "peasant" consciousness that was either naturally pro-monarchist or prorepublican. After the fall of the monarchy and the rise of the republic in 1792–93, rural France fragmented into pro- and antirepublican regions; these divisions were to last in some instances into the twentieth century. The Revolution was a national event, but in rural areas it was a chance to express the deepest sentiments of localism and particularism. Similarly, the response to the escalating radicalism of national politics was determined by its meaning for local life and local institutions, as Lynn Hunt has shown. In the countryside, the response to national events was probably a function of their implications for community autonomy and politics, and we have already seen how different regions of the country responded to the tenurial reforms of 1793 very differently.[105] The same point applies to all the other legislation and policies of the revolutionary governments, and no class logic, with its assumption of a unitary fit between social position and political action, can account for the marked diversity of rural responses to the Revolution. Some communities remained staunchly monarchist and antirevolutionary, while others became strongly republican.[106] Most, however, seem to have maintained a guarded neutrality, accepting revolutionary laws that abolished manorial and aristocratic power, while rejecting novel revolutionary taxes and requisitions. Much depended on whether the new bureaucracy and legal order threatened community institutions, and when they did, local communities were capable of violently resisting the new forces of bureaucratic domination unleashed by the Revolution. For example, national conscription, although dictated by the imperatives of France's war for survival in a world hostile to the revolutionary order, was widely detested in rural France, as were the roaming revolutionary tribunals and requisitioning forces, which have been studied in depth by Richard Cobb. When communities were pushed to the brink of real material hardship by revolutionary taxes, or faced the loss of authority at the hands of revolutionary officials, they tended to fight back or withdraw into a stony isolation and indifference that frustrated revolutionary elites.[107] As Alexis de Tocqueville noted, the Revolution threw up a new bureaucratic machine that gradually extended its grip on all areas of life, and it can be argued that rural communities shaped their overall reaction to the Revolution in terms of their

104. Jones, *The Peasantry in the French Revolution*, 207–40.

105. Hunt, *Politics, Culture, and Class*, 123–48, 213–36.

106. Jones, *The Peasantry in the French Revolution*, 206–47.

107. Cobb, *The People's Armies*, 249–480, and Denis Woronoff, *The Thermidorean Regime and the Directory, 1794–1799* (Cambridge: Cambridge University Press, 1984), 1–28, 99–104.

ability or inability to control the agents of bureaucratic power according to local norms.[108]

An interesting illustration of this comes from the complex and contradictory events that accompanied the revolutionary elite's attempt to purge and radically transform the institutions of the French church.[109] On July 12, 1790, the revolutionary National Assembly passed the Civil Constitution of the Clergy, which transformed all priests and ecclesiastics into paid civil servants who were to be elected by district and departmental assemblies. The total number of clergy was reduced, papal authority over the French church drastically curtailed, and all church property placed in the power of the national state. Large blocks of church land and estates had already been auctioned off as "national properties," and the decision to create a salaried priesthood was a bold attempt to turn the church into a moral arm of bureaucratic power.[110] Finally, by means of the decree of November 27–December 26, 1790, all bishops and priests were required to swear an oath of loyalty to the nation and the Civil Constitution of the Clergy, thereby drawing a clear line between religious propriety and clerical sedition.[111] Priests who refused the oath were subject to a range of penalties, including dismissal from their posts, and the result was a hopeless division of the church into "constitutional" loyalists and "refractories," who resisted both the oath and the Revolution.[112] By 1793, as the Revolution entered its most violent and destructive phase, the revolutionaries escalated the stakes by embarking on a program that would lead to the attempt to de-Christianize France in the name of a new "cult of reason and the supreme being."[113]

Rural responses to the attack on the church varied enormously among regions and localities, although the excesses of de-Christianization probably generated fairly general disgust. Some localities, especially those where the church was part of the aristocratic order, welcomed the abolition of clerical tithes as a blow against seigneurialism, and some cultivators must have benefited from the purchase of church lands.[114] In addition, some communities, never deeply affected by church rituals and dogmas, were immune to the consequences of an attack on a church hierarchy that was often socially alien and physically absent. We might speculate that these were also communities rooted in nuclear villages, where the institutions of the parish had never been central to the regulation of popular life.

In any event, the assault on the church did generate enormous popular resistance in some rural areas, particularly parts of the west. The savage Vendée

---

108. Tocqueville, *The Old Regime and the French Revolution*, 19–21.
109. Sutherland, *France, 1789–1815*, 94–96, 115–17.
110. Tackett, *Religion, Revolution, and Regional Culture*, 3–33.
111. Vovelle, *The Fall of the French Monarchy*, 160–62.
112. Tackett, *Religion, Revolution, and Regional Culture*, 59–74.
113. Sutherland, *France, 1789–1815*, 208–17, 280–82.
114. Jones, *The Peasantry in the French Revolution*, 238–40, 154–66.

uprisings, and the less well known phenomenon called Chouannerie (or small insurrections), were instances of local and regional rebellion against the anti-Catholic policies of the revolutionary elites.[115] These insurrections were radical in their rejection of the revolutionary bureaucracy and its commitment to recasting the politics and religious practices of rural communities. In some cases, the insurrections that grew out of the defense of the local church developed into real counterregimes that challenged the capacity of revolutionary officials to rule the countryside. For example, between 1794 and 1796, Chouan rebels controlled most of Brittany, leading Sutherland to conclude that Chouannerie was "the most extensive, persistent and durable peasant movement of the revolution."[116]

Uprisings of this kind cannot be lumped under the heading of "reactionary" or "counterrevolutionary" movements that were caused and manipulated by reactionary elites. These were genuinely popular events, as Sutherland has shown, and they involved much the same forms of community self-defense and self-mobilization that took place during the antiseigneurial and antitax revolts of 1789–91.[117] In fact, Chouannerie and related forms of violence probably took place in regions where the parish was central to the territorial and political definition of local communities. For instance, in parts of the west the parish church was a key focus of popular politics and ritual, and parish priests were resident locals who came from quite humble backgrounds.[118] As a result, the assault on the church became hopelessly entangled with a more general attack on the autonomy and integrity of community institutions, because any attempt to recast the authority of the parish threatened to unravel the fabric of local leadership and community cooperation. Once again, these attacks led to a political struggle over the definition of who had ultimate jurisdiction in the countryside, and the logic of the contest pitted local communities against the monopolistic claims of the revolutionary state, which could not tolerate the existence of a popular priesthood that could provide a focus for rural opposition to the new order.[119]

As the very diverse reactions to the assault on the church show, the revolutionary years in France do not lend themselves to an analysis that uses a global or

115. See, for example, Harvey Mitchell, "Resistance to the Revolution in Western France," in Douglas Johnson, ed., *French Society and the Revolution* (Cambridge: Cambridge University Press, 1976), 248–85.

116. Sutherland, *France, 1789–1815*, 257; Sutherland, *The Chouans*; T. J. A. Le Goff and D. M. G. Sutherland, "The Revolution and the Rural Community in Eighteenth Century Brittany," *Past and Present* 62 (1974), 96–119.

117. Sutherland, *The Chouans*, esp. 14–82, 127–66, 195–221.

118. For the parish as community and its significance, see Peter Jones, "Parish, Seigneurie, and the Community of Inhabitants in Southern Central France during the Eighteenth Century and Nineteenth Century," *Past and Present* 91 (1981), 74–108.

119. Tackett, *Religion, Revolution, and Regional Culture*, 159–82; Timothy Tackett, *Priest and Parish in Eighteenth Century France: A Social and Political Study of the Curés in a Diocese of Dauphiné, 1750–1791* (Princeton: Princeton University Press, 1977), esp. 151–93, 202–9, 269–306.

national concept of peasant revolution. The evidence presented in this section underscores the importance of looking to local politics for the key to rural behavior in the revolutionary decades. Much of what happened in the countryside after 1789 is best described in terms of the logic of community defense and representative violence. Communities were able to mobilize for a violent and radical challenge to fundamental aspects of both the old order and the new revolutionary dispensation, and violence became a medium of representation through which the formal and informal constitution of rural authority was disputed and recast. In sum, rural France experienced highly fragmented and localized waves of rebellion that never fully crossed over into a genuinely revolutionary assault on all established institutions. For example, community violence rarely challenged the hierarchies of age and gender that were at the heart of community life, and the lack of enthusiasm for national politics and national elections also indicates how local issues continued to dominate rural life even after the proclamation of the republic of equals.[120]

Nor should the waves of rural rebellion that occurred within the larger framework of the Revolution be written off as futile exercises with no lasting effects. Popular violence undoubtedly helped to weaken the French aristocracy permanently, and at least some rural people gained from the sale of church and émigré property. Moreover, rural communities were able selectively to adapt to the policies of various revolutionary governments, and the survival of common-land and use rights in the face of elite opposition demonstrates the tenacity of community practices in an era of expanding commercialization.[121] Rural communities were never opposed to the market as such, but they did try to control the market through local institutions and practices that reserved an economic space for communities outside of the power of elite landlords and middlemen. Finally, the ability of communities to defend their priests and parishes against bureaucratization reveals the inadequacy of any notion of rural passivity and powerlessness.[122]

Many of the reforms initiated by revolutionary elites may have strengthened local autonomy, at least over the short term. The destruction of aristocratic jurisdictions destroyed the manor as a possible threat to community insitutions and eliminated the swarms of seigneurial officials who had interfered with every aspect of popular life. More important, the decision to transform the ancient communauté d'habitants into a modern municipality, fittingly called a commune, gave the imprimatur of state legitimacy to a sphere of community politics that could regulate local behavior according to community conventions.[123] The new

120. L. Hunt, D. Lansky, and P. Hanson, "The Failure of the Liberal Republic in France, 1795–1799: The Road to Brumaire," *Journal of Modern History* 51 (4) (1979), 734–59; Jones, *The Peasantry in the French Revolution*, 206–70.

121. Jones, *The Peasantry in the French Revolution*, 248–70, 124–66.

122. Tackett, *Religion, Revolution, and Regional Culture*, 287–302.

123. Jones, *The Peasantry in the French Revolution*, 86–123, 248–70, 173–80.

communes also provided for fairly regular elections of petty officials, which could only have strengthened the credibility and accountability of community leaders. Indeed, to the degree that they respected traditional community boundaries, the communes introduced by the Revolution may have been the most popular of all the revolutionary innovations, precisely because the new municipalities tacitly recognized the salience of territorial community in rural France.

From Resistance to Accommodation, 1851–1900

In 1851, several waves of rural and small-town insurrection shook the foundations of Louis Napoleon Bonaparte's newly established regime. Napoleon III had recently made clear his intention to replace the Second Republic, the gift of the revolution of 1848, with a personalist and authoritarian regime in which the Bonaparte dynasty would be restored to power.[124] In many parts of France, both urban and rural, Napoleon III was recognized as a heroic savior. But in the thirteen departments in the center, southwest, and southeast, insurgent bands of more than 1,000 fairly well armed men challenged Napoleon's coup in the name of the almost mystical concept of the republic. At its height, this largely decentralized revolt may have involved over 100,000 participants, and at least 26,884 persons were tried by special judicial commissions after the insurrections were repressed. This was a sizable movement by any standards, especially when one remembers that entire departments, like Hérault and the Drôme, took up arms. As Ted Margadant has argued, the events of 1851 constituted the last major rural insurrection in French history, although its significance was lost on contemporaries like Karl Marx, who evidently believed that rural politics were simply unimportant.[125]

In fact, the most striking aspect of 1851 was the strong support for the insurrection shown by rural communities, particularly in the south. Entire communes rose up in defense of the republic, and as Agulhon has demonstrated, the events of 1851 were deeply rooted in the traditional institutions of community solidarity and sociability, which were well established in regions like the south, where nuclear villages and solidary hamlets provided the template for daily life.[126] In such regions common rights to woods and pastures were still defended by local communities, even in the face of the exclusive property claims of large landowners. For example, the commune of Le Tignet was locked in a long struggle with Mme de Navailles, daughter of the former lord, over the control of grazing land known

124. Maurice Agulhon, *The Republican Experiment, 1848–1852* (Cambridge: Cambridge University Press, 1983), esp. 6–10, 149–65.
125. Ted W. Margadant, *French Peasants in Revolt: The Insurrection of 1851* (Princeton: Princeton University Press, 1979), 3–39, xvii–xxiv.
126. Philippe Vigier, "Les mouvements paysans dans le cadre de l'agriculture et de société rurale traditionelles," in *Enquête sur les mouvements paysans dans le monde contemporain* (Moscow, 1970), 1:33–59; Agulhon, *The Republic in the Village*, esp. 21–56, 177–294.

as Les Maures du Tignet. Agulhon has provided many other examples of similar communities that ultimately rallied to the public in 1851.[127]

Yet the events of 1851 cannot be described as a peasant revolution, at least not in the conventional sense of the term. Margadant has shown that the social composition of the revolt was extraordinarily diverse and complex. Cultivators, petty shopkeepers, rural artisans, and village "intellectuals" were all involved. This mixture of occupations and economic strata indicates the difficulty of using class logic to explain what happened in 1851, at least in the countryside. Nor do the events of the insurrection fit a simple "mobilization" model in which external, "modernizing" elites manipulate popular groups in a coordinated insurrectionary plot. To be sure, the rural defense of the republic in 1848 owed something to the spread of rural Montagnard clubs that preached a republican gospel, sometimes in the form of a literal mixing of Christian and republican themes.[128] But, as Agulhon has demonstrated, the reception of the republic in the village was a genuinely popular event, and there was no overarching party or centralized association that led or caused the events of 1851.[129] Mobilization occurred from below in the form of community uprisings that followed the traditional institutional networks of local cooperation and sociability. In short, the rural phase of 1851 took the shape of a series of localized incidents in which the defense of the republic merged with the defense of community autonomy.[130]

For the rural rebels of 1851, the republic had become synonymous with the protection of community rights against the interference of outside elites. The republic seemed to promise a defense of the village against imperious landlords and prying bureaucrats. In addition, the republic promised the freedom for local communities to elect their own mayors and local officials without the constant meddling of prefects and other alien bureaucrats, and this, I think, was the key to popular support for the republic in the villages of the south. The republic meant maximum freedom for municipalities to manage their collective affairs according to their own rules. That, in turn, maximized their ability to defend local institutions, including common-use rights, against the forces of elite constraint. Like L'homme à moustache, the rebels of 1851 represented themselves and their communities through a blend of carnival and violent conflict.[131]

127. Agulhon, *The Republic in the Village*, 36–38.

128. Margadant, *French Peasants in Revolt*, 61–162; and Agulhon, *The Republic in the Village*, 253–304. Also see Theodore Zeldin, *France, 1848–1945*, 2 vols. (Oxford: Clarendon Press, 1973–77), 1:131–97; Edward Berenson, *Populist Religion and Left-Wing Politics in France, 1830–1852* (Princeton: Princeton University Press, 1984), 3–35, 169–202.

129. Agulhon, *The Republic in the Village*, 254–72.

130. Margadant, *French Peasants in Revolt*, 228–301; Thomas R. Forstenzer, *French Provincial Police and the Fall of the Second Republic: Social Fear and Counterrevolution* (Princeton: Princeton University Press, 1981), 149–247.

131. See the discussion in Tony Judt, *Socialism in Provence, 1871–1914: A Study in the Origins of the Modern French Left* (Cambridge: Cambridge University Press, 1979), 1–52.

In 1851, however, rural support for the republic was confined largely to the regions of insurrection, and in many regions Bonaparte rather than the republic was a popular symbol of community defense. Moreover, in parts of the west, rural monarchism and Catholicism were the rallying symbols of popular politics well into the 1900s. These sentiments were deep and difficult to transform, and in 1851 it seemed unlikely that rural republicanism would spread beyond the areas where very specific conjunctures had led to republic support in the early nineteenth century. (The south, for example, was unique in combining political radicalism with anticlericalism and heavy dependence on the wine market.)[132]

Nevertheless, by 1900 the Third Republic (1871–1940) had gained at least marginal support throughout much of rural France, in spite of the survival of enclaves of ultraroyalism and Bonapartism. How did this change occur, and how was it linked to the politics of local community in the countryside? No single factor, or even set of factors, can be singled out as determinative. But it is possible to link the rustication of the republic to at least two major political variables.[133]

First, the introduction of manhood suffrage early in the Third Republic produced a situation that was unique in French history. For the first time, national elites were forced to compete actively for the political support of rural people at election time, and the rise of a complex multiparty order increased the need to gain rural consent, since rural voters remained the majority of the potential electorate well into the twentieth century.[134] To be sure, powerful bureaucrats could still be called on to manipulate the rural electorate; however, in clear contrast to the past, elite power at a national level could no longer be simply imposed from above. The point seems elementary, but its deep implications should not be ignored. Elections and manhood suffrage provided an institutional bridge between community politics and national power. This bridge would work as a source of republican legitimacy only if elites proved willing to accommodate community interests. For example, issues like the forcible dissolution of common rights and active anticlericalism were pushed into the background as the "opportunist" republicans of the 1890s and 1900s struggled to consolidate a secure base of rural voting strength.[135]

Of equal importance was the logic of positive appeals that French politicians made to their rural supporters. The Third Republic was the age of "parish-pump" politics, and many successful parliamentarians owed their longevity to their ability to deliver what Americans would have called patronage, or distributive

---

132. See, for example, Weber, *Peasants into Frenchmen*, 195–376; Zeldin, *France, 1848–1945*, 1:467–503.

133. Jean Marie Mayeur and Madeleine Reberioux, *The Third Republic: From Its Origins to the Great War, 1871–1914* (Cambridge: Cambridge University Press, 1984), 5–41, 55–65, 179–240; Zeldin, *France, 1848–1945*, 1:605–39.

134. Mayeur and Reberioux, *The Third Republic*, 55–65, 81–100.

135. Weber, *Peasants into Frenchmen*, 241–77; Judt, *Socialism in Provence, 1871–1914*, 53–99.

benefits, to rural municipalities. Many of these benefits took the form of local collective goods, including the roads, schools, and (eventually) price subsidies that have become the standard fare of rural politics in the twentieth century. Other benefits were less tangible but no less significant. They included protection from bureaucratic incompetence, access to local officials, and the prestige that came with the ability to call on a national notable for help. To put it bluntly, the rustication of the republic involved a process of mutual adjustment in which votes were traded for the defense of community interests. Along with the "civilizing" forces of mass education, conscription, and economic modernization identified by Eugen Weber, the politics of electoral accommodation helped to bridge the ancient gap between national elites and community autonomy.[136] Rebellion was simply no longer a needed mode of representation, and representation became a ritual of election in the French countryside.

Charles Tilly, in his pathbreaking studies of collective action, has argued that popular collective violence began to fade as more modern forms of representation replaced the old modes of community action.[137] But Tilly was only partly right, and the French story can arguably be read in a very different way. In France, collective violence was replaced by accommodation only after French elites had conceded a legitimate sphere of local community autonomy and self-regulation. The symbol of that concession was the rural municipality, or commune, and its national expression was the rise of a competitive electoral politics in which community interests were taken seriously.[138] Prior to the Third Republic, elites had seen rural France as a "peasantry," which had no legitimate political voice at the national level. The collapse of the ancien régime after 1789 had begun a long process in which that vision was ultimately untenable, and the death of aristocratic domination and unchecked bureaucratic power opened up the need for new channels of politics in which rural people would no longer be treated as captive extensions of elite will and elite interests.

One may go further and argue that this marked the real demise of the French peasantry, if we see peasantry as a mode of political domination characterized by an elite domination and subjugation of rural communities. The destruction of those institutional mechanisms of subjugation radically transformed the political logic of rural France, and by 1900 agrarian politics no longer involved a struggle between authoritarian elites and subject communities over the terms of local autonomy. Interestingly, this way of seeing the issues also forces us to reconsider the impact of commercialization on the decline of the French peasant.[139] As we

---

136. Weber, *Peasants into Frenchmen*, 377–484.

137. Charles Tilly, Louise Tilly, and Richard Tilly, *The Rebellious Century, 1830–1920* (Cambridge: Harvard University Press, 1975), 239–300.

138. Agulhon, *The Republican Experiment*, 105–16.

139. See Duby and Wallon, *Histoire de la France rurale;* George W. Grantham, "Scale and Organization in French Farming, 1840–80," in William N. Parker and Eric L. Jones, eds., *European*

have seen, there is simply no unambiguous evidence to support the notion that market forces necessarily subverted community institutions, and many ordinary rural people gained more than they lost through the market, as the history of wine growing shows. What rural people did resist was the unilateral imposition of a logic of commercialization that deprived them of any political control over the marketplace. In this sense, the solicitude for rural markets and prices displayed by the politicians of the Third Republic was powerful testimony to the radical changes that had transformed French life. In the end, politics determined the long-term development of rural France as much as the deep currents of economic change.

Peasants and Their Markets: Essays in Agrarian Economic History (Princeton: Princeton University Press, 1975), 293–326; Gay L. Gullickson, "Proto-Industrialization, Demographic Behavior, and the Sexual Division of Labor in Auffay, France, 1750–1850," *Peasant Studies* 9 (Winter 1982), 106–18; Peter McPhee, "A Reconsideration of the 'Peasantry' of Nineteenth-Century France," *Peasant Studies* 9 (Fall 1981), 5–25; and, especially, Gregor Dallas, *The Imperfect Peasant Economy: The Loire Country, 1800–1914* (Cambridge: Cambridge University Press, 1982), 3–8, 240–87.

CHAPTER 6

Spain and the Logic of
Community Cohesion, 1800–1939

In 1936, Spain's Second Republic collapsed in a brutal civil war that lasted until 1939. Spain's civil war has long been a focus of scholarly debate and passionate politics. An entire generation of European intellectuals defined itself in terms of the events in Spain. Yet the search for understanding of the civil war has tended to narrow the range of issues that are dealt with in the scholarly study of Spanish history. Enormous attention has been paid to such questions as the origins of the conflict, the degree to which the events of 1936–39 can be viewed as a revolutionary situation, and the ways in which responsibility for the debacle of the republic can be assigned to the various foreign and domestic parties that struggled for hegemony.[1] As a result, we know less about the "deep" contours of Spanish social history than we do about the history of the rest of western Europe; a problem that was compounded by the intellectual rigidity of the dictatorship of Franco, who came to power in 1939. It is therefore necessary for new generations of scholars to rewrite Spanish history from new viewpoints that are not narrowly determined by a search for the origins of the civil war. Fortunately, historians and historically informed anthropologists have begun to embark on a much more detailed and focused study of Spain than was possible during the Franco years, and their work has helped to inform the analysis presented in this chapter.[2]

1. Raymond Carr, *Spain, 1808–1939* (Oxford: Clarendon Press, 1966), 603–95; Ronald Fraser, *Blood of Spain: An Oral History of the Spanish Civil War* (New York: Pantheon, 1979); Burnett Bolloten, *The Grand Camouflage: The Spanish Civil War and Revolution, 1936–1939* (London: Pall Mall Press, 1968).

2. I have found the following useful: Joseph Aceves, *Social Change in a Spanish Village* (Cambridge: Schenkman, 1971); Joseph Aceves and William Douglass, eds., *The Changing Faces of Rural Spain* (Cambridge: Schenkman, 1976); Ruth Behar, "The Web of Use-Rights: Forms and Conceptions of Communal Property among Leonese Labradores," *Anthropological Quarterly* 57 (2) (1984), 71–82; Stanley H. Brandes, *Migration, Kinship, and Community: Tradition and Transition in a Spanish Village* (New York: Academic Press, 1975); Concepción de Castro, *La revolución liberal y los municipios españoles (1812–1868)* (Madrid: Alianza Editorial, 1979); I. Chiva, *Rural Communities: Problems, Methods, and Types of Research,* Reports and Papers in the Social Sciences 10

Locating Community:
Self-Help and Self-Defense in Rural Spain, 1800–1939

In contrast to England and France, Spain was characterized by the dominance of agriculture well into the twentieth century.[3] As late as the mid-1950s, 41.3 percent of the active labor force tilled the land, and agriculturalists formed the majority of the population in thirty-six of Spain's fifty provinces.[4] More important, Spanish agriculture was central to the politics of modern Spain, and no government in Madrid could afford to ignore the social weight of the countryside. For example, the Napoleonic invasion of Spain in the first decade of the nineteenth century might have resulted in the successful absorption of Spain into Napoleon I's empire had it not been for the waves of popular rural revolt that met the French armies. Local "juntas" resisted the invading French in a long cycle of rebellion and repression that some have regarded as Europe's first guerrilla war.[5] Similarly, the tenacious resistance of the rural Basques to the bureaucratic state became a major source of national instability in the late nineteenth century. Finally, the seriousness of what came to be known as the agrarian problem helped to lead the governments of the Second Republic (1932–39) to embark on one of Europe's first experiments in comprehensive land reform.[6]

(Paris: UNESCO, 1959); William A. Christian, Jr., *Person and God in a Spanish Valley* (New York: Seminar Press, 1972); James W. Fernandez, *Persuasions and Performances: The Play of Tropes in Culture* (Bloomington: Indiana University Press, 1986); David Gilmore, "Land Reform and Rural Revolt in Nineteenth Century Andalusia (Spain)," *Peasant Studies* 6 (Fall 1977), 142–46; David Gilmore, *The People of the Plain: Class and Community in Lower Andalusia* (New York: Columbia University Press, 1980); David Gilmore, *Aggression and Community: Paradoxes of Andalusian Culture* (New Haven: Yale University Press, 1987); Davydd Greenwood, *Unrewarding Wealth: The Commercialization and Collapse of Agriculture in a Spanish Basque Town* (Cambridge: Cambridge University Press, 1976); Richard Herr, "La vente des propriétés de main morte en Espagne, 1798–1808," *Annales: Economies, Sociétés, Civilisations* 29 (1) (1974), 215–28; Richard Herr, "El significado de la desamortización en España," *Moneda y Crédito* 131 (1974), 55–94; A. Heutz de Lemps, "Les terroirs en vieille Castile et Léon: Un type de structure agraire," *Annales: Economies, Sociétés, Civilisations* 17 (1962), 239–51; Michael Kenny, *A Spanish Tapestry: Town and Country in Castile* (Bloomington: Indiana University Press, 1962); Carmelo Lison-Tolosana, *Belmonte de los Caballeros: A Sociological Study of a Spanish Town* (Oxford: Clarendon Press, 1966). Jerome Mintz, *The Anarchists of Casas Viejas* (Chicago: University of Chicago Press, 1982); Julian Pitt-Rivers, *The People of the Sierra* (New York: Criterion Books, 1954); M. R. Redclift, "The Future of Agriculture in a Spanish Pyrenean Village and the Decline of Communal Institutions," *Ethnology* 12 (2) (1973), 193–202; Luís Redonet y Lopez Doriga, "Policía Rural en España: Leon," *Archivos Leoneses* 9 (1955), 81–108; Teofilo Ruiz, "The Transformation of the Castilian Municipalities, 1248–1350," *Past and Present* 77 (1977), 3–32; David E. Vassberg, "The Tierras Baldias: Community Property and Public Lands in Sixteenth Century Castile," *Agricultural History* 48 (1974), 383–401; and David E. Vassberg, "Peasant Communalism and Anti-Communal Tendencies in Early Modern Castile," *Journal of Peasant Studies* 7 (1980), 477–91.

3. Carr, *Spain, 1808–1939*, 389–429.

4. Edward E. Malefakis, *Agrarian Reform and Peasant Revolution in Spain: Origins of the Civil War* (New Haven: Yale University Press, 1970), 11–12.

5. Carr, *Spain, 1808–1939*, 80–90.

6. Malefakis, *Agrarian Reform and Peasant Revolution*, 186–257.

Yet rural Spain was not a monolithic mass of faceless peasants. Perhaps to a greater degree than France, Spain was marked by a tremendous diversity of regions and localities. In addition to the linguistic differences that divided Castile from Catalonia, Galicia, Asturias, and the Basque provinces, agrarian Spain was characterized by enormous variations of local circumstance and economic practice.[7] In short, there was no Spanish peasantry, at least not in the sense of a nationwide class that shared identical material and social fortunes, and it is necessary to disaggregate the Spanish "peasant" into more concrete regional categories. For our purposes, the most useful distinction has to do with the very real differences between northern Spain and the south.[8] Although northern Spain is more an analytic convenience than a true economic or cultural region, it is a useful category to the degree that it helps to highlight the complexity of rural Spain.

Northern Spain can be defined as the set of regions that includes Galicia, Navarre-Alava, Catalonia, Aragon, Old and New Castile, the Levante, and the Biscay Coast.[9] What gives this huge area a certain thematic unity has been its key role in the unfolding of modern Spanish history. This was the area from which Christian Spain launched its reconquest of the peninsula from the Moslem kingdoms that had established themselves on the ruins of Visigothic Spain during the eighth and ninth centuries. It was also from this part of Spain that the Hapsburg dynasty of the 1500s and the Bourbon rulers of the 1700s launched their experiments in monarchical centralization, and that face has always given a certain common political fate to the northern lands.[10] We are therefore justified in asking, Do we find traces of what I have called the community of grain in northern Spain?

Nonspecialist readers may be surprised to learn that local, territorial community institutions have a long and significant history in the northern Spanish countryside; indeed, the word "pueblo," or rural community, was originally a Spanish term that referred to the strong bonds of local identity and solidarity that characterized the agrarian north. Since the pioneering work of Julian Pitt-Rivers, anthropologists have taken it as almost axiomatic that local communities were the building blocks of rural society in much of Spain, and this tradition has been enriched by the work of scholars like Ruth Behar, Carmelo Lison-Tolosana, and James W. Fernandez.[11]

---

7. Carr, *Spain, 1808–1939*, 4–37.

8. Malefakis, *Agrarian Reform and Peasant Revolution*, 11–64.

9. Ibid., xvii–xix.

10. Charles Jago, "Philip II and the Cortes of Castile: The Case of the Cortes of 1576," *Past and Present* 109 (1985), 24–43; John Lynch, *Spain under the Habsburgs*, 2 vols. (New York: New York University Press, 1981), 1:1–47 and 2:14–41, 290–303; Carr, *Spain, 1808–1939*, 60–78.

11. The classic statement of this position is found in Pitt-Rivers, *The People of the Sierra*, 6–7. For various analyses that deploy the concept of community in detail, see Ruth Behar, *Santa María del Monte: The Presence of the Past in a Spanish Village* (Princeton: Princeton University Press, 1986), esp. 3–42, 252–85; Lison-Tolosana, *Belmonte de los Caballeros*, esp. 1–14, 313–57; Fernandez,

Underpinning the logic of community were strong institutions of economic, political, and ritual cooperation that I have identified as forming the core of the community of grain, and I will sketch each of these three dimensions in order to show how the Spanish north can be located within a much larger map of European rural history. Although this risks an excess of "ideal-typing," it should help to indicate the limits of a rival explanatory logic framed in terms of peasant classes.

Community economic cooperation was strongly influenced by the special history of agricultural settlement that took place in the north of Spain from the eighth through the early thirteenth centuries. Much of this region was settled in the wake of the devastating wars of conquest that eventually drove Moslem civilization from Spain.[12] Groups of Christian colonists, often acting under royal protection or charter, established "free" villages in the depopulated zones that separated the Christian kingdoms of the far north from the Moslem caliphates of the distant south. The symbol of the relative independence of these communities of colonists was the *presura,* a collective charter that guaranteed free, allodial rights to agricultural colonists. As a result of this mode of demographic repopulation, the north of Spain was not dominated by either a powerful supralocal nobility or strong servile and manorial institutions. Instead, even where great estates existed, they were circumscribed by communities that owed direct allegiance to their king, and this relative autonomy was shown by the institution of *behetría,* the right of rural communities to replace their lord through election if his exactions proved unacceptable.[13] Although seigneurial jurisdictions did exist, they apparently never reached the level of sophistication found in parts of France and England, and, in areas like Vizcaya, the concept of nobility, or *hidalguía,* was widely believed to attach to all free men.[14]

Yet, in spite of the absence of strong manorial institutions, the Spanish north was marked by deeply rooted practices of material cooperation at the local level. Much of the north was composed of nuclear villages and rural towns that displayed the same kinds of scattered strip farming and common-use rights that we saw in France and England. For example, as late as the twentieth century, villages in Castile defended common-grazing and common-forest rights against the "anti-collectivist" thrust of successive Spanish governments. Edward Malefakis has estimated that, as late as 1959, public or community ownership of pasture and forest rights occupied as much as 62.9 percent of the area of forest and pasture

---

Persuasions and Performances, 73–129. Also see Susan Tax Freeman, "Introduction to 'Studies' in Rural European Social Organization," *American Anthropologist* 75 (June 1973), 743–50; Susan Fried Harding, *Remaking Ibieca: Rural Life in Aragon under Franco* (Chapel Hill: University of North Carolina Press, 1984).

12. Ruiz, "The Transformation of the Castilian Municipalities," 3–32; Teofilo Ruiz, *Sociedad y poder real en Castilla: Burgos en la Baja Edad Media* (Barcelona: Editorial Ariel, 1981), 11–48.

13. Malefakis, *Agrarian Reform and Peasant Revolution,* 51–52.

14. John F. Coverdale, *The Basque Phase of Spain's First Carlist War* (Princeton: Princeton University Press, 1984), 263.

owned privately in the regions of the north.[15] In addition, wherever fields were divided into disconnected strips, as they were in some areas into the 1970s, intra- and intercommunity networks of cooperation were necessary in order to provide for smooth rights of access and some degree of common regulation of planting, harvesting, and grazing.[16]

The Spanish north was a world of jealously guarded local rights and privileges in which the territory of the pueblo, the *término,* was a real territorial unit of material life. Neighbors hired neighbors for seasonal farm work; land was rarely sold, even to community members; and strangers settling in a village were often regarded as *forasteros,* permanent aliens who could never fully participate in the rights and responsibilities of community life. Moreover, as scholars like Lison-Tolosana have shown, the north was also a world in which principles of social and territorial endogamy were sufficiently potent to reinforce the sense that one's identity was deeply dependent on membership in a "house" that was embedded in territorial networks of power and production.[17] In this context, property was a trust that men and women held for themselves *and* for the honor and perpetuation of their families and communities. Indeed, I believe that the concept of property as trusteeship was perhaps as deeply rooted in northern Spain as in any part of western Europe, although a detailed monograph would be needed to prove the point.

In any event, it would be hopelessly romantic to argue that northern Spain was deeply egalitarian. The rural communities of the north were marked by real conflicts and entrenched hierarchies of age, sex, and wealth. For example, the community studied by Lison-Tolosana was shot through with clear hierarchies of economic advantage that divided community members. Furthermore, the community as a whole was subject to the control of adult male householders who filled the most important decision-making roles.[18]

Yet it would be a mistake to underestimate the reciprocal foundations of rural hierarchies in northern Spain. In Lison-Tolosana's community, the better-off households were involved in ongoing relations of exchange and patronage with their less well off neighbors that mitigated the effects of inequalities of landholding and lifestyles.[19] Advantaged villagers provided regular field employment for their neighbors, and they also contributed to the upkeep of community rituals that cemented basic relations of territorial identity. More important, the willingness of

15. Malefakis, *Agrarian Reform and Peasant Revolution,* 64. A crude philological analysis of the terms, like *behetría,* drawn from Malefakis did not unearth any great discrepancy between his interpretation and their distant historical referents. For those interested see the *Diccionario crítico etimológico castellano e hispánico* (Madrid: Gredos, 1980 (J. Corominas).
16. Behar, *Santa María del Monte,* 189–264. Also see Redclift, "The Future of Agriculture in a Spanish Pyrenean Village," 193–202; Vassberg, "Peasant Communalism and Anti-Communal Tendencies," 477–91; and T. Lynn Smith, "Fragmentation of Agricultural Land in Spain," *Rural Sociology* 24 (Mar. 1959), 140–49.
17. Lison-Tolosana, *Belmonte de los Caballeros,* 1–14, 15–38. Also see Behar, "The Web of Use-Rights," 71–82.
18. Lison-Tolosana, *Belmonte de los Caballeros,* 10–14, 54–142.
19. Ibid., 11–12, 288–303.

the better-off to contribute to the management of common community affairs is a good indication of their commitment to the community as a whole. The willingness to expend time and resources in this role shows that the advantaged were compelled by the logic of their situation to "pay" for their position.

We should also avoid the mistake of exaggerating the economic distance between the most and least advantaged members of rural communities in northern Spain during the modern period. As Malefakis has demonstrated, the north of Spain was a region of small and medium landholdings in the nineteenth and twentieth centuries, and in regions like Catalonia and Galicia, even tenants were protected by long-term or hereditary forms of tenure that reduced the arbitrary power of owners over their tenants.[20] To be well-off in northern Spain was to be a secure householder with enough land to be able to be self-sufficient in bad times as well as good, and this is a far cry from the world of indolent display that characterized the true aristocracy of southern Spain.

Finally, we should not forget the importance of irrigation in shaping community economic cooperation in agrarian Spain. Especially in areas like the Levante, small-scale irrigation networks, vital to the production of basic food crops, demanded close cooperation between neighbors, regardless of their economic status.[21] Canals and sluices had to be cleaned and maintained, water flows and rights to water had to be negotiated, and conflicting interests over the use of water had to be managed. In addition, much of this work required group labor or at least joint community expenditure on special services like ditch digging and canal cleaning, none of which could be accomplished in the absence of cooperation at the level of the whole community. As Robert Wade has argued in his study of southern India, irrigation is a powerful support for collective action in small-scale rural societies, a point that seems borne out by the Spanish evidence.[22]

Economic cooperation in the north of Spain was reinforced by institutional networks of political decision making that were deeply rooted in Spanish history. The northern regions of Spain had long traditions of community self-government that were partly conditioned by the waves of colonization that had pressed down from the north in the Middle Ages. Even after the "rationalizing" reforms of the eighteenth and nineteenth centuries, northern Spanish communities were responsible for a wide range of public tasks. They controlled common or municipal lands, raised local taxes, maintained roads and canals, and provided a court of first jurisdiction over community behavior.[23]

20. Malefakis, *Agrarian Reform and Peasant Revolution*, 11–34.

21. Arthur Maass and Raymond L. Anderson, *And the Desert Shall Rejoice: Conflict, Growth, and Justice in Arid Environments* (Cambridge: MIT Press, 1978), 11–145. Also see Behar, *Santa María del Monte*, 152–53, 168–69, 290.

22. Robert Wade, *Village Republics: Economic Conditions for Collective Action in South India* (Cambridge: Cambridge University Press, 1988), 1–36, 179–98.

23. Lison-Tolosana, *Belmonte de los Caballeros*, 17, 202–58. Also see José M. Mangas Navas, *El régimen comunal agrario de los concejos de Castilla* (Madrid: Servicio de Publicaciones Agrarias, 1981).

At the heart of this political life was the theory and practice of *concejo,* the Spanish equivalent of the councils of householders or village members that were common in much of rural Europe. But concejo was much more than the formal council of government of a territory or municipality; concejo referred to the whole complex of formal and informal institutional performances that bound the people of a place into a collectivity. It was in the practice of concejo, understood both as a noun and an event, that community members resolved their conflicts and established the rules that would govern them. In concejo, the community was literally represented in a performance of politics that was both intense and constitutive of community power. As Ruth Behar has observed, "To a very great extent the concejo was an acephalous political system. It was the concejo and the vecinos as a single body that ruled in most matters, and especially so in those of some importance to the whole community. And truly no one stood above the concejo; it was the pinnacle of local power and authority, as it still is even today in many Leonese villages."[24]

Yet the practice of concejo as a mode of government was open primarily to those who had established rights of community membership, and those rights were largely confined to those who, through birth or "adoption," had proven themselves able to act responsibly on behalf of kin and community. For example, in the término (pueblo) of Belmonte de los Caballeros, membership was closely dependent on birth in the community or on an official procedure that involved a specific term of residence. As Lison-Tolosana has pointed out, however, gaining real status as a local vecino, or community member, was tied to active participation in community life and the public approval of established householders: "Official procedures, however, do not affect the popular estimation of new residents. If a new family establishes itself in the town [*término*] it will very likely be called by the name of the town it came from. . . . An outsider—forastero— who does not take an active part in social life will never be properly considered as one of the town even if he has married there and lived there several years. A forastero, even if he has been fully accepted by the town, will never be allowed to criticize anything about it without being reminded of the defects of his own town."[25]

Concejo, therefore, was restricted to the core of vecinos who fully accepted each other on the basis of intimate knowledge and constant interaction. This practice, I think, nicely illustrates the principle of territorial membership that I have identified as central to the logic of the community of grain. To be a vecino was to accept a whole range of obligations, including tax paying, conflict mediation, and representation of the community in its relations with the wider world. As Behar has noted:

24. Behar, *Santa María del Monte,* 125–85, quotation on 147.
25. Lison-Tolosana, *Belmonte de los Caballeros,* 9–10.

A village that took in a stranger who turned out to be less than an ideal vecino stood to lose much more than its properties. For there was a fine balance, an essential reciprocity, between what a village offered to its vecinos as a "gift" and what it expected in return from each and every vecino. The vecino, for example, had to participate in the communal prestations of labor known as hacenderas or facenderas for repairing roads and checking boundary markers, attend to the meetings of the concejo, and take on economic, religious, and political responsibilities when his turn was due. In short, he had to be an active member of the concejo, whose task it was to organize all these matters. And only he who lived and worked in the community, and whose own house was bound up in it, was in a position to be a vecino on a par with all the other vecinos.[26]

As Behar's use of the word "prestation" indicates, political life overlapped with ritual exchanges and local festivals that marked out what I have called a folklore of place. For example, many northern communities maintained a very active calendar of celebrations that, although rooted in the rhythms of agriculture, were part of the collective identity of particular localities. In some cases, this collective memory was actually preserved in written village records over several centuries and passed on between generations as a recognition of the permanence of local life. Along with the bullfights, village processions, and street cabarets so beloved by tourists, the village records and the concejo meeting hall show how much of the consciousness of vecinos was formed through the intersubjective performance of common ceremonies. As Fernandez has indicated in his sensitive studies of Asturias, in this realm of community boundaries, even the language of everyday life could be inflected by the metaphors and metonyms of locality.[27]

A rather striking illustration of the ritual performance of community in northern Spain can be found in the survival into the twentieth century of intercommunity faction fighting. Often taking place on the occasion of the feast day of a village's patron saint, these fights involve the exchange of insults and stylized brawling between rival communities. Although particularly associated with the celebratory life of the young, they stand as a token of the extent to which the honor of the self was tied to the honor of one's village or town.[28]

In sum, northern Spain shows strong traces of community stretching from the medieval past to the present. The word "traces" should be emphasized, because much remains to be explored before we can write the history of this region in depth. Nevertheless, the fascination that anthropologists interested in community have demonstrated for this part of Spain helps to reinforce our conviction that

26. Behar, *Santa María del Monte*, 135.
27. Fernandez, *Persuasions and Performances*, 73–99, 103–26.
28. Lison-Tolosana, *Belmonte de los Caballeros*, 10–14. Also see Christian, *Person and God in a Spanish Valley*, esp. 44–48, 61–80, 99; William A. Christian, Jr., *Local Religion in Sixteenth Century Spain* (Princeton: Princeton University Press, 1981), esp. 31–42, 55–59.

community institutions have been significant in shaping the contours of ordinary life.

More important, the survival of community institutions in northern Spain after the medieval Reconquest tends to undermine the notion that strong rural communities are simply expressions of serfdom and the forces of aristocratic domination. In the north of Spain, the comparative weakness of seigneurial jurisdiction did not prevent the development of powerful bonds of popular solidarity focused on territorial communities. This in itself makes the study of northern Spain worthwhile, because it contradicts the belief that popular institutions have no coherent existence apart from elite power.

Furthermore, the communities of northern Spain clearly illustrate the principle of mutual cooperation that seems characteristic of traditional rural communities. Economic, political, and ritual institutions overlapped in territorial networks of action that involved vecinos in ongoing relations of hierarchical reciprocity. One could not expect mutual aid from one's neighbors unless one cooperated with the same set of neighbors in politics and ritual life. Similarly, willingness to bear the burdens of office and ritual prestations was a guarantee that one could call on traditional forms of economic reciprocity. For example, better-off vecinos could count on a compliant labor force at harvest time, while poorer villagers could count on the right to be hired when work was available.[29] A single individual might not benefit equally from participation in all arenas of local life, but it is reasonable to suppose that across arenas and time periods the balance of rights and obligations, benefits and costs, would reach a rough equilibrium. But that equilibrium had meaning only within the reality of institutional practices that took their logic from the patterned production and distribution of the means of subsistence.

Underlying community in northern Spain, as in England and France, were the hard realities of an agricultural civilization that coexisted with a precarious natural environment.

What, then, do we make of southern Spain, and what happens to this picture of community when we move the focus of our analysis to the giant estates of the south? In contrast to the north, southern Spain developed under the auspices of a powerful landed aristocracy. The final phases of the Christian Reconquest occurred in the south, and aristocratic military forces spearheaded the final offensives against Spanish Islam. In particular, the great military crusading orders—Calatrava, Santiago, and Alcántara—preempted royal power in the south, which left little room for the kind of popular freedom that had characterized the north.[30] Moreover, the indigenous Moslem population of the south was either pushed out of the cities or reduced to servile conditions. This was an ideal situation for the

29. Lison-Tolosana, *Belmonte de los Caballeros*, 54–142.
30. Malefakis, *Agrarian Reform and Peasant Revolution*, 53–130.

growth of great estates, and by the 1500s the south was dominated by an entrenched nobility that probably controlled much of the most fertile agricultural land. Part of the land was originally used for sheep grazing, but by the beginning of the 1670s we can see a gradual transition to wheat and (somewhat later) vines, the two crops that had stable internal market prospects.[31]

The south as a whole can be divided into five subregions: the southeast, Estremadura, La Mancha, and western and eastern Andalusia.[32] Great estates, or latifundia, tended to develop and persist in the most productive areas, like parts of Andalusia, where large estates could draw on a dense population of agricultural laborers who may have developed out of the servile or semiservile populations of the Middle Ages.

By the end of the nineteenth century, the great southern estates reached their most developed form. Buttressed by the police powers of the state, and dominated by an absentee nobility of owners and proprietors, the great estates had become central to the agrarian landscape of the south. Often managed by large-scale commercial leaseholders (*arrendadores*), the southern latifundia were either protected by high tariffs for their staple products or ensconced in "safe" international markets for products like sherry and cork.[33]

The power of the latifundia had been further enhanced by the nineteenth-century "reforms" that historians have referred to as *desamortización*.[34] This set of reforms involved the abolition and sale of perpetual forms of corporate landholding, including the landed estates of the church and certain forms of municipal or communal common lands. For example, municipal lands that had been rented to individual proprietors (the so-called propios) were to be sold as freeholds.[35] The ostensible goal of desamortización was to create a "freer," more individualistic land market, but its real consequences varied widely. In the north, the process does not seem to have despoiled municipalities and villages of their common rights, and common lands survived on a significant scale into the twentieth century. But in the South the land made available was purchased by the same nobles and estate operators who controlled the latifundia economy. The result was to reduce further the number of small and medium proprietors in the south.[36]

By 1900 the landless and land poor formed a majority in many southern municipalities, and it was from this group that the great estates drew their

31. Ibid., 50–64; Julius Klein, *The Mesta: A Study in Spanish Economic History, 1273–1836* (Cambridge: Harvard University Press, 1920), 93–94, 322; Lynch, *Spain under the Habsburgs* 2:155–66.

32. Malefakis, *Agrarian Reform and Peasant Revolution*, xvii–xix.

33. Carr, *Spain, 1808–1939*, 278–434.

34. Francisco Tomás y Valiente, *El marco político de la desamortizacíon en España* (Barcelona: Editorial Ariel, 1977); Herr, "El significado de la desamortización en España," 55–94; Gilmore, "Land Reform and Rural Revolt," 142–46.

35. Gilmore, "Land Reform and Rural Revolt," 142–46.

36. Malefakis, *Agrarian Reform and Peasant Revolution*, 61–64.

permanent and temporary labor force.[37] There can be no doubt that this was a poor population characterized by low wages, intermittent employment, and few opportunities to acquire land or an independent material existence apart from the great estates. For our purposes, however, the most important question to ask is simply this: Did the southern laboring population form distinct rural communities or do other categories best describe their social position?

The contours of southern life were strongly shaped by the distinctive physical geography of the region. Much of the population lived in densely concentrated villages or "agro-towns" that existed within or at the margins of the great estates. Much of the laboring population was thus bound by overlapping ties of neighborhood, friendship, and exchange.[38] It was easy in this context for entire communities to see themselves as a common enemy of the great estates and the agents of state power who enforced the will of the estate owners and operators. In short, this was not an atomized or fragmented population; it was a population with clear ties to particular localities.

Moreover, the southern population was not highly migratory, contrary to what one might expect of a landless and land-poor population. The south of Spain had one of the lowest rates of internal and international emigration of any Spanish region. For example, between 1891 and 1895 only 7.1 per thousand inhabitants emigrated from the southern province of Cadiz, while 12.2 inhabitants per thousand emigrated from the northern province of La Coruña. Yet Cadiz had the highest emigration rate of any latifundia province, which indicates that much of the laboring population of the south did not form a fully mobile proletariat.[39] It was "rooted" in the densely nucleated landscape of the great estates. It seems reasonable to suppose that this situation led to a heightened awareness of the importance of territorial community as a basic social framework, particularly because the immobility of ordinary people across generations reinforced the bonds of attachment to the pueblo, or community of birth. Many ordinary landless and land-poor people must have expected to live out their lives in a single village or agro-town, and kin and friends would have correspondingly focused on the opportunities available in a single locality.[40]

The most important source of economic solidarity, however, probably developed out of the logic of labor on the great estates. Ordinary fieldworkers did not work as individuals. They worked in gangs, and during the peaks of the harvest cycle they also ate and slept together in the fields.[41] Laborers worked not with

37. Ibid., 93–130; Temma Kaplan, *Anarchists of Andalusia, 1868–1903* (Princeton: Princeton University Press, 1977), 3–60.

38. Kaplan, *Anarchists of Andalusia*, 204–5. Also see Juan Martinez-Alier, *Labourers and Landowners in Southern Spain* (London: Allen and Unwin, 1971), 39–47, 313–15; Gilmore, *The People of the Plain*, esp. chaps. 1 and 2.

39. Malefakis, *Agrarian Reform and Peasant Revolution*, 104–6.

40. Gilmore, *Aggression and Community*, esp. 1–52, 171–86.

41. Kaplan, *Anarchists of Andalusia*, 7, 25, 63–64; Jerome R. Mintz, *The Anarchists of Casas Viejas* (Chicago: University of Chicago Press, 1982), 47–61.

strangers but with friends and neighbors, thereby strengthening their attachment to territorial networks. Such a situation must have put a premium on the ability of ordinary people to institutionalize forms of economic cooperation that would reduce the possibility of conflict in an environment of extraordinary scarcity. Conflict in the fields, or failure to cooperate in popular work practices, could spill over into damaging conflicts with kin and neighbors that implicated local honor and prestige. As many scholars have shown, southern Spain was a world in which local reputation was central to the identity of ordinary people, and it does not seem unreasonable to suppose that a large part of reputation depended on one's ability to work according to the norms of the local labor gang.[42]

Although the evidence is fragmentary, two points seem quite clear. First, the labor gangs of southern Spain were capable of showing tremendous solidarity during moments of tension and crisis. For example, harvest strikes in areas like Andalusia depended for their success on the ability of field gangs to bid up piece rates and day wages by withholding their collective labor at the key time of the agricultural year.[43] Although often short-lived, the persistence of strike action in the late nineteenth and twentieth centuries can be interpreted as an indirect indicator of local institutions of cooperation, especially because Spain's national labor organizations were usually too weak to provide the resources necessary to instigate and control local strikes. It is difficult to believe that strikes could have occurred at all in the absence of preexisting forms of popular economic cooperation.

Second, the logic of local consumption practices also worked to strengthen the ties of community. The local landless and land poor were forced to rely on economic networks beyond the nuclear family in order to survive.[44] Field wages were often inadequate, and unless they could be supplemented with a garden plot or a piece of rented arable, the deficit could be made up only through the operation of a sideline business or access to credit. Supplementing income, however, required support and cooperation from kin and neighbors, because household resources were severely constricted and migration was unlikely. In short, southern villages and agro-towns can be accurately described as economies of shared poverty in which local communities practiced an enforced distribution of risks and benefits according to a finely graded hierarchy of locally defined rights and responsibilities. For example, in the pueblo of Casas Viejas, the right of the laborer to work was partly determined by local, popular estimations of the family needs of the laborer, and even though bosses were free to hire whomever they pleased, the evidence seems to support the view that laborers were subject to at least some degree of popular regulation when it came to behavior in the economic arena.[45]

---

42. Mintz, *The Anarchists of Casas Viejas*, 33–61.

43. Kaplan, *Anarchists of Andalusia*, 103–8, 149–55, 201–5.

44. Ibid., 12–36, 135–67; George A. Collier, *Socialists of Rural Andalusia: Unacknowledged Revolutionaries of the Second Republic* (Stanford: Stanford University Press, 1987), 4, 103, 187. The latter work is strongly class oriented, but it does not deny the importance of community.

45. Mintz, *The Anarchists of Casas Viejas*, 33–61.

The symbol of this enforced economy of shared poverty was the gazpacho, the heavy garlic soup that was the staple of field laborers during the peak of the harvest.[46] When working in the fields, gangs of laborers shared the gazpacho from a common pot, and this meal was probably governed by strict rules of popular etiquette that determined who could eat how much and what the order of consumption would be. This is precisely what anthropologists would call commensality, the collective consumption of the means of life. The gazpacho served to draw a bright line between the enforced solidarity of the labor gang and the elite of owners and leaseholders, whose absence from the common meal signaled their clear distance from popular life.

In other words, the logic of land and labor in southern Spain reinforced rather than undercut the salience of community economic institutions. Ordinary men and women found themselves dependent on *local* networks of production and distribution for the means of life.[47] In addition to the fact that many fieldworkers combined wage labor with sideline occupations and access to petty tenancies and garden plots, the fieldworkers of the south did not constitute a true proletariat whose life chances were determined by the competitive play of the labor market. Indeed, it is difficult to view southern fieldwork as fitting into any conventional market model. Wage rates seem to have been as much a function of the naked power of owners and bosses as of the free play of supply and demand.[48] Moreover, given low emigration rates, the gradual demographic expansion in the period 1868–1939 only heightened the power of the landed elite unilaterally to control field wages in the absence of popular resistance.[49] Marxists might regard this as simply the logic of capitalist markets. But we can turn this notion on its head and argue that southern Spain represents a deviant rather than typical case of agricultural commercialization that was made possible by an extreme form of coercive commercialization. After all, the political economy of the rural south was the result of an entrenched elite's ability to use concentrated political power in order to monopolize land and dispossess popular communities of common-use rights in the period of desamortización. This was not a normal process of market development, and, in the end, we might follow the insights of William Reddy and view southern Spain as dominated by "sham" markets that used an ideology of market freedom to disguise the realities of an economy shot through with power and politics.[50]

In any case, the evidence indicates that territorial community is *at least* as powerful as class analysis in accounting for the economic logic of rural society in

---

46. Ibid., 52–55, 60–62, plate 29.
47. Malefakis, *Agrarian Reform and Peasant Revolution*, 133–61.
48. Kaplan, *Anarchists of Andalusia*, 26–27, 150–52.
49. Malefakis, *Agrarian Reform and Peasant Revolution*, 98–110.
50. William Reddy, *The Rise of Market Culture: The Textile Trade and French Society, 1750–1900* (Cambridge: Cambridge University Press, 1984), esp. 22–47, 253–325.

southern Spain. Further support can be drawn from a brief consideration of politics and popular culture.

In contrast to the north, ordinary rural people in the south rarely controlled the formal institutions of municipal or village government, except in moments of political upheaval. The agents of the elite and powerful regional political bosses, called caciques, ran the local councils and controlled the appointment of mayors and councillors. Still, this does not mean that ordinary people lacked institutional networks of popular self-regulation.

Beginning in the 1860s and 1870s and extending into the 1930s, popular communities formed a variety of labor and cooperative associations that offered an alternative to the formal institutions of politics. These networks of collective action provided a means of managing conflicts with local bosses, as well as a forum for the expression of grievances and the regulation of popular life.[51] Sometimes associated with a national political current and sometimes completely autonomous, these popular institutions of cooperation should be understood as much more than mere labor unions or bargaining agencies: they should be seen as the institutional expression of popular communities. As Temma Kaplan has observed of the situation in Andalusia:

> The great strength of late nineteenth-century Andalusian anarchism lay in the merger of communal and militant trade union traditions. In towns where the vast majority worked in agriculture, agricultural workers' unions came to be identified with the community as a whole. This was especially true of the hill towns of Grazelema, Alcalá del Valle, Benaocaz, and San José del Valle. . . .
>
> It would be a mistake, then, to argue that "village anarchism" in Andalusia was distinct from militant unionism, or that the movement was a "surrogate religion." The union was the community in places like Ubrique or Arcos."[52]

As these passages imply, the landless and land poor of the rural south drew on preexisting community traditions and boundaries to create an alternative polity in their local workers' unions and cooperative societies. Their exclusion from the formal institutions of government did not render them powerless or atomized; on the contrary, they built institutions of "counterpower" that must have been based in the old traditions of concejo and *vecindad,* or neighborhood, that we saw at work in the Spanish north.[53]

Similar observations can be made about the survival of popular ritual and folklore in the rural south. There can be little doubt that a lively community ritual life survived the rise of the great estates. Many of the same festival practices that characterized the north also could be found in the south, although the situation

51. Kaplan, *Anarchists of Andalusia,* 92–167.
52. Ibid., 204–5.
53. Mintz, *The Anarchists of Casas Viejas,* 79–114.

was somewhat complicated by the decline of the Catholic church and the rise of a self-conscious, popular anti-Christian sentiment. Nevertheless, ceremonial life continued, with or without the patronage of the landed elite, and these ceremonies could provide the basis for a powerful folklore of place, or collective identity, that could survive over the generations.[54] For example, in regions that adopted anarchism, May Day and other secular holidays could rally whole communities around the festival performance of local solidarity. Underlying these performances was a sense of the pueblo, or local community, that combined both a belief in the pueblo as a political collectivity and a ritual union of the poor against the rich outsiders who constrained the autonomy of community life. As Pitt-Rivers argued, the pueblo, in addition to being a territorial people and its government, "has a third meaning: 'people' in the sense of plebs as opposed to the rich . . . for the rich do not belong to the pueblo but to that wider world which has already been delimited as theirs. In this sense, the pueblo is a potentially revolutionary force."[55]

Pitt-Rivers, I believe, can be read as supporting the view that the most fundamental division in southern rural society was between popular communities and elite outsiders and their agents. This was a division that cut across occupational and class distinctions and unified landless laborers, artisans, petty shopkeepers, and small tenants in a common front against the local great estate. Underpinning popular resistance were the institutions of mutually implicated cooperation that bound the poor together in an ongoing community of fate. Admittedly, the traces of the community of grain are weaker in the south than the north, and much of community life in the south could be thought of as residual, rooted as much in myth and remembrance as material power. Nor were popular institutions purely egalitarian and free from all traces of hierarchy, although they were probably more egalitarian than in the north, owing simply to the logic of an economy of shared poverty. For example, areas like Andalusia were deeply involved in the cult of male honor, or macho, that strictly subordinated women to the power of men, and this kind of patriarchy was probably just as typical of popular communities as it was of the landowning elite.[56]

Yet, in spite of these qualifications, I think that the logic of territorial community makes as much sense as class analysis when applied to the broad sweep of history in southern Spain. Skeptics may remain unconvinced, and they will point to the work of scholars like George A. Collier, who have tried to recast the history of southern Spain in class terms.[57] Those who remain committed to class logic, however, must answer two key questions. First, why was so much of popular collective action in the south—especially incidents of popular resistance—delim-

54. See, for example, Gilmore, *Aggression and Community*, 1–52, 171–86.
55. Pitt-Rivers, *The People of the Sierra*, 17–19, quotation on 18.
56. Gilmore, *Aggression and Community*, 129–34.
57. Collier sometimes uses "class" to mean conflict or conflict relations. Collier, *Socialists of Rural Andalusia*, 1–21, 22–44.

ited by the boundaries of local communities? Second, and more important, how do we account for the spread of ideological anarchism among the landless and land-poor people of the rural south? Marx, after all, regarded anarchism as a doctrine specially suited to "petty bourgeois" small commodity producers. It seems odd that the rural poor would have adopted anarchism if they constituted a true proletariat with a common class interest. Or was this just one more case of an unfortunate outbreak of false consciousness?

Anarchism and Community Defense in Southern Spain, 1868–1939

A good synthetic history of rural rebellion in modern Spain has yet to be written. What we do know indicates that rural Spain between 1800 and the civil war of the 1930s was hardly the placid rustic idyll portrayed in tourist brochures. For example, major episodes of rural unrest occurred in the Basque provinces during the Carlist wars, and concerted forms of popular resistance also took place in Catalonia and Galicia during the Second Republic.[58] In addition, the process of desamortización generated its own forms of resistance and revolt, although this is a problem that is not as well understood as it might be.[59] In any event, the drama of the civil war illustrated the ability of rural people to mobilize autonomously in the defense of their interests, in both the north and the south of Spain. Indeed, one indicator of the way the Spanish elite viewed its rural subjects is the Guardia Civil, the semimilitary police force that was installed throughout the countryside in the nineteenth century.[60] That Spain's elites felt the need to militarize its surveillance of the countryside is a good reminder that Spanish elites saw the countryside as a potential threat to peace and order rather than as a docile source of passive compliance. I point this out merely as a way of emphasizing the need to conduct further research in the history of Spanish rural resistance; such research would probably reveal a much richer tradition of rural resistance than we are currently aware of.

In fact, part of the problem may be that one region, the rural south, has overshadowed all others in the study of Spanish rural insurrection. The south had a long history of local resistance stretching from the mid-1800s through 1939.[61]

58. Coverdale, *The Basque Phase of Spain's First Carlist War*, 3–28, 257–83; Carr, *Spain, 1808–1939*, 8–11, 421; and Edward C. Hansen, *Rural Catalonia under the Franco Regime: The Fate of Regional Culture since the Spanish Civil War* (Cambridge: Cambridge University Press, 1977), 24–83.
59. Gilmore, "Land Reform and Rural Revolt," 142–46.
60. Ben Whitaker, *The Police in Society* (London: Eyre Methuen, 1979), 176.
61. Michael R. Weisser, *The Peasants of the Montes: The Roots of Rural Rebellion in Spain* (Chicago: University of Chicago Press, 1976).

According to Malefakis, who is otherwise quite cautious in his attribution of any political initiative to ordinary rural people:

> The tragic confrontation of classes in Southern Spain began to unfold after 1870 as landless workers abandoned Catholicism and turned increasingly to the revolutionary philosophy of anarchism. By the turn of the century village uprisings, insurrectionary strikes, crop burnings and other violent acts of protest had become endemic. At the end of World War I three consecutive years of labor strife shook Andalusia and Estremadura. Socialist labor unions began to compete with the Anarchists for peasant support. The alienation of the landless workers from the prevailing bourgeois society seemed complete. Southern Spain appeared doomed to a state of permanent instability in which the slightest relaxation of surveillance by the authorities or the slightest enthusiasm among the workers would lead to a new period of conflict.[62]

Although I would disagree with his rather loose and metaphoric use of the concept of class, the basic logic of Malefakis's analysis is quite clear: Between the 1870s and 1930s the south of Spain was a kind of social battlefront in which the legitimacy of the great estate was called in question. As Malefakis himself admits, much of this struggle "was sporadic and small in scale."[63] Yet it was also informed by a popular commitment to the ideology of anarchism, and as Malefakis's use of phrases like "village uprisings" and "small-scale" implies, there was something about the combination of localism and anarchist ideas that made the rural south particularly unstable.[64]

At the heart of anarchism was a double rejection of both the modern state and market capitalism. Anarchists like Mikhail Bakunin called for the abolition of all large-scale forms of institutional hierarchy and their replacement by a "free" association of producers.[65] Society would be reorganized as a federation of local communities. Neither competitive capitalism nor state hierarchies would survive the great insurrection that would usher in the new world of anarchist liberty. Although not always clearly thought through, the revolution against the old order was sometimes pictured in terms of a general strike or revolutionary mass uprising that would be brought about through the medium of ceaseless agitation and education by anarchist militants. In contrast to their erstwhile enemies, the

---

62. Malefakis, *Agrarian Reform and Peasant Revolution*, 6.

63. Ibid., 139. For the whole period of unrest in southern Spain, see also Victor G. Kiernan, *The Revolution of 1854 in Spanish History* (Oxford: Clarendon Press, 1966), 177–78, 213–14; C. A. M. Hennessey, *The Federal Republic in Spain: Pi y Margall and the Federal Republican Movement, 1868–1874* (Oxford: Clarendon Press, 1962), 57; Juan Díaz del Moral, *Historia de las agitaciones campesinas andaluzas—Córdoba (Antecedentes para una reforma agraria)* (Madrid: Revista de Derecho Privado, 1929), 79–393; Gerald H. Meaker, *The Revolutionary Left in Spain, 1914–1923* (Stanford: Stanford University Press, 1974), 133–45.

64. Malefakis, *Agrarian Reform and Revolution*, 284–316.

65. James Joll, *The Anarchists* (Boston: Little, Brown, 1964), 84–114; Paul Avrich, *The Russian Anarchists* (Princeton: Princeton University Press, 1967), esp. 24–26.

socialists, the followers of anarchism opposed the creation of a centralized party hierarchy, since this was regarded as merely reinforcing the authoritarian elements of the old order.[66]

Anarchism went through several internal transformations prior to the 1930s, and the original stress on "libertarian" anarchism was modified to take account of the rise of large-scale industry and the increasing complexity of modern societies. For example, anarcho-syndicalism appealed to factory workers by calling for the seizure of power at the point of production through a general strike. Similarly, anarcho-communism, with its stress on an equality of rights in both production and consumption, tried to spread the anarchist message to groups whose poverty cut them off from any degree of economic independence in the productive process.[67]

It is impossible to know how much of the formal doctrine of anarchism was absorbed in the Spanish countryside after 1870. We do know that in 1868, Giuseppi Fanelli, one of Bakunin's followers, toured Spain and gained at least a modicum of support among artisans and other small producers. By 1873, anarchism had gained roughly 28,000 adherents in Andalusia alone. In 1892 a rural insurrection in the south led by rural anarchists resulted in a march by some 4,000 rural people on the city of Jerez, and the events of that year indicate that anarchism was widespread in the rural south by then.[68] Certainly by 1900 the anarchist message had become deeply intertwined with the identity of popular communities in much of the rural south, especially in Andalusia, where anarchist ideas became a discourse of political resistance that the forces of order could not eradicate.[69]

The content of popular rural anarchism has been much discussed, although there is some difference among experts about exactly how we should interpret the meaning of rural anarchist beliefs. For example, J. Díaz del Moral, in his studies of Andalusia, saw anarchism as essentially a surrogate religion for the rural poor, who could derive a kind of secular comfort from anarchism's supposedly millenarian visions.[70] Kaplan has demonstrated, however, that anarchism made a "rational" contribution to popular society in Andalusia, because it allowed ordinary rural people to construct an economic and political alternative to elite power.[71] Kaplan believes that, whatever its millenarian connotations, anarchism met real needs in terms of a plausible theory of the world.

Yet neither the "religious" nor the "secular" interpretation of rural anarchism has fully addressed the most important question: Why did anarchism rather than

66. Meaker, *The Revolutionary Left in Spain*, 133–88.

67. Mintz, *The Anarchists of Casas Viejas*, 23–29; Murray Bookchin, *The Spanish Anarchists: The Heroic Years, 1868–1936* (New York: Free Life Editions, 1977), 89–109, 128–56.

68. Malefakis, *Agrarian Reform and Peasant Revolution*, 137–40; Kaplan, *Anarchists of Andalusia*, 168–205.

69. Meaker, *The Revolutionary Left in Spain*, 133–45.

70. Díaz del Moral, *Historia de las agitaciones campesinas andaluzas—Córdoba*.

71. Kaplan, *Anarchists of Andalusia*, 206–12.

one of many other competing radical doctrines gain widespread rural support in southern Spain? After all, socialism and radical republicanism were also active contenders for the Spanish political left after 1868, and both were capable of attracting limited rural support. But in the south, anarchism became the key ideology of popular radicalism and remained so through the 1930s.[72]

The relative success of anarchism may be due to the strong affinity between anarchist discourse and the institutional logic of a society still deeply embedded in networks of territorial community. Following Max Weber, we can define an elective affinity as a deep similarity or similitude between a body of ideas and the social situation of believers.[73] Anarchism was not simply foisted on "ignorant" masses by scheming intellectuals; no anarchist organization in Spain ever had such power. Ordinary people *chose* anarchism because of what it told them about their lives and futures.

The basis of this affinity was anarchism's commitment to community. The anarchist "utopia" was a world of self-sufficient associations of producers that would combine maximum decentralization with community solidarity. It is easy to see how this vision could appeal to a rural society in which the pueblo was still the focus of popular life.[74] Anarchism promised to restore lost forms of community autonomy on that "great day" when all forms of elite domination would perish. In the meantime, anarchism gained recruits simply because of its strident defense of everything local and communal. Anarchism, in short, was a natural expression of the defense of popular community in Spain's southern countryside.

Long before anarchism had appeared on the scene, southern communities had erupted in intermittent revolts against the latifundia.[75] At the heart of this "little tradition" of insurrection was the community's attempt to regain control over the use of land and labor, reflected in the popular belief in the legitimacy of the *reparto,* the "black" repartition that would destroy elite property and usher in a general redistribution of land and power. Anarchism directly addressed this kind of sentiment through its uncompromising acceptance of the right of popular groups to use violent collective action at any time in defiance of elite power.[76] In contrast to the cautious legalism of the republicans and the ameliorative gradualism of the socialists, Spanish anarchism told rural people that their traditions of community insurrection were appropriate responses to a world gone wrong.

Moreover, anarchism's rejection of both the state *and* capitalism spoke directly to the double bind in which southern communities found themselves at the end of

72. Malefakis, *Agrarian Reform and Peasant Revolution,* 284–316.

73. Max Weber, *Economy and Society: An Outline of Interpretive Sociology,* 3 vols. (New York: Bedminster Press, 1968), 2:479–588.

74. Julian Pitt-Rivers, Introduction to Julian Pitt-Rivers, ed., *Mediterranean Countrymen: Essays in the Social Anthropology of the Mediterranean* (Paris: Mouton, 1963), 9–25.

75. Malefakis, *Agrarian Reform and Peasant Revolution,* 133–37; Weisser, *The Peasants of the Montes,* 2–17.

76. Meaker, *The Revolutionary Left in Spain,* 133–45.

the nineteenth century. In southern Spain the key forces of constraint were coercive commercialization and unchecked bureaucratic domination.[77] The desamortizacíon had forcibly dispossessed communities of church and common lands in the name of commercial freedom, and the resulting decline of living standards and the rise of a "captive" labor market for the great estates must have convinced many ordinary rural people that the market was an enemy of community autonomy, at least in the coercive form it took in areas like Andalusia. Anarchism promised to liquidate markets dominated by the elite in a new world of "free" association in which communities would confederate in purely voluntary relations of exchange.[78]

But anarchists also held out the hope of ending the power of the bureaucratic state, and in southern Spain the character of state power weighed heavily on popular communities. State officials were associated with the defense of the great estates, a defense that, backed by paramilitary forces like the Guardia Civil, could take a very savage form. For example, the waves of harvest strikes and land seizures that occurred during the early post–World War I period were met with swift repression. Civil and military governors were quick to suspend constitutional guarantees, send in the troops, and imprison or even torture suspects.[79]

Nor were the rigors of the state mitigated by the gradual development of the kind of politics of electoral accommodation that characterized nineteenth-century France. Formally, Spain's nineteenth-century constitutional order was "liberal" in the classic sense, and by 1889 universal manhood suffrage had been established for elections to the national parliament, the Cortes. In some parts of Spain this liberalization led to the growth of a genuine patron-client politics that is reminiscent of Third Republic France. In the south, however, the electoral process was rigged by political bosses, caciques, who used a combination of force and fraud to manipulate elections in favor of the ruling government's candidates. Whatever benefits accrued from such manipulation flowed into the hands of the cliques of estate owners, town middle classes, and local strongmen who ruled the countryside; very little patronage of the state made its way into ordinary communities.[80] For instance, the south did not experience any massive influx of resources that might have helped to modernize agriculture through irrigation and soil reclamation, nor did state elites seriously consider breaking up the great estates until the Second Republic, long after anarchism had gained mass support.[81]

In this context of political fraud and open violence, anarchism, with its com-

---

77. Malefakis, *Agrarian Reform and Peasant Revolution*, 64–92; Carr, *Spain, 1808–1939*, 210–56, 473–563.

78. Mintz, *The Anarchists of Casas Viejas*, 79–123.

79. Malefakis, *Agrarian Reform and Peasant Revolution*, 93–161; Shlomo Ben-Ami, *Fascism from Above: The Dictatorship of Primo de Rivera in Spain, 1923–1930* (Oxford: Oxford University Press, 1983), 1–52.

80. Carr, *Spain, 1808–1939*, 355–79.

81. Malefakis, *Agrarian Reform and Peasant Revolution*, 205–35.

plete rejection of all forms of state authority, must have made a good deal of sense to ordinary men and women whose experience of the state was both alienating and threatening. Along with its rejection of commercialism, anarchism seemed to offer a discourse of power and politics that was completely free of any taint of bureaucracy or elite manipulation. Anarchism offered an "antiestablishment" politics that could be used to represent embattled communities in their struggle with the great estates and the Guardia Civil. In the currents of anarchist thought the traditional defense of community mingled with new ideas about land and labor to produce a potent critique of the difficult realities of southern life. In a harvest strike or local land seizure, popular communities violently represented themselves in a struggle for political control of the countryside; similarly, the preaching of anarchist ideas and the formation of anarchist unions and cooperatives helped people to represent themselves and their communities through new institutions of collective empowerment.[82]

Anarchism, then, was a true radical challenge to the politics of Spain's old order; and we should understand rural anarchism as a political movement that, although fragmented by village and small-town particularism, had the capacity to infuse long-standing traditions of village revolt with a sense of newly found moral idealism.[83] Perhaps the closest analogy would be the spread of radical Protestant beliefs in Germany prior to the Bauernkrieg. As readers will recall, the Bauernkrieg involved a traditional village revolt that was partly energized by the spread of Protestant spirituality. Like Protestantism, anarchism in southern Spain was less a revolutionary ideology than a practical radicalism that spoke of old problems and goals through a new language of alternative politics.

An excellent illustration of the ability of anarchism to mix traditional village ideals with a novel political collectivism can be found in the dialogue between two village anarchists that was recorded by Jerome Mintz in his historical reconstruction of the Casas Viejas uprising. The two anarchists, who had lived through the Second Republic, were allowed to reminisce about the kind of rural world they would have created if they had won the civil war.

José Monroy: If we had won, we would have made collectives. Each finca (great estate) would be a collective. One would take what one needed for the day, and in this way we would get rid of egoism. If one had all one needed, why would anyone want more? Each day one would get bread and the other necessities of life. One would have what one needed for each day from a common store. Since this is a small town, everyone knew everyone else's needs. The rich could keep their selfish grasping for money. They could have it. We wanted only the land. We had no intention to take their houses. That was theirs. Each had his own house.

82. Kaplan, *Anarchists of Andalusia*, 135–67; Fraser, *Blood of Spain*, 348–73.
83. Mintz, *The Anarchists of Casas Viejas*, 279–317.

Pepe Pilar [excited]: No! Only what they needed. If they had extra rooms, take them. You here. You there.

José Monroy [tranquil]: Each person had his house. We were interested in the land.

Pepe Pilar [angry]: If one had too large a house, we would use the rooms.

José Monroy: But this situation never occurred. The land would be taken. No, we would not pay for the land. One is born without land. Only the land of the large landowners, those with vast estates that lie unproductive, would be confiscated. We would not bother the small landowners; only if one had 4,000 or 5,000 fanegas [a land measure].[84]

As this exchange indicates, anarchism did not necessarily call for the complete destruction of all property and all forms of inequality. As José Monroy's statement proves, at least some anarchists saw themselves as primarily engaged in a political war against the great estate, and they probably foresaw the survival of household proprietorship at the local level, although it would be the community that would collectively regulate property rights. In fact, the fusion of small proprietorship with community power received formal expression in 1919 when the Spanish anarchist congress accepted the doctrine of *minifundio comunal* (small-scale communal regulation.)[85] According to this doctrine land was to be owned and regulated by the local community as a whole, but cultivation was to be carried out by households working on small plots.[86] This, it seems to me, is a clear statement of the commitment of rural anarchists to what I have called property as trusteeship, and had anarchism triumphed in southern Spain it would ironically have led to a strengthening of local community institutions to such an extent that southern villages would have come to resemble the communities of smallholders in northern Spain. The anarchist collectives of the south would probably have been closer to the traditional concejo than to the "modern" collectives imagined by Mikhail Bakunin and Peter Kropotkin.[87]

It is, then, an error to see rural anarchism as either a secular religion or a doctrine of class consciousness. Anarchists did have great expectations and great moral fervor, and every anarchist center had its radical "men of ideas" and "conscious workers" who spoke constantly of the coming reparto of the latifundia. Yet anarchism gained support because of its plausibility in a world where the defense of community meant more than the struggle of classes.

We may speculate that anarchism would not have gained such a stronghold in the rural south if Spanish political elites of the 1890s and early 1900s had been willing to use parliamentary politics as a bridge between the state and ordinary rural people. What, for example, would have happened if the liberal political

84. Ibid., 151–52.
85. Malefakis, *Agrarian Reform and Peasant Revolution,* 150–51.
86. Fraser, *Blood of Spain,* 348–73.
87. Mintz, *The Anarchists of Casas Viejas,* 151–52.

parties of the early 1900s had appealed over the heads of the southern caciques on a platform of land reform that combined a restitution of common lands with a large injection of distributive patronage? As the history of the Third Republic in France demonstrates, this kind of institutional bridge building was possible, even in the context of a largely agrarian society.

But political bridge building was not to occur in Spain. Spanish elites were intractable when faced with popular rural demands, and in the 1920s they turned to authoritarianism rather than reform as a solution to mounting social tensions.[88] Although this move to the right was temporarily reversed by the republican experiment of the 1930s, conservative reaction became deeply entrenched in the countryside, and when the leftist politicians of the 1930s at last turned to land reform as a solution to the problems of the south they discovered that it was too late to overcome the hostility of landowning elites and the radicalism of the pueblo.[89]

In the south, the failure of parliamentary representation meant that local insurrection continued to be a viable mode of popular politics well into the 1930s. Collective violence was a means of representing community interests against landowning elites and bureaucrats who refused to respect the boundaries of community autonomy. Arson, assassination, violent harvest strikes, and the occasional collective seizure and redivision of estate land can all be seen as popular efforts aimed at reconstituting local authority and political power.[90] The goal was to eliminate the local power of the landed elite and replace it with the authority of the local community. Once again, we see that politics rather than sheer material hardship was at the heart of the logic that led to rural rebellion.

The Politics of Poverty and the Poverty of Theory

Much debate has swirled around the connection between poverty and rural insurrection. During the 1960s it became fashionable to argue that sheer material impoverishment was not a sufficient condition for the occurrence of rural unrest, and the clever work of Ted Gurr can be cited as an attempt to recast the whole study of "civil" violence in terms of a psychological model of subjective rather than objective factors. Similarly, Barrington Moore, although much more "materialist" in his focus than Gurr, argued in his study of injustice that the moral meaning of poverty and degradation should be seen as just as important as

88. Ben-Ami, *Fascism from Above*, 19–77.

89. Malefakis, *Agrarian Reform and Peasant Revolution*, 364–400.

90. Kaplan, *Anarchists of Andalusia*, 206–12. Also see Gerald Brenan, *The Spanish Labyrinth: An Account of the Social and Political Background of the Civil War* (Cambridge: Cambridge University Press, 1967), 89.

material factors in any explanation of rebellion.[91] What most of these studies seem to show is that absolute material deprivation does not make a good basis for collective action, a finding that should actually occasion little or no surprise. As Napoleon recognized in his quip about the relationship between full stomachs and marching armies, starving people are not likely to engage in concerted social action of any kind.

Scott has argued that societies in which the problem of guaranteeing subsistence is a daily reality are not going to have the same political and social logic as societies in which full stomachs are taken for granted. Although much of Scott's analysis may be disputed, he has certainly highlighted the need to rethink the relationship between politics and poverty in a way that does justice to the distinctive logic of poor societies without falling into the trap of assuming that poor people are inherently radical or conservative.[92]

What does the Spanish experience show us about the links between poverty and rural politics? As I have pointed out, Spain, especially the rural south, resembled a third-world country well into the 1950s, and in the south the problem of guaranteeing daily subsistence was a real issue for many ordinary landless and land-poor people. Spain, therefore, has much to teach us about the effect of poverty, or acute subsistence insecurity, on popular behavior.

To begin with it is fairly clear that poverty in southern Spain was not experienced as a purely individual problem, or even as a problem that was specific to certain households. Poverty was evidently experienced as a collective fate that affected entire communities in very visible ways. This, I think, is the underlying fact that explains the extraordinary social resentments that unified southern communities in their hatred of the rich and powerful. These people saw themselves as sharing a common poverty, an enforced economy of shared hardship, that gave them a joint interest and identity. Moreover, they saw poverty as attaching to particular communities or pueblos rather than to abstract class categories. This allowed ordinary people to identify with a group and thus to act collectively as established networks. As many scholars have shown, collective action by national class aggregates is both difficult to organize and almost impossible to sustain.[93] But organization was not a problem for the poor of the rural south of Spain; they could use preexisting community institutions as a foundation for mobilizing themselves *as* communities of the poor. They did not have to create special-purpose poor people's movements or associations. In effect, they were "pre-

91. Ted Gurr, *Why Men Rebel* (Princeton: Princeton University Press, 1970); and see James B. Rule, *Theories of Civil Violence* (Berkeley: University of California Press, 1988), 200–23. Barrington Moore, Jr., *Injustice: The Social Bases of Obedience and Revolt* (White Plains, N.Y.: M. E. Sharpe, 1978), esp. 3–48.

92. James C. Scott, *Weapons of the Weak* (New Haven: Yale University Press, 1985), 304–50.

93. Adam Przeworski, *Capitalism and Social Democracy* (Cambridge: Cambridge University Press, 1985).

organized," and their problem was not how to act collectively but how far to push their assault on elite power.[94]

More important, the causes of rural poverty in the Spanish south were neither mysterious nor hidden from popular consciousness.[95] The causes of community poverty lay in the open encroachment of the great estates on common land and common rights. Many village anarchists alive in 1900 must have personally witnessed the desamortización of the mid-1800s, and many others must have personally experienced the power of local estate managers to rig the labor market and deprive entire communities of access to land. As anyone who reads the interviews recorded by Jerome Mintz will discover, the rural anarchists of places like Casas Viejas had no illusions about who was responsible for their problems. This must have made it easy to mobilize popular anger, because the visible target of the great estate offered an obvious focus for community resistance. Even worse, the rich and powerful were not only the causes of community misfortune; they were idle rentiers who could easily be regarded as parasites, a feature of their social character that made them clear targets for popular animosity. As one of Mintz's informants observed: "Neither the grandees nor the rich worked. The grandees [noble estate owners] lived away. The rich rode their horses around the estates but did not work either with their hands or with their heads in the office. . . . Here in Andalusia the rich do not work."[96]

As this statement implies, the gap between rich and poor was perceived as a moral as well as a material problem. Yet the issue seems to have been more complex than a "moral economy" perspective would lead us to expect. The question was not so much a matter of what the elite refused to provide in the way of "subsistence insurance" as a question of why the elite did nothing useful, even though they drew their wealth from productive communities.

Nor is it very useful to understand poverty and politics in the rural south in terms of a model of relative deprivation.[97] "Relative deprivation" implies a clear connection between individual expectations and some block or impediment that frustrates those expectations. Southern Spain was not a world of upwardly mobile individualists who suddenly found their ambitions blocked by the rise of the great estates. Social identity, like poverty itself, was a collective experience, and it is very doubtful that the landless and land poor of the south saw themselves as having "careers" or mobility possibilities apart from their communities. Naturally, "individualism" did exist in areas like Andalusia, and it manifested itself in the petty struggles for honor that anthropologists have studied in depth.[98] That is simply beside the point, however. The real point is that, however we choose to explain it, the relationship between poverty and politics was a collective and

94. Kaplan, *Anarchists of Andalusia*, 135–67.
95. Ibid., 206–212.
96. Mintz, *The Anarchists of Casas Viejas*, 1–78, quotation on 38.
97. A better approach is offered in Moore, Jr., *Injustice*, 458–505.
98. Gilmore, *Aggression and Community*, 53–76, 126–70.

institutional issue that must be understood in terms of its intersubjective implications for community politics.

In sum, poverty probably did contribute to popular radicalism in southern Spain, although the lines of cause and effect are much more subtle than simple models would predict. Poverty was something that happened to communities, and it could provide a rallying point for mobilization to the degree that community action could be plausibly seen as a means of ending its causes. Poverty could also be a symbol of popular pride when the poor compared their humble but productive lives with the unproductive lives of the rich and mighty. In this sense, it was not the shame of poverty that led to protest, but the ability of poor people to turn their objective circumstances into a badge of honor and defiance. Anarchism probably helped effect this transformation, because anarchism boldly elevated the status of the humble, the plebs, into the vanguard of history. In any case, poverty would not have had political consequences if it had not had causes and consequences that were transparent and intersubjectively understood by whole communities.[99]

I would suggest that, in the absence of these very specific conditions, poverty will probably not provide a focus for popular mobilizations. Naturally, there is much that is simply specific to the Spanish case, and we would not expect certain factors, especially anarchism, to be found in other contexts. I would argue, however, that poverty in rural societies will become politicized only if it affects institutional collectivities as a joint or collective problem that has obvious causes and clear solutions that can be brought about through the mobilization of existing institutional networks. Objective hardship, even threats to some subsistence minimum, cannot automatically generate collective protest, nor do changes in social structure necessarily lead to collective resistance. Between poverty as a material cause and resistance as a collective effect stand the institutional mediations through which an intersubjective awareness of the politics of poverty must be developed.[100]

The situation in southern Spain also illustrates the subtle and ambiguous relationship between commercialization, poverty, and the politics of rural resistance. Coercive commercialization undoubtedly threatened the institutional autonomy of rural communities in southern Spain. For example, the expansion of the sherry industry in Andalusia encroached on common land and reduced the availability of both common pasture and the total area of arable land open to cultivation by smallholders. Local communities lost their ability to control use rights according to local conventions, and the capacity of rural communities to maintain jurisdictional control over property rights was undermined by the offensive launched by the great estates and the bureaucratic supporters of desamortización.

Yet it does not follow that commercialization undermined the institutional

99. This point is drawn from Fernandez, *Persuasions and Performances.*
100. Moore, Jr., *Injustice,* 3–116.

cohesion of popular communities. "Cohesion" means the ability of a group or process to stick together—to cohere—in varying circumstances. At least in areas like Andalusia, the cohesiveness of popular communities was not destroyed by the imposition of supralocal markets, nor was cohesion undermined by growing social differentiation within local communities. On the contrary, ordinary men and women were forced by necessity to stick together in a harsh economy. For example, field laborers had to cooperate in the harvest period if they were to have any control over the labor process, and neighbors had to learn to get along if they were going to exert any power over local governments.[101] In the context of an economy of shared poverty, every occasion, from the consumption of the gazpacho in the fields to a local wedding or funeral, was a community occasion when local solidarity was put to the test. Petty jealousies and conflicts may have been rife, but in the absence of a wide distribution of freehold property, ordinary people needed each other too often and in too many ways to permit them the luxury of breaking ties with their communities.

Similarly, commercialization in southern Spain worked against social differentiation within rural communities. Ironically, the dispossession of common-land and use rights may have led to a greater degree of material equality, because many communities became homogeneous blocks of landless and land-poor people. This result was a form of enforced or involuntary egalitarianism, but it was real nonetheless. It means that ordinary people shared a solidarity in poverty that was capable of mobilizing entire communities against the established order.[102]

Thus, commercialization may work in some cases to reinforce traditional institutional practices of solidarity and cooperation. If commercialization forces entire communities into an economy of shared poverty it may actually heighten the dependence of poor households on the institutional arrangements of community life, especially when there are few alternatives. Too many theories, it seems to me, have assumed that commercial penetration automatically undermines the cohesion of popular institutions, but the evidence from southern Spain indicates a much more complex problem that cannot be reduced to a simple, linear formula.

Nor should the Spanish case be regarded as somehow typical or representative of the impact of commercialization on small-scale rural societies. In France and England, for example, agrarian markets did not necessarily cause the erosion of local institutions, and they certainly did not cause widespread misery. Much of the variation depended on the political context in which market relations were embedded. In France and England, ordinary cultivators had much more control over the course and consequences of commercialization than in Spain. One might go so far as to argue that in England and France, rural communities benefited from commercialization, because they had greater political leverage over the course and conse-

---

101. Kaplan, *Anarchists of Andalusia*, 168–205.
102. Brenan, *The Spanish Labyrinth*, 88, 102–9, 112–13, 118–22.

quences of the process. Southern Spain saw a social war over commercialization because it was imposed from the outside according to a unilateral logic of elite power and privilege.[103]

Finally, a word is in order concerning the relationship between community autonomy and community cohesion. As I have pointed out on several occasions, "community autonomy" can be understood as the ability of local communities to make their own authoritative rules, while "cohesion" refers to the capacity of communities to stick together in varying circumstances. What is intriguing about the situation in southern Spain is that communities lost autonomy but not cohesion. The destruction of common-land and use rights drastically reduced the capacity of local institutions to control land and labor. Yet communities retained enough cohesiveness to challenge elite power repeatedly, and the radical nature of that challenge, including the turn to anarchism, was partly the result of this interesting juxtaposition of limited autonomy and strong cohesion. Cohesive communities struggled to regain a lost but well-remembered history of local control and local empowerment.

Does the Spanish experience have wider comparative implications? I would suggest, at least as a hypothesis, that the juxtaposition of weak autonomy and high cohesion may provide the most likely context in which rural protest can escalate into sustained movements of local insurrection. This is the situation in which ordinary people can act collectively but are simultaneously most threatened by unchecked elite domination. This was certainly true in southern Spain, and I think it also accounts for the ferocity and tenacity of rural collective violence in eighteenth- and nineteenth-century Ireland. It was not, after all, sheer poverty that drove entire communities to rebel. It was the combination of severe material pressure *and* the survival of institutions of cooperation that gave rebellion both a purpose and a means of expression.

---

103. Herr, "El significado de la desamortizacíon en España," 55–94; Gilmore, "Land Reform and Rural Revolt," 142–46.

CHAPTER 7

Russia and the Secession
of Community, 1800–1930

In the summer of 1774, an area of some six hundred thousand square kilometers along the Volga River erupted in one of the most savage rural insurrections in the history of modern Europe.[1] Whole villages rose against their overlords and enemies in a brutal wave of pillaging, plundering, and murder; at its peak, the total number of participants may have reached three million. The rebels aimed their most determined violence against the institutional bulwarks of Russian serfdom, an aim that had a long lineage in the Russian countryside.[2] Russia in the 1770s was a society in which manorial serfdom underpinned every aspect of social and political power. The Russian nobility, although in theory a service aristocracy that existed to execute the will of the tsar, the great autocrat of all the Russias, in practice depended on serfdom for its material existence. Nor was Russian serfdom a mild regime that had little practical effect on the lives of ordinary people. By the 1770s Russian serfdom had become a highly sophisticated form of forced labor, and probably the large majority of Russian villagers paid a substantial part of their harvest and their labor power as a form of tribute to their official owners, the noble serfholders who composed the core of the Russian elite. Although it would be false to assume that there were no practical limits to the effective power of the nobility in the countryside, it is quite clear that serfdom was capable of generating fierce and widespread popular opposition, and the insurrection of 1774 was but one in a long series of serf revolts.[3]

1. Throughout this chapter I have given primary emphasis to the regions of European Russia characterized by repartitional land communes and a history of serfdom. My reasons for this are theoretical, and I do not want to leave the reader with the impression that all of the Russian empire had this particular configuration. A separate study would be necessary to treat the empire's "minority" regions, especially Central Asia and Russian Poland.

2. Paul Avrich, *Russian Rebels, 1600–1800* (New York: Schocken Books, 1972), esp. 180–255. For a very different interpretation of serfdom and the mir, see Steven L. Hoch's *Serfdom and Social Control in Russia* (Chicago: Chicago University Press, 1986), esp. 187–90.

3. Peter Kolchin, *Unfree Labor: American Slavery and Russian Serfdom* (Cambridge: Harvard University Press, Belknap Press, 1987), 37, 244–57.

Historians refer to the events of 1774 as the Pugachev rebellion, or Pugachev-shchina. Pugachev, who claimed to fight on behalf of the "true" tsar, was neither the instigator nor absolute leader of the revolts of 1774, but he became a symbolic rallying point for ordinary villagers, partly because of his willingness to claim legitimacy for a direct and violent assault on the nobility and serfdom.[4] For example, Pugachev had a penchant for issuing decrees and manifestos, many of which promised to liberate rural society and create a new polity in which the "true" tsar, or Pugachev himself, would exercise benevolent power. In one of his decrees Pugachev said:

By this decree . . . we grant to all hitherto in serfdom and subjection the right to be faithful slaves [i.e., subjects] of our crown, and we award them the old cross and prayer, heads and beards, liberty and freedom always to be cossacks, without demanding recruit levies, soul taxes or other monetary obligations, possession of the lands, the woods, the hay meadows, the fisheries and the salt lakes, without payment or obrok [serviled dues], and we free all those formerly oppressed by the villainous nobles and bribe-takers and judges, all peasants and all the people oppressed by obligations and burdens. . . . [As for] those who hitherto were nobles, with their estates, those opponents of our power and disruptors of the empire and ruiners of the peasants, catch, kill and hang them, and treat them just as they, having no Christianity, treated you. With the annihilation of these enemies and miscreant nobles, all may feel peace and a tranquil life, which will last through the ages."[5]

Although Pugachev's followers were harshly treated by the tsarist regime, the memory of the events of the 1770s left the Russian elite with a lasting fear of servile insurrection, a fear that would persist even after serfdom had been abolished in 1861. More important, rural Russia developed what can only be called a tradition of popular resistance to elite rule, and in 1905 and 1917 that tradition exploded in waves of local insurrection that finally liquidated noble privilege and tsarist power in the countryside.[6]

I have chosen in this chapter to emphasize the late nineteenth and early twentieth centuries. My reasons for this are twofold. First, the abolition of serfdom in the 1860s eliminated the manor as a major institution in the Russian countryside, which allows us to gauge the extent to which the institutions of popular community were viable in the absence of supervision and surveillance by the manor. It might be suggested that community was an artificial construct that was imposed by the logic of serfdom, and by focusing on the postserf period we can achieve a clearer understanding of this issue. Second, the period from 1900 to

---

4. Philip Longworth, "The Last Great Cossack-Peasant Rising," *Journal of European Studies* 3 (Mar. 1973), 1–35; John T. Alexander, "Book Review: *Autocratic Politics in a National Crisis: The Imperial Russian Government and Pugachev's Revolt, 1773–1775*," *Canadian Slavic Studies* 4 (1970), 618–19.

5. Kolchin, *Unfree Labor*, 249–50.

6. Graeme Gill, *Peasants and Government in the Russian Revolution* (New York: Barnes and Noble, 1979), 132–87.

1919 saw two major episodes of rural insurrection punctuated by the Stolypin reforms, the first concerted attempt by the tsarist regime to dismantle the institutions of popular community in the countryside. Consequently, this was a period when community institutions were least likely to constitute the primary focus of rural life, and by trying to understand what happened between 1900 and 1919 we can see the underlying logic of community in rural Russia.

Redistributive Communities and Russian History, 1770–1900

Between the 1640s and the 1850s Russia depended on the institutions of serfdom as a basis for state building and economic development. By the reign of Catherine the Great (1762–96), serfs formed 53.9 percent of the adult male population, and as late as 1858, just on the eve of the abolition of serfdom, serfs still made up 39.2 percent of the population.[7] Although usually owned by absentee nobles, serfs were supervised by several layers of manorial administration that theoretically governed all aspects of servile life.[8] At the heart of this relationship of domination were the institutions of forced labor and surplus extraction that provided the material foundations for aristocratic power. Most serfs were agriculturalists who rendered tribute in the form of *barshchina* (forced labor) or *obrok* (dues in lieu of labor), and these were not legally negotiable at the will of the serfs.[9] In theory, serf owners had complete power over the lives and labor of their serfs, and serfs had no legal redress against their owners, save in limited cases of treason on the part of the owner.[10]

Indeed, Russian serfdom is almost a pure case of aristocratic domination. Russian serf owners could arbitrarily increase the dues of their servile tenants, move them from estate to estate, and, in limited cases, buy and sell them like chattel slaves. Serf owners and their agents could also use physical punishment against their serfs, although the tsarist regime attempted, probably unsuccessfully, to forbid the actual murder of serfs. But serf owners provided precious little in return for their domination of the countryside.[11] As absentees, they had little

7. The best starting points for the study of serfdom are Jerome Blum, "The Rise of Serfdom in Eastern Europe," *American Historical Review* 62 (1956), 807–36; Jerzy Topolsk, "The Manorial-Serf Economy in Central and Eastern Europe in the Sixteenth and Seventeenth Centuries," *Agricultural History* 48 (1974), 346–52; Richard Hellie, *Enserfment and Military Change in Muscovy* (Chicago: University of Chicago Press, 1971), esp. 77–92; and Sergei F. Platonov, *The Time of Troubles: A Historical Study of the Internal Crisis and Social Struggle in Sixteenth and Seventeenth Century Muscovy* (Lawrence: University Press of Kansas, 1970); Kolchin, *Unfree Labor*, 27, 365–71.

8. Jerome Blum, *Lord and Peasant in Russia from the Ninth to the Nineteenth Century* (Princeton: Princeton University Press, 1961), esp. 393–401, 570–72; Michael Confino, *Domaines et seigneurs en Russie vers la fin du XVIIIe siècle: Étude de structures agraires et de mentalités économiques* (Paris: Institut D'Etudes Slaves de l'Université de Paris, 1963), 39–105.

9. Blum, *Lord and Peasant in Russia*, 247–61; Kolchin, *Unfree Labor*, 3, 42, 102–10, 142–47.

10. Blum, *Lord and Peasant in Russia*, 8, 428–33, 551–60.

11. Kolchin, *Unfree Labor*, 49–156, 359–75.

interest in their estates apart from a smooth flow of servile rents and taxes, and the Russian nobility did little to improve agriculture until long after serfdom had been abolished. Moreover, the will of the local serf owner was arbitrary and theoretically absolute in all matters save those reserved for the tsar. In sum, Russian nobles (*pomeshchiki*) constituted a "parasitic" stratum of privileged property holders who claimed unchecked and irresponsible dominion over the countryside.[12]

In practice, of course, the realities of serfdom must have varied widely between estates, and the record of *volneniia,* or small-scale antimanorial protests, indicates the power of serfs to resist arbitrary domination. For example, Peter Kolchin has cited figures by Soviet historians that show the occurrence of some 2,261 voleniia between 1796 and 1855. Evidently, serfs were neither passive nor powerless in the face of the rigors of servile agriculture, and we may surmise that, even in the absence of legal modes of redress, serfs were able collectively to influence the daily operation of the manorial economy.[13]

It seems clear that community institutions were significant in defining popular society, at least during the age of serfdom. Serfs were not an atomized mass of poor cultivators who lacked any autonomous political space in which to regulate their common concerns.[14] On the contrary, the Russian landscape was marked by the predominance of solidary villages that resembled the strong communities of the medieval west. As Kolchin argues:

> The village constituted the peasants' world in a literal sense; its central institution, around which revolved their collective lives, was the peasant commune (obshchina or mir; mir also means "world"). A subject of intense ideological debate in Russian history—condemned by pro-Western modernizers for sapping individual initiative and celebrated by Slavophiles for its uniquely Russian character and by socialists for its protosocialism—the commune spread with villages during the early years of serfdom, existed throughout central and northern Russia by the early seventeenth century, and had acquired the sanction of tradition and custom by the early eighteenth. Receiving official government recognition and at least grudging seigneurial toleration, the mir constituted the political representative of the village, "the organizing basis of all village life," through which serfs ordered their lives and expressed their needs.[15]

Russian villages practiced two- or three-field strip farming, and the logic of material cooperation enforced by the regime of common fields and pasture rein-

---

12. Daniel Field, *The End of Serfdom: Nobility and Bureaucracy in Russia, 1855–1861* (Cambridge: Harvard University Press, 1976), 8–34, 359–67.

13. Kolchin, *Unfree Labor,* 241–357.

14. See, for example, the essays in Wayne S. Vucinich, ed., *The Peasant in Nineteenth Century Russia* (Stanford: Stanford University Press, 1969).

15. Kolchin, *Unfree Labor,* 201.

forced the importance of the village as a territorial unit of membership.[16] The village as a whole had to regulate the timing of the agricultural cycle, the conversion of arable to pasture, and the drawing of boundaries between fields. In addition, scattered-strip farming put a premium on the ability to regulate rights of way and resolve intracommunity conflicts over the use of arable and pasture. Whatever the local manor lord may have desired, ordinary villagers had to develop institutional mechanisms for controlling the village economy, and the member households had a strong incentive to resist any changes that would disrupt the collective rights of the community.[17]

So far the Russian village bears a strong resemblance to the open field villages of western Europe. As Kolchin suggests, however, the Russian village showed even stronger traces of economic cooperation owing to the existence of the mir.[18] The mir formed a repartitional land "commune" in which the village or mir as a whole collectively owned the land and other resources that were available to member households. The mir also periodically redistributed land to its households, either on the basis of the number of household members or in proportion to their total labor force. In practice this meant that member households had a hereditary right to use arable land and common fields, and village communes did not hesitate to intervene in the affairs of their members in order to balance the number of member households with the total quantity of available land. As Dorothy Atkinson has pointed out in her pathbreaking study of the mir:

> General redistributions of communal land took place irregularly as the need arose, although some communes held them periodically. Where allotments were based on demographic totals, general redivisions were usually scheduled at the time of a census, that is, about every twenty years. Shorter or longer intervals were not uncommon, but the requirements of the three field system discouraged any general redistribution that did not coincide with the triennial cycle. Between general redivisions, which involved the holdings of all members, more frequent partial redistributions took place among a limited number of households; in some communes these limited transfers of land occurred annually. Voluntary adjustments between individual households could often be arranged without specific authorization from the commune, but communes could interfere in family affairs and at times brought about involuntary divisions of households and their lands.[19]

The redistributive practices of the Russian village provide an excellent illustration of the principle of property as trusteeship. Village households held permanent

16. Dorothy Atkinson, *The End of the Russian Land Commune, 1905–1930* (Stanford: Stanford University Press, 1983), 3–40; R. E. F. Smith, *Peasant Farming in Muscovy* (Cambridge: Cambridge University Press, 1977), 26–33.

17. Kolchin, *Unfree Labor*, 195–240.

18. Ibid., 201–6, 236.

19. Atkinson, *The End of the Russian Land Commune*, 11–12. Also see Teodor Shanin, *The Awkward Class: Political Sociology of Peasantry in a Developing Society, Russia, 1910–1925* (Oxford: Clarendon Press, 1972), 32–38.

and inalienable rights to enough land to maintain themselves across the generations, and this right was tantamount to hereditary proprietorship; however, it was the whole village that controlled the ultimate disposition of local property rights. Member households held their allotments in trust for the entire mir, and the mir was powerful enough actually to divide extended families in order to create new landholding units. Thus, collective institutions determined the economic fate of ordinary rural households, and those institutions subordinated family property rights to the survival of the village as a solidary unit.

Moreover, the Russian village, even in the period of serfdom, was a genuine political community that exercised authoritative jurisdiction over its members.[20] It was the village that defined the nature of land tenure, the collective rights and obligations of its members, and the fundamental conditions of village membership. According to Kolchin:

> The mir performed a host of functions on a regular basis that were of vital concern to the daily lives of their serfs. It exercised broad authority in internal village affairs, settling minor disputes among peasants, enforcing family morality, and maintaining a reserve of money and grain to help the needy in time of crisis. Tradition—together with noble instructions—gave the commune substantial power in selecting recruits to serve in the military levies the government periodically imposed. Although pomeshchiki had the ultimate right to send whomever they wanted into the army and availed themselves of their right by picking special troublemakers as well as by laying down general guidelines for the mir to follow in making their choices, most allowed the serfs themselves "to select . . . in the mir gathering whomever they sentence." The commune was thus able to take account of specific conditions, usually selecting for military service unmarried youths and those from large families, but sometimes resorting to lot.
>
> The obshchina's most important regular function, however, consisted of apportioning land and obligations among the village inhabitants. Because pomeshchiki typically cared little about the internal distribution of work and resources in their villages . . . they usually assigned obligations to villages or estates collectively and allowed the commune to determine, on the basis of local conditions, who owed what.[21]

Institutional expression was given to the political autonomy and cohesion of the village in the regular meetings of the village assembly, the *skhod* or *mirskiiskhod*.[22] Open to all male householders who held land rights, the skhod debated common problems, apportioned rights and duties among members, and passed judgment on the issues of the day. Sometimes led by the village headman, or *starosta*, the skhod was not simply a reflection of the will of the local manor lord; it was a partly autonomous political jurisdiction that constituted the basic "cell"

20. Atkinson, *The End of the Russian Land Commune*, 3–40.
21. Kolchin, *Unfree Labor*, 203–4.
22. Atkinson, *The End of the Russian Land Commune*, 4, 52.

of rural government for ordinary people. Like the Spanish concejo, the skhod should be seen as a performance of politics in which householders enacted the ties of territorial cohesion that made them a real collectivity.[23]

Closely connected to the mir and the skhod were the many ritual practices, often of a "pagan" or pre-Christian origin, that made Russian villages significant arenas of popular identity. For example, religious occasions like Easter provided a moment of celebratory release that strengthened the bonds of communal solidarity.[24] Whole villages participated in the semimythological rites of fertility and renewal that were considered to be nothing more than "superstitions" by the "enlightened" serf owners of the eighteenth and nineteenth centuries. Interestingly, much of the ritual and festival life of the village seems to have been independent of the official doctrines of the Orthodox church, which indicates that there was an autonomous popular culture rooted in a folklore of place. The fact that the word *mir* means "world" as well as "land commune" shows how much of popular cultural identity was dependent on the circumscribed institutional arena of the village. Russian villagers inhabited a world of myth and magic in which every rock could have spiritual meaning, and household hearths were protected or threatened by local tutelary spirits who hid behind the stove by day and roamed the house at night, eating food left out for them by local believers.[25] Village priests who accepted this local folklore were treated as community members, or even as leaders, but priests who bent to the will of the lord or the official church hierarchy could generate popular resistance, as Gregory L. Freeze has shown in his excellent studies of the Russian parish clergy.[26]

The cultural identity of the village was also manifested in bouts of heavy drinking among male householders, a prominent if unfortunate feature of Russian rural society in the nineteenth and twentieth centuries.[27] The brewing and consumption of strong drink can be viewed as a type of male commensality that cemented interfamily alliances and networks of cooperation. Whether it took place legally or illegally, in or outside of the tavern, hard drinking was an

23. Moshe Lewin, *Russian Peasants and Soviet Power: A Study of Collectivization* (Evanston: Northwestern University Press, 1968), 19–40, 65–106.

24. Kolchin, *Unfree Labor*, 195–240.

25. Moshe Lewin, *The Making of the Soviet System: Essays in the Social History of Interwar Russia* (New York: Pantheon, 1985), 49–71.

26. Gregory L. Freeze, *The Russian Levites: Parish Clergy in the Eighteenth Century* (Cambridge: Harvard University Press, 1977), 172–79; Gregory L. Freeze, *The Parish Clergy in Nineteenth Century Russia: Crisis, Reform, Counter-Reform* (Princeton: Princeton University Press, 1983), 103–18, 156–59.

27. For an overview of drink and rural society in Old Regime Europe, see Jerome Blum, *The End of the Old Order in Rural Europe* (Princeton: Princeton University Press, 1978), 48–49, 295–96; Kolchin, *Unfree Labor*, 152–55; R. E. F. Smith and David Christian, *Bread and Salt: A Social and Economic History of Food and Drink in Russia* (Cambridge: Cambridge University Press, 1984), esp. 251–87; and Mary Matossian, "The Peasant Way of Life," in Vucinich, *The Peasant in Nineteenth Century Russia.*

ineradicable component of village ritual life. Although there were more benign expressions of village culture—including the *khorovod,* or village circle dance, during which unmarried boys and girls met and courted, or the *posidelka,* the village spinning party in which village girls met for singing and dancing—heavy drinking was always looming in the background as a grim reminder of the village's collective determination to live according to its own rules of life and leisure.[28]

In sum, there is powerful evidence that Russian serf villages can be accurately described as communities of grain. Villages were territorial collectivities characterized by strong institutions of material, political, and ritual cooperation. Although strongly constrained by serfdom, Russian villages had a wide degree of autonomous control over the production and distribution of the means of life. Russian communities were scarcely egalitarian utopias, and strong hierarchies of age and sex were ingrained in the fabric of village life. Yet the periodic redistribution of land rights probably reduced the absolute levels of material inequality in the Russian countryside and certainly reinforced the cohesion of village communities.[29] The life chances of ordinary men and women were largely determined by the world that existed within the mir. No man could become an independent householder without the consent of the land commune, and no man or woman could establish village membership rights without the approval of the established householders of the village. Prior to the 1860s, the chief threat to community autonomy and cohesion came from the logic of aristocratic domination and the constraints of serfdom; and it is not surprising that serfdom formed the chief focus of popular resistance and collective violence.[30] As Paul Avrich has shown in his study of Russian rebels, serfdom was a major cause of both local struggles (the volneniia) and large-scale uprisings.[31] In addition to the Pugachevshchina, major revolts occurred in 1606–7, 1670–71, and 1707–8. By the time of Pugachev's revolt the rallying cry of village freedom from serfdom had evidently become a deep part of the politics and consciousness of local communities, and some scholars have viewed the eighteenth and early nineteenth centuries as a period of escalating popular opposition to the institutions of serfdom. Whole villages began to refuse the orders of their masters when "they felt that their collective rights were being violated."[32] For example, in one quantitative study of 2,342 volneniia, undertaken by the Soviet scholar B. G. Litvak, a wide variety of specific causes of serf protest were discovered, ranging from inadequate landholdings to cruel treatment.[33] What this shows, I think, is that serfdom was resented less for

28. Lewin, *The Making of the Soviet System,* 72–87.
29. Shanin, *The Awkward Class,* 32–38.
30. Blum, *The End of the Old Order,* 332–53.
31. Avrich, *Russian Rebels,* 229–34, 256–73.
32. Kolchin, *Unfree Labor,* 269–71.
33. Cited in ibid., 304.

its sheer economic exploitation than for its political threat to community institutions, and it is possible that serfdom might have led to the kind of massive antiseigneurial uprisings that occurred in France during 1789.

Yet serfdom was not abolished in this fashion; for whatever reasons, the tsarist regime of Alexander II began to dismantle serfdom from above. In February 1861 the tsar issued a decree proclaiming the commitment of the regime to liquidate serfdom throughout Russia. Between 1861 and 1867 a series of detailed decrees and statutes specified the terms of abolition, the division of land between former serfs and their owners, and the new legal status of ordinary rural people.[34] Henceforth, rural commoners would form an estate (*soslovie*), or peasant status group, that would be personally free from noble jurisdiction and any taint of servile status. At one stroke, the tsarist bureaucracy destroyed manorial institutions and noble control of the countryside. This was probably the most daring attempt at agrarian reform from above undertaken in the nineteenth century, paralleled only by Abraham Lincoln's Emancipation Proclamation.

Land tenure and village politics were the areas in which village institutions were most likely to have been affected by the emancipation process. The disappearance of forced labor, servile dues, and manorial institutions radically transformed the economic relations between farmer serfs and outside elites. Similarly, the creation of new administrative relations between the tsarist regime and the rural "estate," symbolized by the creation of "peasant" law courts and institutions of county and provincial self-administration (the *zemstvos*), altered the balance of political power in the countryside.[35]

The emancipation process did not, however, *legally* undermine the Russian mir, nor did the abolition decrees attempt to create an "individualistic" stratum of yeomen farmers who would become a force for agricultural modernization. In addition to recognizing rural commoners as a distinct social estate with their own laws and particular rights and responsibilities, the drafters of the reform decrees legally sanctioned the mir as the basic organizational structure in the countryside. The mir was officially singled out as the proprietary holder of "peasant," or allotment, land. Allotment land was the portion of former serf estates that passed into the hands of ordinary cultivators after emancipation, and the mir as a whole became legally responsible for the redemption payments that were supposed to reimburse serf owners for the loss of part of their patrimony. Moreover, villages were collectively liable for the behavior of their members, with all tax and judicial

34. Field, *The End of Serfdom*, 35–101, 324–67; Atkinson, *The End of the Russian Land Commune*, 20–28.

35. For the creation of "peasant" institutions after 1861, see Dorothy Atkinson, "The Zemstvo and the Peasants," in Terence Emmons and W. S. Vucinich, eds., *The Zemstvo in Russia: An Experiment in Self-Government* (Cambridge: Cambridge University Press, 1982), 79–132; Peter Czap, "P. A. Valuev's Proposal for a Vyt' Administration, 1864," *Slavonic and East European Review* 45 (1967), 391–411; and Terence Emmons, *The Russian Landed Gentry and the Peasant Emancipation of 1861* (Cambridge: Cambridge University Press, 1968).

responsibilities falling on the shoulders of the collectivity of householders who made up what was now called in government legislation the "rural society."[36]

We should, therefore, not rule out the possibility that the survival of strong community institutions in the postemancipation period was *partly* a function of the support given by the tsarist government to the land commune.[37] It would be a mistake, however, to assume that the tsarist regime had sufficient power to determine the fundamental character of popular institutions. Neil B. Weissman has demonstrated how inept and incapable the tsarist autocracy was when it came to governing the countryside, and, with 6.2 administrators per thousand inhabitants, the tsarist empire was relatively undergoverned in comparison with France and Germany, which had 17.6 and 12.6 bureaucrats per thousand, respectively. The tsarist regime could tax, conscript, and repress—indeed, it could interfere in popular life in a myriad of ways that led to popular indignation and hostility. But a regime that could neither prevent the famines of 1891–92 nor force ordinary villagers to pay their redemption dues on time cannot be regarded as a Leviathan that could create artificial communities in the wake of abolition.[38] One may actually wonder if the decision to give legal recognition to the land commune may have stemmed more from the tenacity of community institutions than the schemes of tsarist officials.[39] Perhaps the grant of legal and corporate status to the mir was a reflection of the fact that the tsarist regime could deal with its rural subjects only through the mediation of the deeply entrenched institutions of the village land commune.

In any case, we are not dependent on tsarist legal definitions for evidence of the postemancipation survival of strong community institutions in the Russian countryside. Atkinson, whose synthesis has done much to illuminate these issues, has provided data that show how vital and vibrant community control of land tenure remained after 1861. For example, in 1905, land tenure in 77 percent of all households in the fifty provinces of European Russia was still communal, and in regions like the mid-Volga communal tenure approached 100 percent. More important, periodic land redistribution continued throughout the period from 1861 to 1917, even though this was one aspect of the village mir that was officially frowned on. For example, laws enacted in 1886 and 1893 made it easier for well-

36. Atkinson, *The End of the Russian Land Commune*, 23–37; Steven Grant, "Obshchina and Mir," *Slavic Review* 35 (Dec. 1976), 636–51.

37. Geroid Tanquary Robinson, *Rural Russia under the Old Regime: A History of the Landlord-Peasant World and a Prologue to the Peasant Revolution of 1917* (Berkeley: University of California Press, 1967), 66–74.

38. Neil B. Weissman, *Reform in Tsarist Russia: The State, Bureaucracy, and Local Government, 1900–1914* (New Brunswick: Rutgers University Press, 1981), 3–39, 202–28. Also see S. Frederick Starr, *Decentralization and Self Government in Russia, 1830–1870* (Princeton: Princeton University Press, 1972); George L. Yarey, "Law, Society, and the Domestic Regime in Russia in Historical Perspective," *American Political Science Review* 59 (1965), 379–90.

39. Robinson, *Rural Russia under the Old Regime*, 94–128.

off rural households to block repartition, but repartitions occurred anyway, with or without official sanction. In the single province of Ekaterinoslav, 140 cases of general redistribution took place between 1864 and 1904 in the 157 communes that made up the district (*uezd*) of Aleksandrov.[40] As Atkinson suggests, this was no isolated phenomenon. The tsarist regime attempted to block repartitions on the correct assumption that constant redistributions led to an acute fragmentation of landholdings that undermined the tax base. Yet repartitions continued, thereby indicating, however obliquely, that the institutional practices of the land commune were entrenched in the political economy of Russian villages.

What is striking about the survival of repartition in the postemancipation period is that it occurred during an era of very rapid population growth. Between 1858 and 1897 the total population of the tsarist empire rose from 74 million to 129 million, and much of this increase took place in rural provinces where the village mir remained a powerful focus of popular life. In the seven regions identified by Atkinson as featuring "nearly universal" communal tenure, the rate of population growth between 1863 and 1914 was a hefty 103 percent.[41] Although demographic pressure may have been mitigated by a comparatively high death rate, there can be little doubt that the forces of demographic erosion were eating away at the subsistence threshold of the Russian countryside. By 1914 Russia was a relatively poor agrarian society, and Russian villages had literally begun to run out of land to redistribute.

Well-off villagers had the most to lose by any redivision of village holdings, yet both well-off and disadvantaged households submitted to redistribution well into the 1920s.[42] Naturally, there were exceptions to this rule, but Dorothy Atkinson has argued that households who removed themselves from the commune did so as a way of avoiding tax liabilities rather than because of any desire for individualized land tenure.[43] Evidently the institutional ties of the village mir were strong enough to deter large-scale defections from the commune, even if it meant subjecting one's family to the repartitional lottery. But this outcome should not have occurred if the Russian countryside had become dominated by a class of protocapitalist farmers, or kulaks, who would have had a structural interest in dissolving the village mir.[44]

40. Atkinson, *The End of the Russian Land Commune*, 4, 29–30.
41. Ibid., 30–32.
42. Shanin, *The Awkward Class*, 32–38.
43. Atkinson, *The End of the Russian Land Commune*, 32–37, 83–92.
44. For some of the roots of rural tenacity, see Edgar Melton, "Proto-Industrialization, Serf Agriculture, and Agrarian Social Structure: Two Estates in Nineteenth Century Russia," *Past and Present* 115 (1987), 69–106; Rodney D. Bohac, "Peasant Inheritance Strategies in Russia," *Journal of Interdisciplinary History* 16 (1985), 27–29; Steven L. Hoch, "Serfs in Russia: Demographic Insights," *Journal of Interdisciplinary History* 13 (1982), 221–46; and Peter Czap, "The Perennial Multiple Family Household: Mishino, Russia, 1782–1858," *Journal of Family History* 7 (Spring 1982), 5–26.

The survival of the repartitional land commune, I believe, can be explained in terms of the logic of mutually implicated forms of cooperation. Readers will recall that mutually implicated cooperation refers to the multiple points of overlapping institutional ties that characterize small-scale agrarian societies. The ability to cooperate successfully in one arena of community life depends on the ability to cooperate in other, "implicated" arenas, and the power and prestige of any individual are based in a continuous flow of reciprocities that cut across institutional boundaries. Thus, the ability of a household to gain community political support depends on its willingness to cooperate in local economic practices, and this, in turn, depends on the willingness of other households to underwrite the ritual and festive performances of community life. In short, the life chances of households are embedded in simultaneous networks of group endeavor that form a kind of circle or unity of institutional action.

Well-off households remained dependent on the willingness of their neighbors to cooperate in every arena of village life.[45] The village as a whole continued to control access rights to common pastures and forests, and the persistence of scattered strips in common, open fields meant that neighbors still had to cooperate in arranging the timing of fieldwork and the organization of field boundaries. Not even the most aggressive kulak could withdraw from the land commune without facing the possibility of serious economic reprisals by his neighbors.[46]

Nor should we follow Lenin in exaggerating the degree of economic differentiation within Russian villages in the postemancipation period. Complete landlessness was apparently rare in the Russian countryside prior to 1917, as Robert Edelman, one of the most cogent critics of the "communal" interpretation of Russian agriculture, has admitted.[47] As long as most families had access to some land, well-off cultivators could not treat poorer neighbors simply as a pool of cheap labor that could be manipulated at will, and the ability of better-off households to hire any labor whatsoever must have been partly a function of the willingness of well-off households to accept the rules of the village mir. After all, Russian kulaks were not wealthy by the standards of the pomeshchiki; their status and survival could be guaranteed only by the local communities in which they claimed the rights and obligations of membership.[48]

Furthermore, there is no reason to suppose that well-off rural households necessarily lost more than they gained from the persistence of communal repartition. According to Shanin, one of the most lucid analysts of the problem, repartitions tended to affect large, extended, or joint families in which older householders with unmarried adult offspring faced pressure from their children to

45. Shanin, *The Awkward Class*, 9–62.
46. Atkinson, *The End of the Russian Land Commune*, 71–82, 155–64.
47. Robert Edelman, *Proletarian Peasants: The Revolution of 1905 in Russia's Southwest* (Ithaca: Cornell University Press, 1987), 1–34, 169–78.
48. Shanin, *The Awkward Class*, 76–95.

establish independent households.[49] In this context, the offspring of better-off families could actually benefit from a general or partial repartition that gave them enough land to be able to support an autonomous family.[50]

In any event, the decision of a rural household to support or oppose repartition cannot be reduced to a simple, economic choice that had no political and social consequences. Both well-off and poorer householders were tied to the political institutions of the village skhod, and there seems to be little evidence that the skhod deteriorated after 1861. Although the tsarist government tried to reformulate local politics through the introduction of local zemstvos, elective organs of administration responsible for the provision of health, education, and agricultural services, the village skhod continued as the basic institutional focus of community politics.[51] It was the skhod that provided the key forum in which group decisions were made that regulated the use of land and labor and resolved local disputes. The rural *volost* courts and zemstvos were "alien" institutions that represented elite rather than community interests, and it is in no way remarkable that the ancient skhod retained its ability to constitute the genuine voice of community needs and popular politics. As Atkinson has remarked with respect to the persistence of village political institutions during the 1920s, "What the law decreed was not necessarily what the peasants practiced. Village life encompassed a range of activities and relationships that had long been regulated by custom rather than formal law, and custom proved tenacious. Moreover, the laws themselves—articulating the norms of a new order while attempting to compromise with the old—were constantly being reshaped in response to changing conditions."[52]

Given this set of circumstances, a household's decision to oppose communal repartition could have grave political as well as economic consequences. Political ostracism, or even violent reprisals, could result from the refusal to abide by a local redivision of holdings. But at a minimum, the failure to support the village mir might lead to a kind of political isolation in which an offending household was left without the political support of its neighbors in its relations with the agents of the tsarist regime. This was a daunting prospect in a society where the lowest official representative of elite power, the land captain (*zemski nachalnik*), had wide discretionary authority to punish those who fell afoul of his power.[53] Often drawn from the ranks of the nobility, the land captains were introduced in 1889 in order to supervise the countryside, and they were capable of corrupt and arbitrary behavior.[54] In this situation it was probably wiser for ordinary rural people to deal

49. Ibid., 63–121.
50. Teodor Shanin, *The Roots of Otherness: Russia's Turn of Century*, 2 vols. (New Haven: Yale University Press, 1986), 2:79–183.
51. Atkinson, "The Zemstvo and the Peasants"; and see Lewin, *The Making of the Soviet System*, 72–87; Shanin, *The Awkward Class*, 203–14, 219–27.
52. Atkinson, *The End of the Russian Land Commune*, 239.
53. George Yaney, *The Urge to Mobilize: Agrarian Reform in Russia, 1861–1930* (Urbana: University of Illinois Press, 1982), esp. 97–351.
54. Weissman, *Reform in Tsarist Russia*, 24–30, 217–18.

with elite authorities through the mediation of village institutions; at least they offered solidarity and group anonymity that might deflect the worst abuses of elite power.

The tenacity of the village community might have been eroded by a comprehensive program of cultural "modernization," which Eugene Weber's *Peasants into Frenchmen* has described as central to the integration of the countryside in Third Republic France. But this was not to be, and the village remained a world of its own.[55] Formal education was limited in spite of the zemstvos' funding of local schools, and national conscription, far from performing integrating functions for the regime, was viewed as a kind of curse that was to be avoided if possible.[56] Perhaps most significant, however, is that village folklore and ritual long outlived the abolition of serfdom. The Orthodox church hierarchy atrophied, and parish priests became a virtually hereditary caste of ritualists who resembled the rural people they served.[57] There was no postemancipation revival of Orthodoxy that, like the transformation of Catholicism in Third Republic France, might have led to a widening of village horizons. On the eve of the revolution of 1905, the village commune clung to its ancient myths and rituals, thereby reinforcing the deep bonds of economic and political cohesion.

It seems reasonable, therefore, to conclude that the abolition of serfdom did not lead to the institutional dissolution of the village mir. Conflicts undoubtedly existed within the village, especially as the pressures of demographic growth made it ever more difficult for ordinary households to gain enough land to become economically invulnerable to periodic subsistence crises. Repartition obviously had natural limits dictated by the total land area available to the mir, and unless that area could be enlarged, repartition would eventually have led to the proliferation of uneconomic smallholdings. It is important to remember that, although land was owned and redistributed by the village, labor was performed by households on their scattered strips of land, much as had been true of the open-field villages of the medieval west. Constant repartition would ultimately have produced a radical imbalance between land and labor, and the existence of households with too many mouths to feed and too little land for the household to exploit could very well have produced a devastating subsistence crisis of the kind that Ladurie discovered in sixteenth- and seventeenth-century France.[58]

Yet, in spite of its problems, the village mir did not collapse, and village solidarity persisted in the face of the constraints on its autonomy caused by tsarist taxes, legal regulations, and the survival of a powerful landowning nobility. Where else but to the village could ordinary rural people turn in order to protect

55. Lewin, *The Making of the Soviet System,* 49–87.
56. Allan K. Wildman, *The End of the Russian Imperial Army,* 2 vols. (Princeton: Princeton University Press, 1980), 1:24–40.
57. Freeze, *The Parish Clergy in Nineteenth Century Russia,* 103–18, 156–59.
58. For the demographic problem, see J. Ansley Coale et al., *Human Fertility in Russia since the Nineteenth Century* (Princeton: Princeton University Press, 1979).

their often precarious hold on economic independence? The tsarist regime offered little or nothing in the way of a comprehensive policy of subsistence insurance for the countryside. There was nothing in Russia analogous to the English poor laws, and loans and other forms of subsidized inputs for agriculture were both expensive and often targeted at the nobility rather than the village.[59] The alternative to a secure if modest place in the village was short- or long-term labor migration, an option that villagers increasingly resorted to prior to 1914.[60] But migration was risky and demeaning, and many migrant villagers preferred a stake in the mir to the problems of urban life.[61]

Instead of turning in on themselves in a wave of internecine struggle, Russian villages in the postemancipation period dealt with demographic pressure by turning their hostility against the surviving landholdings of the nobility and the institutions of bureaucratic domination that underpinned tsarist power. Especially in areas where the landed nobility had preserved a large measure of ownership of arable and forests after 1861, villages became increasingly determined to liquidate aristocratic property rights altogether. As early as 1902, major uprisings took place in the provinces of Kharkov and Poltava in which the legitimacy of noble landholding was called into question.[62] Moreover, the tsarist regime found its own authority challenged on a number of fronts, ranging from the land captains to the tsarist regulations that restricted the right of villagers collectively to control the use of forests. Above all, however, villagers resented the collective redemption taxes imposed as payment for the land they had received at emancipation, and their ultimate response to the burden of redemption dues was simply to stop paying them. By the 1890s accumulated redemption arrears amounted to a sum larger than the total annual rural tax bill; in the southern central black earth region alone, arrears in 1896 came to 127 percent of the annual levy.[63] Although this phenomenal backlog of redemption payments was partly a function of sheer penury, it is clear that village resistance to the levy played a major role in thwarting the redemption process. Only the village as a whole could have organized a tax strike against the tsarist regime.

59. Atkinson, *The End of the Russian Land Commune*, 32–37, 41–70. Also see Alexander Gerschenkron, "Agrarian Policies and Industrialization: Russia, 1861–1917," in H. J. Habakkuk and M. Postan, eds., *Cambridge Economic History* (Cambridge: Cambridge University Press, 1965), vol. 6, part 2, 706–800; and Lazar Volin, *A Century of Russian Agriculture: From Alexander II to Khrushchev* (Cambridge: Harvard University Press, 1970).

60. Robert E. Johnson, *Peasant and Proletarian: The Working Class of Moscow in the Late Nineteenth Century* (New Brunswick: Rutgers University Press, 1979), esp. chaps. 1 and 2.

61. Atkinson, *The End of the Russian Land Commune*, 101–8; Edelman, *Proletarian Peasants*, 38–39, 72–75.

62. Roberta Manning, *The Crisis of the Old Order in Russia: Gentry and Government* (Princeton: Princeton University Press, 1982), 104–5.

63. Atkinson, *The End of the Russian Land Commune*, 26–34; and see Arcadius Kahan, "Government Policies and the Industrialization of Russia," *Journal of Economic History* 27 (Dec. 1967), 460–77.

Rural opposition to noble landholding and tsarist authority was neither irrational nor simply a result of popular envy, although it may be doubted that the destruction of noble estates and imperial taxes would have permanently resolved the demographic problems that weighed so heavily on Russian villages by 1900.[64] At the time of emancipation the total land area under the direct control of the mir was reduced by anywhere from 13 to 18 percent in the major agricultural provinces.[65] This land was legally "cut off" from the village and transferred to former serf owners, who also received payment from the tsarist treasury for the land kept by the mir. It is certainly true that much of the land of the nobility was rented out to former serfs, but the survival of large blocks of noble property offered a visible target for villagers who resented having to pay for access to land they regarded as rightfully theirs.[66] Whether organized in compact estates or scattered strips intermingled with the land of the village, the existence of noble property reduced the amount of land under the autonomous control of the village and represented a constant reminder that emancipation had not fully ended aristocratic domination in the countryside.

Furthermore, Roberta Manning has argued that the late nineteenth century saw an intensification of estate agriculture. Many noble estate owners moved from the cities to the countryside and began to take an active managerial role. They tightened up rent collection, introduced new commercial techniques, and tried to restrict the rights of ordinary villagers. Perhaps, as Manning's evidence suggests, their action can be understood as an instance of coercive commercialization. But there can be little doubt that the new agricultural activism of parts of the pomeshchiki led to increased friction with ordinary villagers, who saw this new activism as one more material threat to the mir. For example, noble proprietors began to eliminate the practice of *otrabotka*, or labor rent, which had at least allowed villagers to supplement their holdings by renting noble land.[67] By breaking with otrabotka the elite signaled its willingness to overturn the postemancipation settlement and launch a new offensive against the village that could only eventuate in a further reduction of the total land available to the autonomous control of the mir.

Finally, one should not underestimate the extent to which popular hostility to the tsarist regime resulted from very real material and political problems. In addition to the burden of redemption dues and the arbitrary quality of local officials, the tsarist government intervened in a variety of ways that were bound to generate popular antagonism. The tsarist bureaucracy taxed a whole range of items of popular consumption, including alcohol, and the state vodka monopoly

---

64. John L. H. Keep, *The Russian Revolution: A Study in Mass Mobilization* (New York: Norton, 1976), 3–15, 156–99.
65. Atkinson, *The End of the Russian Land Commune*, 389.
66. Manning, *The Crisis of the Old Order in Russia*, 4–24, 138–76.
67. Ibid., 4–44.

seemed designed to produce evasion and popular animosity.[68] More important, the tsarist war machine was labor intensive, and in both the Russo-Japanese War (1904–5) and World War I (1914–18), the village yielded up the vast bulk of the conscripts.[69] Given the heavy demands of the tsarist bureaucracy on the countryside it is not difficult to understand why so much popular anger was directed at the agents of tsarist power, particularly after the events of 1905 had begun to shatter the legitimacy of the tsar himself.[70]

On the eve of the 1905 revolution the Russian village was still a cohesive community with at least limited autonomy in terms of its control of local land and labor. But the village was also hard pressed by demographic erosion and constrained by both the tsarist bureaucracy and the persistence of aristocratic power and property. The end of serfdom had neither eliminated the village community nor satisfied deeply held popular desires for a complete redistribution of noble land and political power. The stage was therefore set for the explosion of the period 1905–7.

Communities in Motion in the Russian Countryside, 1905–1907

The first supreme crisis for the tsarist regime since the abolition of serfdom occurred in 1905. Russia's tragicomic defeat in the Russo-Japanese War led to a complex upsurge of political radicalism that nearly destroyed the tsarist empire. Urban workers, students, ethnic minorities, and political radicals managed to coalesce briefly in a revolutionary movement that called for political liberalization and an end to the autocratic power of the tsarist bureaucracy. Although the loyalty of the army allowed the regime to survive until 1917, the tsar was forced to concede Russia's first national representative assembly, the Duma, as well as a number of reforms that concerned the limits of bureaucratic power.[71]

In the countryside the period from 1905 to 1907 was characterized by massive unrest, and in some parts of the empire collective violence reached levels that paralleled the Pugachev uprising. Officials recorded 3,228 "disorders" in 1905, 2,600 in 1906, and 1,337 in 1907. Of these incidents, 979 involved arson and 846 took the form of destruction of local estates. There were also 216 land seizures, 211 rent strikes, 316 seizures of food and fodder, and 205 clashes with estate owners and their agents in addition to the "milder" forms of rural protest, like harvest strikes and illegal timber cutting, that took place during the same period.

---

68. Robinson, *Rural Russia under the Old Regime*, 60–78, 153–54.

69. Wildman, *The End of the Russian Imperial Army* 1:3–74; 2:54–77, 215–25.

70. Abraham Ascher, *The Revolution of 1905* (Stanford: Stanford University Press, 1988), 74–126.

71. Ibid., 152–74, 226–74; Terence Emmons, *The Formation of Political Parties and the First National Elections in Russia* (Cambridge: Harvard University Press, 1983), 11–17.

Although concentrated largely in ten provinces, the uprisings of 1905–7 led to the partial or complete destruction of at least 1,900 estates, a substantial chunk of the elite's landed property, and by 1907 the total monetary value of property damaged or destroyed reached 30 million rubles.[72]

Admittedly these figures are quite crude, and in the absence of more sophisticated measures and accepted comparative criteria, it would be foolish to argue that rural unrest in 1905 and after involved a majority of Russia's rural population or approximated the scale of rural protest in revolutionary France. But both contemporaries and historians have never been in doubt about the widespread character of rural insurrection during this period, and Manning has argued that rural protest had a decisive impact on turning Russia's pomeshchiki in a reactionary direction.[73] In any event, the tsarist elite viewed developments in the countryside with the gravest concern, as indicated by the savage punitive expeditions launched by the regime in an effort to smash village opposition. For example, in the Baltic provinces, where rebel violence had been particularly intense, "entire rebel villages were burned by the authorities; over one hundred riot leaders were publicly beheaded without trials while many were simply shot."[74] Clearly, something profound had happened in much of village Russia, and the panic sales of land by the nobility after 1905 is a striking reminder of how the events of the period helped to undermine the rural elite's confidence in its ability to rule the countryside.

Yet the uprisings of 1905–7 were not led by a unified, supralocal movement or revolutionary party. There was no overarching peasant organization that could have provided national direction, and most of the violence occurred at the level of a single village or group of villages.[75] Outside agitators undoubtedly fanned the flames of rural discontent, but the evidence suggests that the collapse of tsarist authority opened a kind of "window of opportunity" in which villages settled old scores, particularly against the pomeshchiki estates that had survived the abolition of serfdom. Whole villages rose in an autonomous exercise of community power that was aimed at nothing less than the physical destruction of the landed estate and its absorption by the village mir.[76]

The eyewitness accounts cited by Manning are worth reproducing for the light they shed on the politics of rural insurrection in Russia during the 1905 revolution. The first account comes from Baron N. Wrangel, a hostile elite source whose

72. Manning, *The Crisis of the Old Order in Russia,* 141–44, table 10.

73. G. M. Hamburg, *Politics of the Russian Nobility, 1881–1905* (New Brunswick: Rutgers University Press, 1984); Shmuel Galai, *The Liberation Movement in Russia, 1900–1905* (Cambridge: Cambridge University Press, 1973); Robert Edelman, *Gentry Politics on the Eve of the Russian Revolution: The Nationalist Party, 1907–1917* (New Brunswick: Rutgers University Press, 1980).

74. Manning, *The Crisis of the Old Order in Russia,* 171–72.

75. Atkinson, *The End of the Russian Land Commune,* 43–47.

76. Manning, *The Crisis of the Old Order in Russia,* 138–76. Also see Shanin, *The Roots of Otherness,* 2:79–179.

testimony should not show any trace of sympathy for insurgent villagers. What Wrangel's account indicates is the distinctive blending of radical collective action and traditional propriety that we have seen at work in other countries. According to Wrangel:

> In Russia proper, burning and plundering were pretty general too, but the landowner was rarely assassinated, in fact only when he made it unavoidable. Everything went off quite smoothly and without ill-feeling, as a rule, in quite a friendly way as it is right between neighbors who like and respect one another. . . .
>
> Things were generally managed quite pleasantly and in the following manner. Peasants, a whole village of them, would arrive in carts, bringing their wives and children to help with the work. The ambassador, the most respected man of the community, a venerable old gentleman with a white beard, would go to the lord's house and holding his hat in both hands as a mark of respect, would humbly ask for an interview. Then he would sigh and say:
>
> "We're here now, bativshka. We must get away as quickly as possible. That will be much better. The youth might give you a bad time. They might really. Ah, yes. To the young men of today nothing is sacred. They're absolute criminals. And whatever you do, don't forget to give us the keys to the barns. It would be a great pity to have to spoil those fine new doors. We have already told your coachman to harness the horses and to take you to the station or to the town, whichever you prefer. Only see to it that you are well covered, the cold is fearful and I shouldn't advise you to go by the open fields, that road is very bad. And you'd better avoid the bridge, it's rotten and you might have an accident."
>
> When the carriage was brought out, the landowner was helped in with his luggage and his feet were covered with a traveling rug. "Good-bye. The Lord keep you in good health, bativshka. We love you like a little father. Oh dear, we don't want to leave you. One can always come to an understanding if one is well disposed."[77]

Wrangel may have exaggerated the degree of deference shown for the nobility, but his description sounds strongly reminiscent of the mixture of localism, defiance, and residual deference that we have seen at work in other societies. Like England's enclosure rioters, the rebels portrayed by Wrangel were struggling to defend their communities against a powerful landed elite, and they seem to have understood that the problem lay with the institutions of elite property rather than the personality of the landowner. In any event, the rebels mobilized as whole communities in a violent confrontation that was radical but not revolutionary. Villagers challenged the authority of elite power at its roots, yet their focus was exclusively local and very specific. They do not appear to have wanted to destroy the nobility as a whole, nor do they seem to have envisioned themselves as a revolutionary class. They were local people with particular goals who saw the village as their proper world.

77. Manning, *The Crisis of the Old Order in Russia,* 157.

Wrangel's analysis of the events of 1905 was echoed by the more sober voice of the Tambov County zemstvo board, whose report was written at the height of the violence in November 1905: "All agrarian disorders are almost identical in character. The peasants of a given region go to the owner of an estate or to his manager and propose first of all that he leave the estate. Then the destruction of all the property begins. They take away everything in the house, haul away the grain, drive away the cattle and the buildings are burned. In rare cases, the disorders are limited to arson alone."[78]

This kind of raucous violence was accompanied, of course, by bouts of ritual drinking that expressed the sense of community deliverance that followed a "successful" assault on a local estate. But more than alcohol was responsible for the buoyancy of popular consciousness, and the events of 1905 must have seemed to many to be the fulfillment of the *chernyi peredel,* the long-awaited "black repartition" that would forever return all land to the village mir. As a frustrated police chief in Riazan wrote: "The mood of the population is extremely agitated. Not only the landowners but also urban inhabitants are afraid and expect pogroms and looting any minute. The peasants, on the other hand, feel themselves the master of the situation and have become rude, insolent and willful. Already official personnel often hear the peasants say that 'now we are all gentlemen [*gospoda*] and we are all equal' and that the freedoms granted [by the October Manifesto] allow peasants 'to do what we want to do.' "[79]

Ordinary rural people may not have desired equality in the liberal sense, but their determination and willingness to resort to violence was clearly expressed by a villager from Skopin County, Riazan, whose role as a local spokesman led him to a confrontation with the landowner E. N. Miasnikow. The spokesman stated the goals and grievances of the villagers in blunt language: "Evgenii Nikolgevich, I have just returned from Tambov province. There the peasants chase out the landowners, rob them, and burn [their estates] so that they all go to Moscow. We don't want to do this, but you must give us flour for food and all your forest . . . to chop down. If you don't give us this, then your estate will be destroyed and looted."[80]

In sum, rural violence in the 1905 revolution reveals a logic that can be plausibly described as representative violence. Entire communities rose in defense of their autonomy and against the entrenched privileges of the landed elite. Violence became a representative arena in which villages renegotiated the fundamental principles of power and property in the countryside. The Russian term for this sort of violence is *razgrom,* a brief episode of wild destruction designed to humiliate and intimidate its victims. Like the enclosure riot, the razgrom was a

78. Ibid., 141–42.
79. Ibid., 147.
80. Ibid., 152.

210 | Communities of Grain

method the populace used to force an entrenched local elite to submit to the will of the community, although in Russia offending elites were physically expelled also.[81] In the village revolts of 1905 the mir was literally present, or represented, in a moment of political redefinition. Although rooted in very real material problems, the events of 1905–7 transcended a simple struggle over economic resources. The larger issue concerned the authority of elite landowners and tsarist officials and whether that authority would be held accountable to the village mir. At least for a brief period, the village asserted a strong claim to rule itself according to its own rules and conceptions of justice.

Nor did the events of 1905 fail to have a profound impact on the course of Russian agrarian history.[82] In addition to triggering severe repression the revolts of the period caused panic land sales on the part of the nobility and the first appearance of ordinary villagers on the national political stage during the elections to the first two Dumas.[83] Although tsarist officials later regretted their decision, the first two Dumas, or parliaments, granted the "peasant" estate a preponderance of seats; an outcome that allowed ordinary rural deputies to call loudly for a comprehensive redivision of the great estates.

More important, however, the "mad days" of 1905 led to a complete reorientation of the tsarist regime's policy regarding the village mir. In a series of decrees and statutes known collectively as the Stolypin reforms (after Pyotr Stolypin, the prime minister), the regime committed itself to nothing less than the abolition of the land commune.[84] Now regarded as a threat to public order and a drag on modernization, the village mir was to be replaced by a kind of sturdy "yeomanry" of independent farmers who were to cultivate enclosed farms unencumbered by any trace of collective ownership or periodic repartition.[85] The government would support this process of dissolution through the provision of land-surveying services and limited financial assistance, including support for villagers who chose to migrate to Siberia.[86]

The clearest expression of the Stolypin reforms was probably the law of June 14, 1910.[87] According to this statute, any commune that had not carried out a general repartition since 1887 was to be regarded as having shifted to hereditary household tenure. The enactment of this statute was tantamount to abolishing a

81. Ibid., 141–58.

82. Shanin, The Roots of Otherness 2:138–83.

83. Emmons, The Formation of Political Parties, 11–13, 237–53, 297–300, 366–71.

84. Atkinson, The End of the Russian Land Commune, 47–70; Manning, The Crisis of the Old Order in Russia, 223–28, 317–67; Robinson, Rural Russia under the Old Regime, 208–42.

85. Robinson, Rural Russia under the Old Regime, 208–42; Yaney, The Urge to Mobilize, 257–400.

86. Robinson, Rural Russia under the Old Regime, 243–65; Donald Treadgold, The Great Siberian Migration: Government and Peasant in Resettlement from Emancipation to the First World War (Princeton: Princeton University Press, 1957), 130, 153–83.

87. Atkinson, The End of the Russian Land Commune, 61–62.

large number of communes by bureaucratic fiat. In addition, all communes were required to accept at any time the consolidation of a member's plots when, in the judgment of local officials, it would present no special hardships.[88] As Dorothy Atkinson has pointed out, "the legislation left no doubt that the government, with the support of the refashioned Duma [i.e., the landowner-dominated third Duma], was intent on establishing a new class of independent peasant proprietors."[89]

For our purposes the most interesting consequence of the Stolypin reform project was its failure.[90] To be sure, many households availed themselves of the opportunity to leave the mir, and many more may have wished to leave. But, in spite of positive inducements and no small degree of administrative coercion, the regime failed to destroy the land commune before world war and revolution ended the regime.[91] Atkinson has made the point quite clearly:

> The land data support the conclusion that communes still had a strong grip on peasant land at the end of the reform decade. By 1916 over 16 million desiatins (about 14 percent of the 115.4 million desiatins of allotment land in communes in 1905) had been individualized through appropriations and certifications. The remainder, approximately 99 million desiatins, amounted to over 70 percent of all allotment land held by the entire peasantry. Even after allowance for additional losses through consolidations of communal land, fully two-thirds of all allotment land held by the peasantry remained in communes at the end of the old regime.[92]

At another point Atkinson adds, regarding the acquisition of so-called private or nonallotment land by ordinary villagers: "One striking aspect of peasant land gains in this period has drawn little attention. In 1905 slightly over half (54 percent) of the land held privately by peasants was held by individuals, but by 1915 the share held individually had dropped to 49 percent. In other words, during the period of intense government effort to individualize proprietorship, the proportion of private land owned collectively by the peasantry [by rural societies and peasant associations] actually rose."[93] In short, the village mir not only survived the Stolypin reforms but proved capable of continuing an old tradition of collective action.

We may endlessly debate whether the Stolypin reforms could have worked, given enough time and resources. My own opinion is that they could have succeeded if they had not been undertaken as an exercise in authoritarian politics

88. Manning, *The Crisis of the Old Order in Russia,* 346–47; Robinson, *Rural Russia under the Old Regime,* 208–31.
89. Atkinson, *The End of the Russian Land Commune,* 62.
90. This argument is even admitted by Keep, *The Russian Revolution,* 11–15.
91. Shanin, *The Roots of Otherness* 2:190–91, 236–45.
92. Atkinson, *The End of the Russian Land Commune,* 81.
93. Ibid., 82.

in which the reforms were simply imposed from above. But the reforms failed, and two important points follow from that fact.

First, the limited success of the Stolypin project casts rather strong doubts on the notion that the village mir was an "artificial" construct. Ordinary rural people did not stampede their way out of the commune, an indication that the institutions of the village were probably still central to the lives of ordinary people.[94]

Second, and more important, the willingness of the tsarist regime to pressure the mir out of existence enhanced the weight of the forces of bureaucratic domination in the Russian countryside. The tsarist regime had long been a problem in rural Russia, but the Stolypin reforms added a whole new dimension of bureaucratic arbitrariness that directly and openly threatened the very survival of the village community. As George Yaney has shown, the reforming bureaucrats of the Stolypin period saw themselves as engaged in a kind of civilizing mission that was to lead to the complete transformation of the village.[95] Although they failed, their "wager on the strong" must have generated a fund of ill will that matched the bitterness felt for the pomeshchik's estates. How else can we explain the savage violence that was meted out to tsarist officials after 1917?

Viewed from the perspective of the village the events of 1905–7 had very mixed results. The noble estate survived in parts of the empire, although it was badly battered by popular violence, panic land sales, and decades of indebtedness and mismanagement.[96] The tsarist regime had responded to rural violence with its own violence and had embarked on a direct attack on the mir. Nevertheless, something had changed, and perhaps the most important part of that change was a heightened popular distrust of all elite institutions and a readiness to oppose those institutions with grim determination. This was the conclusion of the nephew of Stolypin, the minister whose name has been attached to the post–1905 assault on the mir. According to S. S. Podolinskii:

> The summer of 1905. The revolutionary outburst of 1905 left behind deep traces. Externally everything appeared to have returned to normalcy. . . . Nevertheless, something essential, something irreparable had occurred and within the people themselves. A vague feeling of fear had undermined all trust. . . . Earlier everyone had laughed when in the evenings, often late into the night, the village assembly became too noisy; one was not interested in what these people discussed among themselves. But now the interest of the landowners was awakened: which questions are on the agenda? Will the assembly proceed in peace or not? Which political parties will have the upper hand? How would this night pass? Would not this drinking drive the crowd to commit new disorders?[97]

94. Ibid., 71–100.
95. Yaney, *The Urge to Mobilize*, chaps. 5–9, esp. 144–46, 163–78.
96. See the essays in Leopold Haimson, ed., *The Politics of Rural Russia* (Bloomington: Indiana University Press, 1979); Richard Hennessy, *The Agrarian Questions in Russia, 1905–1907* (Giessen: W. Schmitz, 1977).
97. Manning, *The Crisis of the Old Order in Russia*, 146.

From Community Autonomy to
Community Secession, 1917–1921

In February 1917 the tsarist regime perished in the wake of military defeat and massive popular resistance. As the army mutinied and urban workers began to seize power in their factories and city assemblies, the shattered fragments of national power passed first to a multiparty provisional government and ultimately to the Bolsheviks.[98] These were seen as heroic times, at least for those who sympathized with the revolutionaries, and this view has led to a tradition of heroic history writing that has tended to focus on "great" personalities like Lenin and Trotsky. Only since 1945 have historians begun to focus on the popular history of the revolution; that history has begun to change our understanding of the revolutionary years.[99]

In the countryside the fall of the tsar occasioned a period of cautious waiting that was rapidly followed by an explosion of rural violence and rebellion that had far-reaching effects on the future of Russia. In all regions of the former empire villagers attacked and destroyed landed estates, assaulted the agents of bureaucratic power, and turned against the households who had separated themselves from the mir during the Stolypin period. Although historians disagree about the precise quantitative dimensions, there seems to be general agreement about the sweeping and conclusive nature of what took place. The large estate was destroyed forever, as were all traces of the Stolypin reforms. The village mir, wherever it was established, absorbed almost all the available arable and pasture.[100] Even in areas like Poland, the Baltic provinces, and the southwest, where the repartitional commune was not strongly developed, local insurrections shattered the social and political order. According to a recent estimate cited by Atkinson, as many as 11,364 incidents of rural unrest may have occurred between March and October of 1917, substantially more than in 1905.[101]

Historians as diverse in their judgments and sympathies as John Keep, Moshe Lewin, and Graeme Gill concur in seeing the rural history of 1917 as a frontal attack on all elite institutions.[102] Not only noble estates but monasteries, crown

98. A good overview is Keep, *The Russian Revolution*.

99. See, for example, Alexander Rabinowitch, *The Bolsheviks Come to Power: The Revolution of 1917 in Petrograd* (New York: Norton, 1976); Stephen A. Smith, *Red Petrograd: Revolution in the Factories, 1917–18* (Cambridge: Cambridge University Press, 1983); Oskar Anweiler, *The Soviets: The Russian Workers, Peasants, and Soldiers Councils, 1905–1921* (New York: Pantheon Books, 1975); Victoria Bonnell, *Roots of Rebellion: Workers' Politics and Organizations in St. Petersburg and Moscow, 1900–1914* (Berkeley: University of California Press, 1983); and Reginald E. Zelnik, *Labor and Society in Tsarist Russia: The Factory Workers of St. Petersburg, 1855–1870*, vol. 1 (Stanford: Stanford University Press, 1971).

100. Keep, *The Russian Revolution*, 186–339, 383–463.

101. Atkinson, *The End of the Russian Land Commune*, 149–85, esp. 163, table 12.

102. Keep, *The Russian Revolution*, 385–463; Lewin, *Russian Peasants and Soviet Power*, 21–197; Gill, *Peasants and Government*, 133–69, 189–91.

and state lands, and public offices were ransacked and looted.[103] Government officials were driven from the countryside, and the new agents of the various revolutionary governments were hard put to make their power effective outside of the county capitals.[104] Even the zemstvos, the elective institutions of self-government established in the 1860s, collapsed in the face of popular hostility.[105]

From the standpoint of the provisional government and its Bolshevik successor, the most damaging implication of the fall of the old order in the countryside had to do with the worsening food situation in urban Russia.[106] Already strained to the breaking point by the partial collapse of the transportation network, the food-supply system was further jeopardized by the destruction of established market networks in the countryside. During the late nineteenth and early twentieth centuries Russia had been an exporter of bread grains, especially rye, but much of this commerce had been conducted by elite estate owners and middlemen.[107] Ordinary cultivators were tied to the market to a much lesser extent, and small-holders may have viewed the market more as a means of paying rent and taxes than as a source of profit and prosperity.[108] In any event, the dismantling of estate agriculture wiped out much of the commercial infrastructure of agrarian Russia, thereby presenting the urban population with the grim prospect of starvation. By 1919 the new Bolshevik regime was forced literally to "extract" grain from the countryside through the medium of forced requisitions and local barter. Although Russian villagers were not inherently pre- or anticommercial, ordinary cultivators may have seen large-scale rural commerce as just one more component of an alien elite order.[109]

But not all rural institutions collapsed after 1917. The village mir survived and was strengthened by the destruction of the forces of bureaucratic domination and aristocratic property that had constrained village autonomy. According to Dorothy Atkinson:

Within the limits of the supply of agricultural land, the chernyi peredel (black repartition) was unable to satisfy the exaggerated hopes of the peasants. Yet in the peasants' attempt to apply their own solution to the land problem the Russian land commune "reached the apogee of its power and of its development" in the judgment

103. Atkinson, *The End of the Russian Land Commune*, 149–63; Gill, *Peasants and Government*, 98–132.

104. Gill, *Peasants and Government*, 98–132.

105. Atkinson, "The Zemstvo and the Peasants."

106. Keep, *The Russian Revolution*, 153–71.

107. Volin, *A Century of Russian Agriculture;* Steven Wheatcroft, "The Reliability of Russian Prewar Grain Output Statistics," *Soviet Studies* 26 (2) (1974), 157; Eugene D. Vinogradov, "The Invisible Hand and the Russian Peasant," *Peasant Studies Newsletter* 4 (July 1975), 6–19; Vladimir P. Timoshenko, *Agricultural Russia and the Wheat Problem* (Stanford: Stanford University Press, 1932); Gerschenkron, "Agrarian Policies and Industrialization."

108. Keep, *The Russian Revolution*, 172–85.

109. Silvana Malle, *The Economic Organization of War Communism, 1918–1921* (Cambridge: Cambridge University Press, 1985), 322–78.

of a contemporary scholar who had studied the institution for decades—and had helped to establish the prerevolutionary opinion that the commune was an obsolescent institution. The whole trend of the anticommunal agrarian revolution of the previous decade was abruptly reversed by the 1917 revolutions. The commune that had been whittled back in the course of the preceding decade blossomed over virtually all of the agricultural land in the country. By 1920 the commune encompassed almost all rural households for which data is available. The Stolypin negation of the commune after the revolution of 1905 had undergone in its turn the negation of the revolution of 1917, and the commune had entered a new historical phase.[110]

The most striking illustration of the resurgence of the mir was the local attacks on households who had separated from the commune and the subsequent general or partial land redivisions undertaken by the village. The members of such households, who were often termed *otrubniki,* sometimes voluntarily returned to the mir, but in many cases they were forced to abandon their farms to the village. This attack on separators was followed by a rising crescendo of village repartitions that may have peaked by 1919. By 1920 Russian villages had become collectivities of smallholding households, and any signs of the emergence of a wealthy class of kulak proprietors had disappeared.[111]

It seems obtuse to reduce the subtle and ambiguous events of the period to a simple model of peasant revolution.[112] As in 1905 there was little or nothing in the way of a national peasant organization, and many of the groups that claimed to represent the peasantry as a whole were really associations of urban radicals whose ties to the countryside were minimal. I do not deny that there were some interesting experiments in building supralocal rural organizations during this period; nor do I wish to minimize the radicalizing effect of angry young army veterans who returned to their villages demanding an immediate resolution of the land problem. But I would deny the fruitfulness of reducing the period from 1917 to 1920 to a mechanical class framework that cannot disaggregate events to the village level. Just as in 1905, the main arena of action was the village, and village institutions provided the framework for popular collective action.[113]

Ordinary villagers do not seem to have displayed much of a taste for seizing state power at the national level. They did not revolt en masse when the Bolsheviks seized power and suspended the Constituent Assembly, and they showed a guarded neutrality between Whites and Reds during the civil war that followed.[114] In short, rural Russia did not do any of the things we normally associate with a revolutionary class. Indeed, within their own world, the mir, Russian villagers

110. Atkinson, *The End of the Russian Land Commune,* 185.
111. Shanin, *The Awkward Class,* 14–162.
112. A more subtle approach is offered in Roger Pethybridge, *The Spread of the Russian Revolution: Essays on 1917* (New York: St. Martin's Press, 1972).
113. Atkinson, *The End of the Russian Land Commune,* 149–205.
114. Oliver Radkey, *The Unknown Civil War in Soviet Russia: A Study of the Green Movement in the Tambov Region, 1920–1921* (Stanford: Hoover Institution Press, 1976), esp. 20–41, 78–87.

clung to traditional gender hierarchies and old cultural practices well into the 1920s, much to the dismay of urban revolutionaries.[115]

The events of 1917 and after do make sense, however, when placed in historical perspective. Those events can be understood as a direct continuation of the village insurrections of 1905. Once again, villagers focused their anger on the elite forces of constraint that had circumscribed the autonomy of the mir. Violence represented communities in their ongoing struggle with bureaucratic and aristocratic power, and the limits of the struggle tended to coincide with the well-marked territorial boundaries of the village or estate.[116]

What was distinctive about 1917 was the complete collapse of tsarist power at both national and local levels.[117] In this context there was nothing to prevent the village from rupturing all ties with supralocal authority. To be sure, the village still had kinship links with urban migrants, and villagers had developed a taste for a narrow range of urban products, including kerosene, matches, and processed sugar. But the relative underdevelopment of commercial agriculture meant that the village was still relatively self-sufficient in terms of the production and distribution of the means of subsistence. Unlike the poor Spanish communities of the 1900s, Russian communities had both enough cohesion to act collectively and enough autonomy with respect to their control of the food supply to withdraw temporarily from the networks of urban power. To put the matter bluntly, the failure of the Stolypin reforms had preserved a realm of village economic power that reinforced the political cohesiveness of the mir.[118]

Russian villages, it seems, quite literally seceded from the dying Russian empire after 1917. This process of secession was symbolized by the attempt to destroy all the markers of elite power in the countryside. Manor houses were sacked and looted, and whatever residual deference had existed in 1905 evaporated.[119] In the collective performance of the chernyi peredel, the violent and leveling repartition, the members of the village mir affirmed the boundaries of the village and withdrew the mir from the old order of power.

Toward Social War, 1919–1930

The new Bolshevik rulers of Soviet Russia faced a nearly impossible conjuncture of crises and problems.[120] After fighting a brutal civil war, and nearly destroying themselves through the excesses of war communism, they faced a series of rural and urban revolts that led to the great compromise of the New

115. Lewin, *The Making of the Soviet System*, 91–141.

116. Keep, *The Russian Revolution*, 200–228.

117. Pethybridge, *The Spread of the Russian Revolution*, e.g., 12–16, 83–110, 176–214.

118. Lewin, *Russian Peasants and Soviet Power*, 21–197.

119. Keep, *The Russian Revolution*, 186–215, 394–418.

120. Roger Pethybridge, *The Social Prelude to Stalinism* (New York: St. Martin's Press, 1974), esp. 73–131, 196–251.

Economic Policy. War, hyperinflation, and the sheer carnage of the revolution guaranteed that the Bolshevik regime would be forced to build socialism on the weakest of foundations.

Yet underlying everything else was the problem of the village. All Bolshevik factions agreed that the future of socialist industrialization hinged on the development of agriculture.[121] But whatever they may have believed about their own capabilities, the Bolsheviks could not simply order the countryside to comply with their policies. The village had gained too much autonomy after 1917 to be easily manipulated by slogans or commands, and the future of Bolshevik power depended on the ability of the regime to build institutional bridges between the mir and the urban locus of the Bolshevik state. Somehow, the secession of the village had to be prevented, because a repetition of the events of 1917 would lead to economic and political disaster.[122]

But the Bolsheviks had very little in the way of resources or expertise when it came to the countryside. As Moshe Lewin has shown in his classic study of collectivization, the Bolshevik governments of the 1920s had a remarkably weak presence in rural Russia.[123] The Communist party, the core of the Bolshevik state, was incapable of gaining a popular base, and the soviets, the formal arenas of local administration, were underdeveloped and too underfinanced to make much of a contribution to popular life. Moreover, the fragility of urban industry, especially in the consumer sectors, limited the ability of the regime to "buy" rural consent through the provision of cheap consumer goods and subsidized services.[124]

Even worse, the Bolsheviks had a very poor cognitive map of the countryside. Apart from the pioneering studies of A. V. Chayanov and his students, most Soviet leaders seem to have operated with a rather mechanical class logic that had advanced little beyond Lenin's analysis of "capitalism" in rural Russia.[125] Even Bukharin, who was sympathetic to the countryside, tended to view agrarian society as a more or less differentiated mass of peasants.[126]

---

121. Lewin, *Russian Peasants and Soviet Power*, 198–266; Stephen Cohen, *Bukharin and the Bolshevik Revolution: A Political Biography 1888–1938* (New York: Knopf, 1973), 107–22.

122. Pethybridge, *The Social Prelude to Stalinism*, esp. 196–251; Lewin, *The Making of the Soviet System*, 91–120, 142–77; Donald J. Male, *Russian Peasant Organization before Collectivization: A Study of Commune and Gathering, 1925–1930* (Cambridge: Cambridge University Press, 1971), esp. 120–36; James R. Millar, "Soviet Rapid Development and the Agricultural Surplus Hypothesis," *Soviet Studies* 22 (1) (1970), 77–93; Dorothy Atkinson, "The Statistics on the Russian Land Commune, 1905–1917," *Slavic Review* 32 (Dec. 1973), 773–87.

123. Lewin, *Russian Peasants and Soviet Power*, 81–131. Also see the relevant sections in the following volumes by Edward H. Carr: *The Interregnum, 1923–1924* (New York: Macmillan, 1954), esp. 146–49; *Socialism in One Country*, 3 vols. (New York: Macmillan, 1958–64), 1:189–328, 2:304–56, 362–68; and *Foundations of a Planned Economy, 1926–1929* (New York: Macmillan, 1971), esp. 13–18, 44–89, 95–105, 142–43, 175–79, 255–70.

124. Atkinson, *The End of the Russian Land Commune*, 233–345.

125. Esther Kingston-Mann, *Lenin and the Problem of Marxist Peasant Revolution* (New York: Oxford University Press, 1983).

126. Cohen, *Bukharin and the Bolshevik Revolution*, 146.

If my analysis is correct, however, this was precisely the wrong way to view the Russian countryside. One may argue that the peasantry disappeared after 1917 when the institutional constraints that had defined it were destroyed. What remained was the village mir, and no analysis that failed to focus on the village could avoid inaccurate or even perverse results.[127]

What, then, were the Bolsheviks to do? I would suggest that the Bolshevik regime faced two possible strategies regarding relations with the village. Each had distinct political implications, and each carried costs and benefits for the stability of the regime.

The first strategy, which can be called a policy of indirection, involved a reliance on market forces and representative institutions as a point of mediation between the village and the state. In broadest outlines, this was the strategy followed in the 1920s, and it demanded a willingness to compromise with the partial autonomy of the mir. For example, during the 1920s there was no wholesale assault on the land commune, and the regime relied on market incentives and political concessions to transform instrumental consent into political loyalty.[128] Over time, this way of proceeding might have led to greater cooperation between villagers and party elites, a growing dependence of cultivators on market relations, and a transformed popular consciousness in which national loyalties took precedence over village ties.

Nevertheless, this strategy was neither foolproof nor cost-free. As the grain procurements crises of the 1920s indicated, much depended on the health of the soviet macroeconomy and the availability of resources that could be used to build local patronage networks. Neither could be guaranteed in the 1920s, and any failure of the market could lead to another village secession so long as rural markets remained voluntary and peripheral to the subsistence needs of the village.[129]

The second strategy, which can be defined as direct incorporation, required a return to the politics of the tsarist past. Direct incorporation involved the use of force and authoritarian domination to "capture" the mir and break its autonomy. In short, it meant the recreation of a Russian peasantry through a direct assault on the village, irrespective of what it implied for the long-term loyalty and social identity of the countryside, the point was to capture the land and labor of the mir, even if the attempt generated fierce resistance.

As we know, the Stalinist regime followed this strategy in the 1930s, and the whole process of collectivization is best seen as an attempt to subjugate the village

127. See the essays in A. V. Chayanov, *The Theory of Peasant Economy,* ed. Daniel Thorner et al. (Madison: University of Wisconsin Press, 1986).

128. Lewin, *Russian Peasants and Soviet Power,* 132–97; Yuzuru Taniuchi, *The Village Gathering in Russia in the Mid-1920's* (Birmingham: University of Birmingham Press, 1968).

129. R. W. Davies, *The Socialist Offensive: The Collectivization of Soviet Agriculture, 1929–1930* (Cambridge: Harvard University Press, 1980), 1–109.

through the creation of a novel form of bureaucratic domination, the collective farm and its associated Machine Tractor Stations.[130]

The costs of the Stalinist program are well known and range from widespread popular resistance to a permanent weakening of the agricultural economy.[131] But it is easy to forget that the collectivization drive, with its titanic struggles aimed at transforming villages into socialist collectives, held real advantages for the Stalinist elite. Faced with an uncertain market and failed grain-procurement drives, the regime must have understood that a direct offensive against the village at least offered maximum short-term control of the grain supply. Moreover, the Stalinist elite had been shaped in the fires of revolution and civil war and this kind of military "socialism" was something Stalin and his associates understood.[132]

The moral cost of Stalinism is obvious, and at this late date it is rather banal to launch into a debate with the shade of Stalin. But the Stalinist regime can be accused of more than moral evil; it also stands indicted because of its failure to think past the rigid class categories of the early 1900s. Always hoping for class war in the countryside, always willing to see the rise of a rural bourgeoisie in the slightest signs of social differentiation, the Soviet elite in the 1930s suffered from a failure of imagination that blinded them to the politics of rural Russia. Ironically, as good Leninists, the Stalinist elite believed that it was creating a world in which "archaic" peasants would at last disappear, but their policies led to a reconstitution of a Russian peasantry that would have been easily recognized by Pugachev and his followers.[133]

130. Robert F. Miller, *One Hundred Thousand Tractors: The MTS and the Development of Controls in Soviet Agriculture* (Cambridge: Harvard University Press, 1970), esp. 3–62, 138–87. Also see R. W. Davies, *The Soviet Collective Farm, 1929–1930* (Cambridge: Harvard University Press, 1980), esp. 1–33, 56–67; and Millar, "Soviet Rapid Development," 77–93.

131. See, for example, Robert Conquest, *Harvard of Sorrow: Soviet Collectivization and the Terror-Famine* (Oxford: Oxford University Press, 1986), 117–88; Lynne Viola, *The Best Sons of the Fatherland: Workers in the Vanguard of Soviet Collectivization* (Oxford: Oxford University Press, 1987), 8–35, 90–151, 179–209; and Lewin, *The Making of the Soviet System,* 178–88.

132. Malle, *The Economic Organization of War Communism,* 322–95, 495–507.

133. Atkinson, *The End of the Russian Land Commune,* 346–80.

CHAPTER 8

Japan and the Problem of Community in Cross-Cultural Perspective, 1600–1868

In 1653, Sakura Sōgorō, an elder of Narita village, was executed by order of Hotta Masanobu, daimyo of the Sakura feudal domain. Sakura's crime had been the offense of directly presenting a petition of grievances to the domain's lord (the daimyo), and this sort of direct and forceful demonstration had long been regarded as a threat to the deeply aristocratic and feudal social order that had characterized Japan since the sixteenth century. As the Tokugawa, the supreme feudal overlords of Japan, reminded their vassals, "though your request is righteous, if you do not follow correct procedures, or if you be rude and unseemly in conduct, you will be severely punished." In the case of Sakura Sōgorō this meant ritual crucifixion, a punishment that emphasized the grave seriousness with which the feudal elite viewed any assertion of political autonomy on the part of rural commoners.[1]

Sakura Sōgorō was neither unique nor marginal to the course of early modern Japanese history. In 1746 his memory was invoked by the descendant of the lord who executed him when the domain government began paying a stipend to Sakura's descendants, perhaps in order to still the ghost of the martyred elder. So powerful had the myth of Sakura become that on the 150th anniversary of his death, the domain granted him an honorific posthumous name and erected a gravestone in his honor.[2]

More important, the story of Sakura Sōgorō was but one of many comparable "righteous martyrs," or *gimin,* who sacrificed themselves for the good of a greater

1. Irwin Scheiner, "Benevolent Lords and Honorable Peasants: Rebellion and Peasant Consciousness in Tokugawa Japan," in Tetsuo Najita and Irwin Scheiner, eds., *Japanese Thought in the Tokugawa Period, 1600–1868: Methods and Metaphors* (Chicago: University of Chicago Press, 1978), esp. 47–48; and see Irwin Scheiner, "The Mindful Peasant: Sketches for a Study of Rebellion," *Journal of Asian Studies* 32 (Aug. 1973), 579–91. Also see the wide-ranging study of popular culture in Ann Walthall's *Social Protest and Popular Culture in Eighteenth Century Japan* (Tucson: University of Arizona Press, 1986). I thank Ken Torii for his assistance in reading the Japanese secondary materials.

2. Scheiner, "Benevolent Lords and Honorable Peasants," esp. 48.

collectivity. That collectivity was often the village, and in Tokugawa Japan the defense of rural life against the impact of feudal power became a central theme of Japanese agrarian history. Contrary to many popular stereotypes, early modern Japan was not a "passive" society in which harmony and deference made impossible any serious expression of popular opposition.[3] Between 1600 and 1868, rural Japan was repeatedly shaken by a complex series of protests and disturbances that challenged the power of the samurai (*bushi*), Japan's elite warrior aristocrats.[4] According to the estimates of Aoki Kōji, one of the best-known students of the subject, some 260 years of Tokugawa rule saw 2,809 rural revolts and 1,000 cases of riot.[5] The forms of collective action ranged from illegal and forcible petitions (*daihyō osso*) and violent direct action (*gōso*), to millenarian movements of "world renewal" (*yonaoshi*) and incidents of "smashing and breaking" (*uchikowashi*).[6] Often confined to a handful of villages, the modes of rural insurrection could sometimes escalate into regional rebellions, as in the yonaoshi uprisings of the nineteenth century.[7]

Skeptics may doubt whether aggregate figures of this kind do much to establish the frequency of rural insurrection in early modern Japan. But the point is not that Japan was an inherently rebellious society seething with revolutionary potential.

3. See, for example, Tetsuo Najita, "Introduction: A Synchronous Approach to the Study of Conflict in Modern Japanese History"; J. Victor Koschmann, "Action as Text: Ideology in the Tensu Insurrection"; and Hoshimoto Mitsuru, "The Social Background of Peasant Uprisings in Tokugawa Japan," all in Tetsuo Najita and J. Victor Koschmann, eds., *Conflict in Modern Japanese History: The Neglected Tradition* (Princeton: Princeton University Press, 1982), 3–24, 81–106, 145–63. Also see Herbert B. Bix, *Peasant Protest in Japan, 1590–1884* (New Haven: Yale University Press, 1986), esp. 1–56. For an excellent statement of the anticonsensus position for the postwar period, see Frank K. Upham, *Law and Social Change in Postwar Japan* (Cambridge: Harvard University Press, 1987), esp. 28–77.

4. For the origins of the samurai and Tokugawa Japan, see John Whitney Hall, *Government and Local Power in Japan, 500 to 1700: A Study Based on Bizen Province* (Princeton: Princeton University Press, 1966), esp. 101, 130, 139, 186–90; John Whitney Hall and Jeffrey P. Mass, eds., *Medieval Japan: Essays in Institutional History* (Stanford: Stanford University Press, 1988), esp. Elizabeth Sato, "The Early Development of the Shōen," 91–108; Jeffrey P. Mass, "The Emergence of the Kamakuo Bakufu," 127–56; and Mary Elizabeth Berry, *Hideyoshi* (Cambridge: Harvard University Press, 1982), 10–65.

5. Aoki Kōji, *Hyakusho ikki no nenjiteki kenkyū* (Tokyo: Shinseisha, 1966), esp. 36–37, table 9. There is no consensus about total numbers, and some estimates range as high as 7,000; I have therefore chosen a *conservative* estimate. Also see Toshio Yokoyama, *Hyakushō ikki to gimin denshō* (Tokyo: Kyoikusha, 1977), 38. Finally, see Stephen Vlastos, *Peasant Protests and Uprisings in Tokugawa Japan* (Berkeley: University of California Press, 1986), p. 46, table 1; p. 75, table 2; and p. 78, table 3; and Bix, *Peasant Protest in Japan*, xi–xxxviii, esp. fig. 1. Bix gives an excellent synthesis of Japanese Marxist and quasi-Marxist views of rural Japan.

6. Scheiner, "Benevolent Lords and Honorable Peasants," 39–62. Also see Mitsuru, "The Social Background of Peasant Uprisings"; W. Donald Burton, "Peasant Movements in Early Tokugawa Japan," *Peasant Studies* 8 (Summer 1979), 162–81; Yoshio Sugimoto, "Structural Sources of Popular Revolts and the Tōbaku Movement at the Time of the Meiji Restoration," *Journal of Asian Studies* 34 (Aug. 1975), 875–89; and Patricia Sipple, "Popular Protest in Early Modern Japan: The Būshū Outburst," *Harvard Journal of Asiatic Studies* 37 (Dec. 1977), 273–322.

7. Vlastos, *Peasant Protests*, esp. 1–20, 142–53.

Rather, the point is simply that rural collective violence was a recurrent part of the rural landscape, and Japanese elites regarded it as serious enough to respond with draconian punishments, including the penalty of crucifixion. Even more striking is that rural violence in Japan occurred in a society marked by rigid hierarchies of status and gender that left little room for the formal expression of popular interests.[8] Ordinary commoners could litigate and petition, but they were ultimately at the mercy of their superiors, who regarded any concession to popular wishes as an expression of elite benevolence rather than submission to a popular right. Tokugawa Japan did not have a tradition of popular political rights analogous to the common-law rights of Englishmen, and Japanese commoners had no access to local and nationwide representative assemblies.[9] It is remarkable that popular protest, including collective violence, could take place in a society in which even a violation of the "etiquette" of petitioning could result in death.

How can we explain the logic of rural collective violence in early modern Japan? More specifically, does the Japanese case lend itself to the logic of community defense that we have seen at work in Europe? Or is Japan too distinctive to be captured by comparative categories?

Before launching into the core of the analysis, a word is in order with regard to cross-cultural research. Cross-cultural work lies at the heart of comparative history and social science.[10] No theoretical framework that claims general applicability can afford to forgo at least a weak test that involves the extension of theoretical categories to diverse cultural contexts. One of the problems in the study of rural society has been a tendency to construct theory on the basis of a single case, often a case drawn from a society that seems unrepresentative because of one or more "peculiar" features that are distinct to that society. As a result, it has been difficult to decide whether conclusions drawn from that case can be generalized to other contexts. It is important, therefore, to expose theory to "strange" or "alien" cultural data; by doing this we can stretch a theoretical framework to its limits, thereby showing the boundaries of an argument. Japan serves this purpose quite nicely, because it is often portrayed as a unique culture with a distinctive history that cannot be easily reduced to comparative categories.[11] Consequently, if the theoretical framework presented in this book is limited

8. Herman Ooms, *Tokugawa Ideology: Early Constructs, 1570–1680* (Princeton: Princeton University Press, 1985), 162–93, 287–98; Hall, *Government and Local Power in Japan;* and Berry, *Hideyoshi,* 99–146.

9. See, for example, Harold Bolitho, *Treasures among Men: The Fudai Daimyo in Tokugawa Japan* (New Haven: Yale University Press, 1974); Kate Wildman Nakai, *Shogunal Politics: Arai Hakuseki and the Premises of Tokugawa Rule* (Cambridge: Harvard University Press, 1988), esp. 132, 142–49, 162–65; Conrad Totman, *Politics in the Tokugawa Bakufu, 1600–1843* (Cambridge: Harvard University Press, 1967), 204–33; and Conrad Totman, *The Collapse of the Tokugawa Bakufu, 1862–1868* (Honolulu: University Press of Hawaii, 1980).

10. See, for example, Reinhard Bendix, *Kings or People: Power and the Mandate to Rule* (Berkeley: University of California Press, 1978), esp. 61–87.

11. Chie Nakane, *Japanese Society* (Berkeley: University of California Press, 1970).

by a Euro-centric bias it should simply not work when applied to Tokugawa Japan. Tokugawa Japan was quite literally cut off from most foreign influences by the so-called "seclusion policy" that confined external contacts to a minimum.[12] In this context Japanese culture was free to develop many of the characteristics that are now thought of as distinctively Japanese. What we need to do is to explore Tokugawa agrarian history in order to gain at least a basic understanding of the logic of rural institutions and their relationship to "deep" cultural practices.[13]

Locating Community in the Japanese Countryside, 1600–1868

In 1600 the Tokugawa house defeated its rivals at the great battle of Sekigahara and brought to an end the savage period of warfare that had fragmented Japan into a patchwork of warlord domains.[14] The head of the Tokugawa house assumed the ancient title of shogun, or supreme military overlord, thereby announcing his political supremacy over the whole of Japan. Although Japan was still divided into more than 250 feudal domains (han), the bakufu, or government of the shogun, had broad powers of supervision and control that extended beyond the roughly one-quarter of the country directly ruled by the Tokugawa house. The shogun could transfer or depose the daimyo, the rulers of the various han, and all daimyo were required to practice alternate attendance (sankin-kotai) at Edo (Tokyo), the shogun's capital and the castle towns of their own domains. Indeed, the only possible rival to the shogun's hegemony was the emperor, who lived in a kind of splendid captivity until the Meiji Restoration overthrew bakufu power.[15]

The early Tokugawa rulers committed themselves to a rigid and authoritarian politics that saw all social and political relationships as static exemplars of a universal and cosmic ethos. Formally, Japanese society was divided into four

12. Ronald P. Toby, "Reopening the Question of Sakokui Diplomacy in the Legitimation of the Tokugawa Bakufu," *Journal of Japanese Studies* 3 (Summer 1977), 2:323–63.

13. For overviews of agrarian history, see Thomas C. Smith, *The Agrarian Origins of Modern Japan* (Stanford: Stanford University Press, 1959); Thomas C. Smith, "Farm Family By-employments in Preindustrial Japan," *Journal of Economic History* 29 (Dec. 1969), 687–715; E. Sydney Crawcour, "The Tokugawa Heritage," in William W. Lockwood, ed., *The State and Economic Enterprise in Japan: Essays in the Political Economy of Growth* (Princeton: Princeton University Press, 1965), 17–44; William B. Hauser, *Economic Institutional Change in Tokugawa Japan: Osaka and the Kinai Cotton Trade* (Cambridge: Cambridge University Press, 1974), esp. 117–73, 180–82; Susan B. Hanley and Kozo Yamamura, *Economic and Demographic Change in Preindustrial Japan, 1600–1868* (Princeton: Princeton University Press, 1977), esp. 91–198; and Kazushi Ohkawa et al., eds., *Agriculture and Economic Growth: Japan's Experience* (Princeton: Princeton University Press, 1970).

14. Asao Naohiro, "Shogun and Tennō," and Sasaki Junnosuke, "The Changing Rationale of Daimyo Control in the Emergence of the Bakuhan State," both in John W. Hall et al., eds., *Japan before Tokugawa: Political Consolidation and Economic Growth* (Princeton: Princeton University Press, 1981), 248–94.

15. Bolitho, *Treasures among Men*, 1–41; Totman, *Politics in the Tokugawa Bakufu*, 35–36, 97–99, 204–61.

inflexible status groups—samurai, cultivators, artisans, and merchants—and strict sumptuary rules prescribed and proscribed the entitlements of each group.[16] In theory, and to a considerable degree in practice, status was hereditary, and inequality permeated every aspect of daily life, even the discourse of everyday social encounters. For example, commoners (that is, all people who could not claim samurai status) were required to be highly deferential to all authorities at all times; only samurai could participate in domain and bakufu politics; and only samurai could wear swords, the supreme mark of elite status.[17] In short, Tokugawa Japan was a society strongly marked by aristocratic domination, and, perhaps to an almost exaggerated degree, Japan's warrior aristocracy saw itself as ruling by a divine and inalienable dispensation that was unchecked by formal law or representative institutions. Although the rigor of samurai power was mitigated by a neo-Confucian ethos that stressed "benevolent" rule, as well as by the slow growth of bureaucratic procedures that limited arbitrary rule, it would be absurd to deny the pervasiveness of hierarchy and deference in all spheres of Tokugawa life.[18]

The first of three Tokugawa shoguns saw himself as laying the foundations for a social order that would remain fixed forever, and the creation of a static world was seen as a positive good.[19] But Tokugawa Japan was neither static nor doomed to merely cyclical change with no lasting consequences. The Tokugawa "peace" made possible a whole series of complex changes that some historians have interpreted as marking a process of indigenous economic development that would eventually lead to industrialization.[20] Between 1600 and 1721, Japan's population grew from some 10 million to 18 million to over 26 million, and although population growth flattened out after the latter date, the increase in numbers contributed to a burst of economic innovations and transformations that made late Tokugawa Japan one of the most commercialized East Asian societies.[21] Rapid urban growth, especially in Edo and Osaka more than compensated for the decline of older castle towns (*jokamachi*), and a sophisticated merchant population devel-

16. Ooms, *Tokugawa Ideology*, 18–62, 106, 119–20, 162–93, 291–94.

17. For the origins of the sword as status symbol, see Berry, *Hideyoshi*, 102–6, 198.

18. Marius B. Jansen and Gilbert Rozman, eds., *Japan in Transition from Tokugawa to Meiji* (Princeton: Princeton University Press, 1986), esp. Marius B. Jansen, Introduction to part 1, "Administration," 29–35, and Albert M. Craig, "The Central Government," 36–67; Michio Umegaki and Herschel Webb, *The Japanese Imperial Institution in the Tokugawa Period* (New York: Columbia University Press, 1968).

19. Harry Harootunian, *Things Seen and Unseen: Discourse and Ideology in Tokugawa Nativism* (Chicago: University of Chicago Press, 1988), 1–75; H. D. Harootunian, "The Functions of China in Tokugawa Thought," in Akira Iriye, ed., *The Chinese and the Japanese: Essays in Political and Cultural Interactions* (Princeton: Princeton University Press, 1980), 9–36.

20. Hanley and Yamamura, *Economic and Demographic Change;* Thomas C. Smith, *Native Sources of Japanese Industrialization, 1750–1920* (Berkeley: University of California Press, 1988).

21. Smith, *Native Sources of Japanese Industrialization*, 103–32; Thomas C. Smith et al., *Nakahara: Family Farming and Population in a Japanese Village, 1717–1830* (Stanford: Stanford University Press, 1977), 5–14.

oped complex commercial institutions and market networks that cut across the fragmented boundaries of feudal domains.[22] In the countryside, artisanal by-employments and local markets for staple goods and specialty products helped to propel many ordinary cultivators into the market.[23] The developments of the Tokugawa period set the stage for Japan's rapid industrialization after 1868, as well as undermining the power of the samurai, who increasingly found themselves indebted to urban merchants.[24]

The whole edifice of Tokugawa Japan rested on the ability of ordinary cultivators to produce a surplus large enough to support both the samurai elite and the large population of urban merchants, artisans, and laborers. In the fifteenth and early sixteenth centuries much of the samurai population lived in scattered villages and hamlets, and these Ji-samurai, or village warriors, were probably little different from ordinary cultivators.[25] But by the end of the sixteenth century the samurai had, as we have seen, become a closed, hereditary caste, and samurai no longer lived in the countryside but were confined instead to castle towns and cities.[26] Samurai households were supported by fixed stipends in kind or cash paid by the lord of the domain, who had learned by painful experience that this kind of material dependence of vassals on their lords greatly simplified the politics of loyalty and control. Everything depended, therefore, on the capacity of the lord's administration to extract from the countryside a regular flow of tribute sufficiently great to maintain the entire vassal band and their servants, kinsmen, and retainers.[27] In contrast to the elite in Europe, the Japanese warrior elite did not exercise manorial jurisdiction over agriculture, nor did individual samurai have specific territorial control of parts of the countryside.[28] Instead, the agricultural population of a single domain dealt with the domain lord and his vassals as a group through the mediation of a land tax (*nengu*), typically paid in kind on an annual

22. Thomas C. Smith, "Premodern Economic Growth: Japan and the West," *Past and Present* 60 (Aug. 1973), 127–61; Gilbert Rozman, *Urban Networks in Ch'ing China and Tokugawa Japan* (Princeton: Princeton University Press, 1973), 105–40.

23. See, for example, Hauser, *Economic Institutional Change in Tokugawa Japan*, 117–20, 136–48, 157–58, 165–73; but also see Frances V. Moulder, *Japan, China, and the Modern World Economy: Toward a Reinterpretation of East Asian Development, ca. 1600 to ca. 1918* (Cambridge: Cambridge University Press, 1977).

24. Smith, *Native Sources of Japanese Industrialization*, esp. 133–72 and 50–70.

25. Cornelius J. Kiley, "Estate and Property in the Late Heian Period"; Jeffrey P. Mass, "The Emergence of the Kamakura Bakufu"; Jeffrey P. Mass, "Jito Land Possession in the Thirteenth Century: The Case of Shitaji Chubun"; and David L. Davis, "Ikki in Late Medieval Japan," all in Hall and Mass, *Medieval Japan*, 109–24, 127–56, 221–47.

26. John W. Hall, "Feudalism in Japan: A Reassessment" and "The Castle Town and Japan's Modern Urbanization," in John W. Hall and M. Jansen, eds., *Studies in the Institutional History of Early Modern Japan* (Princeton: Princeton University Press, 1968), 15–51, 169–88. Also see Wakita Osamu, "The Kokudaka System: A Device for Unification," *Journal of Japanese Studies* 1 (Spring 1975), 312–15.

27. Smith, *The Agrarian Origins of Modern Japan*, esp. 100–101, 181–86; Vlastos, *Peasant Protests and Uprisings in Tokugawa Japan*, 21–34.

28. Hall, *Government and Local Power in Japan*, 330–423.

basis.[29] Usually levied in units called *kokudaka*, a measure of rice output linked to field size and quality, the land tax was the chief point of contact between rural commoners and the samurai elite, just as it was the key political obligation levied on the countryside by feudal institutions. In contrast to early modern Europe, Japanese elites during the Tokugawa period seem to have been relatively uninterested in interfering in the lives and agricultural practices of rural commoners.[30] Domain lords periodically issued pious injunctions about the need for frugality and loyalty on the part of commoners, and during the Tokugawa period rural households were supposed to form five-man groups (*gonin-gumi*) for mutual surveillance and moral exhortation.[31] But apart from episodic famine relief and some investment in roads and large-scale water control, feudal lords and their retainers did little either to change or to maintain established agricultural practices.[32] Samurai never became improving landlords of the European type, and it is interesting that even in the area of property law the Tokugawa administration may have done little to regulate contracts and property rights.[33] Evidently this was perceived to be an area of jurisdiction over which commoners themselves should exercise control, subject to the proviso that such control would remain revocable at the will of the feudal lord. Indeed, the chief form of intervention in economic affairs undertaken by feudal authorities, especially after the mid-1700s, was the creation of chartered merchant monopolies as sources of domain revenue.[34]

The land tax, then, was the political and economic linchpin that held Tokugawa Japan together. The land tax was the symbol and substance of the political subjection of the countryside to an urbanized aristocracy of warrior administrators. Moreover, the land tax made possible the spectacular commercial development of the Tokugawa period. The need to convert tax rice into the full range of goods and services required by a high-status elite of urban samurai encouraged the growth of a money economy and the rise of an urban service population.[35] In

29. Thomas C. Smith, "The Land Tax in the Tokugawa Period," *Journal of Asian Studies* 18 (Nov. 1958), 3–20; Hanley and Yamamura, *Economic and Demographic Change in Premodern Japan*, 19–28.

30. The clearest statement is Dan Fenno Henderson, "Contracts in Tokugawa Villages," *Journal of Japanese Studies* 1 (1974), 51–90, esp. 62; and see the documents in John H. Wigmore, ed., *Law and Justice in Tokugawa Japan, Being Materials for the History of Japanese Law and Justice under the Tokugawa Shogunate, 1603–1867* (Tokyo: University of Tokyo Press, 1967–86). My readings of the latter do not support the notion of an "active" as opposed to exhortatory or exemplary political elite.

31. George Sansom, *A History of Japan*, vol. 3, *1615–1867* (Stanford: Stanford University Press, 1963), 30, 100–103.

32. See Smith, *The Agrarian Origins of Modern Japan*, esp. 67–86, 180–200. This statement, of course, must be qualified by pointing to the constant stream of exhortations and injunctions enacted by the bakufu and the domains, but the *administrative* machinery to enforce them was lacking.

33. Henderson, "Contracts in Tokugawa Villages," 51–90. But also see Ann Waswo, *Japanese Landlords: The Decline of a Rural Elite* (Berkeley: University of California Press, 1977), 12–23.

34. Smith, *Native Sources of Japanese Industrialization*, 23–25; William W. Kelly, *Deference and Defiance in Nineteenth Century Japan* (Princeton: Princeton University Press, 1985), esp. 3–25, 34–49. Also see Hauser, *Economic Institutional Change in Tokugawa Japan*, esp. chaps. 5 and 6.

35. Smith, *The Agrarian Origins of Modern Japan*, 67–86.

addition, tax rice had to be transported to both the domain's castle town and Edo, where all lords were required to spend half of each year in attendance on the shogun, and thus stimulated the development of long-distance trade and credit.[36]

An important feature of Japan's agrarian history is the long-term persistence of nucleated habitats.[37] According to Scheiner, "most peasants in the Tokugawa period lived in homogeneous hamlets (villages) of fifty to one hundred households," and this was apparently true of all regions during the period.[38] The feudal elite tacitly recognized the importance of the village as the basic unit of social organization by making it collectively responsible for the payment of all taxes and the punishment of offenses. The imposition of collective responsibility made sense, because the nucleated village was a visible and permanent organization of people and territory that long predated the victory of the Tokugawa.[39]

But the Japanese village was much more than a unit of territorial neighborhood and collective political responsibility. It was also an ensemble of economic institutions that focused on the control of village land and labor. This point has been well made by Thomas C. Smith who, although also emphasizing the salience of intravillage competition, has written: "Historians and anthropologists have emphasized the solidarity of the traditional Japanese farming village, and unquestionable solidarity was one of its major characteristics. Exchange of labor between neighbors and kin was the rule; compromise and accommodation were highly valued; universal observance of holidays and festivals was enforced. Speech, clothing, farm tools, custom, and religious observances all differed between villages but were remarkably homogeneous within them. Dissent from village opinion on important issues brought ostracism or expulsion."[40]

Village institutions regulated irrigation, the layout of fields, and the timing of the agricultural cycle.[41] Villages also held common land and water rights, and according to Smith, time itself was regarded as a kind of corporate or group property right subject to village regulation: "Nevertheless, time was regarded as fleeting and precarious, and great moral value attached to its productive use.

36. Rozman, *Urban Networks in Ch'ing China and Tokugawa Japan*, 112, 117; James L. McClain, *Kanazawa: A Seventeenth Century Japanese Castle Town* (New Haven: Yale University Press, 1982).

37. See, for example, William Jones Chambliss, *Chiaraijima Village: Land Tenure, Taxation, and Local Trade, 1818–1884* (Tucson: University of Arizona Press, 1965); Ronald P. Dore, *Land Reform in Japan* (London: Oxford University Press, 1959); John Embree, *Suye Mura: A Japanese Village* (Chicago: University of Chicago Press, 1939); Tadashi Fukutake, *Japanese Rural Society* (Tokyo: Oxford University Press, 1967); Social Science Research Institute, *The Power Structure in a Rural Community: The Case of Mutsuzawa Mura* (Tokyo, 1960); and Thomas C. Smith, "The Japanese Village in the Seventeenth Century," *Journal of Economic History* 12 (Winter 1952), 1–20. Much of this literature uses class terms but also can be read to support community as an analytic category.

38. Scheiner, "Benevolent Lords and Honorable Peasants," esp. 44.

39. Davis, "Ikki in Late Medieval Japan."

40. Smith et al., *Nakahara*, 114.

41. The most balanced source is Smith's *Agrarian Origins*, which gives weight to intravillage cooperation and conflict. See Smith, *The Agrarian Origins of Modern Japan*, 50–64, 157–79.

Farmers made elaborate efforts to coordinate work and to stretch nature's constraints by the skillful use of early and late varieties, between row planting, straw-covered planting beds, fast acting fertilizers, and other time-saving devices. None of this ingenuity, however, was for the benefit of individuals. Time was not a personal possession but belonged primarily to families and, through them, to kin, neighbors, and villages."[42]

Moreover, the village exercised broad if highly local control over the definition and enforcement of property rights to land and labor. Beginning at least in the fifteenth century, villages pressed for transfer of these matters from outside elites to the village, exactly what we would expect in a society characterized by the importance of local community institutions.[43] Davis has argued that the rural uprisings, or *ikki*, of the fifteenth century must be understood in part as struggles for the empowerment of the village in regard to property rights: "First, the new peasant political associations, forerunners of the characteristic village governments of the Edo [Tokugawa] period, aimed to assume all essential governmental functions relating to the daily life of the peasantry. These involved such matters as the management of projects requiring communal labor, but most important, the transfer of adjudication of peasant disputes over land ownership and other vital matters from a shōen's (estate's) headquarters to the village itself. This led to an enhancement of the average peasant's security of tenure."[44]

Now it is certainly true that land tenure during the Tokugawa period was held by households, and especially in the 1700s, a lively local market for land rights developed in commercial farming regions. But it seems safe to argue that, like productive time, property rights were regulated first and foremost by village institutions, and established village households may be seen as enjoying a kind of hereditary tenure that depended partly on village membership. This was reinforced during the period from roughly 1600 to the 1750s by the practice called *tezukuri*, a form of cooperative farming in which a "superior" householder (*oyakata*) and a number of attached "lesser" houses (*nago*) and hereditary servants (*fudai*) cultivated their joint holdings as a collective enterprise. Even after tezukuri began to give way to tenant farming in some regions, farm families still clung to the land as a hereditary patrimony, and many tenant households must have had what amounted to permanent tenure.[45]

Yet it would be false to view the Japanese village as economically egalitarian, and Tokugawa villages did not have a Japanese version of the Russian land commune. As the example of tezukuri suggests, village economic relationships were always hierarchical, and member households differed in terms of wealth, landholdings, and economic opportunities.[46] Still, these were reciprocal hier-

42. Smith, *Native Sources of Japanese Industrialization*, 202.
43. Ibid., 199–235.
44. Davis, "Ikki in Late Medieval Japan," 226–27.
45. Smith, *Agrarian Origins of Modern Japan*, 140–56, 50–64, 5–11, 22–23, 124–39.
46. Smith et al., *Nakahara*, 34–46.

archies, at least to the extent that advantaged households had to work through established institutions in order to mobilize labor and support. As long as the property rights of even well-off households depended on the village for enforcement and definition, the situation worked against a unilateral assertion of the prerogatives of wealth.[47] In short, this was a society that required some degree of reciprocal cooperation between all village households. For example, tenants could and did demand a reduction of rents in bad times, and nago or other dependent households shared to some degree in the status and economic security of the established households to which they belonged.[48]

Occasionally, domain governments reinforced the logic of local economic solidarity by forbidding land alienation and issuing decrees protecting tenant rights. But given the relative weakness of elite administration outside of the area of tax collection, it is reasonable to argue that economic reciprocity, like property rights, was largely a function of the strength and salience of village institutions. This is a point made in an indirect but illuminating way by Ann Waswo in her discussion of the post-Tokugawa regime's efforts to create a "modern" system of exclusive property rights. According to Waswo:

> The deeds which the government began issuing in 1871 were given to those people customarily recognized as landowners, but in a society in which there had been no clear [read *national*] conception of property rights in the past and where local practices and attitudes regarding both land ownership and tenancy had varied widely, the determination of ownership was no easy matter. In many parts of the country, for example, where the ban on the alienation of land had been rigorously enforced, the tenant and not the landlord had paid the land tax and had been listed in official registers as the holders of the land. Unaware of local differences and impatient to get the new tax system under way, however, the government generally gave deeds to anyone receiving rents or holding mortgages. . . . Two forms of permanent tenancy had existed during the Tokugawa period (of which the government was apparently unaware, . . . but . . . failed to gain legal recognition, and many cultivators became ordinary tenants at will of their landlords.[49]

Once again, what this suggests is that it is simply meaningless to view property rights and economic relationships in the Tokugawa period as the reflection of either national market forces or elite politics. The village was the institutional matrix of both property and production, and economic rights were held in trust for both the household or lineage *and* the village as a community.[50] Indeed, the notion of property as trusteeship, which we have seen at work in all the European cases, may have been just as powerfully institutionalized in the Tokugawa countryside.

47. Smith, *Native Sources of Japanese Industrialization*, 199–235.
48. Smith, *Agrarian Origins of Modern Japan*, 154–57.
49. Waswo, *Japanese Landlords*, 12–34, quotation on 17–18.
50. Henderson, "Contracts in Tokugawa Villages," 51–90; Dan Fenno Henderson, *Conciliation and Japanese Law: Tokugawa and Modern*, vol. 1 (Seattle: University of Washington Press, 1965).

As Smith points out, Tokugawa villages could exercise potent controls over the economic behavior of their members:

> No doubt because the village was considered a single moral sphere, efforts were made to monitor and improve the use of time in the community. . . . The Hōtokusha, a society inspired by the teachings of the late Tokugawa agrarian moralist Ninomiya Sontoku (1787–1856), gave much attention to the proper use of time and to the abolition of singing, dancing and theatrical performances in villages. A certain follower of Ninomiya's named Furuhashi made up a time schedule . . . and exhorted fellow villagers to follow it; another made the rounds of the village each morning wakening people to the sound of a wooden clapper.
>
> The language of Tokugawa agriculture was rich in vocabulary expressing work in a context of obligation to others. Suke was labor given by a dependent to a protector in return and gratitude for benefits such as the loan of land, animals, and a house. Yui was an equal exchange of like labor such as mutual help in transplanting rice. Hōkō was service while living as a servant and quasi member of another's family. There were numerous words for work apart from social relations, but these refer to the physical act or effort of work (shigoto, hataraki, kasegi). It is difficult to find any word that suggests work in a social context without carrying a sense of obligation to others.[51]

These paragraphs strikingly illustrate the principle of reciprocal hierarchy, and they underscore the importance of the Japanese village as a sphere of economic production and distribution. Undoubtedly, much conflict and competition took place in the most solidary of villages. But that observation does not undermine the validity of seeing the village as the key arena in which both cooperation *and* conflict were embedded within the institutional arrangements of village life. Class logic does little to explain the Tokugawa village, at least if we mean by class logic the analysis of societies in terms of large-scale, supraterritorial social groups that share common class interests and identities. There were simply no classes in this sense in Tokugawa rural society, and village membership was arguably more important than class position in determining the life chances of ordinary people. To be an established village householder was to have a secure if subordinate role in a profoundly hierarchical world.[52]

It is tempting to speculate that village institutions in Japan were deeply affected by irrigated, small-scale agriculture, especially in regions where wet-rice cultivation had developed. Irrigation demanded a high level of local cooperation among farming households to apportion water rights, time the flow of water and the flooding of fields, and arrange for the upkeep of irrigation canals and ditches.[53] In

---

51. Smith, *Native Sources of Japanese Industrialization,* 219–20.
52. Scheiner, "Benevolent Lords and Honorable Peasants," 39–62.
53. See, for example, R. Beardsley, "Ecological and Social Parallels between Rice-Growing Communities of Japan and Spain," in Viola Garfield and Ernestine Friedl, eds., *Symposium on*

the absence of an external enforcement agency, these ongoing problems could be managed only by village institutions. Moreover, wet-rice agriculture lent itself to seasonal cooperation among farm families, since rice plants had to be transplanted according to a fairly strict schedule. It took advantage of group labor, and it also offered opportunities for households to exchange labor at peak periods. Finally, it should be kept in mind that Japanese field designs paralleled their European counterparts to the extent that fields were scattered in numerous fragments rather than arranged in large-scale enclosures. This put a premium on cooperative arrangements that could guarantee a minimum of friction over access rights and a maximum of agreement about what and when to plant.[54]

Ironically, therefore, the material logic of Japanese agriculture may have strengthened community institutions and weakened the significance of class forces. Territory was central in shaping the basic material dynamic of small-scale agriculture, and rules of territorial membership made up the economic "code" of daily life. Some readers may find this too "functionalist," but I would claim on behalf of the argument that it at least captures the nature of the Japanese village more accurately than a disembodied class analysis.

Economic cooperation in the Tokugawa village was closely linked to the political institutions that made the village a distinct political jurisdiction. The village was always characterized by a village assembly (*yoriai*) that had wide powers over all matters of local concern.[55] The assembly could mobilize local land and labor for village projects, and it was probably the assembly that divided taxes among member households.[56] At the head of the village as a whole was the headman (*shōya*), an important figure who mediated between the village community and all outsiders, including the feudal authorities.[57] Sometimes hereditary, the office of headman was often risky and expensive; headmen were expected to lead their villages in both good and bad times, even if this meant defying the rigid rules of the feudal hierarchy. In extreme cases, headmen may have been expected to sacrifice their lives on behalf of their villages, a tradition of expectation and propriety that has been skillfully reconstructed by Irwin Scheiner.[58] In any event,

Community Studies in Anthropology (Seattle: American Ethnological Society, 1964), 51–63; Ronald Dore, "Modern Cooperatives in Traditional Communities," in Peter Worsley, ed., *Two Blades of Grass: Rural Cooperatives in Agricultural Modernization* (Manchester: Manchester University Press, 1971), 43–60; Ronald Dore, *Shinohata: A Portrait of a Japanese Village* (London: Allen Lane, 1978); J. Eyre, "Water Controls in a Japanese Irrigation System," *Geographical Review* 45 (Apr. 1955), 197–216; Y. Hayami, "The Economic Approach to Village Community and Institution," *Journal of Rural Development* 3 (Apr. 1983), 27–49; and M. McKean, "Management of Traditional Common Lands in Japan" (Department of Political Science, Duke University, 1984, Mimeographed). These sources reinforce the view of Japanese villages as communities of grain.

54. Beardsley, "Ecological and Social Parallels."
55. Smith, *The Agrarian Origins of Modern Japan*, 50–64, 180–200.
56. Smith, "The Japanese Village in the Seventeenth Century," 1–20.
57. Scheiner, "Benevolent Lords and Honorable Peasants," 43–47.
58. Scheiner, "The Mindful Peasant," 579–91.

the headman symbolized the political cohesion of the village as a collectivity that dealt as a group with external authorities.

The political power of the village is nicely illustrated by the practice called *muraharai,* or "cleansing of the village."[59] Anyone who transgressed village rules or refused to rectify abuses of the village code could be expelled from the village and deprived of membership rights. This practice was called "cleansing," and it shows both the power of the community to make and enforce rules for its members and the strong forces of cohesion that underpinned village life. Only a community with a high degree of political autonomy could have so completely determined its own conditions of membership. One may suggest that the power of the village in most areas of daily concern must have mitigated local conflicts that might otherwise have undercut community solidarity. Anyone who pressed a conflict in unacceptable ways by turning it into a confrontation between the offending individual and the community risked banishment. This must have been a daunting prospect in a society that lacked rudimentary welfare institutions apart from the village and household.[60] Strangers, wanderers, and masterless men were political outcasts in Tokugawa Japan; anyone who desired a secure and respectable existence had little choice but to obey the rules of his house and village.[61]

The political control of the village was not, of course, absolute. Many disputes could not be regulated through local rules, and many households could manipulate village rules for their own ends.[62] More important, the political autonomy of the village was constrained by the institutions of feudal power. Feudal authorities may not have interfered with the village to the degree practiced by European manor lords. But samurai power was real, and at any time the lord of the domain might embark on a new project that could wind up threatening the economic and political autonomy of the village. In this context it would have been foolhardy for village assemblies to be too brazen in their policies or too forthright in their assertion of political independence. This must have limited to some extent the kinds of claims that village assemblies could make on their member households, and political innovation was probably not a frequent occurrence in community political life.[63]

Nevertheless, it is clear that the village was the major political focus of popular life in the Tokugawa countryside. This fact was reinforced by the role played by village institutions in the ritual and religious experience of ordinary people. Every village formed a single sacrificial or cultic organization with its own village deity, a sure indication of the importance of the village as a source of popular identity. In

59. Smith, *The Agrarian Origins of Modern Japan,* 61.

60. Some domains tried to maintain "relief" granaries, but there seems to have been nothing like the English poor laws. "Failed" farming families of ten simply disappeared from their villages. See, for example, Smith et al., *Nakahara,* 33–46, 147–56.

61. Smith, *Native Sources of Japanese Industrialization,* 199–235.

62. See, for example, Smith, *The Agrarian Origins of Modern Japan,* esp. 180–200.

63. Scheiner, "Benevolent Lords and Honorable Peasants," 39–62.

some regions a group of families, called *miyaza,* exercised exclusive ceremonial control over the village rites, and less privileged households participated in a subordinate capacity.[64] But in spite of its hierarchical character, village religious life was deeply embedded in the daily experience of all households, thereby drawing the village as a whole together in a "folklore of place" that invested rural routines with spiritual significance. No one could escape the fact that the village was the home of the ancestral deities and the site of the major rites of passage for every householder. Japanese villages were more than simple networks of power and production; they were focused communities of ritual performance that shaped the loyalties and discourse of their members.[65]

Underpinning the ritual cohesion of the village was a system of kinship that placed extraordinary emphasis on preserving the household against any threats that might rupture intergenerational continuity. Japanese villages were both patriarchal and patrilocal, and marriage was strictly regulated by family and village elders. In extreme cases, a house that failed to produce an heir through marriage or adoption could have an heir appointed by the village, and a variety of strategies, including infanticide, were used to balance family size against available resources. Naturally, many households failed and died out, but the evidence suggests that farm families operated according to a calculus in which the chief goal was to preserve the status of the house as an established village kin group.[66] What this mode of operation shows, I think, is how strongly Japanese kinship was affected by the logic of the village, and how deeply village practices affected every realm of ordinary life.

In sum, the concept of the community of grain seems to capture much of the historical pattern of popular life during the Tokugawa period. Village communities had a large degree of autonomy in the basic matters that affected the village and its component households, and the village had enough cohesion to stick together even in adverse circumstances.[67] Reciprocal hierarchies of economic, political, and ritual cooperation bound member households together in mutually implicated networks of practice and performance. The villages, of course, also faced the same ongoing problem as the other agricultural societies discussed in this book: how to arrange the production and distribution of the means of life in a context of political and economic uncertainty. Conflict and competition undoubtedly existed, but it is difficult to avoid the conclusion that conflict took place within the rules of the village rather than against the village as a collectivity.

But village institutions were not immutable, and profound changes certainly

---

64. Smith, *The Agrarian Origins of Modern Japan,* 58–59, 188–200.
65. See, for example, Scheiner, "Benevolent Lords and Honorable Peasants," 39–62.
66. Smith et al., *Nakahara,* 107–46, 59–85.
67. Richard E. Varner, "The Organized Peasant: The Wakamonogumi in the Edo Period," *Monumenta Nipponica* 32 (Winter 1977), 459–83. Also see Carol Gluck, "The People in History: Recent Trends in Japanese Historiography," *Journal of Asian Studies* 38 (Nov. 1978), 25–50.

234 | Communities of Grain

did occur in the Tokugawa countryside. The expansion of rural markets drew village households into a cash economy, and the spread of new techniques and new crops may have made Tokugawa agriculture among the most productive and adaptive economies in the early modern world.[68] In addition, tenant farming replaced older forms of economic hierarchy as farm servants and dependent households were given leasehold farms in exchange for rents in cash and kind.[69] Money lending, land mortgaging, pawnbroking, and sake brewing provided novel opportunities for families to enhance their prosperity and security, and many villages also turned to artisanal by-employments that led to complex occupational differentiation in the more commercialized regions of the country.[70] By 1868 Japanese agriculture was capable of producing a "surplus" large enough to finance Japan's first wave of industrialization.

These are the kinds of changes that Japanese historians have pointed to as evidence of village disintegration. For example, Sasaki Junnosuke, one of the best scholars to have studied Tokugawa rebellion, has developed an ingenious set of class categories that supposedly demonstrate how class divisions ruptured the unity of the Tokugawa village.[71] Sasaki sees late Tokugawa Japan as increasingly divided between a rural "semiproletariat" and a variety of other classes and class fragments, and his research has been followed by many other historians who continue to deploy one or another mode of class analysis. As Scheiner has argued, Sasaki, and by extension other quasi-Marxist scholars, have a tendency to use an analytic framework that is "too mechanical, too peremptory in its determination of the political substance of a movement from the apparent social class and the social-economic relations of its members."[72] Nevertheless, both Marxist and non-Marxist specialists have shown how important change was in the Tokugawa countryside.

Still, we should not exaggerate the rate or extent of change, especially with respect to the growth of tenant farming. For example, Ann Waswo points out that roughly 27 percent of Japan's arable land was controlled by landlords in 1868, and this simple but striking figure should caution us against assuming too great a degree of agricultural transformation prior to the twentieth century.[73] Moreover, the spread of markets and tenant farming did not necessarily lead to class polariza-

68. Crawcour, "The Tokugawa Heritage," 17–44; Jansen and Rozman, *Japan in Transition from Tokugawa to Meiji,* esp. Kozo Yamamura, Introduction to part 4 ("Rural Economy and Material Conditions"), 372–81, and "The Meiji Land Tax Reform and Its Effects," 382–99; Osumu Saito, "The Rural Economy: Commercial Agriculture, By-Employment, and Wage Work," 400–420; Shunsaku Nishikawa, "Grain Consumption: The Case of Chosnu," 421–46; and Susan B. Hanley, "The Material Culture: Stability in Transition," 447–70.
69. Smith, *The Agrarian Origins of Modern Japan,* 140–56.
70. Smith, *Native Sources of Japanese Industrialization,* 71–102.
71. Sasaki Junnosuke, "Yonaoshi nojokyō," in Kōza Nihonshi, ed., *Nihonshi Kenkyōkai* (Tokyo, 1970), 94–101; Sasaki Junnosuke, *Bakumatsu shakai ron* (Tokyo: Hanawa Shobo, 1969).
72. Scheiner, "Benevolent Lords and Honorable Peasants," 42; and see Irwin Scheiner, "Review of Roger Bowen, Rebellion and Democracy in Meiji Japan: A Study of Commoners in the Popular Rights Movement," *Journal of Japanese Studies* 8 (Winter 1982), 179–86.
73. Waswo, *Japanese Landlords,* 16.

tion. After all, the transition from older forms of agricultural dependency to tenant farming may have increased the economic independence of many rural households who could use the tenant contract as a way of increasing autonomy from outside control. In contrast to the nago, tenant families evidently had much more freedom to make basic economic decisions, and it seems difficult to explain the gradual spread of tenancy unless we can assume that it offered benefits as well as costs and risks.[74] Tenant farming was not imposed by the feudal elite; it was created through the institutional relations of the village. Is it unreasonable to suppose that tenant farming would not have spread if it had represented a disaster for village solidarity? Certainly, we need at least to entertain the possibility that Tokugawa tenant relations were constructed through a long process of bargaining and negotiation that was possible only because of the survival of village institutions in which both well-off and poor households had a stake.

More important, however, we know that village institutions continued to play a significant role in agrarian life well into the twentieth century; indeed, local communities sometimes even voted as solidary groups as late as the 1970s.[75] Anthropologists, including Tadashi Fukutake, have shown the continuing power of the village as a material and political framework, in spite of the vast changes that took place after 1868, and it is difficult to think of organizing research about rural Japan without focusing on the village as a "natural" unit of analysis.[76] Indeed, we are probably safe in assuming that Tokugawa villages were more cohesive than their twentieth-century counterparts.

Much of the debate about the decay of the Tokugawa village assumes a stark dichotomy between precommercial communities and the supposedly corrosive forces of the market.[77] Any evidence of economic change becomes automatic proof of village dissolution, even though we can point to other evidence that shows the stability of community institutions. Yet this kind of argument is too mechanical and logically suspect. Rural markets did not necessarily lead to community decay in Europe, and there is no reason to suppose that Japan was different in this respect. Perhaps we should reconceptualize the whole issue by turning from a narrow debate about village decline to a very different strategy that focuses on the specific ways in which village institutions changed in response to economic forces. The real question is not whether the village disintegrated, but how material change was connected to transformations in the rules governing village membership. For example, the rise of tenant farming brought new economic roles and new conceptions of economic rights, but it did not destroy the significance of the village as the key political arena in which these changes were worked out. As Dan Fenno Henderson has argued, "the Tokugawa village was

74. Smith, *The Agrarian Origins of Modern Japan*, 67–123.
75. Smith et al., *Nakahara*, 114; and see Upham, *Law and Social Change in Postwar Japan*, 28–77.
76. See, for example, Dore, *Shinohata.*
77. See, for example, Sasaki, *Bakumatsu shakai ron,* esp. chaps. 2 and 3.

empowered and obligated by the feudal authorities to manage its own internal affairs in accordance with its customary law with minimal intrusion from the law of the overlord [*hatto*] so long as the tax was paid."[78] Surely this means that the sweeping economic changes of the Tokugawa period were managed by local communities, and what we need to know is how the village adapted to those changes through a reconstitution of its rules and rights.

In any event, those who argue for the disintegration of the Tokugawa village must deal with one simple but decisive fact: small-scale household farming did not disappear in the post-Tokugawa period, and as late as 1945, Japanese agriculture was characterized by small but intensive units of production that were closely tied to family labor and family proprietorship.[79] No enclosure movement liquidated the Japanese "peasantry," and no transition to large-scale capitalist farming took place.[80] Indeed, new market crops, especially the spread of commercial silkworm production, may have worked in favor of small-scale agriculture because of their tendency to be labor intensive.[81]

But if Tokugawa agriculture had been transformed by the division of the village into "semiproletarians" and protobourgeois farmers, the result should have been the rise of large-scale consolidated farming operated by wage labor.[82] Yet this result did not occur, and even before the post-1945 land reform, the dominant profile of Japanese agriculture combined tenant farming with small owner-occupied landholdings.[83] This picture is simply incompatible with a rigid class analysis of Tokugawa history that reduces the Japanese village to a passive object of social forces. Somehow small-scale farming survived, and it does not seem fanciful to argue that its survival was partly a function of village autonomy and cohesion. Smallholders and tenants could use the reciprocal hierarchies and cooperative arrangements of village life to protect themselves against the shifting fortunes of the market. Of course, many failed while others prospered, but a sufficient number survived to preserve the family farm in modern Japan.[84]

78. Henderson, "Contracts in Tokugawa Villages," 51–90, esp. 62.

79. For all its problems this is a point well made by Richard J. Smethurst, *Agricultural Development and Tenancy Disputes in Japan, 1870–1940* (Princeton: Princeton University Press, 1986), esp. 43–104. Also see R. Dore, "Agricultural Improvements in Japan: 1870–1900," in "City and Village in Japan," ed. Thomas C. Smith, *Economic Development and Cultural Change* 9 (Oct. 1960), 69–91.

80. Yujiro Hayami, *A Century of Agricultural Growth in Japan: Its Relevance to Asian Development* (Minneapolis: University of Minnesota Press, 1975); William W. Lockwood, *The Economic Development of Japan: Growth and Structural Change* (Princeton: Princeton University Press, 1968), 99–100, 277–78, 295–97, 552–54.

81. Smethurst, *Agricultural Development and Tenancy Disputes in Japan*, 55–57, 153–64, 170–83, 185, 228–31.

82. This is, after all, the standard Marxist argument. See Robert Brenner, "The Agrarian Roots of European Capitalism," in T. H. Aston and C. H. E. Philpin, *The Brenner Debate: Agrarian Class Structure and Economic Development in Pre-Industrial Europe* (Cambridge: Cambridge University Press, 1987), 213–327.

83. Dore, *Land Reform in Japan*, 3–127.

84. James I. Nakamura, *Agricultural Production and the Economic Development of Japan, 1873–1922* (Princeton: Princeton University Press, 1966).

A final illustration of the limits of class analysis when applied to the Tokugawa countryside can be found in the complicated history of the *uchikowashi*, the violent episodes of "smashing and breaking" that became relatively frequent in the late eighteenth century.[85] According to Aoki, 153 of these events occurred between 1751 and 1800, and another 187 took place in the period from 1801 to 1850.[86] Although it is dangerous to generalize, three salient features of the uchikowashi stand out in the historical literature. First, these were small-scale affrays, usually confined to a single village or group of villages.[87] Second, the targets seem to have been individuals who violated popular norms of justice and fair play by refusing to abide by village rules regarding the use of land and labor; typical targets included "bad" village headmen, pawnbrokers and money lenders accused of usury, and cultivators who had somehow "cheated" less fortunate neighbors. Finally, the uchikowashi shows strong traces of ritual prescription and self-control, because the targets of popular violence were usually humiliated by having their houses or property destroyed but were otherwise spared much personal injury.[88]

A good example of the logic of the uchikowashi comes from Stephen Vlastos's account of one such episode that occurred in 1866 in the Shindatsu region. It resulted from complicated conflict that grew out of the politics of the local marketplace. According to Vlastos:

> Early in the evening of 6/15, the second day of the boycott of the silk fair [a struggle over silk taxes was the immediate cause of the trouble], about fifty peasants gathered in Oka village. They lit bonfires, drummed on pots, blew conches, shouted, shrieked, and whistled. More people came, carrying torches, staves, hoes, axes, and shovels. They marched to the house of Umaji, the village headman and recently appointed silk inspector. As they circled the house, a leader stepped forward and shouted: "Be especially careful with fires! Don't spill and scatter rice! Don't carry off pawned goods, because they belong to other people! Don't steal money! This is being done to help the people, not for selfish reasons. But smash everything in this man's house, even the cat's dish." Whereupon they fell upon the house, knocking down the doors and screens; they stormed inside and smashed everything in sight. Nobody was hurt, but Umaji's property lay in ruins.
>
> That evening they attacked Bun'emon, the assistant headman of the village; Banroku, the headman of neighboring Nagakura; and the other inspectors who lived in the area. After the first attacks, the leaders drafted a manifesto which they circulated throughout the district:
>
> "Acting selfishly and avariciously, Umaji of Oka village, Banroku of Nagakura, and six others have turned their backs on the hardship they cause the people by

---

85. Scheiner, "Benevolent Lords and Honorable Peasants," esp. 40–41.

86. Aoki, *Hyakushō ikki no nenjiteki kenkyū*, 36–37; Aoki Kōji, *Hyakushō ikki sōgō nenpyo* (Tokyo: San'ichi Shobō, 1971).

87. Vlastos, *Peasant Protests and Uprisings*, 42–91; also see Bix, *Peasant Protest in Japan*, xix, 81, 104, 169, 198–99.

88. Vlastos, *Peasant Protests and Uprisings*, 73–92.

collecting taxes under the new system. This year crops have been poor, and many silkworms did not spin proper cocoons. Just when everyone was struggling to eke out a living, the new regulations were put into effect. Now we cannot even market our goods, and the poorest are on the verge of starvation. Several attacks have already occurred, and greater disturbances are imminent. We will not tolerate the calamity that is upon the land."

The text was written on a thick sheet of paper of the type used in egg-card manufacture, and around the message the names of seventy-four villages. Each village which received the circular marked its name and sent it to the next destination. This way the peasants knew which villages had withheld support. To them they sent runners carrying the following message:

"Our purpose is to aid poor and impoverished people, and therefore everyone must lend support. If you refuse, we will gather a great force and descend on your village, set fires, and burn everything down."

The leaders planned to mobilize peasants from every part of Shindatsu, march on Koori, and demand cheap rice and the cancellation of taxes.[89]

I have cited this lengthy passage from Vlastos because of the light it sheds on the uchikowashi and related forms of violence. Sasaki Junnosuke and like-minded historians would probably interpret the Shindatsu incident as a straightforward expression of class struggle, but Vlastos's reconstruction leaves little doubt that much more than class power was at stake. The participants seem to have mobilized as village communities, and their willingness to smash anyone, rich or poor, who stood in their way suggests that they did not see themselves as members of a specific class.[90] On the contrary, their appeal to notions of correct conduct and their rhetorical assault on selfishness implies a standard of local propriety that cut across mere economic divisions.

More important, the targets of popular violence were carefully chosen, and they seem to have been individuals who threatened the integrity of the village community through corrupt or unscrupulous abuse of village institutions.[91] The rioters did not attack the rich as a social category; instead, they singled out specific village officials who had collected unpopular taxes or who had in other ways violated the trust of their communities. Their behavior, of course, was the exact opposite of the kind of selflessness that characterized village leaders like Sakura Sōgorō, and Scheiner has shown how "righteous" leaders like Sakura provided a clear standard by which ordinary villagers could evaluate correct political behavior.[92] Is it possible that uchikowashi represented an attempt on the part of villagers to force advantaged village members to play by the rules of reciprocal hierarchy? After all, the Shindatsu villagers do not seem to have despised wealth

89. Ibid., 123–24.
90. Ibid., 114–41, 73–91.
91. Scheiner, "Benevolent Lords and Honorable Peasants," esp. 52–56.
92. Scheiner, "The Mindful Peasant," 579–91.

or power as such; their anger was directed more at the failure of particular households to live up to community standards.[93]

The economic changes of the Tokugawa period generated a window of opportunity in which at least some households could escape the institutional network of the village, especially by manipulating the market economy against the village as a whole. But village institutions retained sufficient cohesion to enable the village population to fight back, and in the uchikowashi ordinary villagers drew a symbolic and coercive boundary around what would count as acceptable behavior.[94] By "smashing and breaking" the property of its victim, the uchikowashi forced the victim to submit to the will of the village and resume his place as a village member with all the rights and obligations attached to his position.[95] Rather than a class war, the uchikowashi was an intravillage struggle that sought to rectify the proper performance of roles and protect the village against threats to its autonomy and cohesion. In fact, the ability of villages to act in this way may have helped to preserve the continuity and stability of the village in the face of rapid change.

From Violent Representation to Community Secession, 1600–1868

Vlastos has argued that "one of the salient factors about peasants' movements in the Tokugawa period is that there were a great many of them," and this conclusion is supported by the work of Irwin Scheiner, Herbert P. Bix, and other Western and Japanese scholars who have done so much to reconstruct the popular history of early modern Japan.[96] The generic term for all forms of popular insurrection is *ikki*, a word that means "one goal" or "in agreement." However, the literature disaggregates the concept of *ikki* into a complex and rich set of subtypes that range from regional insurrections to illegal partitioning campaigns.[97] With the exception of the uchikowashi and other intravillage struggles (called *murakata*), most of the forms of popular collective violence mobilized whole villages behind their headmen in a confrontation with the feudal elite. Irwin Scheiner has made this point quite clearly:

> For most of the Tokugawa period peasants revolted as whole villages under the leadership of the headman, who represented the intent of the collectivity. Just as a headman's success in governing depended on a consensus for his policies, his prestige and authority depended on his representation or leadership of the village in revolt.

93. Vlastos, *Peasant Protests and Uprisings*, 114–41.
94. This idea is drawn from Scheiner, "The Mindful Peasant," 579–91.
95. That the point of the smashing was to force people in some sense to "repent" may explain why few were actually killed outright.
96. Vlastos, *Peasant Protests and Uprisings*, 10.
97. See the complex typology in Bix, *Peasant Protest in Japan*, xi–xxxviii.

Hayashi Hachiemon, village headman and leader of the Maebashi rebellion in 1821, explained his participation as both a duty and responsibility of a village leader. "I was aware of the confusion [due to my rebellion] but if I had ignored the pain of my villagers I could not keep my office as village head. To do so would be like leaving my own wounds uncared for."[98]

A further point about which there seems to be fairly broad agreement is that taxation somehow generated much, perhaps most of the insurrectionary violence of the Tokugawa period. For example, Aoki has shown that taxation overshadowed all other causes of rural unrest between 1590 and 1699, and this conclusion can be generalized to the whole Tokugawa period (see table).[99] Probably one-half to two thirds of the rural protests stemmed from taxation and its associated problems.[100] For instance, between 1650 and 1720 direct and forcible appeals for tax relief (*daihyo osso* and *jikiso*) dominate the historical record, and although other issues began to appear after the mid-1700s, taxes and tax policy was an almost constant source of popular protest right down to the fall of the bakufu in 1868.[101] I would hesitate to be any more precise than this, because the nature of the evidence makes exactness impossible. Interested readers are invited to consult either Aoki Kōji or the work of Yokoyama Toshio in order to confirm my estimates.[102]

In any event, tax protest was itself a complex and diverse phenomenon, and it ranged from illegal and direct petitioning to domain-wide revolts in which villagers assaulted the whole infrastructure of feudal power. Somewhere in between was the *gōso,* a violent collective action that resembled the tax revolts of seventeenth-century France. According to Stephen Vlastos: "Not all protests in the early Tokugawa period were as peaceful and respectful of authority as direct appeals. Sometimes unruly crowds marched on the lord's castle town and refused to disband until promised satisfaction."[103]

Like the Croquandage of rural France, violence in the gōso was a medium of representation that allowed the village to establish a clear claim to a sphere of autonomous jurisdiction in which the feudal lord ought not to intervene. In the estimation of Scheiner, this notion of village autonomy from at least some forms of feudal power was expressed within the discourse of a "covenant" ideology that portrayed lordship as legitimate only as long as it was benevolent.[104] Scheiner argues:

98. Scheiner, "Benevolent Lords and Honorable Peasants," esp. 45.
99. Aoki, *Hyakushō ikki no nenjiteki kenkyu,* 36–37.
100. Aoki, *Hyakushō ikki sōyō nenpyo.*
101. Scheiner, "Benevolent Lords and Honorable Peasants," esp. 40–43, 60 n. 24.
102. See n. 5 above.
103. Vlastos, *Peasant Protests and Uprisings,* 59.
104. Scheiner, "The Mindful Peasant," 579–91.

Rural Protests, 1601–1867

	Number	Average number per year
1601–1650	209	4.2
1651–1700	211	4.2
1701–1750	422	8.4
1751–1800	670	13.4
1801–1850	814	16.3
1851–1867	374	22

Source: Kōji Aoki, Hyakushō ikki no nenjiteki kenkyu (Tokyo: Shin'seisha, 1966), 36–37.

Implicit in the traditional sense of the covenant is the idea that the well-being of a society cannot simply be based on socially organized force.

This principle was understood in Japan. Lords such as Matsudaira Sadanobu in the late eighteenth century, much influenced by Neo-Confucianism, spoke of the necessity of the moral duties of the just and benevolent lord (jinkun), and the importance of establishing moral priorities for his benevolent rule (Jinsei).[105]

Evidently, ordinary villagers understood this principle as cogently as their rulers did, and many of the revolts of the Tokugawa period were informed by a demand for benevolent rule. Often this was accompanied by very specific demands for tax reductions or remissions, but the call for benevolence indicated a popular commitment to a practical theory of the rights of the village as a community. Once again, Scheiner makes this point quite well:

Peasants sought justice and reason, or ri; they criticized harsh actions of the domain as an injustice, or mutai. A peasant rebel leader in Mimasaka in 1726 defied lower officials of the domain, since, as he said, "they broke rei," or rites and propriety, and betrayed michi, or the Way. He described this break with propriety as "the origin of the peasants' uprising." As used by Matsudaira Sadanobu, rei signified the importance of the ruler as well as the ruled, and thus the regulation of the use of material resources for each according to his status. It also indicated the limits of arbitrary actions of the ruler, since his authority was not ultimate but inherited from heaven through his ancestors, and his right to partake of it came from the practice of virtuous rule. Rule by status, therefore, assigned certain roles of servitude to the peasant, but quite clearly it also implied that status rights of peasants as well as ruler would be honored. When peasants were referred to as onbyakushō, peasants of the domain . . . the lord acknowledged that by right of their status as peasants of his domain they could count on his adherence to certain promises.[106]

105. Scheiner, "Benevolent Lords and Honorable Peasants," esp. 46.
106. Ibid., 47.

It is correct, therefore, to argue that ordinary villagers saw feudal authority as limited by the collective rights of the village, in spite of the absence of formal institutions of popular representation. Japanese feudalism had a strong undertone of arbitrary power and aristocratic privilege, and many feudal lords may have regarded rural commoners as little more than a source of revenue.[107] Yet the record does not support the belief that rural commoners passively accepted the pretensions of the feudal elite. After all, Tokugawa rural commoners called themselves *onbyakushō*, honorable people who should have a dignified and secure status at the base of the feudal hierarchy.[108]

The significance of taxation as a source of rural unrest in Tokugawa Japan may strike some readers as paradoxical. Smith has provided impressive evidence that the real material burden on the village caused by taxation has been exaggerated.[109] Nominal tax rates could range up to 50 percent or more of total village production, and the fact that nengu was often paid in kind interfered with the ability of cultivators to take advantage of periodic episodes of monetary inflation.[110] Yet tax assessments, measured in kokudaka, were rarely adjusted upward after they had been established, nor were they revised to take account of the reclamation of new arable and the growing productivity of family labor. Taxation was a real material burden, but it may have become less significant as a share of rural output as the Tokugawa period neared the nineteenth century.[111] In effect, an ever larger share of the village harvest was untaxed, something that could not have been overlooked by village farmers. According to Smith:

> In many villages the land tax and komononari [supplementary taxes] were static or even declined slightly, although the productivity of land was generally rising. Thus a larger and larger surplus was left by these two taxes in the hands of peasants. . . .
>
> Other types of taxes may have reduced the "surplus," but the reduction was probably not drastic in most cases. The facts of this matter are, of course, obscure. But no one doubts that other taxes were quantitatively much less significant than the land tax, and there was necessarily a tendency to hold them within limits tolerable to the average peasant family. They were therefore unlikely to have offset entirely the increment that accrued to improving peasants from the combination of rising yields and a static land tax; in no case would they have canceled the comparative advantage of such peasants.
>
> It seems likely that for many peasant families in the Tokugawa period farming paid—for some it may even have paid handsomely by the standard of the times.[112]

107. Hall, *Government and Local Power in Japan*.
108. Scheiner, "Benevolent Lords and Honorable Peasants," esp. 47.
109. Smith, *Native Sources of Japanese Industrialization*, 50–70.
110. Kelly, *Deference and Defiance*, 3, 187–205.
111. See Hanley and Yamamura, *Economic and Demographic Change in Preindustrial Japan*, 91–198.
112. Thomas C. Smith, "The Land Tax in the Tokugawa Period," in Smith, *Native Sources of Japanese Industrialization*, 69.

Why, then, did taxation figure so prominently in the grievances of rural rebels in the Tokugawa period? A simple materialist explanation that sees tax revolts as mechanically linked to economic hardship scarcely fits the facts of the case. We need a more subtle interpretive framework.

First, taxation was a permanent problem from the standpoint of village cohesion. Taxes were the collective responsibility of the community, but households were not taxed equally.[113] The household's tax bill depended on the size of its holdings, the quality of its land and labor, and its ability to take advantage of economic change.[114] A well-off household might pay a real tax bill much below its nominal assessment, while a poorer family would pay a much larger real share of its harvest to the tax collector. This was a situation ripe for endless conflicts over who should pay how much of the tax bill, and especially in bad harvest years the solidarity of the village must have been strained as more and less advantaged households struggled over the question of which families should shoulder the major part of the burden.[115] It must have been obvious, however, that the real source of this threat to community cohesion lay with the lord's administration rather than the vicissitudes of village fortunes. Why not strike at the root of the problem by demanding a reduction or even cancellation of the year's taxes? If the lord capitulated, and there was at least the possibility that he would, this year's temporary gains might be turned into customary rights that the lord would not dare infringe.[116] In any event, the solidarity and honor of the village would be preserved, and well-off households who participated in village revolts could point to their involvement as a vindication of their obligations to the community.[117]

A second and perhaps more important source of popular discontent concerning taxation can be explained in terms of the logic of elite forces of constraint presented in earlier chapters. I have argued that European aristocracies displayed a dual character: they claimed a right to rule on the basis of the "protective" functions they performed for ordinary people, yet they also claimed unilateral and unchecked power over the countryside. When their protective role began to wane they found themselves increasingly vulnerable to the charge of parasitism, and rural communities could easily turn against a landed elite that was imperious enough to take much and give little in return.

This logic, I believe, captures the predicament of the Japanese samurai during the long years of the Tokugawa peace. Divorced from the land and deprived of any real opportunity to use their martial skills, the samurai had become an urban elite of officials and leisured gentlemen, whose real contact with the countryside was

---

113. Ibid., 50–70.
114. Also see Yamamura, "The Meiji Land Tax Reform and Its Effects," 382–99.
115. Smith, *Agrarian Origins of Modern Japan*, 180–85.
116. Vlastos, *Peasant Protests and Uprisings*, 21–41.
117. This set of circumstances, I think, explains the "village martyr," the good headman who sacrificed himself for the "whole" of the village.

limited to the problem of taxation.[118] In short, whatever protective division of labor had once characterized the relations between villagers and samurai had evaporated after the Tokugawa victory, and it would not be surprising if village commoners began to view samurai privileges as a parasitic imposition on the village. Aristocratic domination was, therefore, the chief threat to community autonomy and cohesion. It intruded in the form of taxes that undercut village institutions, and it was constantly enacted through the rigid rules of hereditary privilege claimed by the samurai elite. That elite was committed to the subjection of the village to aristocratic power; it was committed to the creation of a Japanese peasantry made up of captive communities that would exist to serve the will of the aristocratic elite. But this vision became increasingly difficult to sustain as villagers learned how to oppose the pretensions of their overlords.[119] The key expression of that opposition was the tax revolt. Although willing to petition for redress, the village was also willing to use force in order to draw boundaries around aristocratic power.

Interestingly, some support for this interpretation can be found in the work of intellectual historians, especially Tetsuo Najita and Harry Harootunian. They have shown how novel intellectual movements in the later Tokugawa period provided a new discourse for rural commoners that challenged the rigidly hierarchical constructs of neo-Confucian orthodoxy, the intellectual foundation of samurai power. For example, the school known as *kokugaku,* or school of native learning, sought to recover an authentic Japanese conceptual language rooted in ordinary life. According to Harootunian, rural commoners could use kokugaku as a basis for legitimating the autonomy of the village, because it focused on agriculture rather than aristocratic power as the true foundation of the realm.[120] Similarly, the Tokugawa period saw the proliferation of practical farming manuals and village schools, both of which emphasized the dignity and centrality of agricultural life. Increasingly, villagers could draw on all these unorthodoxies as a support for their vision of a fully autonomous village free from feudal power. Harootunian, for example, has written of kokugaku:

> Thus kokugaku, in its rural appropriation, sanctioned the elevation of the village as substitute for the whole, just as phenomenal life merely called attention to its noumenal and hidden origins. The argument for an autonomous village standing for the whole, apart or separated from the world of public authority, was authenticated by appeals to the Izumo versions of mytho-history. Much of it hinged upon the duty to return blessings to the creation deities from which all things literally flowed, and the subsequent obligation to replicate the archetypal creative acts through agricultural

118. Hall, *Government and Local Power in Japan,* 330–74.
119. Vlastos, *Peasant Protests and Uprisings,* 42–72.
120. Tetsuo Najita, *Visions of Virtue in Tokugawa Japan: The Kaitokudo Merchant Academy of Osaka* (Chicago: University of Chicago Press, 1987); Harootunian, *Things Seen and Unseen,* 1, 17, 25–33, 218–325.

work and reproduction. This duty was invariably described as a form of entrustment (yosashi, mi-yosashi). . . .

Late Tokugawa kokugakusha (invariably village leaders) such as Miyahiro Sadao and Hirayama Chūeimon saw the idea of entrustment as a means of emphasizing the central importance of agricultural life, not to mention their own position in such a world. . . . The upshot was increasingly to see kokugaku as a method for solving problems in the countryside. Such a method was dramatized in this conception of caring, assistance, and mutual aid, which also could be justified under the aspect of entrustment; in the end, entrustment so conceived became grounds for village self-sufficiency and secession.[121]

It is revealing that kokugaku thinkers talked about "entrustment"; it may indicate that kokugaku spread partly because of its deep affinities with the notion of property and power as trusteeship that I have argued was central to the Japanese village.[122] Like Spanish anarchism, kokugaku made sense as a defense of community against an entrenched outside elite. But, whatever the case, late Tokugawa life was marked by growing dissatisfaction with feudal rule, and village commoners could find a variety of discourses to support their opposition to aristocratic domination.[123]

Another form of opposition to feudal power was the *yonaoshi*, a violent movement of "world renewal" that drew on millenarian themes in its confrontation with the status quo.[124] Although yonaoshi episodes apparently took place even in the early Tokugawa period, they evidently became more frequent in the late eighteenth and nineteenth centuries as feudal authority weakened. In yonaoshi, villagers rebelled against both feudal power and "greedy or avaricious" individuals who violated local conceptions of justice and propriety.[125] Yonaoshi were often accompanied, therefore, by uchikowashi, but they differed in terms of their scale, violence, and radicalism. Sometimes engulfing whole domains, yonaoshi revolts demanded nothing less than a reconstitution of the position of rural society in Japan. As Scheiner argues:

> Yonaoshi revolts, therefore, represented a more drastic revision of peasants' sense of ordering the world. . . . Peasants initially waited on their lord's judgment and his explanation for not redressing evil. "Can someone give us a reasonable explanation?" they asked. "So far we have had none." But they quickly deemed themselves

121. Harry Harootunian, "Ideology as Conflict," in Najita and Koschmann, *Conflict in Modern Japanese History*, 50–51.

122. Smith, *Native Sources of Japanese Industrialization*, 199–235.

123. Harootunian, *Things Seen and Unseen*, 218–325; Tetsuo Najita, "Method and Analysis in the Conceptual Portrayal of Tokugawa Intellectual History," in Najita and Scheiner, *Japanese Thought in the Tokugawa Period*, 3–38.

124. George Wilson, "Pursuing the Millennium in the Meiji Restoration," in Najita and Koschmann, *Conflict in Modern Japanese History*, 176–94, esp. 184–88.

125. Vlastos, *Peasant Protests and Uprisings*, 142–53.

"righteous men" and outlined objectives much broader than the simpler redress of past evils. In the same way Murayama [domain] rebels wanted to "save the poor." Both rebel movements acted to "punish the unrighteous," but the Chichubu [domain] peasants also "would help the poverty-stricken people of Japan." In both cases their direct hostility was aimed at the "merciless and greedy"; they would "get" or "slay" the greedy "puffed up in vanity who treat us as dogs or horses."[126]

Historians like Vlastos and Sasaki have seen the yonaoshi as somehow flowing from the logic of class antagonism, largely because the rebels attacked headmen, merchants, and usurers in typical episodes of "smashing and breaking."[127] My interpretation, however, is quite different and follows the logic of community defense that we have seen at work in earlier revolts. I suggest that we see the yonaoshi revolts as movements of community "secession" in which villagers acted to "rectify" all the abuses that had threatened the autonomy and cohesion of the village community. By taking up arms the yonaoshi rebels signaled a determination to withdraw or secede from the decaying feudal order.[128] It is interesting that the rebels drew on the millenarian teachings of Maitreya Buddhism with its emphasis on rebirth and renovation, and the expression of rebel beliefs in this deeply religious idiom shows that the rebels saw themselves as ushering in a new world cleansed of the feudal past.[129]

Moreover, the yonaoshi revolts were fragmented and highly particularistic.[130] They rarely flowed over the boundaries of a single domain, and they did not form parts of a single national "peasant" movement. For example, in Aizu domain, the rebels concentrated on rectifying village government by ejecting village headmen and replacing them with more worthy candidates, thereby revealing how important the integrity of the village was in the minds of the rebels. In other domains, however, tax protests and violent direct action against the feudal elite also occurred. As Vlastos points out:

> The Aizu peasant movement was only one of many yonaoshi-type movements in the closing years of the Tokugawa period. Most of the large uprisings occurred in eastern and northeastern Japan between 1866 and 1869. It is easier to draw valid generalizations concerning the social and economic character of the uprisings than about their political character. The common characteristic of all of the uprisings was attacks by poor peasants against the wealthy peasant elite, but the political character of the uprisings varied considerably from locality to locality. On the whole the uprisings that occurred in 1868–1869 within the context of the civil war and the visible collapse of daimyo rule, as in Aizu, Echigo, and Kōzuke, were primarily rebellions against the

126. Scheiner, "Benevolent Lords and Honorable Peasants," 57.
127. Sasaki, "Yonaoshi nojokyō," 87–112; and Sasaki, Yonaoshi (Tokyo: Sai'nich, 1979). Also see Vlastos, Peasant Protests and Uprisings, 141–67.
128. For the concept of "secession," see Harootunian, "Ideology as Conflict," 25–61.
129. Scheiner, "Benevolent Lords and Honorable Peasants," 56–59.
130. Vlastos, Peasant Protests and Uprisings, 142–67.

political authority of the village elite, whereas the uprisings in Shindatsu and Bushu in 1866 resembled Tokugawa period gōso, though with millenarian overtones.[131]

It is significant that Vlastos, although committed to class analysis, admits that political issues rather than simple class struggle underlay the yonaoshi, even in cases like Aizu, where village leaders were attacked. It does not seem unreasonable to conclude that the yonaoshi rebels were trying to reinforce the integrity of community institutions by punishing villagers who had withdrawn from the controls and obligations of the village. As Vlastos concludes in his study of the Aizu events, "The 'world' of the revolutionary peasant movement in Aizu was the village and not the state."[132]

A useful analogy from Russian history will help to clarify the point. In 1917, when Russian villages attacked all the constraints that threatened the village, among their targets were the so-called separators, the village households who had physically and socially withdrawn from the land commune in the wake of the Stolypin reforms. They were attacked because they had violated the institutional integrity of the village, and they were forced to return to village membership. It is possible that a very similar logic came into play during the yonaoshi rebellions. Villagers acted as communities in their struggle with "greedy and avaricious" households who had turned away from their communities. By smashing their targets' property, ordinary villagers demonstrated that the village was the ultimate source of legitimate power and property rights.

Like earlier tax revolts, therefore, the yonaoshi uprisings can be understood as examples of representative violence. Violence was not simply an expression of "primitive" or "atavistic" minds. It was a medium of community politics that literally represented community households against the specific individuals who had violated community institutions.[133] To be sure, yonaoshi rebels gained an additional measure of radicalism from a millenarian worldview, just as the Bauernkrieg rebels gained moral reinforcement from radical Protestantism. But we should beware of reducing the yonaoshi to a "moment of madness"; whatever we ultimately decide about its class composition, the yonaoshi formed but one part of a long tradition of rural politics and protest. Rural unrest continued into the Meiji and Taisho periods, and tenant unrest and "popular rights" movements kept the problem of the village at the center of the political agenda into the 1930s.[134]

131. Vlastos, "Yonaoshi in Aizu," in Najita and Koschmann, Conflict in Japanese History, 164–76, quotation on 167, n. 7; and see Sipple, "Popular Protest in Early Modern Japan."

132. Vlastos, "Yonaoshi in Aizu," 174.

133. Scheiner, "The Mindful Peasant."

134. See, for the post-Tokugawa period, Roger Bowen, Rebellion and Democracy in Meiji Japan: A Study of Commoners in the Popular Rights Movement (Berkeley: University of California Press, 1980), esp. chaps. 1 and 2; and Thomas R. H. Havens, Farm and Nation in Modern Japan: Agrarian Nationalism, 1870–1940 (Princeton: Princeton University Press, 1974).

Locating Culture

The years of Tokugawa peace allowed Japanese elites to develop a highly distinctive culture that helped to set the stage for Japan's plunge into the industrial world. It would be absurd to deny the many ways in which Japanese culture diverged widely from the West.[135] Religious sentiments, attitudes toward loyalty and politics, even the aesthetic sensibilities of a deeply Buddhist society—all these dimensions of elite values and discourse differed fundamentally from their Western counterparts. There is, for instance, no exact analogue of the Japanese imperial house with its profound combination of hereditary continuity and sacred authority.[136]

Yet, popular rural society can be shown to share a common institutional logic with the agrarian West, even if we break with class analysis. The problem of producing and distributing the means of existence seems to have led to many of the same problems of territorial organization and community membership that were at work in Europe. Moreover, Japan had a "peasantry," but not in the usual sense of the term. Japan had a powerful aristocratic elite that was able to construct a long-lived but contested mode of political domination of the countryside. The institutions of domination that made samurai rule possible defined the Japanese peasantry. But beneath those institutions were partly autonomous and cohesive village communities that were capable of surviving in the absence of samurai power. The tension and ambiguity in this situation is neatly captured by the term *onbyakushō*, or honorable peasant. When Japanese villagers used this form of self-identification, it signaled their unwillingness to accept servility and degradation, the two logical end points of uncontested aristocratic power.[137] In short, the Japanese village resisted its transformation into a peasantry in the usual sense of the term, and that resistance was a political rather than a merely economic fact.

At least in preindustrial rural societies, ordinary rural people thus may have shared more with their counterparts in other societies than they shared with the elites who ruled them. Ordinary people had a common institutional and existential predicament that was ultimately related to the logic of agriculture. Ironically, however, that logic did not lead toward the development of national or even supralocal peasant classes. Instead, it cut in exactly the opposite direction, toward territorial particularism and a profound suspicion of outsiders, a rational response to rural life.

Elites, especially powerful landed elites, had both the resources and the incentive to become cultural innovators. They could afford to adopt new fashions and ideas, and they had the leisure to create a written culture that could emphasize

135. See, for example, Marius B. Jansen, ed., *Changing Japanese Attitudes toward Modernization* (Princeton: Princeton University Press, 1965).
136. Carol Gluck, *Japan's Modern Myths* (Princeton: Princeton University Press, 1985), 73–101.
137. Ooms, *Tokugawa Ideology*, 110, 143–51, 293–95.

precisely those rarefied differences that would eventually congeal into national traditions. Moreover, landed elites had a potent institutional incentive to differentiate themselves from ordinary people. They claimed to rule by a special dispensation, and they had every interest in marking themselves off in speech and dress from the "rustics" they ruled. As Jack Goody has shown, this kind of social marking could even take the form of special elite cuisines that eventually became the basis for "national" cooking styles.[138]

We must therefore consider the possibility that what we now think of as national cultures can be traced to the inventions and innovations of elites, who had both the means and the need to create a distinct cultural style. That style should not be seen simply as abstract categories in a larger cognitive map; it should be understood in terms of the institutions and performances that carved up social and political space in particular ways. For example, to be a samurai was more than a state of mind; more yet than the spirit of *bushido,* or martial valor. It was an ongoing exhibition of status and power that almost consciously exaggerated the social distance between samurai and commoners.

Popular culture is not, of course, an unimportant or uninteresting category. We have seen on many occasions how the ritual and discourse of rural communities gave focus to everyday life. We require no functionalist analysis to explain the importance of the ideas and identities that emerged out of the folklore of place. We need only point to their existence as part of the institutional architecture of community organization, and, as anthropologists have done, we can then begin to read the "text" of what David Sabean has called village discourse in order to evaluate its particular significance.[139] From such a viewpoint, we can ask more focused questions about popular culture, which combine the specificity of ethnography and the broad agenda of comparative research. Why, for example, did the Japanese village develop a "martyrology" of sacrifice, and how did that influence the behavior of Japanese communities? How did this differ in its logic from rural Christian cults in Europe, and what do those differences mean for the trajectory of agrarian history in the two cases? These are the kinds of issues that can link anthropology, history, and comparative research in a common project that cuts across the somewhat stale debates about generalization versus case-specific description.

The concept of culture is too valuable to lose, and this volume should not be read as a simplistic attack on culture and its supporters. But we need to rethink the concept to meet the kinds of challenges and paradoxes that a close examination of culture exposes. We have become too used to arguing about culture as if it were an all-or-nothing proposition. Either culture is a single, national system that explains

---

138. Jack Goody, *Cooking, Cuisine, and Class: A Study in Comparative Sociology* (Cambridge: Cambridge University Press, 1982), 10–40, 191–215.

139. David Warren Sabean, *Power in the Blood: Popular Culture and Village Discourse in Early Modern Germany* (Cambridge: Cambridge University Press, 1984), 1–36.

key behavior, or it is an empty category that can be reduced to ideology or insignificance. Surely this way of viewing the matter is too crude, and we need to break with this sort of dichotomous argument if we are to gain a clearer understanding of what culture is about. As the historical events in Japan show, supposedly monolithic national cultures may mask a significant plurality of cultural voices. More important, there may be deep cultural similarities, at least at the level of rural society, that cut across the boundaries of national states. We need to know more about these similarities and much more about the conditions in which they are subject to change. In the end, we may discover that culture is a more basic category than we had thought, although that discovery cannot be made without prior reconceptualization.

CHAPTER 9

The Limits of Community

Autonomy, Cohesion, and the Dissolution of Community

Small-scale rural societies are characterized by two basic problems that jointly influence rural institutions. First, all rural societies must be able to produce and distribute the means of subsistence according to rules that apportion rights and responsibilities to the harvest. Second, the organization of territory is a basic part of any stable set of such rules. Land and labor must be coordinated in a determinate pattern, and territorial rules of membership serve to allocate a stable relationship between people, production, and the agricultural cycle. Community institutions based on hierarchical networks of reciprocal interaction, communities of grain, can be understood as at least one mode of organizing agricultural space. These community institutions cut across what we usually think of as economics, politics, and culture. But this interlinkage should not be thought of as a "system" or systematic whole. Each arena or realm of community life is implicated in all others, and the interaction among institutions strongly shapes the kinds of conflict and cooperation that can occur. For example, the dependence of rural households on the economic, political, and ritual cooperation of neighboring households strongly reinforced their willingness to support the community as a whole, even during times of crisis. Perhaps the most striking illustration of this was the willingness of whole villages to revolt, in both Europe and Japan.[1]

Still, community institutions should not be thought of as monolithic and unchanging. Communities change in response to historical forces; for instance, enclosure changed the character of the English rural community. And commu-

1. See Friedrich Katz, ed., *Riot, Rebellion, and Revolution* (Princeton: Princeton University Press, 1988), esp. Friedrich Katz, "Introduction: Rural Revolt in Mexico," 3–20, and John Coatsworth, "Patterns of Rural Rebellion in Latin America: Mexican Comparative Perspective," 21–62.

nities vary historically and comparatively: the impoverished communities of southern Spain differ markedly from the more robust villages of Russia.

We can, then, distinguish among communities in terms of their varying patterns of autonomy and cohesion.[2] Autonomy and cohesion may vary independently, as was true in southern Spain, but we might expect them to be closely associated in most cases. For instance, the medieval English village seems to have combined a relatively high degree of cohesion with broad autonomy in the determination of manorial custom.

A complete theory of rural community should be able to show the causal factors that determine the balance of autonomy and cohesion, and it should also be able to explain variations in community politics that result from various mixes of that balance. Although this is clearly an area for future research, the information provided in the case studies in the preceding chapters does allow for some interesting generalizations about the possible forms of community life. In order to simplify the discussion I will concentrate on the issue of property rights, even though this is only one dimension of community that might be selected.[3]

First, community institutions with the largest measure of autonomy and cohesion should be found in societies where the community is the effective owner of productive property. In Russia the village mir, or *obshichina,* was the locus of proprietorship over land and labor; similarly, in parts of Mexico, the village exercised ownership long before the land reforms of the 1930s.[4] In both cases community institutions limited the ability of households to break with community practices, whether for reasons of economic advantage or factional conflict. More important, the community as a whole periodically reassigned rights to productive property among its member households; this sort of episodic intervention underpinned the significance of community membership for the survival of the family. We may refer to institutional arrangements of this kind as redistributive communities, because they formed the basic mechanisms through which flowed the resources necessary for agricultural production.

---

2. Earlier community-focused concepts that approximate my own include George M. Foster, "Peasant Society and the Image of Limited Good," in Jack M. Potter, et al., eds., *Peasant Society: A Reader* (Boston: Little, Brown, 1967), 300–323; Eric R. Wolf, "Closed Corporate Peasant Communities in Mesoamerica and Central Java," *Southwestern Journal of Anthropology* 13 (1957), 1–18. Also see the recent discussion in A. Douglas Kincaid, "Peasant into Rebels: Community and Class in Rural El Salvador," *Comparative Studies of Society and History* 29 (3) (1987), 466–94.

3. See Douglas C. North, *Structure and Change in Economic History* (New York: Norton, 1981), 3–44. Also see the important essays in Jules S. Coleman, *Markets, Morals, and the Law* (Cambridge: Cambridge University Press, 1988), esp. 28–66, 153–201.

4. Katz, *Riot, Rebellion, and Revolution,* esp. John Tutino, "Agrarian Social Change and Peasant Rebellion in Nineteenth-Century Mexico: The Example of Chalco," 95–140; Evelyn Hu-DeHart, "Peasant Rebellion in the Northwest: The Yaqui Indians of Sonora, 1740–1976," 141–75; Eric VanYoung, "Moving toward Revolt: Agrarian Origins of the Hidalgo Rebellion in the Guadalajara Region," 176–204; and William B. Taylor, "Banditry and Insurrection: Revolutionary Unrest in Central Jalisco, 1790–1816," 205–46.

Second, many of the societies we have considered struck an institutional balance between household proprietorship and community control. We may call these regulative communities, since community practices regulated what owner households could do with their land and labor. For example, in the common-field village, families owned land, and in some cases they could buy and sell property rights.[5] The village as a whole, however, regulated the agricultural cycle and controlled such matters as common grazing and gleaning. We should expect community institutions of this type to fall somewhere toward the center of a continuum ranked according to autonomy and cohesion. The community is still the focus of definition and enforcement of property rights, but ultimate ownership has been vested in households, which have greater autonomy in controlling agricultural practices. Nevertheless, they remain tied to the fate of the community, and their security is closely linked to the survival of community institutions.

Finally, we can identify a range of residual communities in which local institutions play a marginal and episodic role in the allocation of productive property. In late-nineteenth-century England the village was only a residual source of authoritative rules, and property law was generated by Parliament and the courts.[6] The village still formed an important source of identity, but its practical autonomy and cohesion were probably low. In this sort of context we have reached the limits of the concept of community, and beyond this point community will no longer work as an explanatory category.

If my division of communities into redistributive, regulative, and residual categories makes sense, we must ask an important question: What are the factors that account for the range of variation among communities; and can we arrive at a parsimonious explanation of why communities can be located at distinct points on the continuum?[7]

The key, I think, lies with the elite forces of constraint. Most of the strong communities examined in this book were located in societies in which entrenched landed elites tried to rule the countryside through authoritarian relations of domination and submission. They tried, in effect, to capture community institutions through a combination of coercion and social distance. As a result, they continually threatened the survival of local institutions, although they rarely had sufficient power to eliminate a realm of popular power and politics outside of their effective control. In southern Spain, for example, the latifundia, or great estate, never eliminated the pueblo as a focus of ordinary life.[8]

5. Carl Dahlman, *The Open-Field System and Beyond: Social Change and Agrarian England, 1660–1900* (Cambridge: Cambridge University Press, 1980), esp. 1–15, 93–145.

6. See K. D. M. Snell, *Annals of the Labouring Poor: Social Change and Agrarian England, 1660–1900* (Cambridge: Cambridge University Press, 1985), 138–227.

7. See Craig Calhoun, *The Question of Class Struggle: Social Foundations of Popular Radicalism during the Industrial Revolution* (Chicago: University of Chicago Press, 1982), 149–82.

8. See Julian Pitt-Rivers, *The People of the Sierra* (New York: Criterion Books, 1954).

Ironically, therefore, community institutions may have been strongest in societies in which local communities had the least measure of practical control over the exercise of elite power. In these societies ordinary people had a strong incentive to cling to community institutions as a source of security and status. More than subsistence was at stake; community defined the only "safe" territorial arena in which rural men and women could exercise effective power over their lives. Moreover, local institutions offered the one certain set of arrangements through which elite power and demands could be resisted. Far from being "unnatural" or imposed from above, the territorial community was a genuinely popular expression of the ongoing problems of agrarian life.[9]

To be sure, landed elites often traded protection and patronage for a presumptive right to rule.[10] But the "services" elites provided were not effectively accountable to popular control; they depended on a shifting and uncertain balance of local power that was always subject to revision. How could ordinary people know if the manor lord or the tax collector would keep his promises? How, indeed, could they know if today's benefits might not turn into tomorrow's threats and burdens? They could not, because they lacked effective and permanent institutions that would hold elites accountable, even when elite and popular interests came into conflict. No amount of patronage or paternalism could change the fact that supralocal elites were potentially dangerous outsiders, whose commitment to domination reinforced the significance of the reciprocal hierarchies of community life. At least one had some certainty about the role and responsibilities of the village headmen or the local elders, and they could be held accountable for their actions as long as they were embedded in local networks of cooperation.[11]

The implications for the dissolution of community are clear. First, community institutions will remain the focus of popular life as long as there are no effective representative institutions through which outside elites can be held regularly accountable to popular interests. Once such representative mediations have appeared they can constitute the basis for a complete redefinition of the relations underpinning rural society. Ordinary rural people need no longer fear that their cooperation with outsiders will lead to their entrapment by elites they cannot control, and the expansion of effective accountability means that community institutions no longer provide the only certain source of politial security. For example, community members need no longer fear that their opposition to community practices will lead to disaster; they can even withdraw from community membership without facing the possibility of being manipulated by unchecked

---

9. See, for example, Susan Reynolds, *Kingdoms and Communities in Western Europe, 900–1300* (Oxford: Clarendon Press, 1984), 79–154.

10. James C. Scott, "The Erosion of Patron-Client Bonds and Social Change in Rural Southeast Asia," *Journal of Asian Studies* 32 (Nov. 1972), 5–38.

11. For reciprocity generally, see Marshall Sahlins, *Stone Age Economics* (Chicago: Aldine-Atherton, 1972), 149–275.

elite power. In short, community begins to become residual when there are alternative networks of power that allow ordinary rural households to control supralocal elites.[12]

Second, community loses its significance for popular life when there are extracommunity arrangements for the definition and enforcement of property rights more stable and secure than the institutions of local communities. It is unsurprising that property rights are so important in rural societies, because they affect the capacity of every household to survive across generations. But in many rural societies the only certain and accountable source of property rights is the local community; elite definitions of property are too remote and too precarious to become the basis for stable expectations. When the institutions of supralocal power become more effective in guaranteeing enforceable property rights for ordinary households, however, we should expect the situation to change radically. Ordinary people will no longer have a permanent interest in defending community practices; instead, they will have an equal or greater interest in supporting the supralocal arrangements that are central to the acquisition and transmission of property. For example, in early modern England and postrevolutionary France, rural families found the courts and law of the nation-state increasingly useful in securing the proprietary interests of their households, and novel institutions like the Napoleonic Code became a more certain guarantor of family interests than the village.[13] I would argue that it was exactly at this point that the logic of the community of grain began to dissolve.

The community of grain should not be expected to disappear before the appearance of supralocal institutions that represent the interests and enforce the property rights of ordinary rural households. But the establishment of such institutions is an intrinsically political process; it involves nothing less than a fundamental alteration of the relations between rulers and ruled. It cannot, therefore, be predicted on the basis of economic or cultural change alone. Other conditions may or may not be important, but the development of responsible and accountable institutions of elite power is a *necessary* condition for the transformation of the logic of community.

The emergence of an accountable elite, however, does not explain the factors that lead to redistributive communities in some contexts and regulative communities in others. Here I can only appeal to the specific histories of the various societies in which these two forms of community have appeared. For example, the conditions that led to the Russian land commune are deeply tied to the geopolitical and economic specifics of Russian history, especially the late and failed expansion

12. See Joel Migdal, *Strong Societies and Weak States: State-Society Relations and State Capabilities in the Third World* (Princeton: Princeton University Press, 1988), 52–72, 259–77.

13. Jack Goody et al., eds., *Family and Inheritance: Rural Society in Western Europe, 1200–1800* (Cambridge: Cambridge University Press, 1976), esp. Jack Goody, Introduction, 1–9, and V. G. Kiernan, "Private Property in History," 361–98.

of rural commerce. Similarly, the combination of household property and community regulation in the west of Europe had much to do with the spread of popular Christianity and the characteristics of the three-field system.[14] These are not the kinds of factors that can be deductively established, and I would argue that the range of variation at this level is so great that it makes hazardous any generalizations aimed at the community level. Political factors, on the other hand, show much greater uniformity across societies.[15]

Three linked hypotheses clearly state the argument put forth in this section:

1. Stable redistributive and regulative communities are most likely to persist in societies with weak supralocal representative institutions and precarious or uncertain supralocal property rights.

2. Conversely, residual communities are most likely to appear in societies in which supralocal elites are held effectively accountable to representative institutions, and community institutions are less effective than national institutions in defining and enforcing the property rights of ordinary rural households.

3. Hypothesis 1 is most likely and hypothesis 2 is least likely in societies dominated by landed aristocracies or bureaucratic elites that are unaccountable to popular control. (Hypothesis 3 follows from the logic of aristocratic and bureaucratic domination discussed in earlier chapters; indeed, the very existence of an aristocracy is incompatible with ongoing popular control and supervision.)

Admittedly, a thorough operational use of these hypotheses would require a great deal more specification, but at least they ought to illuminate the precise issues at stake. The application of these hypotheses, even to third-world countries, may help to explain much about the nature of rural politics.

For example, we know that Mexico experienced an extraordinary decade of rural violence and insurrection after 1910, yet it has been difficult to interpret the logic of what occurred.[16] Neither revolutionary nor clearly reactionary, rural revolt after 1910 was highly particularistic and focused on the defense of local interests. According to Alan Knight in his history of the Mexican Revolution:

> The peasant community, be it Indian or Mestizo, was important in providing the cell of revolution, in both classic agrarian and serrano movements. It was not just that forms of communal tenure (whose importance varied greatly from place to place) or corporate civil/religious hierarchies came under sustained attack from engrossing landlords and the expanding state; it was also the case that the very existence of the

14. Jack Goody, *The Development of the Family and Marriage in Europe* (Cambridge: Cambridge University Press, 1983), 6–33, 103–56.
15. See Samuel P. Huntington, *Political Order in Changing Societies* (New Haven: Yale University Press, 1968), esp. 8–71.
16. Katz, *Riot, Rebellion, and Revolution*, esp. 3–62.

community actively facilitated resistance, and that, without such organizational facilities, resistance was at a discount. The community, it could be said, afforded both the casus belli and the modus operandi of the revolutionary war.[17]

Would it be unreasonable to suppose that the communities Knight refers to could be explained in terms of redistributive and regulative communities threatened with a radical loss of autonomy at the hands of unresponsive and irresponsible elites? The picture drawn by Knight bears a remarkable family resemblance to the cases we have examined in Europe and Japan. It seems to indicate that even colonial and postcolonial societies may share a great deal with societies that did not experience colonial domination, at least with regard to the broad problems of political change in the countryside. It is interesting, for example, that rural insurrection in Mexico began to cease after the postrevolutionary governments began to guarantee the property rights of "traditional" communities through "official" land reform and the restitution of *ejidal* (collective) tenure. In addition, the postrevolutionary regimes were forced to grant more effective representation to rural communities through the "corporatist" institutions of the ruling party. Naturally, these concessions did not alleviate rural poverty, nor did they effectively apply to the whole rural population. But, in areas where they were granted, they may have helped to eliminate the causes of rural rebellion *and* undermine the significance of community institutions in the lives of ordinary people.

In any event, I think that the concept of the community of grain can be applied far beyond the range of cases discussed in the previous chapters. At a minimum, I believe that it could be fruitfully applied to Andean Latin America, Mexico, and parts of sub-Saharan Africa and Southeast Asia.[18] Still, the most important point is that the limits and dissolution of rural community may be more a question of politics than a question of world systems or colonial capitalism.

17. Alan Knight, *The Mexican Revolution*, 2 vols. (Cambridge: Cambridge University Press, 1986), 1:158.
18. For Mexico, see ibid., esp. 1:78–170; John Tutino, *From Insurrection to Revolution in Mexico: Social Bases of Agrarian Violence, 1750–1940* (Princeton: Princeton University Press, 1986); Katz, *Riot, Rebellion, and Revolution;* and Arturo Warman, *"We Come to Object": The Peasants of Morelos and the National State* (Baltimore: Johns Hopkins University Press, 1980). For the Andes, see Florencia E. Mallon, *The Defense of Community in Peru's Central Highlands: Peasant Struggle and Capitalist Transition, 1860–1940* (Princeton: Princeton University Press, 1983); Karen Spaulding, *Huarochini: An Andean Society* (Stanford: Stanford University Press, 1984); Steve Stern, ed., *Resistance, Rebellion, and Consciousness in the Andean Peasant World, 18th to 20th Centuries* (Madison: University of Wisconsin Press, 1988). For Southeast Asia, see Robert Jay, *Javanese Villagers: Social Relations in Rural Modjokuto* (Cambridge: MIT Press, 1969); Clifford Geertz, *The Religion of Java* (Glencoe, Ill.: Free Press, 1960); and Anthony Reid, *Southeast Asia in the Age of Commerce, 1450–1680*, vol. 1 (New Haven: Yale University Press, 1988). For Africa, see David Lan, *Guns and Rain: Guerrillas and Spirit Mediums in Zimbabwe* (Berkeley: University of California Press, 1985); and Karen Field, *Revival and Rebellion in Colonial Central Africa* (Princeton: Princeton University Press, 1985).

Rebellion, Representative Violence, and the
Logic of Constitution and Secession

There is no such thing as a generic "peasant" rebellion. It makes little sense to work with an image or metaphor of national peasant classes who rise up in revolt against the whole social order. Those who do work with this image are likely to be disappointed by the evidence, and they may wind up falsely concluding that "peasants," after all, are "classes of low-classness" incapable of concerted, collective action. Recall for example, that even during the French and Russian revolutions—often taken as paradigmatic peasant revolutions—there were no national peasant classes or movements.[19] Yet a great deal happened in the countryside; indeed, the *micro* balance of power was changed forever, even though the many disaggregated revolts that took place did not add up to a revolution in the classic sense.

I have suggested that we should simply stop worrying about the "revolutionary potential of the peasantry" and concentrate on accurately interpreting the logic of rural collective violence. When we do this, however, we are at once faced with an apparent but tractable paradox: we discover what seems to be a curious combination of radicalism and conservatism. Rural rebels offered a radical challenge to one or more of the institutional foundations of elite power. But this challenge was meant to preserve community institutions in the face of elite threats, and many of the institutional practices in question were shot through with hierarchies that would be unacceptable to modern intellectuals. For example, every case we have examined displays very strong traces of patriarchy; even the egalitarian Russian village was a world of paternalism and gerontocracy.[20] Some scholars have seen these hierarchies as a sure sign of the "primitivism" and "atavism" of rural collective violence, but this viewpoint is hopelessly condescending and leads to the kinds of logical paradoxes with which we began.

My own way out of this problem was to interpret the case studies as instances of representative violence. I argued that representative violence can be understood as the violent presentation, or literal re-presentation, of community interests and grievances that center on the preservation of community autonomy and cohesion. From the viewpoint of elite privilege, violence of this kind can be understood only as rebellion or insurrection, because it is a radical (or root-and-branch) challenge to the institutions of elite constraint that underlie elite power in the countryside. From the standpoint of rural communities, however, collective violence was one among a number of modes of community politics that mediated between elite and

19. Here I am following and adopting the logic in Theda Skocpol, *States and Social Revolutions: A Comprehensive Analysis of France, Russia, and China* (Cambridge: Cambridge University Press, 1979).

20. Goody et al., *Family and Inheritance,* esp. Jack Goody, "Inheritance, Property, and Women: Some Comparative Considerations," 10–36.

popular interests. As James C. Scott has shown, traditional rural societies have developed a variety of mechanisms for coping with elite power, and in the case studies we saw that even the most rigid agrarian societies offered at least some modes of "peaceful" redress, although those modes were too uncertain and arbitrary to constitute a permanent and effective mechanism of popular representation.[21] (For example, all the societies we have considered made provisions for popular petitioning of elite authorities, but the problem was that petitions could always be rejected, or in some cases redescribed as subversion.)

I prefer the phrase "representative violence" to "bargaining by riot," because the latter phrase draws on too many misplaced analogies with urban labor movements. Undoubtedly, representative violence involved a large measure of negotiation, but the fact is that violence adds a highly distinctive logic to the expression of popular demands. Violence, to put it bluntly, vastly expands the possibility of escalation and unintended consequences. Innocent or unintended victims may die, elite repression may be so savage as to threaten community survival, and a violent act may set off a long cycle of popular violence and elite counterviolence that neither side desired. In many cases, of course, popular violence may be quite controlled and successful, as was true in France and Russia. Yet collective violence is not a labor strike; violence needs to be understood according to its own logic.

The kinds of collective violence discussed in this book were not simply "distributive" bargaining games that took place within otherwise accepted rules of elite power and popular politics. Instead, the "little" insurrections were about the rules themselves; they were focused on a radical redrawing of the institutional conventions that linked rural communities to supralocal elites. In this sense, they can be seen as a moment during which community members represented themselves in an enactment, or "performance," of fundamental political redefinition that recast the boundaries of community autonomy. Even the English enclosure riot can be interpreted as a war of local social hegemony in which the basic question was clear: Would the lord of the manor or the community have the ultimate power to control community institutions?[22]

Representative violence can be further differentiated into two kinds of community movements: movements of secession and movements of reconstitution. The revolts discussed in this book vary in terms of their goals and consequences, although all of them can be understood as expressions of community defense. In Russia in 1905 and 1917, and in Japan during the yonaoshi uprisings, community violence seems to have led to a secession of whole communities from the networks of elite power. But in England, France, and Spain, representative violence

21. James C. Scott, *Weapons of the Weak* (New Haven: Yale University Press, 1985).

22. For example, see Roger Manning, *Village Revolts: Social Protest and Popular Disturbances in England, 1509–1640* (Oxford: Clarendon Press, 1988).

is probably best understood as an attempt to recast, or reconstitute, the links between local communities and supralocal institutions. For example, English and French villages do not seem to have understood the moment of violence as an occasion for completely withdrawing from the market and the state; instead, they used violence in order to make outside elites and market networks accountable to popular interest.

The difference between representative violence as secession and reconstitution is most strikingly illustrated by the contrasting characteristics of the English enclosure riot and the Russian razgrom. In the enclosure riot there was a good deal of property damage and ritual humiliation, but there was no effort to expel the manor lord and withdraw the community from all supralocal institutions. Rather, the enclosure riot signaled the determination of the community to protect its definition of property *and* hold to account landlords, middlemen, and other outsiders who linked the community to wider social networks. But in the razgrom, or violent "turning upside down," the situation worked out very differently. The local lord, or *barin,* was often physically expelled, his property was demolished completely, and the village simply turned in on itself. As we have seen, it was precisely this secession of the Russian village that left the Bolsheviks with so little room to maneuver after 1917.[23]

But if the distinction between secession and reconstitution makes sense, how can we account for it? Once again, I do not think that any simple theory of modernization, underdevelopment, or capitalist penetration clearly explains the difference. It is true that England was a much more commercial society during the period of enclosure rioting than Russia was during the 1905 and 1917 revolts. Yet, according to some accounts, Russia was already a "late-developing" society by 1905, and Lenin himself saw prerevolutionary Russia as embarked on the same general process of capitalist development that had characterized sixteenth- and seventeenth-century Europe.

One way of cutting through this thicket of conflicting interpretations is to reject the notion that the problem can be reduced to developmental levels and stages and to concentrate instead on the political institutions that underlay the expansion of commercial networks in the countryside. In Russia, the market was imposed on the village by tsarist taxation policies and the unilateral shift to market agriculture on the part of a segment of the landed elite. I have called this coercive commercialization in order to highlight the fact that market networks in this sort of case were marginal to community practices and threatening from the standpoint of community institutions. It would not be surprising if communities faced with this kind of "alien" and imposed market structure would reject supralocal links and try to withdraw into self-sufficiency.

23. Moshe Lewin, *Russian Peasants and Soviet Power: A Study of Collectivization* (Evanston: Northwestern University Press, 1968), 107–97.

To be sure, enclosure in England might also be seen in some instances as coercive commercialization, yet this does not mean that commercialization there was identical to the Russian experience. By the 1500s, ordinary rural commoners in England were involved in complex networks of local and regional exchange over which they could exercise some measure of control.[24] For example, the grain trade could often be worked to the advantage of small farmers, who had considerable discretion in terms of when and where they could sell. In addition, the growth of numerous by-employments and occupational specialties in the countryside reinforced the horizontal market ties between village communities and the larger social order. In contrast to those in Russia, these networks may have been built from below, and they were probably much more subject to community regulation than their Russian counterparts.[25]

Thus, movements of secession are most likely to take place when commercialization occurs "from above" through political coercion and an attack on community institutions. Conversely, commercialization "from below" produces many overlapping horizontal networks of exchange that may enhance the economic welfare of ordinary rural households. In this context, representative violence is more likely to focus on a reconstitution of supralocal institutions, because community members have an interest in preserving their ties to the wider world. Admittedly, this assessment is impressionistic, but it highlights the importance of politics in any theoretical understanding of popular collective violence, particularly in our effort to understand why rural rebellion seems to take on a distinctive logic in different societies.

Finally, a word is in order about the frequency of rural collective violence. Some critics may argue that agrarian rebellion is too rare or episodic to be of any theoretical interest. But to put the matter this way begs a very large question: How many episodes of collective violence must occur before we can say that such behavior is frequent or chronic? To my knowledge, no one has answered this question decisively; indeed, it is all too rarely asked in serious research. Assertions are made, but those assertions are not infrequently lacking in firm conceptual and theoretical foundations.

The compilation of aggregate statistics on the number of rural revolts in different societies is, to be sure, an important task, but it is ultimately of greatest use in answering the comparative question of why some societies had more of such episodes than others. First, however, we must first decide if rural rebellion, or representative violence, is *significant* enough to subject to more sophisticated measures.

---

24. William N. Parker and Eric L. Jones, *European Peasants and Their Markets: Essays in Agrarian Economic History* (Princeton: Princeton University Press, 1975).

25. See Sahlins, *Stone Age Economics*. Also, for coercive commercialization, see Amartya K. Sen, "Starvation and Exchange Entitlements: A General Approach and Its Applications to the Great Bengal Famine," *Cambridge Journal of Economics* 1 (Mar. 1977), 33–59.

Representative violence was *dispositional* in certain kinds of rural societies. Now, "disposition" denotes, among other things, a person's way of acting toward others or thinking about things, and this neatly captures the role of representative violence in the societies we have considered.[26] Such violence was a way of representing community interests in societies where elites were socially distant and politically insulated from most other forms of popular action. It was, of course, not the only way, the everyday way, or the way that most people preferred most of the time. It was probably less frequent than the "silent" forms of resistance identified by James C. Scott, and it did not always succeed (nor, however, did it always fail).[27]

But all these qualifications do not undercut the plausibility of seeing small-scale rebellion as one mode of "doing" politics in authoritarian societies. This follows *not* from the recurrence of the phenomenon, but from the logic of political institutions in the societies considered in this book. In those societies, elites did not see themselves as the representatives of ordinary rural people; they saw themselves as the masters of the countryside who had wide prerogative powers over popular life. Rebellion was one way of bringing this elite to account, and its logic had special force in societies where the relations between elites and ordinary people were probably marked by a net balance of conflict rather than cooperation.

The alternative to this view is a vision of rural rebellion as atavistic, arational, and ultimately inexplicable. After all, if rural rebellion was not a logical response to political conditions it must have been simply a desperate act of rage. But this implies that ordinary rural people did not know what they were doing or why, and in an age that has broken with most forms of the theory of false consciousness, this seems to be a rather incredible position to maintain.

An acceptance of the idea that representative violence was a "disposition" but a denial of its application to the post-1945 period leads to the notion that elites now possess such a preponderance of organized violence that they can easily crush any open revolt, and as a result, representative violence will no longer constitute a logical way of representing community interests. Ultimately, this objection may have real force, but it should be stated in a way that does not work out as a tautology in which people cannot revolt because they do not revolt. Instead, we should carefully investigate the ways in which elites do or do not possess a preponderance of violence, and we should be especially cautious about assuming that "modern" military techniques have rendered popular rebellion meaningless or obsolete. (The word "Vietnam" unfortunately comes to mind here as an inevitable counterexample).[28]

26. This idea is drawn from John R. Searle, *Speech Acts: An Essay in the Philosophy of Language* (London: Cambridge University Press, 1969), esp. 3–21.

27. Scott, *Weapons of the Weak.*

28. See, for example, Alexander B. Woodside, *Community and Revolution in Modern Vietnam* (Boston: Houghton Mifflin, 1976), 109–59.

In any event, even if rebellion is now out of date, the cases discussed in this volume underscore the significance of political institutions in producing the conditions in which collective violence is likely to take place. If collective violence is no longer on the agenda in many parts of the agrarian world, it may have more to do with changes in the logic of politics than it does with changes in economic conditions or coercive technologies. At least this way of stating the issues has the advantage of allowing us to explore rival interpretations in a clear and explicit fashion.

Hypotheses 4–6 state the argument in this section.

4. Representative violence is "dispositional" in societies dominated by landed and bureaucratic elites who are only intermittently and contingently responsive to popular demands. (A marker of this kind of society is a political order in which petitioning is the chief peaceful means of popular redress.) Differences *among* societies in terms of their levels of representative violence, however, should vary as a function of the political institutions through which elite power is exercised. (The greater the degree of elite authoritarianism, the greater the likelihood of popular violence as a way of "doing" politics. Therefore, societies dominated by aristocratic elites are most liable to face recurrent periods of insurrection.)

5. Representative violence can be disaggregated into movements of secession and movements of reconstitution. Secession is most likely to occur in societies where market networks are built "from above" through coercive means. Reconstitution is most likely in societies where commercial networks are built "from below" and where we can show that community members have a demonstrable interest in maintaining supralocal institutions.

6. Changes in the political relations between elites and rural communities should be the best single predictor of the presence or absence of a sustained tradition of rural insurrection. Economic and technological changes should be significantly less important in influencing the outcome.

Ritual and Focus in Rural Communities

In my discussion of Japan, I indicated the importance of rethinking the concept of culture. But throughout this volume I have emphasized the significance of community rituals as a focus for community identity. For example, the "perambulation" of the village in England was an enactment of what the community meant. It drew boundaries between insiders and outsiders, and it focused the consciousness of participants in a celebratory moment of ritual solidarity. Similar rituals can be found in a variety of social and historical contexts. Some, like the charivari in England and France, enacted community hierarchy and membership rules in a raucous sanctioning of deviant behavior; others, including the cult of the sacrificial martyr in Japan, marked out the village as a "sacred" realm of reverential concern.[29]

Rituals of this kind expressed a "folklore of place" that tied ordinary people together in a discourse of community. An emphasis on their performance rather than their value shows community rituals as recurrent, intersubjective events that do not depend for their reference on purely "subjective" factors that cannot be recovered from the historical record. As Fernandez has shown, the performative approach to culture has much to offer in comparison with the older emphasis on culture as a subjective state of mind.[30]

Still, a number of interesting questions can be raised about the character of community ritual and local culture that bear on the wider comparative concerns of this study. First, is there any theoretical significance to the fact that community rituals vary in terms of their substantive content and specific focus? (For example, should we see the charivari as simply the functional equivalent of Japanese or Russian rituals, or do the specific differences have important implications for community cohesion?) Second, how does elite culture shape the culture of rural communities; and, more specifically, can we say something about the impact of the "great" religious and political traditions on the folklore of place?

We may speculate that local ritual practices have divergent implications for the cohesion of rural communities. For example, rituals that emphasize the ongoing sharing of food and spirits may enhance the incentives of even less well off community members to cooperate in other arenas of community life. Conversely, "underdeveloped" local rituals might have reduced cohesion to the extent that there was less of a standing focus for popular action. For instance, the attack on rural customs by English Puritans produced factional conflicts that undermined village solidarity.[31]

More important, we might ask if certain ritual practices are more likely than others to provide a clear, transparent focus for community action. For example, the charivari offered a clear target for community mobilization in the form of fairly specific rules about village propriety; people who violated those rules were subject to humiliation according to deeply embedded forms of action. Everyone in a village knew who had violated its code, and everyone knew how to respond. It is possible that this kind of clarity may have varied across societies. We know that languages differ in the divisions they make among objects in the world, and I would suggest that a similar logic can be applied to community rituals, whether

29. Irwin Scheiner, "Benevolent Lords and Honorable Peasants: Rebellion and Peasant Consciousness in Tokugawa Japan," in Tetsuo Najita and Irwin Scheiner, eds., *Japanese Thought in the Tokugawa Period, 1600–1868: Methods and Metaphors* (Chicago: University of Chicago Press, 1978), 39–62.

30. James W. Fernandez, *Persuasions and Performances: The Play of Tropes in Culture* (Bloomington: Indiana University Press, 1986).

31. David Underdown, *Revel, Riot, and Rebellion: Popular Politics and Culture in England, 1603–1660* (Oxford: Clarendon Press, 1985), 239–70.

viewed linguistically or nonlinguistically.[32] Some may have been capable of providing highly focused cognitive maps that drew hard-and-fast boundaries between friends and enemies, insiders and outsiders. Other ritual traditions may have been less focused, and therefore less capable of generating a "common sense" of the community with regard to the source and solution of community problems. For instance, the cult of the sacrificial martyr in village Japan left no doubt about who was a "good" village leader, and it also left little in the way of ambiguity about how such a leader would respond to a threat to his community: a good leader would risk death. Naturally, not everyone could or would live up to the standard, but its persistence as a ritual focal point was a standing rebuke to those who refused its clear moral implications.

We are, therefore, faced with the intriguing possibility that clearly articulated ritual focal points may enhance collective action by rural communities. Cognitive ritual maps that generate obvious rules of problem identification and solution might allow ordinary rural people to agree more easily on common concerns and common action. For example, the rigid moral code of the Spanish pueblo might have facilitated the ability of community members to reach a rough consensus on the identification of moral targets, whose behavior could then be sanctioned through gossip and ostracism. I do not claim to have the kinds of data that would permit me to prove or disprove this line of reasoning, but I think that the case studies show that this approach to understanding the cultural sources of community cohesion may prove fruitful.

In addition, we may discover that certain ritual practices were more conducive to local cohesion because of their capacity to effect a kind of "politics of reconciliation" in divided communities. Throughout this book I have emphasized the logic of agrarian societies, but I have tried to qualify it by pointing to the existence of ongoing conflicts within popular communities. We all know that small communities contain a good measure of factionalism, envy, and outright social hatred. Although quite real, these divisions must be put in perspective, and they must be interpreted within the context of mutually implicated forms of cooperation.

I have not emphasized the important ways in which community rituals may facilitate at least a temporary reconciliation of community conflicts, partly because I lack the ethnographic data necessary to the task. Nevertheless, there is some suggestive evidence that communities with traditions of ritual reconciliation may have been more cohesive than societies in which such traditions were weak. In both Russia and western Europe the comradeship offered by the local tavern or alehouse may have helped to bond people together (although it may also have led to the occasion for some rather nasty fights). Moreover, events such as village festivals and weekly church services must have offered symbolic moments in

32. George Lakoff, *Women, Fire, and Dangerous Things: What Categories Reveal about the Mind* (Chicago: University of Chicago Press, 1987), 269–370.

which local conflicts could be worked out. But, as James Obelkevich has shown, the absence of these community events in late-nineteenth-century England weakened the territorial bonds and ties of village life.[33] We may, therefore, discover that strong traditions of reconciliation through ritual performance underpin community cohesion in economic and political matters.

But the various ritual and cultural dimensions of rural community were not simply generated by the community itself. They were often derived in part from the so-called great traditions of religion and political philosophy that ultimately traced their roots back to the world of elite culture. Popular Christianity in agrarian Europe, like folk Buddhism in Japan, was somehow refracted through popular consciousness in ways that produced a distinctively rural religious tradition. Similarly, anarchism became a means of expressing village sentiment in southern Spain, and in Andalusia, anarchism may have even replaced the church as a focus of popular culture.

It is no longer necessary to argue against the old notion that these patterns of belief were simply imposed on rural society by powerful elites (indeed, in the case of Spanish anarchism, the suggestion would be absurd). Scholars like Natalie Z. Davis have helped us to see the ways in which popular culture emerged out of an interaction between elite ideas and popular beliefs, and it is simply no longer useful to reduce rural society to a "part culture" with no cultural integrity of its own.[34] What we must ask, then, is why certain elite traditions rather than others were selectively adapted by rural communities? Is there some comparative logic that lies behind this process, or is it merely a random phenomenon?

A tradition like anarchism is most likely to gain community support if it represents a worldview compatible with the logic and predicament of rural communities. More specifically, anarchism has a strong conceptual "affinity" with the defense of community institutions. Anarchism stresses the importance of reorganizing society along the lines of a federation of autonomous local units of production and consumption, and this neatly captures the traditions of the Spanish pueblo as an autonomous community.

This logic can be extended far beyond the particularities of rural Spain. For example, Christianity spread at the end of the Roman Empire partly because of its capacity to make sense of the lives of ordinary rural people, and the subsequent development of the parish as a unit of ecclesiastical administration may have owed something to its logical affinity with preexisting forms of rural community.[35] Even in Japan the spread of certain types of popular Buddhism, especially the sect called Ikko-shu, has been shown to be a result of its popular appeal to and

33. James Obelkevich, *Religion and Rural Society: South Lindsey, 1825–1875* (Oxford: Clarendon Press, 1976), esp. 23–102, 259–300.
34. Natalie Z. Davis, *Society and Culture in Early Modern France: Eight Essays* (Stanford: Stanford University Press, 1975).
35. See Goody, *The Development of the Family and Marriage*, 157–93.

reinforcement for rural communities. In fact, popular Buddhism, like Spanish anarchism, could help to generate a popular ideology of resistance that was ultimately turned against feudal power. As John W. Hall and Toyoda Takeshi point out, "whatever may be said about the purity of their religious beliefs, these communities were welded together by spiritual bonds of extraordinary strength. At the popular level, Buddhism had reached so great a degree of penetration that whole communities were willing to risk their lives for their right to separate existence."[36]

It seems reasonable, then, to argue that elite beliefs and ideologies are most liable to be accepted by rural communities if those beliefs and ideologies speak a discourse that works for rather than against the autonomy and cohesion of community institutions. The pure case would probably be an ideology that was not associated with the official ideas of elite power and that portrayed a utopia in which maximum decentralization and community autonomy were valued goals.

Some readers may object that the whole of the preceding analysis of ritual and culture is hopelessly "functionalist."[37] My only response is that I am a functionalist if this means nothing more than an attempt to think through the determinate effects of institutions and cultural practices. But my argument is not functionalist in the sense of ascribing teleological ends to social arrangements, nor is it functionalist in the sense of trying to explain the origins of ritual practices in terms of the effects they may have on the incentives of individuals at some point after they have become established. My only point is that specific institutional arrangements have a particular logic that should be explored to the limits, and, I think, all social scientists are "functionalists" at this level.

Three final hypotheses will highlight the main features of my analysis of the comparative dimensions of rural ritual:

7. We should expect community cohesion to be strongest in societies in which there are ritual practices that provide a clear focus, or focal point, for the identification of community problems and their solution. In order to test this proposition fully we would need data about the discourse of popular communities in order to draw a cognitive map of community members' understanding of their world.

8. The economic and political cohesion of rural communities should be greater in communities that have an ongoing series of rituals of reconciliation that provide the occasion for the management of intracommunity conflicts. There is, to be

36. In John W. Hall and Toyoda Takeshi, eds., *Japan in the Muromachi Age* (Berkeley: University of California Press, 1977), 312; see also Nagahara Keiji and Kozo Yamamura, "Village Communities and Daimyo Power," in the same volume, 107–23.

37. For a cogent critique of functionalism, see Jon Elster, *Ulysses and the Sirens: Studies in Rationality and Irrationality* (Cambridge: Cambridge University Press, 1979), 28–35.

sure, no *necessary* causal connection, but the existence of an occasion for reconciliation should increase the likelihood of its occurrence.

9. "Great" or elite traditions of religion and politics are most likely to be adopted in rural communities if they reinforce the defense of community autonomy and cohesion.

I would also add as a qualifier to this list that there will always be some degree of overlap between ritual practices and the other forms of cooperation that make up community life. As the case studies indicate, however, ritual has sufficient integrity to be studied independently, and this integrity provides the basis for evaluating its contribution to community cohesion without falling into tautology.

Rethinking the Limits of Analogy

The hope (and fear) of community has a long pedigree in Western political thought. Thinkers as diverse as Rousseau, Hegel, and Marx can be interpreted as having adopted a defense of community in the midst of a world increasingly individualistic and anticommunitarian.[38] Nor does community lack persuasive defenders in the American tradition of political theory. Since the founding, there has been at least a minor theme of community in American public discourse; and this theme has been articulated by Alasdair MacIntyre, Michael Sandel, and Michael Walzer, among others, as well as by legal scholars like Jerold Auerbach and Laurence Tribe.[39]

The defense of community advanced by this tradition is straightforward. Community is seen as necessary to the creation of an arena of genuinely public values and political participation in which consensus rather than conflict prescribes the rules of the game. In contrast to the supposedly atomized world of liberalism, the politics of community has been interpreted as both more secure and more enriching. Indeed, for the most determined advocates of community, especially Benjamin Barber and Roberto Unger, only a revival of community can genuinely empower ordinary people, in the sense of providing an authentic forum for face-

38. For an excellent critique of communitarian thought, see H. N. Hirsch, "The Threnody of Liberalism: Constitutional Liberty and the Renewal of Community," *Political Theory* 14 (Aug. 1986), 423–49. Also see Judith N. Shklar, *Men and Citizens: A Study of Rousseau's Social Theory* (London: Cambridge University Press, 1969), esp. 165–214; and Judith N. Shklar, *Freedom and Independence: A Study of the Political Ideas of Hegel's "Phenomenology of Mind"* (Cambridge: Cambridge University Press, 1976).

39. Alasdair MacIntyre, *After Virtue: A Study in Moral Theory* (Notre Dame: University of Notre Dame Press, 1981); Michael Sandel, *Liberalism and the Limits of Justice* (Cambridge: Cambridge University Press, 1982); Michael Walzer, *Spheres of Justice: A Defense of Pluralism and Equality* (New York: Basic Books, 1983); Jerold Auerbach, *Justice without Law* (New York: Oxford University Press, 1983); Laurence Tribe, "Structural Due Process," *Harvard Civil Rights* 10 (2) (1975), 269–321.

to-face discourse and decision making that is egalitarian and subject to immediate control by all participants.[40]

The communitarian tradition is too rich to dismiss out of hand, and I do not have any particular complaint against the tradition as a whole. But my analysis of rural community does suggest that there are clear limits to the kinds of analogies that communitarian theorists should draw on in formulating a communitarian alternative to the liberal order.[41] Specifically, the practices of traditional rural communities cannot be used as the basis for the retrieval of community. Although contemporary communitarian theorists are chiefly interested in the problems of industrial societies, there are many who do see rural community as a possible source of inspiration, if not an explicit blueprint for the design of contemporary communities. For example, Michael Taylor is quite specific in his praise of traditional rural communities, and thinkers like Roberto Unger and Benjamin Barber reveal a similar preoccupation with a metaphor of community that is indebted to a certain understanding of the agrarian past.[42] I am less interested, however, in an exegesis of their work than I am in establishing the dangers of modeling community on the basis of the rural experience.

Rural communities were not egalitarian; they were shot through with hierarchies that subordinated many individuals to many other individuals across a wide range of daily experience. It is true that these hierarchies were reciprocal, and they were much less pronounced or "oppressive" than the relations between rural communities and outside elites. But contemporary defenders of community see community as a *more* egalitarian polity than the present social order; indeed, part of their defense of community stems from their support for a more equal distribution of effective political rights.[43] I do not see how this commitment can be grounded in any defensible reading of the agrarian experience; even the Russian land commune was sufficiently patriarchal to disqualify as a case of communitarian equality. What such hierarchies show is that rural history may not have anything substantive to offer contemporary communitarians, at least if they retain their commitment to equal rights.

This, in fact, leads to a more important problem, which cuts to the heart of the problem of community in the contemporary world. I have argued that the extraordinary autonomy and cohesion of rural communities were linked to the reciprocal

40. Benjamin Barber, *Strong Democracy: Participatory Politics for a New Age* (Berkeley: University of California Press, 1984), 213–60; Roberto M. Unger, *Politics: A Work in Constructive Social Theory*, 3 vols. (Cambridge: Cambridge University Press, 1987), esp. 2:172–206.

41. See, for example, William M. Sullivan, *Reconstructing Public Philosophy* (Berkeley: University of California Press, 1982), 23–55.

42. Michael Taylor, *Community, Anarchy, and Liberty* (Cambridge: Cambridge University Press, 1982), esp. 1–38.

43. For further discussions of community, see Jane Mansbridge, *Beyond Adversary Democracy* (Chicago: University of Chicago Press, 1983), esp. 3–35, and Wilson Carey McWilliams, *The Idea of Fraternity in America* (Berkeley: University of California Press, 1973).

hierarchies of daily life. Those hierarchies made possible a degree of collective discipline and group mobilization that underpinned the survival of the community in adverse times. People who refused to abide by community rules could be held to account through the performance of hierarchical sanctioning. Is it possible that the survival of rural communities would not have been so likely if those hierarchies had not been available to control collective and individual behavior? In short, would community have failed if it had been genuinely egalitarian?

Contemporary communitarians would be well advised to consider this possibility, because it bears directly on the ability to reconstitute community in the contemporary world. Communitarian theorists see their communities as voluntary and grounded in the equal distribution of the rights and responsibilities of membership. But traditional rural communities were both unequal and founded on a notion of involuntary participation. (For example, there was often a strong assumption that one born into a community was involuntarily obligated to support it.) Although not all forms of community must follow this logic, it does indicate that anyone who would redesign community in the contemporary world must show how community can be combined with voluntarism and equality. To my knowledge, only Michael Taylor has undertaken this task in a serious way, but his argument is limited by his tendency to draw on a flawed reading of traditional communities.[44] Those who work in the communitarian tradition must do more than merely invoke the concept as an antidote to alienation; they must show how we can create stable community institutions that do not collapse in the face of internal and external problems. Unfortunately, the history of agrarian society may have little or nothing to offer in the way of appropriate analogies.

A related problem has to do with scale. The rural communities discussed in this volume were small assemblies of neighbors and kin who had little alternative but to cooperate, at least in those areas that were vital to the survival of the household. Agriculture, as I have tried to show, enforced a very specific logic in which territory and community membership shaped the contours of everyday life in a way that insured some degree of face-to-face interaction on a regular basis.

But much of this argument seems simply irrelevant when applied to the contemporary industrial world.[45] Many of our current problems are obviously large-scale, and they do not lend themselves easily to small-scale solutions. For example, industrial pollution has become a national, even international, problem, and its resolution cannot be undertaken by neighborhood groups. At a minimum, groups of this kind must federate at a supralocal level in order to be effective. Agricultural societies faced a very different world, in which many or all of the key problems associated with the production and distribution of the means of life could be managed locally, and it is unclear if there are any real analogies in advanced industrial societies.

44. Taylor, *Community, Anarchy, and Liberty*, esp. 1–38.
45. See Mansbridge, *Beyond Adversary Democracy*, 278–302.

Of course, many communitarians recognize the differences time has brought, and their solution to the problem of scale is to combine large-scale federal institutions with the maximum feasible decentralization of politics to the local level. But is this really compatible with the reconstitution of community, or is it simply a formula for decentralization that does not differ in kind from liberal politics? I do not claim to know the answer, but I do think it misplaced to draw on analogies from rural societies that simply cannot be transposed to contemporary contexts. It may be that industrial societies are inherently large-scale and impersonal; in that case, communitarian solutions may be not so much perverse as simply irrelevant.

A final point has to do with the theory and practice of citizenship. Individuals in the societies discussed in the case studies lacked citizenship rights in the modern sense. Rights and obligations were linked to the conditions of membership in local communities, and this was one reason why communities were able to hold their members' loyalty. If communities lost membership they faced a rather grim future, and all of the societies I have considered made life difficult for wanderers, strangers, and anyone who was not part of a specified group. In the contemporary world, citizenship provides ordinary people with national and transferable rights that are not constrained by the political definitions of local territorial groups. Indeed, the creation of transferable rights may have contributed to the decline of the salience of rural communities, because rural men and women were able to leave their communities without having to fear permanent marginality in their own societies.

How, then, do contemporary communitarians hope to combine citizenship rights with the kinds of intense loyalties that characterized rural societies? Once again, if community is voluntary, and people are free to exit during periods of dissatisfaction and difficulty, the result may be the creation of community institutions too fragile to survive. I would not suggest that this problem is impossible to solve, but communitarian theorists should avoid drawing on analogies from rural societies to prove their case for the possibility of community in present times. The creation of national citizenship rights may be incompatible with the resilient forms of community that existed in the past, and I doubt if any communitarians would want to extinguish citizenship in their quest for community.[46]

In sum, the logic of rural community cannot and should not be used as a metaphor for the possibility of community in the contemporary nation-state. Communitarian theorists should draw their blueprints from industrial societies, and they should resist any nostalgia for a vanished agrarian fraternity that may never have existed, except in very particular circumstances. More important, modern notions of community are too committed to equality to be comfortably

---

46. For the concept of citizenship, see T. H. Marshall, *Citizenship and Social Class, and Other Essays* (Cambridge: Cambridge University Press, 1950); reprinted in T. H. Marshall, *Class, Citizenship and Social Development* (Chicago: University of Chicago Press, 1977), 70–134.

situated in the kinds of institutions that underpinned the communities of grain. If we are to avoid a retreat into the obscure we must face the problems of the industrial world resolutely and without any fantasies about our agrarian past. To put the matter bluntly, we must draw clear boundaries around our theoretical concerns, boundaries that are appropriate to the age. In the end, this may be the real lesson to be learned from the study of rural history. Ordinary rural people understood the limits and boundaries of their world very clearly, and they fashioned a politics that was appropriate to the conditions of the times. We should and must do the same.

Index

273

Library of Congress Cataloging-in-Publication Data

Magagna, Victor V., 1954–
    Communities of grain : rural rebellion in comparative perspective/Victor V. Magagna.
        p.   cm.—(The Wilder house series in history, politics, and culture)
    Includes index.
    ISBN 0-8014-2361-9 (alk. paper)
    1. Rural development—Social aspects—Europe—History—Cross cultural
studies.   2. Rural development—Social aspects—Japan—History—Cross-cultural
studies.   3. Peasantry—Europe—History—Cross-cultural studies.   4. Peasantry—
Japan—History—Cross-cultural studies.   5. Village communities—Europe—
History—Cross-cultural studies.   6. Village communities—Japan—History—Cross-
cultural studies.   I. Title.   II. Series.
HN380.Z9C66   1991
307.1'412'094—dc20   90-55720